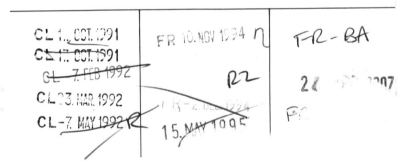

Visions
and blueprints

VISIONS
AND
BLUEPRINTS

Avant-garde culture and radical politics
in early twentieth-century Europe

edited by EDWARD TIMMS and
PETER COLLIER
with an introduction by Raymond Williams

Manchester University Press

Distributed exclusively in the USA and Canada
by ST. MARTIN'S PRESS, New York

Published by Manchester University Press,
Oxford Road, Manchester M13 9PL
and Room 400, 175 Fifth Avenue, New York, NY 10010, USA

Distributed exclusively in the USA and Canada
by St. Martin's Press, Inc.,
175 Fifth Avenue, New York, NY 10010, USA

British Library cataloguing in publication data

Visions and blueprints : avant-garde culture and radical politics in early
   twentieth-century Europe.
   1. Arts, European   2. Arts, Modern – 20th century – Europe   3. Avant-
   garde (Aesthetics) – Political aspects – Europe
   I. Timms, Edward   II. Collier, Peter
   700'.94   NX542

Library of Congress cataloguing in publication data applied for

ISBN 0–7190–2261–4 *paperback*

Photoset in Linotron Sabon
by Northern Phototypesetting Co., Bolton

Printed in Great Britain
by Bell & Bain Ltd., Glasgow

Contents

III   Masses and minorities

IV   Medium and message

Illustrations

Preface

The achievements of early twentieth-century modernism have an enduring fascination. The poets, painters, theorists, dramatists and film directors of this generation were not only radical artistic innovators. They saw themselves as members of a cultural 'avant-garde', helping to bring about – through the medium of art – a fundamental reorientation of society. But cultural modernism interacted with political revivalism in complex and unpredictable ways. Political events stimulated the development of new means of expression, while experimental forms had unforeseen ideological repercussions. This book offers a challenging reassessment of these artistic and political debates from a variety of critical viewpoints.

The political events which shaped the minds of that generation still cast a long shadow: the First World War and the Russian Revolution, the triumph of Mussolini in Italy and of Stalin in the Soviet Union, the Nazi seizure of power in Germany, the Popular Front in France and the Civil War in Spain – foreshadowing the Second World War. Many writers of the 1920s and 1930s experienced a profound disillusionment with democratic politics and with the capitalist system, which were blamed for the horrors of the First World War as well as for subsequent social and economic chaos. This condemnation of 'bourgeois' society (as Raymond Williams's Introduction shows) requires differentiated analysis, if we are to understand the polarised alternatives which emerged. Some of the finest minds were drawn towards radical political remedies – communism at the one extreme, Fascism at the other. The fact that their reactions were so extreme gives them – for better or worse – an exemplary quality. The 'avant-garde', which Williams distinguishes from earlier, less militant forms of 'modernism', was politically extremely volatile. And radical artistic experiments were capable of generating either revolutionary or reactionary impulses.

The structure of this book is designed to clarify these dynamic tendencies. Part I, Culture, Ideology, Commitment, explores the political aesthetics of theorists of the avant-garde. The crisis of the Weimar Republic impelled leading German writers to seek salvation in political extremes – Benn in National Socialism, Brecht in communism (Chapter 1). Political developments in other European countries contributed to divergent forms of theorising about what might constitute a revolutionary culture. Trotsky emphasised the social function of art in shaping a new society; Gramsci saw education as the crucial factor for the attainment of cultural and political hegemony; while Breton and the Surrealists made a cult of dream and desire (Chapter 2).

Revolutionary Marxism thus inspired divergent conceptions of the significance of experimental art. Arguing against what he saw as the self-destructive tendencies of Expressionism, Lukács reaffirmed the value of realist narrative as a medium for expressing social conflicts (Chapter 3). By contrast, Walter Benjamin devised a theory of history in which radical modes of deconstruction, inspired in part by Surrealism, subvert the confident bourgeois creed of progress (Chapter 4).

Part II, Modernism and Politics, explores the ways in which these theoretical debates are reflected in the work of a wide range of creative writers. In Italy the interaction of Marinetti's Futurist aesthetics with emergent Fascist politics provides a particularly complex example of the interpenetration of revolutionary and reactionary impulses (Chapter 5). In Britain, too, the most innovative poets, Eliot and Pound, developed right-wing sympathies which distort their poetic achievement (Chapter 6). These tendencies were identified and resisted during the 1930s by the broad alliance of anti-Fascist writers which was formed around the periodicals *Left Review* and *New Writing* (Chapter 7).

Both in Britain and in France, leading individual poets on the left – notably Auden, Aragon and Eluard (Chapter 8) – adapted modernist poetic forms in order to express revolutionary commitments. An ambiguous attitude towards political violence, however, meant that the left-wing commitment to revolution shaded off at certain points into that cult of self-assertion through action which was so characteristic of the political right. This paradox is memorably expressed in the novels of Malraux, analysed in Chapter 9. The quest for a revolutionary idiom was also taken up by writers on the periphery of Europe, notably Nâzım Hikmet, the poet of Kemalist Turkey who wrote some of his most powerful work either in prison or in exile (Chapter 10).

Part III, Masses and Minorities, focuses on new ways of defining the interaction between the individual and the collective. The mass societies of the twentieth century provoked divergent reactions: towards populism and totalitarianism on the one hand (with racialist and sexist undertones); and on the other towards elitism, individualism and depth psychology. Freud developed categories derived from the psychology of the individual to construct a model for the analysis of collective behaviour (Chapter 11). But he hesitated, perhaps because of his sensitivity to anti-semitism, to carry his argument through to its logical conclusions.

The more resolute response of the Zionists, on the other hand, expressed itself in an alternative political vision: Herzl's programme for a Jewish state, which – as it began to be implemented – provoked a variety of responses among German–Jewish authors (Chapter 12). Paradoxically, the Zionists' appeal to the solidarity of the Jewish 'people' has underlying affinities with that concept of the *Volk* which inspired the German national revival. Similarly, ambiguities can be identified in the appeal to the *pueblo* by cultural theorists in Spain. This concept, variably defined by members of the cultural elite, was a crucial reference point for both the traditionalists of the 1920s and the radical Republicans of the 1930s (Chapter 13). The dilemma of dissenting groups opposed to the dominant (patriarchal) order also found expression in the sexual politics of the period. Aggressively 'avant-garde' programmes for sexual liberation often betrayed a phallocentric confidence in male superiority; but the more subtle insights of writers like Proust and Virginia Woolf led them to develop narrative strategies which subvert the prevailing patriarchal modes (Chapter 14).

Fundamental to all these controversies is the relationship between Medium and Message, the theme of Part IV – the concluding section of the book. This question acquired particular urgency in the visual and performing arts – the spheres in which society and its image were most directly confronted. In Nazi Germany this confrontation expressed itself in official policy, which juxtaposed authentic 'Aryan' painting with so-called 'degenerate' art. The work of avant-garde painters was exposed to public ridicule, while the revival of national grandeur was celebrated in monumental and classical forms (Chapter 15). In the Netherlands, by contrast, the avant-garde theories of art and design associated with the journal *De Stijl* proved to be elitist and even authoritarian in their ideological implications (Chapter 16). It becomes clear that there is no easy equation between experimental art and progressive politics.

It was in the theatre and cinema that new artistic techniques had their greatest political impact. The theatre, particularly in Germany, became a political forum. Its persuasive power depended not simply on the message conveyed, but on a critical awareness generated by the deconstruction of theatrical illusion – notably in the work of Piscator and Brecht (Chapter 18). Piscator, in his most innovative productions, juxtaposed individual scenes with cinema newsreels which established a wider political context. The work of avant-garde film-makers showed, however, that the camera could project both disruptive and hypnotic images. It could thus either challenge or reaffirm established systems of authority and communication, as the contrast between *Battleship Potemkin* and *The Cabinet of Dr Caligari* (Chapter 17) graphically demonstrates. The poster advertising *Potemkin*, which forms our cover design, highlights a recurrent theme of the book: the problematic interaction between systems of communication and political power. Do the urgent signals of the semaphorist merely obey – or do they challenge – the awesome authority of the guns?

No study of European culture and politics of the early twentieth century can be comprehensive. But we hope that this book (developed from a course of lectures given in Cambridge) will succeed in mapping the essential landmarks. The aim is to reassess the whole concept of a cultural 'avant-garde' through a detailed reconstruction of intellectual debates and political positions. Our title, *Visions and Blueprints*, is taken from a poem written in 1936 by one of our senior contributors, Margot Heinemann:

> For seeing visions on the evening sky
> I can do tolerably well; but I
> can read no blue prints and erect no schemes.

The paradox which emerges from this book is that the poets frequently did attempt to provide blueprints for a new society, while the politicians were often predominantly inspired by imaginative visions. Art and politics interacted in complex and unpredictable ways. And it becomes clear that 'modernism' is a mercurial phenomenon which requires continuous redefinition under changing historical circumstances.

Edward Timms and Peter Collier
Cambridge, January 1987

The politics
of the avant-garde

In January 1912 a torchlight procession, headed by members of the Stockholm Workers' Commune, celebrated the sixty-third birthday of August Strindberg. Red flags were carried and revolutionary anthems were sung.

No moment better illustrates the contradictory character of the politics of what is now variously (and confusingly) called the 'modernist' movement or the 'avant-garde'. In one simple dimension the acclamation of Strindberg is not surprising. Thirty years earlier, presenting himself, rhetorically, as the 'son of a servant', Strindberg had declared that in a time of social eruption he would side with those who came, weapon in hand, from below. In a verse contrasting Swartz, the inventor of gunpowder – used by kings to repress their peoples – with Nobel, the inventor of dynamite, he wrote:

> You, Swartz, had a small edition published
> For the nobles and the princely houses!
> Nobel! you published a huge popular edition
> Constantly renewed in a hundred thousand copies.[1]

The metaphor from publishing makes the association between the radical, experimental, popular writer and the rising revolutionary class explicit. Again, from 1909, he had returned to the radical themes of his youth, attacking the aristocracy, the rich, militarism and the conservative literary establishment. This association of enemies was equally characteristic.

Yet very different things had happened in the intervening years. The man who had written: 'I can get quite wild sometimes, thinking about the insanity of the world', had gone on to write: 'I am engaged in such a revolution against myself, and the scales are falling from my eyes.'[2] This is the transition which we shall come to recognise as a key movement in modern art, and which already in 1888 enabled Nietzsche to write of Strindberg's play *The Father*: 'It has astounded me beyond measure to find a work in which my own conception of love – with war as its means and the deathly hatred of the sexes as its fundamental law – is so magnificently expressed.'[3] Strindberg confirmed the mutual recognition: 'Nietzsche is to me the modern spirit who dares to preach the right of the strong and the wise against the foolish, the small (the democrats).'[4] This is still a radicalism, and indeed still daring and violent. But it is not only that the enemies have changed, being identified now as those tendencies which had hitherto been recognised as liberating: political progress, sexual emancipation, the choice of peace against war. It is also that the old enemies have disappeared behind these; indeed it is the strong and the powerful who now carry the seeds of the future: 'Our *evolution* . . . wants to protect the strong against the weak species, and the current aggressiveness of women seems to me a symptom of the regress of the race.'[5] The language is that of social Darwinism, but we can distinguish its use among these radical artists from the relatively banal justifications of a new hard (lean) social order by the direct apologists of capitalism. What emerges in the arts is a 'cultural Darwinism', in which the strong and daring radical spirits are the true *creativity* of the race. Thus there is not only an assault on the weak – democrats, pacifists, women – but on the whole social and moral and religious order. The 'regress of the race' is attributed to Christianity, and Strindberg could hail Nietzsche as 'the prophet of the overthrow of Europe and Christendom'.[6]

We have then to think again of the torches and red flags of the Workers' Commune. It is important, in one kind of analysis, to trace the shifts of position, and indeed the contradictions, within complex individuals. But to begin to understand the more general complexities of the politics of the avant-garde, we have to look beyond these singular men to the turbulent succession of artistic movements and cultural formations which compose the real history of modernism and then of the avant-garde in so many of the countries of Europe. The emergence of these self-conscious, named and self-naming groups is a key marker of the movement in its widest sense.

We can distinguish three main phases, which had been developing rapidly during the late nineteenth century. Initially, there were innovative groups, which sought to protect their practices within the growing dominance of the art market and against the indifference of the formal academies. These developed into alternative, more radically innovative groupings, seeking to provide their own facilities of production, distribution and publicity; and finally into fully oppositional formations, determined not only to promote their own work but to attack its enemies in the cultural establishments and, beyond these, the whole social order in which these enemies had gained and now exercised and reproduced their power. Thus the defence of a particular kind of art became first the self-management of a new kind of art and then, crucially, an attack in the name of this art on a whole social and cultural order.

It is not easy to make simple distinctions between 'modernism' and the 'avant-garde', especially as many uses of these labels are retrospective. But it can be taken as a working hypothesis that modernism can be said to begin with the second type of group – the alternative, radically innovating experimental artists and writers – while the avant-garde begins with groups of the third, fully oppositional type. The old military metaphor of the vanguard, which had been used in politics and in social thought from at latest the 1830s – and which had implied a position within a general human progress – was now directly applicable to these newly militant movements, even when they had renounced the received elements of progressivism. Modernism had proposed a new kind of art for a new kind of social and perceptual world. The avant-garde, aggressive from the beginning, saw itself as the breakthrough to the future: its members were not the bearers of a progress already repetitiously defined, but the militants of a creativity which would revive and liberate humanity.

Thus, two years before the Workers' Commune homage to Strindberg, the Futurists had published their manifestos in Paris and Milan. We can catch clear echoes of the Strindberg and Nietzsche of the 1880s. In the same language of cultural Darwinism, war is the necessary activity of the strong, and the means to the health of society. Women are identified as special examples of the weak who hold back the strong. But there is now a more specific cultural militancy: 'Take up your pickaxes, your axes and hammers, and wreck, wreck the venerable cities, pitilessly. Come on, set fire to the library shelves. Turn aside the canals to flood the museums [. . .] So let them come, the gay incendiaries with charred fingers [. . .] Here we are! Here we are!' The directions are more particular, but we can remember, as we listen to them, Strindberg's celebration of dynamite in 'a huge popular edition'. Except that his violence had been linked with those 'who came, weapon in hand, from below': a central and traditional image of revolution. There is a significant difference in the Futurist commitment to what looks, at first glance, like the same movement: 'We will sing of great crowds excited by work, by pleasure and by riot [. . .] the multicoloured, polyphonic tides of revolution.'[8] Anyone with a ear for the nuances of talk of revolution, down to our own time, will recognise the change, and recognise, also, the confused and confusing elements of these repeated calls to revolution, many of which, in the pressures of subsequent history, were to become not only alternatives but actual political antagonists.

The direct call to political revolution, based in the workers' movements, was rising through just this period. The Futurist call to destroy 'tradition' overlaps with socialist calls to destroy the whole existing social order. But 'great crowds excited by work, by pleasure and by riot', 'the multicoloured polyphonic tides of revolution': these, while they can appear to overlap, are already – especially with the advantage of hindsight – a world away from the tightly organised parties which would use a scientific socialism to destroy the hitherto powerful and emancipate the hitherto powerless. The comparison bears both ways. Against the single track of proletarian revolution there are the 'multicoloured, polyphonic tides'. 'Great crowds excited . . . by riot' carries all the ambiguities between revolution and carnival. Moreover, and crucially, though its full development is later, there is the decisive difference between appeals to the tradition of reason and the new celebration of creativity which finds many of its sources in the irrational, in the newly valued unconscious, and in the fragments of dreams. The social bases which had appeared to fuse when the Workers' Commune honoured Strindberg – a writer who had intensively explored these unconscious sources – could now be equally strongly contrasted: the organised working class with its disciplines of party and union; the cultural movement with its mobile association of free and liberating, often deliberately marginal individuals.

What was 'modern', what was indeed 'avant-garde', is now relatively old. What its works and language reveal, even at their most powerful, is an identifiable historical period, from which, however, we have not fully emerged. What we can now identify in its most active and creative years, underlying its many works, is a range of diverse and fast-moving artistic methods and practices, and at the same time a set of relatively constant positions and beliefs.

We have already noticed the emphasis on creativity. This has precedents, obviously, in the Renaissance, and later in the Romantic Movement when the term, at first thought blasphemous, was invented and heavily used. What marks out this emphasis in both modernism and the avant-garde is a defiance and finally violent rejection of tradition: the insistence on a clean break with the past. In both the earlier periods, though in different ways, there was a strong appeal to *revival*: the art and learning, the life of the past, were sources, stimuli of a new creativity, against an exhausted or deformed current order. This lasted as late as that alternative movement of the Pre-Raphaelites – a conscious modernism of its day; the present and the immediate past must be rejected, but there is a farther past, from which creativity can revive. What we now know as modernism, and certainly as the avant-garde, has changed all this. Creativity is all in new making, new construction: all traditional, academic, even learned models are actually or potentially hostile to it, and must be swept away.

It is true that, as in the Romantic Movement, with its appeal to the folk art of marginal peoples, there is also a sidelong reference. Art seen as primitive or exotic but creatively powerful – and now within a developed imperialism available from much wider sources, in Asia and in Africa – is in several different movements, within this turbulent creative range, taken not only as exemplary, but as forms that can be woven into the consciously modern. These appeals to the 'Other' – in fact highly developed arts of their own places – are combined with an underlying association of the 'primitive' and the 'unconscious'. At the same time, however, and very marked in the competition between these movements, there is a virtually unprecedented emphasis on the most evident features of a modern urban industrialised world: the city, the machine, speed, space — the creative engineering, *construction* of a future. The contrast with the central Romantic emphases on spiritual and natural creativity could hardly be more marked.

Yet also, and decisive for its relations with politics, the range of new movements was operating in a very different social world. To the emphases on creativity and on the rejection of tradition we must add a third common factor: that all these movements, implicitly but more often explicitly, claimed to be anti-bourgeois. Indeed 'bourgeois', in all its rich range of meanings, turns out to be a key to the many movements which claimed to be its opposite. Schools and movements repeatedly succeeded each other, fused or more often fragmented in a proliferation of *isms*. Within them individuals of marked singularity pursued their apparently and in some ways authentically autonomous projects, readily linked by the historian but often directly experienced as isolated and isolating. Very diverse technical solutions were found, in each of the arts, to newly emphasised problems of representation and narration, and to ways beyond what came to be seen as these constrictions of purpose and form. For many working artists and writers, these working considerations – the actual methods of their art – were always uppermost in their minds; indeed they could sometimes be isolated as evidence of the singularity and purity of art. But whichever of these ways was taken there was always a single contrast to it. Hostile or indifferent or merely vulgar, the bourgeois was the mass which the creative artist must either ignore and circumvent, or now increasingly shock, deride and attack.

No question is more important to our understanding of these once modern movements than the ambiguity of bourgeois. The underlying ambiguity is historical, in its dependence on the variable class position from which the bourgeois was seen. To the court and the aristocracy the bourgeois was at once worldly and vulgar, socially pretentious but hidebound, moralistic and spiritually narrow. To the newly organising working class, however, not only the individual bourgeois, with his combination of self-interested morality and self-serving comfort, but the bourgeoisie as a class of employers and controllers of money, was at centre stage.

The majority of artists, writers and intellectuals were in none of these fixed class positions. But in different and variable ways they could overlap with the complaints of each other class against the bourgeois reckoning of the world. There were the dealers and booksellers who, within the newly dominant cultural market, were treating works of art as simple commodities, their values determined by trading success or failure. Protests against this could overlap with the Marxist critique of the reduction of labour to a traded commodity. Alternative and oppositional artistic groups were defensive attempts to get beyond the market, distantly analogous to the working-class development of collective bargaining. There could thus be at least a negative identification between the exploited worker and the exploited artist. Yet one of the central points of their complaint against this treatment of art was that creative art was more than simple labour; its cultural and spiritual or then its aesthetic values were especially outraged as the commodity reduction took hold. Thus the bourgeois could also be seen, simultaneously or alternatively, as the vulgar, hidebound, moralistic and spiritually narrow figure of the aristocratic complaint.

There are innumerable variations on these essentially distinguishable complaints against the bourgeoisie. How each mix or variation came out, politically, depended, crucially, on differences in the social and political structures of the many countries within which these movements were active, but also, in ways often very difficult to analyse, on the proportions of the different elements in the anti-bourgeois positions.

In the nineteenth century the element derived from the aristocratic critique was obviously much stronger, but it found a metaphorical form of its own, which was to survive, pathetically, into the twentieth century, to be taken up by even the most unlikely people: the claim, indeed the assertion, that the artist was the authentic aristocrat; had indeed to be, in the spiritual sense, an aristocrat if he was to be an artist. An alternative vocabulary gathered behind this assertion, from Arnold's culturally superior 'remnant' to Mannheim's vitally uncommitted intelligentsia, and more individually in the proposition – eventually the cult – of 'the genius' and 'the superman'. Naturally the bourgeoisie and its world were objects of hostility and contempt from such positions, but the assertion did not have to be made very often to extend to a wholesale condemnation of the 'mass' that was beyond all authentic artists: now not only the bourgeoisie but that ignorant populace which was beyond the reach of art or hostile to it in vulgar ways. Any residues of an actual aristocracy could at times be included in this type of condemnation: worldly barbarians who were offensively mistaken for the true creative aristocrats.

On the other hand, as the working-class, socialist and anarchist movements developed their own kind of critique, identifying the bourgeoisie as the organisers and agents of capitalism and thus the specific source of the reduction of all broader human values, including the values of art, to money and trade, there was an opportunity for artists to join or support a wide and growing movement which would overthrow and supersede bourgeois society. This could take the form of a negative identification between the artists and workers, each group being practically exploited and oppressed; or, though more rarely, a positive identification, in which artists would commit themselves, in their art and out of it, to the larger causes of the people or of the workers.

Thus within what may at first hearing sound like closely comparable denunciations of the bourgeois, there are already radically different positions, which would lead eventually, both theoretically and under the pressure of actual political crisis, not only to different but to directly opposed kind of politics: to Fascism or to communism; to social democracy or to conservatism and the cult of excellence.

This synchronic range has, moreover, to be complemented by the diachronic range of the actual bourgeoisie. In its early stages there had been an emphasis on independent productive and trading enterprise, free of the constraints of state regulation and both privilege and precedent, which in practice closely accorded with the life-situation and desires of many artists, who were already in precisely this position. It is not really surprising that so many artists, including, ironically, at later stages of their careers, many avant-garde artists, became in this sense good and successful bourgeois: at once attentive to control of their own production and property and, which mattered more in public presentation, ultimate apotheoses of that central bourgeois figure: the sovereign individual. This is still today the small change of conventional artistic self-presentation.

Yet the effective bourgeoisie had not stopped at these early stages. As it gathered the fruits of its free and independent production it placed a heavy emphasis on the rights of accumulated (as distinct from inherited) property, and thus on its forms of settlement. Though in practice these were interlocked, in variable ways, with older forms of property and settlement in state and aristocracy, there was a distinctive emphasis on the morality (rather than only the brute fact) of property and order.

A particular instance, of great importance to modernism and the avant-garde, is what came to be called the *bourgeois family*. The actual bourgeois family was not the inventor of propertied marriage, nor of the inclusion within it of male domination over women and children. The bourgeois initiative within these established feudal forms had been an emphasis on personal feeling – at first derided as sentimental – as the proper basis for marriage, and a related emphasis on the direct care of children. The fusion of these ideas of the family with the received forms of property and settlement was a hybrid rather than a true bourgeois creation.

Yet, by the time of modernism, the contradictions of this hybrid were increasing. The emphasis on personal feeling was quickly developed into an emphasis on irresistible or even momentary desire, which it would be a thwarting of humanity to suppress. The care of children could be resented as an irksome form of control. And the repression of women, within a restrictive social system, was increasingly challenged. Nor is it any reduction of the nature of these developments to note how much more vigorous they became as the bourgeoisie moved, by its very economic success, into more funded forms. The economic constraints by which the older forms had maintained practical control were loosened not only by general changes in the economy and by the availability of new (and especially professional) kinds of work, but by a cruder consideration: that the son or daughter of a bourgeois family was financially in a position to lay claim to new forms of liberation; and in a significant number of cases could actually use the profits of the economic bourgeoisie to lead political and artistic crusades against it.

Thus the growing critique of the bourgeois family was as ambiguous as the more general critique of the bourgeois as such. With the same vigour and confidence as the first bourgeois generations, who had fought state and aristocratic monopolies and privileges, a new generation, still in majority by practice and inheritance bourgeois, fought, on the same principle of the sovereign individual, against the monopoly and privilege of marriage and family. It is true that this was most vigorous at relatively young ages, in the break-out to new directions and new identities. But in many respects a main element of modernism was that it was an authentic avant-garde, in personal desires and relationships, of the successful and evolving bourgeoisie itself. The desperate challenges and deep shocks of the first phase were to become the statistics and even the conventions of a later phase of the same order.

Thus what we have observed synchronically in the range of positions covered by the anti-bourgeois revolt we observe also, diachronically, within that evolution of the bourgeoisie which in the end produced its own successions of distinctively bourgeois dissidents. This is a key element of the politics of the avant-garde, and we need especially to remember it as we look at forms which seem to go beyond politics or indeed to discount politics as irrelevant. Thus there is a position within the apparent critique of the bourgeois family which is actually a critique and rejection of all social forms of human reproduction. The 'bourgeois family', with all its known characteristics of property and control, is often in effect a covering phrase for those rejections of women and children which take the form of a rejection of 'domesticity'. The sovereign individual is confined by any such form. The genius is tamed by it. But since there is little option for celibacy, and only a limited option (though taken and newly valued, even directly associated with art) for homosexuality, the male campaign for liberation is often associated, as in the cases of Nietzsche and Strindberg, with great resentment and hatred of women, and with a reduction of children to elements of struggle between incompatible individuals. In this strong tendency, liberation translates desire as perpetually mobile: it cannot, in principle, be achieved in a settled relationship or in a society. Yet at the same time the claims of human liberation, against forms of property and other economic controls, are being much more widely made, and increasingly – for that is the irony of even the first phase – by women.

Thus we have seen that what is new in the avant-garde is the aggressive dynamism and conscious affront of claims to liberation and creativity which, through the whole modernist period, were in fact being much more widely made. We have now to look at the variable forms of its actual intersections with politics. These cover, in effect, the whole political range, though in the great majority of cases there is a strong movement towards the new political forces which were breaking beyond old constitutional and imperial politics, both before the war of 1914–18 and with much greater intensity during and after it. We can briefly identify some of the main strands.

There was, first, a strong attraction to forms of anarchism and nihilism, and also to forms of revolutionary socialism which, in their aesthetic representation, had a comparably apocalyptic character. The contradictions between these varying kinds of attachment were eventually to be obvious, but there was a clear initial linkage between the violent assault on existing conventions and the programmes of anarchists, nihilists and revolutionary socialists. The deep emphasis on the liberation of the creative individual took many towards the anarchist wing, but especially after 1917 the project of heroic revolution could be taken as a model for the collective liberation of all individuals. Hostility to the war and to militarism also fed this general tendency, from the Dadaists to the Surrealists, and from the Russian Symbolists to the Russian Futurists.

On the other hand, the commitment to a violent break with the past, most evident in Futurism, was to lead to early political ambiguities. Before 1917 the rhetoric of revolutionary violence could appear congruent with the Italian Futurists' explicit glorification of violence in war. It was only after 1917, and its consequent crises elsewhere, that these came to be fully distinguished. By then two Futurists, Marinetti and Mayakovsky, had moved in quite opposite directions: Marinetti to his support for Italian Fascism; Mayakovsky to his campaigning for a popular Bolshevik culture. The renewed rhetoric of violent rejection and disintegration, in the Germany of the 1920s, produced associations within Expressionism and related movements which by the end of the decade, and then notably with the coming of Hitler, led different writers to positions on the extreme poles of politics: to both Fascism and communism.

Within these varying paths, which can be tracked to relatively explicit political stations, there is a very complex set of attachments which could, it seems, go either way. It is a striking characteristic of several movements, within both modernism and the avant-garde, that rejection of the existing social order and its culture was supported and even directly expressed by recourse to a simpler art: either the primitive or exotic, as in the interest in African and Chinese objects and forms; or the 'folk' or 'popular' elements of their native cultures. As in the earlier case of the 'medievalism' of the Romantic Movement, this reach back beyond the existing cultural order was to have very diverse political results. Initially the main impulse was, in a political sense, 'popular': this was the true or the repressed native culture which had been overlain by academic and establishment forms and formulas. Yet it was simultaneously valued, in the same terms as the exotic art, because it represented a broader human tradition, and especially because of those elements which could be taken as its 'primitivism', a term which corresponded with that emphasis on the innately creative; the unformed and untamed realm of the pre-rational and the unconscious; indeed that vitality of the naive which was so especially a leading edge of the avant-garde.

We can then see why these emphases went in different political directions as they matured. The 'folk' emphasis, when offered as evidence of a repressed popular tradition, could move readily towards socialist and other radical and revolutionary tendencies. One version of the vitality of the naive could be joined with this, as witness of the new kinds of art which a popular revolution would release. On the other hand, an emphasis on the 'folk', as a particular kind of emphasis on 'the people', could lead to very strong national and eventually nationalist identifications, of the kind heavily drawn upon in both Italian and German Fascism.

Equally, however, an emphasis on the creativity of the pre-rational could be co-opted into a rejection of all forms of would-be rational politics, including not only liberal progressivism but also scientific socialism, to the point where, in one version, the politics of action, of the unreflecting strong, could be idealised as necessarily liberating. This was not, of course, the only conclusion from an emphasis of the pre-rational. The majority of the Surrealists, in the 1930s, moved towards resistance against Fascism: of course as an active, disrupting resistance. There was also a long (and unfinished) interaction between psychoanalysis, increasingly the theoretical expression of these 'pre-rational' emphases, and Marxism, now the dominant theoretical expression of the revolutionary working class. There were many attempted fusions of the revolutionary impulse in both, both generally and in particular relation to a new sexual politics which both derived from and contested early modernist sources. There was also, however, an eventual rejection of all politics, in the name of the deeper realities of the dynamic psyche; and, within this, one influential strand of option for *conservative* forms of order, seen as offering at least some framework of control for the unruly impulses both of the dynamic psyche and of the pre-rational 'mass' or 'crowd'.

The diverse movements which went in these different and opposed directions continued to have one general property in common: all were pioneering new methods and purposes in writing, art and thought. It is then a sober fact that, for this very reason, they were so often rejected by mainstream political forces. The Nazis were to lump left, right and centre modernists together as *Kulturbolschewismus*. From the middle and late 1920s, the Bolsheviks in power in the Soviet Union rejected virtually the same range. During the Popular Fronts of the 1930s there was a reassembly of forces: Surrealists with social realists, constructivists with folk artists, popular internationalism with popular nationalism. But this did not outlast its immediate and brief occasion, and through the war of 1939–45 separate directions and transformations were resumed, to reappear in further brief alliances in the post-war years and especially, with what seemed a renewal of the original energies, in the 1960s.

Within the range of general possibilities it mattered greatly what was happening in the different countries in which the avant-garde were based, or in which they found refuge. The true social bases of the early avant-garde were at once cosmopolitan and metropolitan. There was rapid transfer and interaction between different countries and different capitals, and the deep mode of the whole movement, as in modernism, was precisely this mobility across frontiers: frontiers which were among the most obvious elements of the old order which had to be rejected, even when native folk sources were being included as elements or as inspiration of the new art. There was intense competition but also radical coexistence in the great imperial capitals of Paris, Vienna, Berlin, and Petersburg, and also, in more limited ways, in London. These concentrations of wealth and power, and of state and academy, had each, within their very complexities of contact and opportunity, drawn towards them those who most opposed them. The dynamics of the imperialist metropolis were, then, the true bases of this opposition, in ways that have already been explored in the volume *Unreal City*.[9]

This was to happen again, but in essentially different ways, after the shocks of the 1914–18 war and the Russian Revolution. Paris and Berlin (until Hitler) were the new major centres, but the assembly now was not only of pioneering artists, writers and intellectuals, seeking contact and solidarity in their multiplicity of movements, but to a much greater extent of political exiles and emigrés: a movement later to be repeated, with an even greater emphasis, in New York.

Thus there is a certain structural continuity within the changing situations of the metropolitan capitals. Yet, wherever the artists might be, or settle, the quite new political crises of the post-1917 world produced a diversity different in kind from the mobile and competitive diversity of the years before 1914. Thus the Russian modernists and avant-gardists were in a country which had passed through revolution and civil war. Blok, in *The Twelve*, could write a late Symbolist poem of twelve Red Army soldiers led by Christ through a storm towards the new world. Mayakovsky could move from the liberated detachment of *A Cloud in Trousers* (1915) to *Mystery Buffo* (1918), acclaiming the revolution, and later, after the official rejection of modernist and avant-garde art, to the satirical observation of the supposed new world in *The Bedbug* (1929). These are examples among many, in the turbulence of those years, when the relation between politics and art was no longer a matter of manifesto but of difficult and often dangerous practice.

The Italian Futurists had a very different but comparable experience. The earlier rhetoric had led them towards Fascism, but its actual manifestation was to impose new tests, and varieties of accommodation and reservation. In the Weimar Republic there was still an active and competitive diversity, with the current running strongly against bourgeois culture and its forms. But while Piscator could move from the Spartakus League to the Proletarian Theatre, the poet Tucholsky, verifying a point in our earlier analysis, could declare that 'one is bourgeois by predisposition, not by birth and least of all by profession':[10] bourgeois, that is to say, not as a political but as a spiritual classification. The eventual crisis of the end of the Republic and the Nazi rise to power forced a polarisation which can be summarily represented, among writers who had been closely involved with Expressionism, by Brecht on the revolutionary left and Gottfried Benn on the Fascist right (a polarisation explored in greater detail in Chapter 1).

In countries in which during this period there was no radical change of power in the state, the effects, though no less complex, were often less dramatic. There was a notable rallying of Surrealist writers to the anti-Fascist cause in France, but there, as in Britain, it was possible to sustain a certain political solidarity against war and against Fascism within a diversity of literary movements and cultural principles. In the Popular Front period, also, that element of the original avant-garde position which had rejected official cultural institutions and sought new – and in some instances, as in the early Soviet Union, new *popular* – audiences for more open kinds of art, was widely emphasised. There was the leftist tendency of the Auden and Isherwood plays, borrowing from German Expressionism; but there was also an avant-garde colouring in the social–realist and documentary film and theatre movements, offering to break from fixed fictional forms and enclosed bourgeois institutions.

Also in Britain, however, there was a significantly different tendency, in which literary modernism moved explicitly to the right. Wyndham Lewis's Vorticism, a version of Futurism, developed idiosyncratically, but Pound's characteristically total avant-garde position ended in Fascism, and Yeats' version of the 'people', sustained at first by a broad and diverse movement, became a right-wing nationalism. The most interesting because most influential case is that of Eliot, seen from the 1920s to the 1940s as the key modernist poet. Eliot developed what can now be seen as an Ancient-and-Modern position, in which unceasing literary experiment moved towards a conscious elite, and in which an emphasis on tradition (so distinct from earlier modernist and avant-garde rejections of the past) was offered as in effect subversive of an intolerable because shallow and self-deceiving (and in that sense still *bourgeois*) social and cultural order.

In the chapters which follow, these issues are analysed in greater detail. The war of 1939–45 brought an end to many of these movements and transformed most of the earlier positions. Yet, though it requires separate analysis, the period since 1945 shows many of the earlier situations and pressures, and indeed many – though, at their most serious, altered – recurrences of position and initiative. Two new social factors have then to be noted, since continuities and similarities of technique, affiliation and manifesto can too easily be isolated in a separated aesthetic history: itself one of the influential forms of a post-war cultural modernism which had observed the complexity of the many political crises.

First, the avant-garde, in the sense of an artistic movement which is simultaneously both a cultural and political campaign, has become notably less common. Yet there are avant-garde political positions, from the earliest stages – dissident from fixed bourgeois forms, but still as *bourgeois* dissidents – which can be seen as a genuine vanguard of a truly modern international bourgeoisie which has emerged since 1945. The politics of this New Right, with its version of libertarianism in a dissolution or deregulation of all bonds and all national and cultural formations, in the interest of what is represented as the ideal open market and the truly open society, look very familiar in retrospect. For the sovereign individual is offered as the dominant political and cultural form, even in a world more evidently controlled by concentrated economic and military power. That it can be offered as such a form, in such conditions, depends partly on that emphasis which was once, within settled empires and conservative institutions, so challenging and so marginal.

Secondly, especially in the cinema, in the visual arts, and in advertising, certain techniques which were once experimental and actual shocks and affronts have become the working conventions of a widely distributed commercial art, dominated from a few cultural centres, while many of the original works have passed directly into international corporate trade. This is not to say that Futurism, or any other of the avant-garde movements, has found its literal future. The rhetoric may still be of endless innovation. But instead of revolt there is the planned trading of spectacle, itself significantly mobile and, at least on the surface, deliberately disorientating.

We have then to recall that the politics of the avant-garde, from the beginning, could go either way. The new art could find its place either in a new social order or in a culturally transformed but otherwise persistent and recuperated old order. All that was quite certain, from the first stirrings of modernism through to the most extreme forms of the avant-garde, was that nothing could stay quite as it was: that the internal pressures and the intolerable contradictions would force radical changes of some kind. Beyond the particular directions and affiliations, this is still the historical importance of this cluster of movements and of remarkable individual artists. And since, if in new forms, the general pressures and contradictions are still intense, indeed have in many ways intensified, there is still much to learn from the complexities of its vigorous and dazzling development.

Notes to introduction

1   Quoted in O. Lagercrantz, *August Strindberg*, London, 1984, p. 97.
2   *Ibid.*, p. 122.
3   Quoted in M. Meyer, *August Strindberg*, London, 1985, p. 205.

4 *Ibid.*
5 *Ibid.*
6 *Ibid.*
7 *Futurist Manifestos,* ed. U. Apollonio, London, 1973, p. 23.
8 *Ibid.,* p. 22.
9 *Unreal City: Urban Experience in Modern European Literature and Art,* ed. Edward Timms and David Kelley, Manchester, 1985.
10 See A. Phelan, 'Left-wing melancholia', in *The Weimar Dilemma,* ed. A. Phelan, Manchester, 1985.

PART I

CULTURE, IDEOLOGY, COMMITMENT

Treason of the intellectuals?
Benda, Benn and Brecht

What is to be done? This challenging question, title of a pamphlet by Lenin published in 1902, reverberates through the work of European intellectuals of the early twentieth century. These were writers with an unprecedented concern to change the world, not merely to reinterpret it. Lenin insisted that great historical changes do not occur spontaneously, as a result of impersonal economic forces. Given the instability of the capitalist system (particularly in Russia), a small, intellectually advanced 'vanguard' could play a decisive role. This 'committee of professional revolutionaries', supported by 'allies in the ranks of the liberals and intelligensia', is for Lenin the essential factor in 'bringing about' a revolution.[1] Although this pamphlet was not widely read outside Marxist circles, the abortive Russian Revolution of 1905 soon made the importance of Lenin's ideas spectacularly clear.

The signal sent out by the Petersburg revolutionaries of 1905 was that an organised group of activists was indeed capable of destabilising the old order in Europe. This principle was grasped by self-styled 'avant-gardes' of very different ideological persuasions, from the Futurists in Paris and Milan to the Expressionists in Berlin. During the years of political crisis between 1905 and 1914, European literature acquired a consciously prophetic quality, as Trotsky records in *Literature and Revolution*: 'The armed peace, with its patches of diplomacy, the hollow parliamentary systems, the external and internal politics based on the system of safety valves and brakes, all this weighed heavily on poetry at a time when the air, charged with accumulated electricity, gave sign of impending great explosions'.[2] Following the Futurists, avant-garde authors began to see themselves as agents of social protest and cultural transformation.

The outbreak of war in 1914 jolted even the academics and aesthetes out of their attitude of cultivated disdain for politics. For the first time there was a sense of collective participation in the destinies of the nations. Leading writers in every belligerent country began to define the war, not primarily in political terms, but as a cultural crusade. The military conflict was conceived as a struggle for supremacy between different systems of ideas.[3] This ideological struggle acquired a sharper political focus in 1917, after the American entry into the war and the outbreak of revolution in Russia. At both extremes political aims now began to be defined not by statesmen but by intellectuals: Lenin, whose grasp of the 'algebra of revolution' had enabled him to seize political power; Trotsky, both literary theorist and military genius of the Russian Revolution; Woodrow Wilson, the university professor who brought the United States into the war in order to make the world 'safe for democracy'; and Thomas Masaryk, the philosopher who created the democratic republic of Czechoslovakia out of the ruins of the Austro–Hungarian Empire. The ancient dream of the philosopher–king seemed on the verge of fulfilment, as a war of unprecedented horror ended on a note of hope.

Could the intellectuals perhaps succeed – where the statesmen had failed – in providing a more rational blueprint for European politics? This was the hope that inspired the writers and artists who plunged into the political struggles which followed the collapse of the old order in 1918. But the electoral defeat of Wilson, together with the punitive terms imposed on Germany by the Treaty of Versailles, dispelled the illusion that the peace settlement would make the world a safer place. And during the 1920s the triumph of Mussolini in Italy, together with the growing domination of Stalin in the Soviet Union, set up a stark choice between political extremes. These developments, so sinister in retrospect, exerted a remarkable fascination on leading European writers of this period. So strong was the sense of disillusionment with capitalism and democratic politics, which were blamed not only for the horrors of the war but also for the post-war economic malaise, that many of the finest minds were drawn towards ideologies which promised more radical solutions – communism at the one extreme, Fascism at the other. For intellectuals with an uneasy conscience about their own privileged backgrounds, these new systems seemed glamorous and dynamic, offering visions of fraternal solidarity and collective action. There was consequently a polarisation of attitudes, with the advocates of communism or Fascism seeing themselves not as fellow-travellers, but as dedicated apostles of a new creed.

The Nazi seizure of power in 1933, followed by the outbreak of civil war in Spain three years later, made it clear – even to writers who had previously shunned political engagement – that it was necessary to take sides. But by aligning themselves with ideological factions, the writers of this generation ran the risk of forfeiting that critical independence which had traditionally been the source of their authority. In a situation of unprecedented crisis the question was not only: 'What is to be done?' The question was also: 'How can political commitment be reconciled with intellectual integrity and artistic vision?'

A diversity of response to these questions is explored in this book. The fact that many of the reactions were so extreme gives them – for better or for worse – an exemplary quality. The present chapter will focus on three authors whose positions are in this sense exemplary: Bertolt Brecht, the left-winger closely aligned with communism: Gottfried Benn, the irrationalist who sought his salvation in Fascism; and Julien Benda, the apostle of political detachment. The argument begins with Benda, because his account of *The Treason of the Intellectuals* defines the absent centre from which the polarised positions of left and right diverged.

Benda's impartial clerisy

Julien Benda (1867–1956), who came from a prosperous Jewish family, dedicated himself from an early age to intellectual pursuits. But he lived through a period when French cultural life was becoming aggressively politicised, and his mind was shaped by a series of ideological confrontations. The Dreyfus case, in which an army officer of Jewish extraction was victimised by the French authorities, demonstrated the strength of the threat posed by the power of the state to the ideals which Benda espoused. A second ideological danger, which he attacked in a series of pamphlets, arose from the cult of vitalism and irrationality in the philosophy of Henri Bergson. These two currents – political chauvinism and philosophical irrationalism – became fused in the wave of nationalism and xenophobia to which so many intellectuals succumbed during the First World War. This led Benda to analyse the historical sources of these phenomena, which he traced back to the cult of the state in nineteenth-century Germany.

Against these ideological pressures Benda sought to uphold the values of rational discourse and political impartiality. *The Treason of the Intellectuals (La Trahison des clercs, 1927)* is the classic statement of his position.[4] Although the book was widely read, and soon translated into English, the uncompromising rigour of Benda's argument made him an isolated figure, whose merits are still not fully recognised. For his concept of the *clerc* – a word which seems to echo Coleridge's notion of a secular 'clerisy' – challenges the modern conception of the politically committed intellectual. And his powerful indictment convicts the leading European writers of his day for the '*intellectual organization of political hatreds*' (27).

By *clercs* Benda means those 'philosophers, men of religion, men of literature, artists, men of learning' whose lives have been lived 'in direct

opposition to the realism of the multitudes'. They either, like Leonardo da
Vinci, Malebranche and Goethe, dedicated themselves to 'the purely disinterested activity of the mind' and held aloof from political passions; or, like
Erasmus, Kant and Renan, 'they preached, in the name of humanity or
justice, the adoption of an abstract principle superior to and directly
opposed to these passions' (44). When such men entered the political arena,
they did so not for narrowly political ends but in defence of 'abstract
justice', as when Voltaire fought for the Callas family and Zola defended
Dreyfus (50–1).

Modern intellectuals (Benda argues) have betrayed the true calling of
the *clerc* by adopting the slogan: 'My country right or wrong!' He singles
out for attack the leading figures in each country who have subordinated
ethical principle to national policy: Barrès in France, d'Annunzio in Italy,
Kipling in England, William James in the United States. Their political
writings are seen as both intellectually and ethically flawed, for they give
instinct precedence over rationality, and promote collective political
hatreds through a pernicious cult of the state. The state is celebrated not as a
rational political entity, but as a metaphysical concept – the embodiment of
Bergsonian vitalism or the Nietzschean will to power.

Benda conducts his critique of this great betrayal with eloquence and
impartiality, and his exposition is supported by a suggestive analysis of
causes. His dedication to the life of the mind makes him hesitate to adopt
the Marxist theory of material determinants, which would relate the intellectual betrayal to the politics of imperialism and the class interests of the
capitalist bourgeoisie. And yet the account he offers does have Marxist
undertones. He sees the modern intellectual, who is prepared to sacrifice
ethical principles for political influence and practical success, as the servant
of the bourgeoisie. The modern bourgeoisie are in a state of acute anxiety,
'terrified' by the progress of the working class and 'solely anxious' to retain
their privileges. Hence the appeal of writers who denounce the liberal and
democratic virtues and proclaim 'doctrines of arbitrary authority, discipline, tradition, contempt for the spirit of liberty, assertion of the morality
of war' (164–8).

The treason of the intellectuals arises not only from 'changes in their
social status', but also from 'changes in the structure of their minds', above
all the denial of reason and the cult of 'artistic sensibility':

> Artistic sensibility is far more gratified by a system which tends to the
> realization of force and grandeur than by a system which tends to the
> establishment of justice [. . .] Artistic sensibility is especially flattered by the
> spectacle of a mass of units which are subordinated to each other up to the
> final head who dominates them all (167–70).

In such passages Benda acutely identifies the aesthetic appeal of Fascism (he is less perceptive about the complementary appeal of communism). And he recognises that ideologies of 'power' and 'discipline' are all the more seductive in an age when there are no intellectual certainties and when the great philosophical systems 'collapse upon each other as they cry to heaven their contradictory absolutes'. A further factor is the artist's sense that authoritarian systems recognise 'the rights of genius' and satisfy the 'thirst for sensations' – that 'need for cruelty' which some writers claim to be the sign of 'noble minds', but which Benda denounces as 'intellectual sadism' (171–5).

There is no doubt about the force of Benda's critique. But what is his solution? His repeated appeals for 'impartiality' seem inadequate to the crisis he has diagnosed, particularly as he sees the study of the Greek and Latin classics as the essential source of 'intellectual discipline'. His clerisy, like that defined by Coleridge, inhabits a world of the spirit which is remote from effective action.[5] Through his insistence that the true *clerc* should stand aloof from practical politics, Benda has painted himself into a corner. The result is a kind of fatalism – even a cult of failure. The true intellectual must be like Socrates or Christ, his moral authority sealed by practical defeat: hemlock or crucifixion. He should declare to mankind 'that his kingdom is not of this world, that *the grandeur of his teaching lies precisely in this absence of practical value*'. For Benda the betrayal begins the very moment the *clerc* 'claims to be practical' (190–1).

At this point in his argument there seems to be a failure both of nerve and of internal consistency. In his initial definition, Benda had identified *two* authentic models of intellectual life: those (like Goethe) who stand aloof from politics, and those (like Voltaire and Zola) who have decisively intervened in order to uphold an abstract principle. In Benda's summary this second category is lost from sight, as he seems to deny all possibility of principled political intervention. Thus Benda's defeatism is as problematic in its own way as that sacrifice of intellect which he condemns.

The main targets of Benda's attack are the French advocates of irrationalism: Barrès and Maurras, Bergson and Sorel. But the special value of his book derives from its international range of reference. He attacks intellectual treason on a European scale (just as he was later to argue for a united European nation guided by rational principles).[6] Apart from France, it is German intellectual life which commands Benda's main attention. For he sees the nationalistic intellectual as essentially a 'German invention' and bewails the 'victory of Germany' in the spiritual realm (58). The very success of the alliance in Germany between intellectual and political power has compelled intellectuals in other countries to adopt a stance of national fanaticism. Nietzsche, Hegel and the German Romantics are severely censured. But Benda's perspective on German affairs is not only retrospective; it anticipates the rationalisations of political tyranny that were to occur in the 1930s.

Benn's ambiguous radicalism

Treason of the Intellectuals defines the norms against which we may assess the polarisation of political sentiment in Germany. The test case is provided by Gottfried Benn (1886–1956). Benn was one of the most influential figures in the Expressionist movement and exemplifies its political volatility – its tendency to generate impulses towards both left-wing and right-wing extremes. Unlike his gifted contemporaries Georg Trakl and Ernst Stadler, Benn survived the First World War – after serving as an army doctor in German-occupied Brussels – to become a dominating presence in modern German poetry. His writings blend intellectual sophistication with a powerful appeal to the emotions, expressing a cynical disillusionment with modern civilisation and a longing for the simplicities of primal being. He was thus admired by the radical left for his sceptical intelligence, and by the right for his regressive cult of more primitive values.[7]

In a remarkable essay on Expressionism, published in November 1933, Benn analysed the presuppositions of avant-garde European art since 1910. Its essential principle (he argues) is the 'deconstruction of reality', or *Wirklichkeitszertrümmerung*. This subversion of the conventions of realism reflects the fact that 'reality' as an intellectual and social norm is also disintegrating. Modern science has undermined traditional conceptions of a stable universe, reducing space and time to mental functions. Society and the state are now perceived as functional constructs, not substantial entities. Economic analysis reveals that the notion of a stable 'reality' is a 'capitalist concept', concealing the underlying anarchy of production and profiteering, war and hunger, lawlessness and the lust for power. The First World War, with its turbulent aftermath, has transposed these disintegrative tendencies into political terms. There is thus a historical legitimation for the excesses of modern art, with its irrationality and distortions. But Benn also insists that Expressionism, like Futurism and Cubism, is not only an art of disintegration. Its exploration of the debris of bourgeois civilisation is also inspired by a positive impulse to 'get to the root of things' – *An-die-Wurzel-der-Dinge-gehen* (1, 240–56).

The radicalism which Benn so persuasively defines contributed to the

political indeterminateness of the avant-garde, particularly the Expressionists. These artists and writers may be united in their desire to return to the roots of human experience, but there is no consensus about what is to be found there. For some the essential nature of man is mystical, for others psychological (with a new emphasis on sexuality and the unconscious). Politically, the essential man who is discovered when the superstructure of bourgeois civilisation is swept away may equally well be the primitive predator or the exploited proletariat. This explains why among the writers of the Expressionist generation some (like Brecht and Becher) supported the communist movement while others (like Benn and Johst) gravitated towards National Socialism.

Benn's radical questioning of the values of rational man led him into wide-ranging speculations about the prehistory both of the human species and of the natural world. His cast of mind was essentially regressive. He began to speculate (in the manner of Nietzsche) about primitive human society, picturing an authentic community in which the strong could exult in their vitality – uninhibited by Christian morality or humanistic scruples. He sought to return to the roots of biological evolution, identifying that instinctual self which existed prior to that overdevelopment of the brain centres which has made us over-intellectual and endlessly at war with ourselves. He even began to invoke the findings of modern geology in order to measure the paltry achievements of *Homo sapiens* against the mindless grandeur of the millennia.

These primitive yearnings were a source of entrancing poetry. Benn combined his fragmented vision with a gift for melodic diction, and few poets have so eloquently expressed the longing to return to the womb of time:

> O daß wir unsere Ururahnen wären.
> Ein Klümpchen Schleim in einem warmen Moor.
> Leben und Tod, Befruchten und Gebären
> glitte aus unseren stummen Säften vor.
>
> Ein Algenblatt oder ein Dünenhügel,
> vom Wind Geformtes und nach unten schwer.
> Schon ein Libellenkopf, ein Möwenflügel
> wäre zu weit und litte schon zu sehr.
>
> (Would that we were a prehistoric horde.
> A lump of mucus in the dank, warm earth.
> Out of our silent juices would be poured
> life, death, fertility and giving birth.

> Sea-weed or sand-dune underneath the sky,
> shaped by the wind and weighty to the touch.
> A seagull's wing, head of a dragonfly
> would have evolved too far, suffer too much.) (2, 25)

These early 'Incantations' ('Gesänge', 1913) continue with two further strophes which conjure up images of a primeval forest, with an unnamed god lurking in the background. The god to whom the poet longs to return is clearly Nietzsche's Dionysus, presiding over a pre-Darwinistic landscape of organic harmony. But Benn cannot simply be discounted as a romantic or irrationalist. His poetry of urban disillusionment uses sophisticated montage techniques to create a patchwork of conflicting historical references and psychological perspectives, before culminating in images which lure the reader towards an oceanic self-immersion – 'hin in des Meeres erlösend tiefes Blau' (2, 31). Drugs, sexuality and the rhythms of the blood are blended with Spenglerian myths in an attempt to escape from individuality and cerebration.

Benn was not the only poet of his generation to derive potent images from such dubious intellectual sources (there are parallels with Yeats and Pound). The problem arises when the poet begins to confuse vision with blueprint, poetic image with political programme. In a series of essays, Benn asserts that the random processes of social development and biological evolution must be brought under control. The ills of our alienated civilisation are due to a biological imbalance between overdeveloped brain centres and an enfeeblement of the blood. This leads him to endorse eugenic theories and argue for a new social 'discipline' based on selective 'breeding' (Benn's keyword, 'Zucht', combines both meanings). These ideas brought him, even before 1933, into proximity with the racialist theories of National Socialism. Indeed, the fundamental aim of his essay on Expressionism was to show that the radical artistic tendencies of which he was the leading exponent were not degenerate, but derived their vitality 'from Germany's loyal blood'.

It is easy with hindsight to see the links between the regressive poetry and the reactionary politics. But Benn's public support for National Socialism was nevertheless a spectular betrayal of values he had hitherto upheld. During the early years of the Weimar Republic he had prided himself on his position as an outsider, holding aloof from both journalistic cliques and political factions. He lived a 'double life', gaining few financial rewards from his poetry, but scraping a living in one of the less salubrious suburbs of Berlin as a doctor specialising in the treatment of venereal diseases. There is a certain dignity about his attempts, towards the end of the 1920s, to maintain a 'reserved' position while all around him were becoming political 'fellow-travellers'.[8] But even at this stage it is clear that his hostility to 'politics' is directedly primarily against writers of the left, especially Johannes Becher, the Expressionist poet who had become a committed communist.

It was the political crisis which followed the Wall Street collapse of October 1929 which brought Benn into the limelight. Germany, whose financial recovery had been dependent on American loans, was plunged into three years of economic and political chaos, during which the institutions of parliamentary democracy became almost totally discredited. In a series of fiercely fought elections, which frequently erupted into violence, the political struggle became polarised between anti-democratic extremes. For writers like Benn it was tempting to see the political anarchy as a vindication of the Expressionist vision. The political ambivalence of his position was identified as early as autumn 1930 in a perceptive essay by his admirer Klaus Mann. And in 1931 Benn found himself simultaneously being attacked by the Fascist journal *Der Angriff* for his internationalist and 'defeatist' outlook; and denounced by the left-wing *Tagebuch* for sliding so far towards the 'Fascist camp' that he was becoming a 'spiritual comrade' of Hitler.[9] In January 1932, at the height of the crisis, Benn was elected to the Literary Section of the Prussian Academy of Arts, a prestigious body which supposedly stood above politics but which was also becoming sharply polarised, with the novelist Heinrich Mann the leading figure on the left. Benn had been one of Mann's most fervent admirers. But as the political struggle reached its climax, the former allies were to become bitter antagonists.

From the moment in January 1933 when Hitler was appointed German Chancellor, Benn swung his intellectual prestige behind National Socialism. And for almost eighteen months he was to be Hitler's most prominent literary supporter. He immediately joined forces with the right-wing clique in the Prussian Academy, in order to force Heinrich Mann and other left-wingers to resign. And he greeted the burning-down of the Reichstag, which gave Hitler the pretext to start a reign of terror, as the signal that a 'new epoch' had begun.[10] After the general election in March, which enabled the Nazis (with forty-four per cent of the vote) to assume dictatorial powers, Benn made the first of his notorious statements in support of the regime. Using the most public medium available – a radio broadcast – he denounced all those who opposed the new German state: intellectuals, liberals, democrats, internationalists and Marxists. A 'new biological type' (he proclaimed) had triumphed over 'disintegrating European democracy' with its spurious ideal of intellectual freedom ('Der neue Staat und die Intellektuellen', 1, 440–9).

The same sad story continued in a series of further broadcasts, speeches and essays. Against left-wing writers like his erstwhile admirer Klaus Mann, who had been forced into exile, Benn deployed the full range of his biologising pseudo-history in order to defend Nazism as 'the last grandiose project of the white race' (4, 239–48). The great enemy to be destroyed (he argued in subsequent statements) was 'intellectualism'.[11] There must be a return from the corruption of the great metropolis to a more authentic 'feeling for the soil' ('Ackergefühl', 1, 231). The 'purification of the body politic' requires that the state should stop wasting its resources on handicapped children. These inferior elements are to be 'eliminated' ('auszuscheiden', 1, 235). 'German eugenics' require that 'Offices of Health and Heredity' should be set up to regulate all marriages according to a 'system of points'. The values of the mind ('Geist') depend on race and breeding ('Rasse und Züchtung') (1, 232–9).

It is a dismal spectacle to see so gifted a writer lending his intellectual prestige to such arguments. Benn also spoke with the authority of a specialist in sexually-transmitted diseases (the sordidness of his medical experience may even have contributed to his longing for racial purity, as in the case of Céline – a writer whom he admired). A further irony is that as late as March 1934 Benn was still trying to convince himself that Fascism was the fulfilment of the avant-garde artistic vision. In the spring of 1934 Marinetti arrived in Berlin as leading literary representative of Mussolini's Italy. And it was appropriately Benn himself who delivered the official speech of welcome. Speaking in the name of the 'Führer, whom we all without exception admire', Benn sought to identify Marinetti's Futurist Manifesto of 1909 as the inspiration, not only of Italian Fascism, but also of the German national revival (1, 478–81). Benn's speech echoes the hope expressed in his essay on Expressionism that radical art might gain recognition from a reactionary regime. But he was labouring under a double misapprehension. The relationship between Futurism and Fascism was much more complex than Benn supposed (as Judy Davies shows in Chapter 5). And Expressionism, far from gaining recognition as authentic German art, was soon to be publicly vilified in the Exhibition of Degenerate Art (analysed in Chapter 15 by Frank Whitford).

By the summer of 1934 it was becoming clear that Benn's position was untenable. He might capitalise on attacks by literary opponents abroad. But he was vulnerable to accusations from within the German Reich that he himself was in reality one of those rootless intellectuals he despised. His poems were denounced by a right-wing opponent as 'masterpieces of typically Jewish art'. And rumours were soon in circulation that Benn himself was of Jewish origin (his name sounded suspiciously similar to the

Hebrew prefix *ben*). Benn hastened to have his papers authenticated by the Office of Racial Purity, in order to establish that he was '100% Aryan', for the allegation of Jewish origins threatened not only his literary reputation in Germany, but also his livelihood. Nazi edicts had deprived Jewish doctors of the right to practice in certain areas, and the ensuing shortage of qualified medical staff offered Benn the prospect of professional advancement and increased earnings. Hence his panic when the German Medical Association threatened to strike Benn himself off the register, because of alleged Jewish antecedents.[12]

Benn's public pronouncements became increasingly tight-lipped, and his private letters from July 1934 onwards express his disillusionment with Nazism: 'No words are adequate for this tragedy. A German dream – has once against come to an end.' As both his intellectual and his professional position became untenable, he opted for what he called 'the aristocratic form of emigration' – service in the German army.[13] And this enabled him to survive the Nazi reign of terror, even though in 1938 he was officially banned from writing and expelled from the writers' union. The poetry which he wrote in this period expresses a stoical fortitude. Its restrained resonance was to win the poet, despite his Nazi past, a new reputation after the Second World War, as one of the tragic survivors of the Expressionist generation. But it remains an unresolved paradox that one of Germany's greatest modern poets should have been so deeply implicated in intellectual treason.[14]

Brecht's alternative Marxism

The career of Bertolt Brecht (1898–1956) is an inverted image of that of Benn. Conscripted to serve as a medical orderly during the final months of the First World War, he too began to write a poetry of radical disillusionment. And a similar cynicism about the values of bourgeois civilisation led him to celebrate sexual pleasure and the power of the instincts. His first play, *Baal,* strongly coloured by the language of Expressionism, exults in anarchic individualism. And his cynicism about the possibility of effective political action extended to the communist rising of 1919 in Berlin, which in his second play, *Drums in the Night,* forms an ironic counterpoint to the hero's pursuit of physical survival. There are few signs in the early Brecht of any political commitment. His early radicalism was ideologically as ambivalent as that of Benn. And as late as 1928, when *The Threepenny Opera* (set to music by Kurt Weill) won him international fame, his work still revealed an anarchic indeterminateness.

Brecht, too, was not immune to the appeal of collective ideologies. The politicisation of the German theatre during the 1920s, especially in Berlin, inevitably brought him into contact with Marxism. From 1929 onwards he immersed himself in Marxist theory, under the guidance of friends in the communist movement. The attraction of Marxism, to Brecht as to so many writers of his generation, was that it offered a comprehensive explanatory system – not simply a cluster of redemptive myths. And this explanation, at least in Germany, seemed to square with the facts. The polarisation of class conflict had been predicted in the *Communist Manifesto*. So had the crisis of the capitalist economic system, which plunged Germany into chaos after the Wall Street collapse. And no one had foreseen as acutely as Lenin and Rosa Luxemburg the extent to which the official Social Democratic Party would betray revolutionary socialism by making common cause with the political establishment. For Brecht, Marxism was not an abstract theory. It explained what he saw going on outside his window. He was present in Berlin on May Day 1929, when working-class demonstrations were so brutally suppressed by the police that thirty-five people were killed. The chief of police was a Social Democrat.[15]

Brecht had always been sceptical about the Expressionist dream that great art could inspire a transformation of society. But during the crisis years of 1930–3 it was plausible to believe that a radical political theatre, allied to the cultural organisations of the working class, might help to tip the balance towards socialist revolution. His plays of these years, especially the political parable *The Measures Taken* (*Die Maßnahme*, 1930) were a direct contribution to the political struggle. But even in this most explicitly revolutionary play, he avoided political rhetoric and adopted the cool, distanced approach which is characteristic of his conception of epic theatre. The action is set in China, a country which was attracting widespread attention among writers of the left (including Tretiakoff and Malraux) owing to spectacular advances by the communist movement. And its explicit theme is the need for the individual political activist to accept the discipline of the Communist Party.

Technically as well as thematically, the play was a new departure. For in place of the bourgeois audience of passive cultural consumers, *The Measures Taken* involved the active participation of three large workers' choirs, which recited the part assigned to the Control Chorus in Hanns Eisler's musical setting. The workers' choirs thus acted as both performers and audience. For Brecht's primary aim was not to proclaim a dogma, but to provoke discussion about revolutionary tactics among political activists. Questionnaires were distributed at the first performance on 13 December 1930, and a public meeting was held a week later to assess the value of this new style of political art. Further productions followed during 1931 and 1932, until the play was finally banned by the Nazis in January 1933, on the eve of Hitler's accession to power. The lively discussion which this play provoked, both among participants and in the press, led Brecht radically to revise his orginal picture of the relationship between the individual and the Party.

The first version had emphasised the need for political subordination. It tells the story of a Young Comrade, whose undisciplined and emotional response to the sufferings of the Chinese people threatens the success of a political mission. After he has been recognised by the authorities, his fellow agitators feel obliged to kill him and destroy his body, in order to complete their mission without being detected. The play takes the form of a distanced reconstruction of these events, so that the Control Chorus (representing the Party) can evaluate what has occurred. But Brecht's overemphasis on the need for self-subordination (visually accentuated by the use of masks to erase the individual human face) was sharply criticised by fellow revolutionaries who believed in a more participatory form of communism. In the light of the ensuing debate Brecht rewrote a crucial scene, giving his definition of the Party a more democratic character.[16]

It was argued that Brecht's orginal authoritarian emphasis was a sign of the immaturity of his conception of communism. Perhaps he was compensating for his middle-class background and his earlier anarchic individualism. The irony is that for all its theoretical deficiencies, his original image of the Party was to prove so prophetic. The Show Trials in the Soviet Union during the later 1930s were gruesomely to confirm his picture of an impersonal Party apparatus approving the liquidation of dissenting individuals. In this sense a play designed to give ideological support to the communist movement may be seen as a tragic indictment. But the foreground emphasis on Party discipline is interwoven in this play with a second theme, which was to prove in the longer term even more significant for Brecht's development: the theme of learning from mistakes.

Even in his most committed and didactic phase Brecht's writings were infused with a spirit of sceptical inquiry which sets them qualitatively apart from party–political propaganda. The fact that *The Measures Taken* is not a representation but a re-enactment – a play-within-a-play, with echoes of Pirandello – is a further safeguard against dogmatism. And Brecht's subsequent development, after the Nazis forced him into exile, was towards a more flexible alternative form of Marxism which retained the right to dissent. Among the communist fellow travellers of the 1930s (as David Caute has shown), Brecht's independence of judgment places him in a category all of his own.[17]

With little more in his suitcase than the manuscript of his greatest plays, Brecht escaped from Nazi-dominated Europe through Scandinavia to the Soviet Union. But unlike his friend Johannes Becher, he did not remain in Moscow to become integrated into the Party apparatus. In a journey of great symbolic as well as practical value, he travelled across the Soviet Union to Vladivostok – and thence to the United States. The working diary which he kept during this period is testimony to his openness of mind – his ability to recognise the deficiencies of revolutionary communism, as well as of the capitalist alternative.[18] And when he returned to Berlin in 1948, to support Becher – now Minister of Culture – in the construction of the first German Socialist State, he retained that willingness to dissent.

Brecht's alternative Marxism made a cult of contradictions. It has thus become the focal point for a wide-ranging critical debate (further aspects of which are explored in subsequent chapters by David Midgley and Raymond Williams). His significance for the present argument is that he shows in an exemplary way that it is possible to combine political commitment with intellectual integrity. He never succumbed to the treason of the intellectuals, although he was aware of the concessions that even the most independent-minded person must make in order to survive. Indeed, the problematic relationship between individual conscience and political authority forms the theme of one of his greatest plays, *Life of Galileo*: a tragedy which testifies – even under the most adverse circumstances – to the enduring value of the inquiring mind.

Notes to chapter 1

1 V. I. Lenin, *Collected Works*, Vol. 5, Moscow, 1961, pp. 433, 452, 462, 520.
2 Leon Trotsky, *Literature and Revolution*, tr. Rose Strunsky, London, 1925 (reprinted Ann Arbor, Michigan, 1960), p. 126.
3 See Roland N. Stromberg, *Redemption by War: The Intellectuals and 1914*, Lawrence, Kansas, 1982.
4 Julien Benda, *La Trahison des clercs*, Paris, Les Cahiers Verts, 1927; tr. Richard Aldington under the title *The Great Betrayal*, London, 1928. Page references in the text are to the reprint of this translation, under the title *The Treason of the Intellectuals*, New York, The Norton Library, 1969.
5 Coleridge's concept of a 'National Church' or 'Clerisy' is analysed in Raymond Williams, *Culture and Society 1780–1950*, London, 1958, Ch. 3.
6 Julien Benda, *Discours à la nation européenne*, Paris, 1933. For further discussion of Benda's work, see Robert J. Niess, *Julien Benda*, Ann Arbor, Michigan, 1956, and Ray Nichols, *Treason, Tradition and the Intellectual: Julien Benda and Political Discourse*, Lawrence, Kansas, 1978. Benda's revulsion against right-wing ideologies led him later in life to develop communist sympathies.
7 Quotations from Benn's writings are based on his *Gesammelte Werke in vier Bänden*, ed. Dieter Wellershoff, Wiesbaden, 1959–61, and are identified by volume and page

number. English translations are by the present author. For a selection of Benn's writings in English, see *Primal Vision: Selected Writings of Gottfried Benn,* ed. E. B. Ashton, London, 1961.

8   See *Benn Chronik: Daten zu Leben und Werk,* ed. Hanspeter Brode, Munich, 1978, p. 70.
9   *Ibid.,* pp. 76, 79.
10   *Ibid.,* p. 90.
11   *Ibid.,* p. 96.
12   *Ibid.,* pp. 105–11.
13   Gottfried Benn, *Briefe an F. W. Oelze 1932–1945,* Wiesbaden, 1977, pp. 36, 39.
14   For a wide-ranging review of the debate about Benn's politics, see Jürgen Schröder, *Gottfried Benn: Poesie und Sozialisation,* Stuttgart, 1978.
15   For details of Brecht's developing interest in Marxism, see Klaus Völker, *Brecht – A Biography,* London, 1979, esp. Ch. 12.
16   For the textual variants, together with a comprehensive account of the play's intention and reception, see *Die Maßnahme – Kritische Ausgabe,* ed. Reiner Steinweg, Frankfurt, 1972.
17   David Caute, *The Fellow Travellers,* London, 1973.
18   Bertolt Brecht, *Arbeitsjournal 1938–1955,* 3 volumes, Frankfurt, 1973.

Dreams of
a revolutionary culture –
Gramsci, Trotsky and Breton

The social responsibility of the intellectual and the relationship between culture and politics have always been urgent questions. But there has occurred an epistemological shift since the end of the nineteenth century. The theories of Freud and the experience of the Great War came to suggest an unconscious, irrational, lustful and destructive drive behind *culture* as well as politics. An age-old belief in the meliorative tendency of culture was shaken. And man's most spectacular intellectual advances – that is, his scientific inventions and discoveries – undermined the unity of art and science. Painting and theatre have been radically transformed by the development of photography and the cinema. The realisation of man's oldest dream, flight, and the resolution of his oldest riddle, the nature of matter, were rehearsed in one war and accomplished in the next. The supremacy of scientific rationalism and nationalist culture was perfected and demolished at Verdun and Guernica, Auschwitz and Hiroshima. In his 'Theses on the philosophy of history', Walter Benjamin describes the angel of history facing the past, wings caught in its whirlwind, rubble piling up at his feet. Benjamin pessimistically rejects organic historical or fictional narratives which try to impose meaning on the past; he sees ironic surrealist recuperation of objects and images as the only sane riposte to discredited theories of progress.[1]

In 1938 the Surrealist leader André Breton declared that our century was the century of Lautréamont, Freud and Trotsky.[2] This libertarian triad, associating irrational erotic violence with therapeutic depth-psychology and the totalitarian intellect, seems to characterise clearly enough the anguished world of a certain 'avant-garde' – not least through Breton's reference to the mental, the past, and the literary, in order to transcend reason, shape the future, and mould society.

What makes this avant-garde ethos particularly relevant is that we continue to live in the grip of its self-destructive, or 'agonistic' paradigm.[3] For it is the unprecedented intellectual self-negation of their models of individual and political liberation – systems based on paradox and tending towards the unknown – which distinguishes them from their positivist predecessors.

Thus a section of the European avant-garde intelligentsia came to attack the very concepts of culture and progress, in a once-for-all-time rejection of art and its institutions, in favour of life.[4] The purpose of this chapter is to explore this crisis through an analysis of three theorists of the avant-garde: André Breton, who represents an 'agonistic' extreme; and the contrasting positions of Leon Trotsky and Antonio Gramsci, who tried to assimilate and transcend the crisis and produce a theory of a new, post-avant-garde culture for a new, post-capitalist society.

Antonio Gramsci: the hegemony of culture

The twenties were a period of great ferment for the European Left. The Russian Revolution seemed to have rendered all things possible. But a wave of imitative revolutions had been crushed. It was clear to a number of Marxist thinkers that the economic infrastructure could not, through its 'inevitable' contradictions, usher in a new world unaided, and that intellectual and moral intervention was both necessary and possible.

Antonio Gramsci had initially made his name through his journalism.[5] In 1922, after Mussolini's seizure of power, Gramsci went to Moscow for two years; between 1924 and 1926 he was the Communist Party leader in Italy, protected by parliamentary immunity. But in 1926 he was arrested with all the anti-Fascist deputies, and spent the next decade in jail. His *Prison notebooks*,[6] however, continue the profound analysis of culture he had initiated as a journalist. His work constitutes a continuous search for a programme of socialist culture.[7]

Gramsci's writing was nourished by his parallel activities as academic linguist, Communist militant, theatre critic and Marxist theoretician. Gramsci, like Croce before him, criticises the orthodox Marxist view of culture as merely a superstructural phenomenon, dependent on a 'deified' economy.[8] Gramsci evolved the idea of the 'historical bloc',[9] where instead of the economic infrastructure determining cultural activity, ideas and economic forces interact mutually; and he argued that intellectual activities influence politics through a process of 'hegemony'.[10] Gramsci's voluntarist interpretation of Marxism leads him to see the education of the people as the vital task of the intellectual. Other, more artistic cultural manifestations would also have their role to play in fertilising the widespread revolution of the mind which would *prepare* the social revolution.[11]

Gramsci's model of hegemony takes its authority from his understanding of the process of socio-linguistic change, whereby a prestige language secures the active consent of lower-prestige speech communities. He argued that linguistic innovations radiate outwards from a prestigious core or elite, as when, during the Renaissance, there was a diffusion of vernacular linguistic innovation from below (the rich, creative flourishing of Tuscan Italian, due to the rise in the power of Florentine commerce) directed from above (the vital, prestigious formulation of a new literary language by Dante, Petrarch and Boccaccio). So, too, a new civilisation expresses itself in literary form before the creation of a new state; indeed, its literary expression creates the intellectual and moral conditions which are then expressed in legislature and the state.[12] Gramsci therefore argues that a proletarian revolution presupposes a new kind of moral life, a new psychology and new feelings, so that the proletariat need to win *intellectual* power, to organise themselves *culturally*.[13]

Gramsci shared with Trotsky the belief that socialism should redesign the whole aesthetic and cultural as well as social and political context of human life. He was enthusiastic, for instance, about the new Italian 'Rationalist' architecture (inspired by architects as politically diverse as Sant' Elia, Le Corbusier, van Doesburg and Gropius), with its emphasis on functionalism and on the planning of complete urban complexes catering for the social needs of the people, which must take precedence over decorative architectural pretensions. All over Europe in the twenties and thirties there was a strange concordance of left- and right-wing impulses towards such an aesthetic and social totalisation of the environment.

Like Trotsky, Gramsci was struck by the possibilities and the dangers of the cinema. Perceptively, Gramsci saw that the cinema had exposed the false illusionism and intellectualism of the theatre. But he argues that the cinema's very superiority in producing realistic decor and mechanised imagery should allow the theatre to revert to exploration of the language of the classic theatre, rather than try to compete commercially with the cinema.[14] Gramsci's view of culture as a whole nexus of ideas, the concrete manifestation of 'the vague concept of freedom of thought' [SCW 25], led him to argue that theatrical entertainment ought to be removed from the control of the entrepreneurs who, in Gramsci's Turin, seemed to be peddling only music hall acts along with peanuts and iced drinks, and exploiting the actors. Gramsci expects theatre to promote moral progress, and castigates the Italian bourgeois and petty-bourgeois public as a 'hypocritical animal' [SCW 71], disdainful of Pirandello's *Liola* (1917), a Sicilian dialect play, for its failure to end in a knifing or a marriage. Gramsci includes in his condemnation bourgeois women ('potential cocottes'), who can only accept free women if they *are* cocottes, and who reject the serious analysis of the problems of female liberation presented in Ibsen's *Doll's House*.

Gramsci's approval of modernism leads him to praise Pirandello for deprovincialising the audience's taste, and destroying the philistine, petty-bourgeois culture inherited from the late nineteenth century: 'Luigi Pirandello is a "stormtrooper" of the theatre. His comedies are so many hand grenades that explode in the brains of the spectators, bringing down banalities, wrecking feelings and ideas.' [*SCW* 83].

In a review in *Avanti!* in 1920, he berates the bourgeois audience which fails to respond to the moral seriousness of Andreyev's modern Russian play, *Anfisa* (1909). Although unhappy with the 'cinematic' style of the acting, Gramsci seems to look ahead confidently to the marrying of new theatrical forms with a new social morality, necessitating a new audience: Andreyev's play may be a passionate *bourgeois* drama, but it presupposes a new, educated, *proletarian* audience.

Gramsci is convinced that the past needs to be assimilated for the future to be created. The Marxist Gramsci sympathises with the Christian Dante, whose art explores the problems of the intellectual in a period of ideologically motivated conflict (the bloody clashes between Papal Guelfs and Imperial Ghibellines in late thirteenth-century Italy). In contemporary literature, too, Gramsci avoids simply wishing to replace a bourgeois or right-wing content with a socialist or left-wing content, recognising the complexity of the relationship of artistic form to social context. Gramsci rejects both the contention of the Italian 'Calligraphists' that writers can remain aloof from politics, and the claim of the 'Contentists' to decree the (generally Fascist) content of culture from above.[15]

When Trotsky was writing *Literature and Revolution* in 1922,[16] and wanted to explore the paradox that Italian Futurism had helped spawn Fascism, whereas Russian Futurism was vociferously Bolshevik, he addressed himself to Gramsci, who stayed in Moscow from 1922 to 1924. In reply, Gramsci said that Italian Futurism had become almost as irrelevant to reaction as to revolution.[17] But Gramsci had at first been attracted by the Futurist attack on the bourgeoisie, and by the futurist equation of artistic modernism, social progress and technological innovation. He preferred the Futurists to the 'sausage fodder' of official literature, which was 'the pimp of the newspapers'. [*SCW* 47]. In 1913 he welcomed Marinetti's experimental text 'Adrianopoli assedio orchestra' as the linguistic equivalent of Picasso's painting, with its 'noun-planes' intersecting as do Picasso's visual images. [*SCW* 48]. Even as late as January 1921, in *Ordine nuovo*, he approves the Futurists' innovation and audacity, their attempt to destroy ossified bourgeois culture: 'In their field, the field of culture, the Futurists are revolutionaries.'[18]

In Turin in 1920 Gramsci set up an Institute of Proletarian Culture, affiliated to *Proletkult*, inspired, perhaps, by the factory councils in Turin in 1919 which he saw as centres of education for a proletarian state. Gramsci's idea was to train a new type of proletarian intellectual, wresting the privilege of education away from the bourgeoisie, obviating the need for the 'dead weight' of a 'bureaucratic caste'. [*SCW* 18, 22]. For he thought that the rank and file of working-class socialists should be able to have their say in the formulation of political theory, which had been monopolised by middle-class intellectuals. Gramsci's model is based on his interpretation of the way the Renaissance bourgeoisie, on coming to power in the fourteenth century, rejected the Establishment and created their own intellectuals (politicians, scholars, artists, etc.) from among their own ranks, ultimately challenging the authority of the church and aristocracy. He contrasts this procedure with that of the Catholic Church, which creates its own caste of 'intellectuals' (the clergy), but only by raising selected individuals out of their class. The people – from whom the clergy stem, and whom they address – are excluded from intellectual debate, since this is conducted by mandarins manipulating an arcane Latin discourse. Thus Gramsci approves an aspect of dynamic bourgeois individualism, and suggests that it be adopted as a model for creating a popular political culture. As Raymond Williams shows in his Introduction, this imitation of the dynamic and creative side of the bourgeoisie is an important and surprising feature of the avant-garde. Gramsci's view of a whole people raising its consciousness and becoming able to participate in social debate and political decision-making was in opposition to that of the other main Italian Communist theoretician, Bordiga, who believed strongly in a Leninist-style party, with an intellectual elite directing the obedient masses.

Gramsci did not underestimate rival forces in 'popular' culture. He proposed teaching folklore to teachers, to make them familiar with the irrational world that rivalled their scientific views; and he wanted newspapers to persuade Italian writers to produce popular fiction expressing the feelings of ordinary people, rather than translate pretentious foreign (usually French) literature. Gramsci criticises socialist weeklies for adapting themselves to the average level of culture of their readers, instead of trying to educate readers to a higher level, 'to consolidate their spirit in a higher critical perception of history and the world in which they live and struggle'. [*SCW* 33].

Gramsci's vision of a wholly educated and creative populace is influenced by his work as a historical linguist, working until 1918 on a thesis on

Italian dialects. Thus he attacks the vogue for Esperanto in a finely argued piece in *Il Grido del popolo* in 1918, explaining that language is a complex social activity, where the form of the language is even more important than its message. When we need to express concepts and arguments which have a long history, we must avoid dangerous simplifications and generalisations, whereas Esperanto will not allow the shifts in meaning that natural languages do.

However, Gramsci opposed the liberal policy, broached in Croce's *Aesthetics* of 1902 and, ironically, implemented in the Fascist minister G. Gentile's supposedly liberal Education Act of 1923, of allowing children to maintain their dialectal idiosyncracies. The idea (now widespread among educationalists in Britain) was that language should be the subject of creative self-expression rather than normative analysis and prescription. But Gramsci believed that such *laissez-faire* actually *reinforced* class divisions, since bourgeois children speaking standard Italian adapted more easily to the school system. Although Gramsci argues that the process of linguistic innovation cannot be stopped – for grammar is not static, but is driven by a process of reciprocal social monitoring – his desire for the construction of a culture at once national and popular makes him reject some avant-garde poetry, with its neologisms, and ungrammatical associations of words, as exemplified in the 'baroque' and 'incomprehensible' poetry of Ungaretti, with its 'Frenchified conceits'. [SCW 97, 203]. Such apparent contraditions are probably to be explained by the fact that Gramsci thinks that the *educational system* should provide all citizens with the standard linguistic skills which grant access to knowledge, communication, culture and power; but that there should not then be artificial blocks to *creative exploitation* of language – indeed only a properly educated public can enjoy such ludic, avant-garde creativity.

Gramsci continued in his Fascist jail to be committed to violent communist revolution (he was transferred to hospital in 1933 and died in 1937). He persisted, however, in his complex analysis of problems of language, education and culture, believing that the aim of the revolution was to create a new culture, but also that the new culture was too important to be left until after the revolution. It is one of the ironies of history that Marinetti, Ungaretti and Pirandello, who helped create the avant-garde culture in which Gramsci saw hope for radical political change, should have welcomed the Fascist regime which tried to stifle that hope.

Leon Trotsky – the hammer and the mirror

Trotsky published *Literature and revolution* in 1923, during Gramsci's stay in Moscow, at a time when the mutual relevance of artistic and political experiment seemed urgent, exciting – and self-evident – in the USSR. He addresses himself to the question of the role of the writer in a newly created socialist society. His position thus diverges both from that of Breton, preoccupied with the role of the writer fomenting revolution in an apparently terminal capitalist democracy; and from that of Gramsci, debating how to create a new popular culture in order to lay the foundations of a socialist society. Trotsky had been the key ally of Lenin in gaining revolutionary power for the Petersburg Soviet and overthrowing Kerensky's provisional government in 1917. Despite his originally Menshevik views, he became the virtual second-in-command of the whole Bolshevik apparatus. He was a brilliant orator, administrator and man of action, entrusted with the military fate of the whole country as Commissar of the Red Army. Yet he was a profoundly literary man, who read French novels during dull moments in Tsarist jails or Soviet Politburo meetings,[19] and who poured out an astonishing series of biographical, historical and literary studies, before, during and after the period when he held supreme power and responsibility. As passionately as Marx and Lenin he pursued action through the word, in tract, manifesto, pamphlet, newspaper article, oration and book.

His initial assumption in *Literature and Revolution* is that art follows economic developments. But he is at pains to argue that the relationship is so delayed and complex that there is no justification for a socialist government attempting to prescribe artistic form. There must be a time-lag between the activity of revolution and revolutionary art: 'The nightingale of poetry, like that bird of wisdom, the owl, is heard only after the sun is set . . . all through history, mind limps after reality.' [*LR* 19]. Trotsky rejects a theory of simple reflexion of the type 'style is class', and argues that 'a class finds its style in extremely complex ways', seeing literary movements as evolving dialectically from previous movements. [*LR* 205–6]. This implies a partial autonomy of the history of forms, mediated by social factors: 'Artistic creation is always a complicated turning inside out of old forms, under the influence of new stimuli which originate outside of art.' [*LR* 179]. Not only can there be no proletarian culture, as the proletariat will not have time to create art during the decades of struggles involved in this period of transition to socialism, but there will be no proletarian art, because 'before the proletariat has passed out of the stage of cultural apprenticeship, it will have ceased to be a proletariat' [*LR* 194], and thus socialist art will be classless. Trotsky unequivocally rejects the absolutist claims of socialist realism, which he finds tainted with naive sentimentality: 'The Revolution is not at all a torn boot, plus romanticism.' [LR 88].

Yet, although unwilling to delineate a socialist art, he is anxious to recuperate progressive forces in all kinds of culture, even that not sympathetic to Bolshevism, for political ends. Despite his acceptance of the Marxist view that the economic infrastructure is predominant, Trotsky also allows art a prophetic function: 'Works of art are the embodiments of presentiments; therefore pre-revolutionary art is the real art of the Revolution'. Since 'the new art . . . is as yet unborn', he judges that the most urgent task is to use *existing* culture to educate the proletariat. [LR 110, 56]. Breton's Surrealists revalued the unconscious, the marginal and the *maudit*, and Marinetti's and Mayakovsky's Futurists were champions of the mechanical. Both rejected the classical heritage, as well as the cultural status quo. But Trotsky argues that the working classes must first master the classical Pushkin they do not know, absorb him and overcome him, before rejecting the art of the past. The Futurist rejection of the past is 'bohemian nihilism'. [LR 131]. After all, Marx and Engels were brought up on the culture of petty-bourgeois democracy; and Trotsky, like Gramsci, looks forward to the time when the education of the working class will remove the chasm between the creative intelligentsia and the people.

Just as Trotsky places the determination of artistic form beyond the competence of the party and government, so he denies the party competence to accept or reject innovations in scientific theory, including atomic theory, Freud's psychoanalysis, and Einstein's relativity: 'What are the metaphysicians of a purely proletarian science going to say about the theory of relativity?' [LR 219].

Although he is sympathetic to the Futurists' search for a rational and functional art, exemplified by Mayakovsky's direction of LEF ('Left Front of the Arts'), a Petersburg Futurist review and group, founded in 1923, Trotsky finds them guilty of 'Utopian sectarianism', of anticipating and 'prescribing' history. [LR 134]. He reproaches LEF's figurehead, Mayakovsky, with trying too rationally to write progressive poetry, and ignoring the fact that art involves 'one's whole mind, which includes the irrational, in so far as it is alive and vital'. [LR 143]. He prefers Mayakovsky's pre-revolutionary futurist poetry, like *A cloud in trousers*, for, he argues, poetry 'deals with the process of feeling the world in images', as opposed to 'the process of knowing the world scientifically'. [LR 147, 157].

Yet although Trotsky acknowledges the relative self-sufficiency of art forms, he is hostile to what he sees as the futility of the Formalist conception of poetry, which, in Jakobson's perspective, would be a mere combination of sounds: 'Having counted the adjectives, and weighed the lines, and measured the rhythms, a Formalist . . . throws out an unexpected generalisation which contains five per cent of Formalism and ninety-five per cent of the most uncritical intuition.' [*LR* 172]. Thus, for Trotsky, the meaning of Cologne cathedral comes not from measuring it, but from understanding the organisation and function of medieval city and religion. Trotsky's example of such medieval, spiritualised craft as an artistic archetype shows that he is aware that art is spiritual vision at the same time as social production. He insists on including the vision as an integral part of the social project:

> To reject art as a means of picturing and imaging knowledge . . . is to strike from the hands of the class which is building a new society its most important weapon. Art, it is said, is not a mirror, but a hammer: it does not reflect, it shapes. But at present even the handling of a hammer is taught with the help of a mirror, a sensitive film which records all the movements. . . . If one cannot get along without a mirror, even in shaving oneself, how can one reconstruct oneself or one's life, without seeing oneself in the 'mirror' of literature? Of course no one speaks about an exact mirror. No one even thinks of asking the new literature to have a mirror-like impassivity. The deeper literature is, and the more it is imbued with the desire to shape life, the more significantly and dynamically it will be able to picture life. [*LR* 137].

As this crucial allusion to the power of photography and cinema suggests, Trotsky, like Gramsci, realises the enormous potential impact of the visual and performing arts for a society moving towards new forms of social integration. He hopes for a new theatre which will 'emerge out of its four walls and will merge in the life of the masses'. [*LR* 239]. But he is somehow unable to envisage its form, and merely calls for new versions of old forms: 'a Soviet comedy of manners', or an updated tragedy, where the conflict between man and a divinely controlled destiny will be replaced by 'the conflict between the individual and the collectivity'. [*LR* 238, 243]. And when faced with genuine experiment, Trotsky reveals a formal conservatism, accusing 'the passionate experimenter, Meyerhold' of disguising weakness of dialogue in his actors by making them act with 'bio-mechanic' rhythms. Meyerhold stands convicted of 'provincial dilettantism', for trying to guess the future before it is ready. [*LR* 135]. Similarly with modern architecture: Tatlin's famous design for a Soviet meeting hall, with its central cylinder rotating somewhat gratuitously inside a leaning tower of girders, is dismissed as 'a beer bottle in a spiral concrete temple'. [*LR* 248].

Ultimately, however, Trotsky shares part of the Futurist creed, hoping for an end to the separation of culture from technology, arguing that barriers will fall 'not only between art and industry, but simultaneously

between art and nature also', not through a Rousseauesque return to nature, but a transformation of nature into something more artificial: 'The machine is not in opposition to the earth'. [*LR* 250, 252].

Thus Trotsky's vision of the future is a bold projection, feeding on spiritual as well as technical optimism. He foresees an era of abundant resources and energy, releasing 'the liberated egotism of man' which 'will be directed wholly towards the understanding, the transformation and the betterment of the universe – in such a society the dynamic development of culture will be incomparable with anything that went on in the past' [*LR* 188–9] – a passage quoted admiringly by Breton.[20]

These new developments will also affect the position of women. Trotsky's models are not the great female poets Tsvetaeva and Akhmatova, whose mystical tendencies he derides, [*LR* 41] nor does he see woman as a source of transcendental inspiration for man, as Breton tended to. Trotsky looks forward to completely rethinking the role of woman within a socialist culture, and sees such new relationships as inseparable from a new educational system: 'Woman will at last free herself from her semi-servile condition. Side by side with technique, education . . . will take its place as the crown of social thinking. Powerful "parties" will form themselves around pedagogic systems.' [*LR* 253–4]. Trotsky argues that under socialism competition will no longer take the form of class struggles, but of debates over technique, art, style, and education. Here he seems to hope, like Gramsci, that these will help direct the political machine, rather than the reverse.

True to his own theories, Trotsky's analysis tends to use the history of literary forms (formalism, futurism, realism) as an index of historical development and political awareness, scrutinising intellectual and aesthetic arguments as if they were the vital focus of the struggle for power. Although in *Literature and Revolution* Trotsky is unwilling to allow the Party to dictate artistic norms, he did in fact support Lenin's policy of massive state intervention in and encouragement of the arts, with the appointment of the dynamic Lunacharsky as Commissar for Education and Culture, and the setting up of such organisations as *Proletkult*. Artists as various as Chagall, Gorki and Mayakovsky initially joined in the production and administration of a new Soviet culture. Sadly, the Soviet Union was all too soon to turn its back on such creative stylistic pluralism and dynamic cultural experimentation. The exile of Trotsky in 1929, followed by the suicide of Mayakovsky a year later, signalled the supression of artistic and political dissent under Stalinism, just as the imprisonment of Gramsci by Mussolini in 1926 put an end to the pretensions of Fascism to encourage social and cultural vitality. Under these circumstances, even before Hitler's suppression of the ebullient culture of Weimar in 1933, the centre of gravity of the debate about a revolutionary culture understandably shifted to France.

André Breton – dreams and demonstrations

By the end of the twenties in France all the vital forces of artistic creativity and social protest seemed to be channelled through Surrealism. The earlier artistic protest movement, Dadaism, born of disgust with a whole system of official morality and culture which the Dadaists accused of underpinning the massacres of the First World War, was so negative that it imploded. But in 1924 some of the liveliest spirits involved founded a new movement, Surrealism. This movement aimed at nothing less than the radical transformation of society through a revolution in art. Surrealists like André Breton, Louis Aragon, and Paul Eluard became successful writers, and many key figures of avant-garde French culture, like Jean Cocteau, Antonin Artaud, Michel Leiris and Georges Bataille, not to mention Picasso and Dali, went through a Surrealist phase. The famous Surrealist films *Un chien andalou* ('An Andalusian Dog', 1929) and *L'âge d'or* ('The Golden Age', 1930), made by the Spaniards Dali and Buñuel, were inspired by Breton's Movement.

Yet the lastingly popular achievements of the Surrealists – typified by the Dali–Buñuel films – have only the loosest connection with the Surrealists' political ambition to found a new society. There are moments of a healthy but old-fashioned anarchist derision, as there are too in René Clair's film *Entr'acte* ('Intermission', 1925), made in co-operation with the Surrealist painters Marcel Duchamp and Francis Picabia, but no sense of any constructive vision, once the liberatingly irreverent humour has liberated.

In his *Manifesto of Surrealism*, in 1924, Breton claimed that Surrealist poetry should arise from the dream imagery and sexual desire foregrounded by Freud. Artistic creativity, whether driven by associations originating in the private unconscious, or by the group coincidence of collective automatic writing, becomes equivalent to uncontrolled libidinous desire, with its random verbalisation or visualisation. But this self-expressive aesthetics coexists, in the very first issues of his review *La révolution surréaliste* in 1924, with urgent political anarchy, calling for an end to family, nation, army, prisons and religion. 'Open the prisons, disband the army', Breton demanded in the second issue of *La révolution surréaliste*.[21] In the first issue the anarchist assassin Germaine Berton (who had gunned down an *Action*

Française leader in 1923) was idolised, whilst in the third issue Artaud wrote a delirious open letter to the Dalai Lama. Artistic, erotic, spiritual and political liberation seemed happily coextensive in early surrealism.

This open-ended dream of an anarchist, pacifist, erotic liberation (inherited no doubt from Fourier, Proudhon and Sorel) looked incongruous in the face of the realities of political power. The strength of French colonialism, manifest in France's repression of a Moroccan rising in 1925 ('La guerre du Riff'), could not be broken by such methods. The anarchic strain was then revised, when Breton agreed to co-operate with militants working for *Clarté*, a communist review directed by Jean Bernier. The Surrealists had to publicly reject Utopianism, and accept Bernier's announcement in *l'Humanité* that there was 'no Surrealist theory of Revolution'. [N 85, 87]. Having officially admitted that individualistic anarchic revolt was ineffectual, Breton embraced the theory of the class struggle, and joined the Communist Party in January 1927, together with Eluard and Aragon – although, according to *Légitime défense* (1926), he still hoped to subordinate this 'minimum' programme to a transcendental mental revolution. Breton's review, with a change of title in 1930 from *La révolution surréaliste* to *Le surréalisme au service de la révolution*, continued to pursue its parallel revolutions. Accounts of the Surrealists' dreams are juxtaposed with impetuous telegrams to Moscow pledging support for a revolution in Western Europe.

One moment of effective joint cultural action was achieved when in 1931 the Surrealists helped the Communists protest at the French Government's Colonial Exhibition in Paris, by mounting an alternative, anti-colonial exhibition, using primitive works of art in their possession, wittily contrasted with commercial Catholic knick-knacks representing imperialist art.[22] Yet despite Breton's basic premise that the barriers between art and real life should be overthrown, and that artists should intervene in politics, many of the Surrealists' interventions appeared somewhat symbolic. But then political activity is perhaps as replete with symbolic gesture as is cultural activity. In the same spirit with which Diaghilev had unfurled the red flag at the first night of *Parade* in 1917, Breton staged a mock trial of the nationalist writer Barrès in 1921, using a dummy on stage, instead of the (wisely) absent novelist. Of many such scandals, suffice it to recall two examples. Paul Eluard, present with Eisenstein at the first night of Jean Cocteau's play *La voix humaine* in 1930, interrupted the play with insults shouted at the author. The same year, Louis Aragon made a physical attack on a journalist who had attributed Mayakovsky's recent suicide to Soviet persecution, rather than an unhappy love-affair. This cultural agitation should no doubt be read in the context of an equally effervescent right-wing activism. In 1930 Léon Daudet's *Action Française* militants caused riots at the Paris premiere of *L'âge d'or* (with its scandalously rampant desire and obviously anti-bourgeois irony), causing the film to be banned in the interest of public order after a few chaotic evenings; whilst in Germany Nazis threw stink bombs during the Frankfurt production of Brecht's *Mahogonny* and released white mice at the Berlin premiere of Lewis Milestone's anti-war film *All Quiet on the Western Front*.[23]

The exile of Trotsky was the subject of inconclusive debate by the Surrealist group in 1929. Breton, in his *Second Surrealist Manifesto* (1930), hedges his bets, declaring that both Trotsky and Stalin stand for equally valid revolutionary tactics.[24] But Surrealism's privileged *means* of destroying the *bourgeois* order is still supposed to be the *inner* revolution: 'Our aim must be the absolute destruction of all the pretensions of the caste to which we involuntarily belong, pretensions which we can only help to abolish outside ourselves when we have managed to abolish them within us.' [*SM* 87]. Thus culture and consciousness take precedence over politics, as in Gramsci. But Breton did not find it easy to translate his theoretical desire for action into concrete and positive results. He reports on his disappointing experience as secretary of his local gas workers' branch, for whom the Communist Party had asked him to prepare a report on the social and economic structure of Mussolini's Italy, instructing him to 'avoid ideology, above all'. [*SM* 99]. Breton refused to accept a task which must have seemed either too mundane or even too contradictory. He continues to maintain a rigid compartmentalisation of ideas on the role of the artist, arguing simultaneously that artistic activity should be free, but that a proletarian revolution was needed first in order to liberate the mind.

Breton's *Second Manifesto* still promulgated an almost totally anarchist programme: mocking the family, the French flag, the clergy, and traditional sexual morality, and even proposing as the ultimate surrealist act the absurdly gratuitous violence of firing a revolver into the crowd at random. Breton's review continued to champion female assassins, such as the Papin sisters (two Parisian maids who had murdered their oppressive employers) and Violette Nozière (a teenage prostitute who had poisoned her debauched father). Meanwhile Breton pursued his parallel mental revolution in such artistic efforts as his elaborate imitation of the language of insanity in *L'Immaculée conception* (1930), written in collaboration with Eluard.

In 1930, with Trotsky temporarily forgotten, Breton rallied to the Third International, and despatched Aragon to the Soviet city of Kharkov with Georges Sadoul to represent the Surrealists at the Second International Congress of Revolutionary Writers. But Breton was betrayed by his two emissaries, who publicly denounced Freud and Trotsky, and abjured any extra-Party action. Aragon's violently and explicitly revolutionary poem, 'Front rouge' (analysed in detail in Chapter 8), provoked Breton into reaffirming his belief in the political irrelevance of poetry. Aragon left the Surrealist group over this issue, and Breton's enthusiasm for the Communist Party was further undermined.

Breton, Eluard and Crevel were finally expelled from the Communist Party in 1933. Despite this new-found independence, Breton remained a political activist, joining a group of anti-Fascist intellectuals to sign an *Appel à la lutte* on 10 February 1934 (the start of a 'united front' left-wing opposition to Fascism in France, sparked by the French Fascists' abortive attempt on 6 February to take parliament by storm). Breton also signed a tract protesting at France's refusal to grant Trotsky a residence permit in April 1934, and joined the Intellectuals' Committee of Vigilance, alongside André Malraux, in 1935.

In May 1935 Stalin and Laval signed a mutual assistance pact. And the French Communist Party, for the first time ever suspending its aim of overthrowing the French Government by revolutionary violence, now supported the foreign policy of its class enemies. 'Position politique de l'art aujourd'hui', a lecture delivered by Breton in Prague on 1 April 1935, attacks the new united-front policy as a betrayal of the Communists' revolutionary intentions, and criticises Stalin for destroying democracy in 'the homeland of the working classes'. Breton conducts a lively attack on servile art – from Claudel's pious drama *l'Annonce faite à Marie* ('The Annunciation'), on tour in the USSR, to the competition run by *L'Humanité* for the best bust of Stalin. And he accuses the USSR of driving poets like Mayakovsky and Essenin to suicide by obstructing all attempts to 'translate the world into a new language'.[25] He suggests a sinister parallel with Hitler's repressive equation of avant-garde art and Marxist culture – for in Europe, since the Nazis' burning of the books in 1933, it was clear (even before the 1937 Munich exhibition of 'degenerate art') that civilisation itself could be threatened by apparently aesthetic discriminations between 'degenerate' and orthodox artistic styles.

The 'International Congress of Writers for the Defence of Culture' held in Paris in June 1935, whose patrons were the well-known writers Romain Rolland and Henri Barbusse,[26] was a vital platform for European Communist parties, attempting to rejoin the mainstream of democratic culture after over a decade of self-exclusion. The new united-front politics were dramatised by the limelight shed on such moderate writers as Forster and Huxley, Malraux, Gide and Pasternak. But Breton, in his 'Discours au congrès des écrivains' of June 1935, was to confront the Congress with his hostility to the recent pact between Stalin's USSR and Laval's bourgeois France, which revived a nationalism capable of setting French workers to attack German workers.

Breton's political stand throughout the twenties and thirties had consistently been to preach permanent, international revolution. But Breton continued to feel that this revolution must be accompanied by a revolutionary liberation of mind and mores. He included in his speech an apparently tangential claim that the genuinely pre-revolutionary works of art are not the bourgeois classics (as Lukács's defence of Balzac, for instance, or Trotsky's of Pushkin, would suggest) but the works of Baudelaire, Nerval, Lautréamont, and Jarry. No doubt there is something subversive in this recuperation of the avant-garde art of the past, at a moment when defence of the existing revolution in the USSR was supposed to go hand-in-hand with a return to traditional artistic styles. Breton's whole philosophy is threatened if one cannot pursue psychic and moral liberation simultaneously with social revolution: ' "Transform the world", said Marx; "Change your life", said Rimbaud: these two slogans are inseparable for us.' [PPS 82–93] But at this 'Congress for the Defence of Culture' Breton was not allowed to deliver his own speech, although Paul Eluard was enabled *in extremis* to read it out on his behalf.[27] Moreover, a suspiciously well-timed power-cut truncated debate on the speech.

Breton had already exchanged punches in the street with Ilya Ehrenburg, the president of the 1935 Congress, who had hoped to discredit the Surrealists before the Congress by describing them in a newspaper article as 'pederasts'.[28] And after the Congress Eluard was duly attacked in *L'Humanité* by Barbusse for criticising the Franco–Soviet pact. But Breton, Dali, Eluard, Magritte, Ray, Tanguy, and Ernst hit back in August 1935 in 'Du temps que les surréalistes avaient raison', with a demand for creative freedom – criticising socialist realism in Soviet cinema and in 'proletarian' art. (Since 1934 Zhdanov had sought to impose socialist realism as the official communist aesthetic, with varying success). They praised the congress speeches of Gide and Malraux. Gide had not yet published his disillusioned account of the Soviet Union, *Retour de l'URSS* (1936), but Malraux had already been praised by Trotsky for his novel *La Condition humaine* ('Man's Estate', 1933), which exposed Stalin's cynical *realpolitik* in supporting Chang Kai Shek's nationalist Kuomintang movement against the Chinese Communists during the abortive Shanghai rising of 1927.[29] Breton hardly needed to object to the 'deification' of Lenin and the systematic condemnation of any deviants as Trotskyists or Fascists. [PPS 100–4]. His arguments were objectively Trotskyist, and unacceptable to the Communist Party. But in Breton's optic the fundamental aim of creating revolution in France, rather than trying to save what he saw as a doomed capitalist democracy in Europe, was threatened by the return to the Soviet Union of the kind of conservative, philistine, oppressive society he had been fighting against for so long.

In his disgust with the reformism of official left-wing politics as manifested at the 1935 Congress, Breton helped to found *Contre-attaque, union de lutte des intellectuels révolutionnaires*, with that other unreconstructed adept of Trotskyist permanent revolution, Georges Bataille.[20] *Contre-attaque*, in October 1935, attacks the Popular Front politics linking Communists and Socialists as violently as it does Italian and German Fascism. It proposes a Marxist class struggle, but it does so with a fanatical, visceral appeal to physical violence which smacks more of the *Collège de sociologie* which Bataille later helped found (and which mooted human sacrifice), than of Breton's familiar brand of ironic verbal excess.[31] Breton finally parted company with Bataille, after a spate of tracts and meetings calling for 'the physical destruction of the slaves of capitalism',[32] and Breton accusing Bataille of being a *surfasciste*.[33] In fact one might argue that the very success of the united front movement in France, culminating in Léon Blum's 1936 Popular Front Government, made the Surrealists' contribution, whether hyper-leftist or proto-Fascist, increasingly irrelevant.

Breton never quite resolved the conflict between his belief in independent thought and artistry, linked with anarchic individual revolt, and the disciplined proletarian revolution he tried to ally himself with. In his association with Georges Bataille to found the anti-Fascist alliance *Contre-attaque* in 1935, or his agreement with Trotsky in Mexico in 1938 to launch a *Fédération de l'art révolutionnaire indépendant*, Breton was certainly an effective animator and publicist. But in general Breton overestimated the public impact of poetic experiment, and weakened the force of Surrealist revolt both by squabbling repeatedly with his Surrealist rivals, and by insisting on the divorce between poetic and political activities. The Surrealists, with their films, paintings, poetry and *objets trouvés*, however, certainly undertook a kind of cultural subversion of the capitalist appropriation of art. They sabotaged its moral as well as its commercial utility, in a way that understandably earned the admiration of Walter Benjamin. The problem is that they also undermined the potential revolutionary or socialist utility of art.

Breton, Trotsky and Gramsci were highly conscious of the lessons of the past, the artistic pitfalls of political commitment, and the arbitrariness of theoretical visions of the future. They based their critique of society on an ideal horizon – Breton's liberated unconscious, Gramsci's educated populace, Trotsky's post-industrial society of artistic debate. In refusing to break

with values of the past and the irrational, in insisting on the social importance of artistic experiment, they demonstrated an intellectual courage and
a vision which makes a mockery of so-called 'postmodern' theory, which
argues that the 'Modernists' were prisoners of a naive, positivistic belief in
progress.[34] Breton, Trotsky and Gramsci knew that a certain kind of
positivistic search for a future culture had collapsed. But they wished to
move forward into a future that they would construct rather than suffer,
and they engaged in a close dialectic with the past in order to focus their
vision. Despite their fundamental allegiance to Marxist revolution, each in
his own way was led to give precedence to the cultural superstructure of
society over its economic infrastructure. Their ideas seem as relevant as
ever. For it is certain that European society has a long way to go before it
successfully reconciles the divergent liberations of intellect and desire,
education and popular culture, technology and dream.

Notes to chapter 2

1   See W. Benjamin, 'Theses on the philosophy of history', in *Illuminations*, London,
    1973.
2   M. Nadeau, *Histoire du surréalisme*, Paris, 1964, p. 6 (abbreviated as N, followed by
    page number).
3   See R. Poggioli, *The Theory of the Avant-garde*, Cambridge, Mass. and London, 1968.
4   See P. Bürger, *Theory of the Avant-garde*, Minneapolis and Manchester, 1984.
5   Between 1915 and 1919 he wrote for the Socialist papers *Il grido del popolo* and
    Avanti! (the Socialist paper edited, then abandoned by Mussolini), and in 1919, after
    the Fascists sacked *Avanti!'s* offices, he founded his own Socialist paper, *Ordine nuovo*,
    which became Communist after the 1921 split at Livorno between Socialists and
    Communists.
6   See A. Gramsci, *Selections from Prison Notebooks*, London, 1971.
7   See A. Gramsci, *Selections from Cultural Writings*, London, 1985 (abbreviated as
    SCW).
8   See C. Buci-Glucksmann, *Gramsci and the State*, London, 1980.
9   See M.–A. Macciocchi, *Pour Gramsci*, Paris, 1974.
10 See Buci–Glucksmann, *op. cit.*
11 See J. Joll, *Gramsci*, London, 1977.
12 'Every new civilisation, as such (even when held back, attacked and fettered in every
    possible way), has always expressed itself in literary form before expressing itself in the
    life of the state. Indeed its literary expression has been the means with which it has
    created the intellectual and moral conditions for its expression in the legislature and the
    state.' (*SCW* 117).
13 Maria–Antonietta Macciocchi underlines Gramsci's distinction between 'political
    society' – the state with its direct legal control and force – and 'civil society' – the
    ideological and educational organisations which perpetuate hegemony through con-
    sensus: 'This ideological system which surrounds the citizen on all sides, integrates him
    from childhood into the world of the school and, later, that of the church, the army,
    justice, culture, leisure and even the trade union, and so on until death, without leaving
    him the least respite; this prison with a thousand windows symbolises the reign of a

hegemony whose strength resides less in coercion than in the fact that its bars are all the more effective for being less visible' (Macciocchi, *op. cit.* p. 165, tr. P.J.C.).

14   Similarly, Walter Benjamin was torn between his enthusiasm for the infinitely reproducible medium of film, dramatically bereft of the unique 'aura' of the oil painting, and his condemnation of the exploitation of film's hypnotic qualities by Nazi sympathisers (W. Benjamin, 'The work of art in an age of mechanical reproduction', in *Illuminations*, London, 1973).

15   *SCW* 90–1, 117–18.

16   L. Trotsky, *Literature and Revolution*, Moscow 1923, London, 1925 (reprinted with same pagination, Ann Arbor, 1960) (abbreviated as *LR*).

17   'Nearly all the intelligentsia have become reactionary. The workers, who had seen in Futurism the elements of a struggle against academic Italian culture, fossilised and remote from the popular masses, had to fight for their freedom with weapons in their hands and had little interest in the old arguments. In the big industrial centres the programme of Proletkult, aimed at educating workers in the fields of literature and art, absorbs the energy of those who still have the desire and the time to occupy themselves with these problems.' (*SCW* 54). For the full text of Gramsci's reply see *SCW* 52–4, or L. Trotsky, *Littérature et révolution*, Paris, 1974, pp. 185–8. See also I. Deutscher, *The Prophet Unarmed: Trotsky 1921–1929*, London, 1959, p. 185.

18   He continues: 'In this field it is likely to be a long time before the working classes will manage to do anything more creative than the Futurists have done. When they supported the Futurists, the workers' groups showed that they were not afraid of *destruction*, certain as they were of being able to create poetry, paintings and plays, like the Futurists; these workers were supporting historicity, the possibility of a proletarian culture created by the workers themselves.'

19   See T. Ali and P. Evans, *Trotsky for Beginners*, London, 1980, pp. 39, 122.

20   A. Breton, 'Second manifeste du surréalisme', in *Manifestes du surréalisme*, Paris, 1966, p. 114 [abbreviated as *SM*].

21   *N* 64.

22   M. Haslam, *The Real World of the Surrealists*, New York, 1978, p. 207.

23   J. Willett, *The New Sobriety*, London, 1982, p. 208.

24   However, Breton admired an article by Trotsky, 'Révolution et culture', published in *Clarté* in 1923 (and reprinted in *Literature and Revolution*), and endorsed Trotsky's rejection of 'proletarian art'. (*SM* 113–14).

25   A. Breton, *Position politique du surréalisme*, Paris, 1972, p. 31 (abbreviated as *PPS*).

26   Authors, respectively, of the pacifist manifesto *Au dessus de la mêlée*, 1915, and the anti-war novel *Le Feu*, 1917.

27   This may have been allowed by the organisers largely to mute the scandal caused by René Crevel committing suicide on the eve of the Congress, allegedly from despair at the obvious intention of the Communist organisers to silence or discredit the Surrealist group.

28   The sexual liberation preached by Breton in his manifesto was patchily practised. The genuinely obsessional Artaud, Bataille and Dali soon left the Movement. In a pro-Trotsky review, *La Critique sociale*, in 1931–2, the ex-Surrealist Georges Bataille, inspired by Freud, had argued that sexual perversion would survive even in a Socialist regime, whilst the earnest Marxist Jean Bernier dismissed perversion as bourgeois degeneracy (Georges Bataille, *Oeuvres complètes*, Vol. I., Paris, 1970, pp. 275–6, 656–60). The mainstream Surrealists disliked homosexuality, and tended to publicise affairs which were not only heterosexual, but also largely monogamous, and usually romantic.

29   This may be contrasted with Brecht's Leninist *Lehrstück*, *The Measures Taken* (1930), which used the failed Chinese experience as an object lesson in subordinating emotive revolutionary enthusiasm to amoral, long-term political calculation in the service of the Party.

30   See R. S. Short, 'Contre-attaque', in F. Alquié, *Entretiens sur le surréalisme*, Paris, 1968.
31   See D. Hollier, *Le Collège de sociologie*, Paris, 1979, and Georges Bataille, *Visions of Excess*, ed. A. Stoekl, Manchester, 1985.
32   Georges Bataille, *Oeuvres complètes*, Vol. I, p. 382.
33   M. Nadeau, *Documents surréalistes*, Paris, 1948, p. 341.
34   For the seminal definition of postmodernism, see J. F. Lyotard, *The Postmodern Condition*, Manchester, 1984. For a highly intelligent critique of 'postmodern' ideology, see V. Burgin, *The End of Art Theory: Criticism and Postmodernity*, London, 1986.

Communism
and the avant-garde:
the case of Georg Lukács

The road to hell is paved with good intentions. All of us who take our own development seriously, and therefore subject it to ruthless and objective criticism, sooner or later recognise the truth of this old adage.
— Georg Lukács (1938)

The writings of Gottfried Benn (whose problematic position has already been alluded to in Chapter 1) provided the point of departure for a polemical exchange of views in the German exile periodical *Das Wort* between September 1937 and June 1938. Commonly referred to as the 'Expressionism debate', this exchange has become justly famous as an articulation of the inherent tensions between avant-garde art and revolutionary politics. It is therefore an appropriate place to begin an exposition of the views of Georg Lukács.

The periodical had been established in 1936 specifically to provide German writers in exile from National Socialism with an independent forum for discussing literary questions, for which there was no adequate provision in other, predominantly political, exile journals. Given the scattered (and select) nature of the potential readership, and in view of the swift financial failure of earlier attempts to float such a publication, it is clear that this undertaking needed substantial financial backing. Politically, circumstances were in one sense favourable towards obtaining such support from the Soviet Union, which was keen to cultivate a broad alliance with non-Communist opponents of Fascism: it was, as Margot Heinemann shows in Chapter 7, the era of the Popular Front. On the other hand, publication in Moscow constituted a hostage to the fortunes of Soviet domestic politics as they entered their most intense phase of repression and terror. At the international Writers' Congress for the Defence of Culture against War and Fascism, held in Paris in 1935, support was secured from the director of the Moscow-based publishing house Jourgaz. Publication began the following year under the titular editorship of Bertolt Brecht, Willi Bredel and Lion Feuchtwanger, of whom only Bredel was a Communist Party member and resident in Moscow. Actual editorial power rested in the hands of an experienced Communist propagandist, Fritz Erpenbeck, who maintained a degree of tolerance in the range of views he published, while also ensuring that editorial policy ultimately reflected prevailing attitudes within the Party.[1]

The Expressionism debate itself was triggered by a contribution from a decidedly non-Marxist source. Klaus Mann, the son of Thomas Mann and author of one of the earlier failed attempts to establish an exile literary journal, submitted an essay tracing Gottfried Benn's progression from revered poet to vituperative advocate of National Socialism. Mann was at pains to represent Benn's stance as exceptional, as the sole instance of a writer of stature submitting to the barbaric allure of Hitler – even Marinetti remained undeceived by comparison, he argued. Benn's case was 'the crassest example of the fall, the degradation, the self-destruction of an intellectual who betrays the ideas of progress and humanism to this pseudo-ideology of "form" and "breeding" '. [ED 49][2] It was an anguished lament for that primacy of intellectual values which the German idealist tradition entails, and which Klaus Mann saw the literary exiles as upholding. His essay was published alongside an analysis of the same theme from the pen of a Party functionary, Alfred Kurella (under the pseudonym Bernhard Ziegler), which purports to have been prompted by a recent chance encounter with an early publication by Benn. But when Kurella's essay is read in conjunction with Klaus Mann's, it is clear that his purpose is to demonstrate that Benn was not an isolated phenomenon; that it will not do to present him as some kind of renegade; that the primitivism, fragmentation and irrationalism of the avant-garde constitute a linear connection to the descent of bourgeois society into Fascism. Kurella acknowleges that the poetry of Gottfried Benn had formed an inescapable element in his own intellectual development during the decade 1910–20, but only in order to present it as something which should now be repudiated along with the whole historical phase to which it belongs. [ED 60] The spirit of Popular Front fraternity is subordinated to a vehement dogmatism which is palpably influenced by the ferocious campaign against 'Formalism' which was being conducted during the period in question within the Soviet Union.[3]

The simplistic crudity of Kurella's assertions provoked a welter of responses, some from self-avowed former Expressionists sharply protesting at his undifferentiated denunciation of the movement, others from Party intellectuals eager to provide substantiating arguments for Kurella's line. Most of the contributions at least reject the fatalistic notion of an inevitable link between Expressionism and Fascism, distinguishing between those Expressionists whose work is patently mystical and irrational in character, and those whose social radicalism subsequently led them to more rational forms of political commitment – or indeed to communism. Of particular interest here is the article by Herwarth Walden, founder and editor of the leading Expressionist journal *Der Sturm*, whose close sympathy with the working-class movement in the 1920s had led him into exile in Moscow. With the allusive and urbane wit of a veteran literary campaigner, Walden defends the Expressionist exploration of vital rhythms and primitive styles as a quest for the appropriate artistic mode to match the times. He emphasises the oppositional character of Expressionist art and literature in the context of the Wilhelmine Empire, and pleads for recognition of the avant-garde as a still active component of the Popular Front. [*ED* 75–90] Rudolf Leonhardt, writing from Paris as the head of the German Writers' Union in exile, makes a similar point, presenting the Expressionist heritage (the one worth cultivating, that is) as the very antithesis of the bourgeois descent into world war. [*ED* 172–9] And Ernst Bloch (to whom we shall return at the end of this chapter), after pointing to the Nazis' own rabid rejection of Expressionist art as an objective refutation of Kurella's thesis, argues for a dialectical understanding of the diffuseness of Expressionism, its appearance of chaos and decay, as an intrinsic feature of the historical transition from one world order to another. [*ED* 180–91][4] When Kurella assumed the task of winding up the debate in the summer of 1938, he was bound to acknowledge that his initial thesis had been disproved (while disputing, of course, Bloch's insinuation of an astounding congruity between his own attitude to Expressionism and Hitler's). He nevertheless remains profoundly contemptuous towards what he sees as the dehumanised abstraction of Expressionist art, and insistent on the primacy of popular appeal (*Volkstümlichkeit*) as a criterion for what is acceptable in artistic creation. If Kurella's arguments remain apodictic and undeveloped, however, this is largely because he can now draw authority and assurance from the contribution of Georg Lukács, the penultimate (and most comprehensive) essay in the whole debate.

What Lukács had provided, in this essay 'Es geht um den Realismus', was the sustained argument needed to demonstrate that the literature of conventional Realism alone could lay claim to serving the interests of democratic revolution (as he defines the objectives of the Popular Front). It is the novels of Gorky and Romain Rolland, of Thomas and Heinrich Mann, with their rounded characters and traditional narrative techniques, that Lukács sees as providing a broad readership with an authoritative and easily assimilable overall view of contemporary society. And he endorses the condemnation of avant-garde movements from Naturalism to Surrealism on the grounds that they abjure the presentation of human society as a coherent system, as a totality. Where they confine themselves to the recording of empirical perceptions (which is what enables Lukács to classify Joyce as a Naturalist), they remain merely superficial, lacking an intellectual grasp of the determining forces at work in history, its *Gesetzmäßigkeit*. Where they provide intellectual insights, these appear (as in the prose works of the Surrealists) as abstracted *aperçus* embedded, as Lukács puts it, in 'tatters of reality'. The whole sequence of would-be pioneering literary developments from the 1880s to the 1920s aims, he argues, at the 'liquidation of Realism'. Their relation to the best traditions of bourgeois culture is one of a closing-down sale. That is what explains the sense of the title he gives this essay; what is truly at issue is not the cynicism and nihilism of a Gottfried Benn, nor even the true character of Expressionism (on this subject Lukács passes rapidly over the vexed question of who the representative Expressionists were, in order to concentrate on what he calls the 'principles' underlying literary history). It is the artist's relationship to a whole coherent conception of reality that is at stake: 'Es geht um den Realismus'. What Lukács is championing is an ideal mode for the artistic reflection of social reality, one which is defined as independent of the personal political views of the author and even capable of 'triumphing' in spite of those views, as exemplified by the novels of Balzac in particular. History itself will prove whether an author belongs to the real avant-garde: 'it does so by showing that an author has recognised important characteristics, tendencies and social functions of human types correctly, and crafted (*gestaltet*) them in a manner that remains lastingly effective'. [*ED* 217][5]

This was not the first occasion on which Lukács had seemed to perform the function of establishing an official line on literary practice. In 1932 he had published a series of articles in *Die Linkskurve*, attacking the narrative techniques of certain politically radical authors. *Die Linkskurve* represented perhaps the most significant achievement of a group of writers, under the leadership of the former Expressionist poet Johannes R. Becher, in creating space for independent literary activity within the German Communist Movement. It had not been easy to promote such a venture against the predominant instincts of the Central Committee, who had tended to view literature as an activity that could safely be left to useful bourgeois fellow-travellers, whereas Party members were needed for more urgent political business. As the theatrical innovator Erwin Piscator found in 1920, the official Party organ *Rote Fahne* took a positively conservative view of his experiments in populist theatre, arguing that art was too hallowed an institution to be sullied with propaganda material.[6] It was from Moscow, again, and in particular from the Russian Association of Proletarian Writers (RAPP), that Becher was able to call on support for the establishment within the German Party of a League of Proletarian–Revolutionary Writers (BPRS). When this group set up their own journal in 1929, funded partly from private sources and partly from Moscow, the 'leftward curve' of their title was also markedly apparent in editorial policy. In anticipation of the political polarisation of Germany that was to follow the Wall Street crash later that year, *Die Linkskurve* delivered sharp rebukes to potential allies among left-wing liberal intellectuals, such as Döblin, Toller and Tucholsky, for their alleged lack of dedication to the proletarian struggle. The editorial board was vulnerable to shifting power-relations in Moscow, however, and when the RAPP was dissolved along with other left-wing literary groups in 1932, the position of the radical left on *Die Linkskurve* was also weakened. (The journal in fact folded by the end of 1932, before Hitler came to power, owing to lack of finance.)

Lukács appears to have taken advantage of this shift in editorial power in order to pronounce an anathema on documentary technique in the novel.[7] He chose as his immediate target a work by Ernst Ottwalt which demonstrates the operation of class bias within the German legal system (its title was *For They Know What They Do*). Lukács is entirely in sympathy with the author's objectives in this respect. The substance of his criticism is rather that Ottwalt confines his narrative perspective within the machinery of the law which he is seeking to expose, with the result that the reader is not able to see that machinery as part of a historical process which can lead to the abolition of class justice. What is needed in a work of literature is a sense of context, a sense of the social connections of which the individual case depicted is itself but a typical example. In 1932 Lukács is simply advocating the fully crafted authorial narrative (*Gestaltung*) as a more effective means of presenting social issues than the mere 'reportage' which had enjoyed a considerable vogue in Germany since the mid-1920s.[8]

By 1938, the argument had acquired an unashamedly prescriptive note. The formal criteria of an earlier historical period are presented as guidelines to be unswervingly followed by writers confronting the altered realities of the twentieth century. This aspect of Lukács's argument was confirmed when he was subsequently challenged by the Communist novelist Anna Seghers, writing from Paris. Even though the Expressionism debate in *Das Wort* had been brought to a close, her exchange of letters with Lukács was published in the Party journal *Internationale Literatur* in 1939. With the tact and intimacy of a close acquaintance from pre-Nazi Berlin days, Seghers questions whether Lukács's absolute criteria for Realism should be rigidly applied to creative writing in the present day; whether they do not run the risk of suppressing artistic originality while encouraging mediocre talents to think they have found a sure-fire method. She flatters Lukács with a parabolic reference to Goethe who, as she puts it, had been blinded by his own methodological assumptions to the artistic flair of some of his younger contemporaries, notably Kleist. And she illustrates the problem of creative writers in communicating the intensity of their own direct experience of the world by quoting one of Lukács's favoured Realists, Tolstoy, who distinguishes two phases in the process of artistic creation: the first step consists in a direct apprehension of reality 'as if it had never been seen before', and only the second, methodological stage renders this quasi-unconscious perception susceptible once more to conscious discourse. Lukács remains unmoved on all essential points. He calls Tolstoy's distinction a psychological one, whereas he sees his own role as a literary theorist to be to establish a definition of the purpose of 'Realism as such', without which any discussion of 'Realism now' is doomed to remain eclectic. [*ED* 265–84]

From Denmark, Brecht also questioned Lukács's dogmatism, but in sharper terms than Seghers. For someone who was seeking to lay down the law about Realism, he found, Lukács appeared disconcertingly remote from the realities of life. Brecht's own close contacts with the workers of Berlin around 1930 (the phase of his *Lehrstücke*) had taught him that their appreciation of literature was by no means as limited and unsubtle as the doctrines of Lukács and Kurella suggested. These workers had shown a robust sense of the real nature of social forces which were being represented and criticised in literature, and their criteria were not formal but functional: they accepted whatever artistic techniques were required to get to grips with the reality they had experienced. Above all, as the rising social class, they took as their departure point not what was good about the old times, but what was bad about the new. What Brecht missed most in Lukács's writings was a reflection of the human struggle with contemporary conditions, out of which the possibility of social advance arises. The trouble with Lukács's concept of Realism was that it was formalistic. [*ED* 302–36]

Brecht's comments were not published at the time, appearing only in 1967, in Volume 19 of his collected works. The fact that Brecht's strong views remained entirely unrepresented in *Das Wort*, a journal of which he was a titular editor, has sharpened subsequent controversy over the Expressionism debate. It is indeed likely that the terms of the debate were manipulated in Moscow in such a way as to deny Brecht the opportunity for an effective riposte to Lukács's arguments.[9] From conversations which Walter Benjamin had with Brecht in Denmark in late July 1938, moreover, we have a record of the intense suspicion with which Brecht privately regarded the attempts of Lukács and Kurella to 'play the apparatchik' and impose their own tight control on artistic activity.[10] In the climate of the times, the harshness of the remark is understandable: Ernst Ottwalt, the butt of

Lukács's criticisms in 1932 and a former close associate of Brecht's, had already been arrested in Moscow; others among his former associates were to disappear in the Soviet Union in subsequent years, as indeed did Herwarth Walden in 1941. However, when assessing Brecht's position with regard to these menacing developments, we must also bear in mind the sentiment which Benjamin records at the beginning of August 1938: Brecht was not prepared to distance himself from the dictatorship prevailing in the Soviet Union so long as that regime appeared to be making a practical contribution to the interests of the proletariat generally.[11] It was probably for this reason that Brecht decided to avoid any public rupture between himself and his opponents within the Communist Party, preferring silence for the time being to the prolongation of literary debate in terms which he could not endorse.

It is in any case important that this mystery should not lead to an overestimation of Lukács's personal influence in Moscow, nor to a distortion of his motives in arguing his case so vehemently. At least one account indicates that Lukács himself was briefly arrested during the period we are considering.[12] (In 1941 he was to spend several months in prison, accused of being a Trotskyite.) If Lukács's essays of the 1930s give the impression of studiously importing the campaign against 'Formalism' into the German Communist Movement, then this is explicable in terms of a historical coincidence between his own theoretical orientation and the trend enforced within the CPSU under Stalin and Zhdanov. When we find Lukács asserting [ED 221–2], ingeniously but firmly, that there is a close association between the resurgence of Realism and the consolidation of the Communist regime in the USSR (as opposed to the period of revolutionary upheaval immediately following 1917), then we should see in this a reflection of Lukács's personal intellectual development, as much as a need for him to protect his person in the Moscow of the late 1930s. In essence, Lukács's theory of literature was entirely his own, and the vehemence with which he denounces Expressionism in 1939 is a reflection of the sense in which he, like Kurella and other participants in the famous debate, was fired with the will to repudiate erroneous positions which he had himself previously held.

The aesthetic categories which Lukács applies to twentieth-century culture, and to avant-garde literature in particular, were developed in his writings of the pre-1918 period, before he became committed to Marxism. The most significant early influence on Lukács is the Berlin philosopher Georg Simmel, whose *Philosophy of Money* (1900) expounded a pessimistic view of modern capitalism as subjecting all cultural products to the mechanisms of the market and bringing about an irredeemable condition of social 'alienation' by reducing human creativity to the status of a commodity. Lukács's earliest publication, a *History of the Development of Modern Drama* (1911), adopts the position that drama in the strictest sense of the word can only be produced in communities which possess an integral sense of their cultural identity: there will not be an absence of social conflict in such societies, but they retain the potential for the dialectical representation of conflict in a form (the drama) which can be recognised and appreciated by author and public alike. Ancient Greece and Renaissance Europe both constitute societies where drama, typically, reflects the heroic phase in the decline of a dominant social order (Athenian culture and the feudal nobility respectively). The prospects for drama in post-Renaissance Europe, on the other hand, are vitiated by the progressive fragmentation of society, its trend towards liberal individualism, under the development of modern capitalism.

In the preface to this work, Lukács asserts that the truly sociological dimension of literature is form.[13] In practical terms, this is an argument which runs the risk of becoming tautological: the cultural integrity which Lukács attributes to certain societies existing in the past is arrived at intuitively through the formal integrity of the drama those societies produced. But this persistent preoccupation with literary forms also reveals something more fundamental to his outlook. In *Soul and Form* (1911) Lukács is insistent that the idea of poetry is something which pre-exists all concrete manifestations of poetry: it is only through the apperception of forms as absolutes, as platonic ideals, that he can conceive of an intellectual escape from that alienated state of humanity that Simmel had described.[14] It is this commitment to the primacy of a priori concepts that still speaks through Lukács's response to Anna Seghers in 1939, as we have seen. But in the meantime he had found a means of reconciling the claim of the absolute on the one hand and his painful awareness of historical progression on the other. He found it in the philosophy of Hegel, who interprets history as a progress towards enhanced rational consciousness, which compensates for the loss of cultural integrity experienced by mankind. By 1916 Lukács had been able to argue, in *The Theory of the Novel,* that the fragmented culture of the modern age has developed its own representative literary form, characterised especially by an ironic self-awareness on the part of the author. This is what explains the extraordinary value which Lukács attaches to the works of Thomas Mann in particular: it is irony in the novel which constitutes for Lukács the possibility of surmounting the limited subjectivity of authorial narration and thus regaining a 'concrete totality' in cultural awareness.[15]

There is, moreover, a direct connection between Lukács's dedication to formal absolutes and his conversion to communism. As late as December 1918 we find Lukács expressing severe moral reservations about the methods of the Bolshevik Revolution: party dictatorship would, he argued, serve to prolong a cycle of social oppression rather than terminating it.[16] Before the year was out, however, he had joined the newly formed Hungarian Communist Party, while continuing to plead the case for moral regeneration, without which, he maintained, the elimination of class distinctions was in itself meaningless.[17] As the volume of Lukács's *Political Writings* available in English shows, many of his publications during the next few years were devoted to the moral justification of Bolshevism in the terms of German idealist philosophy. But the specific premises for Lukács's intellectual commitment to communism are to be found rather in an essay of mid-1919 entitled 'The Old Culture and the New'. It is here that Lukács rehearses his arguments about culture reflecting the inherent historical development of an epoch (of the dominant social class in that epoch); about an integral, unalienated 'humanity' which is the ultimate aim of culture; and about the inherent contradiction of a bourgeois society, which proclaims the universal ideal of individual liberty while predicating that liberty on conditions of 'capitalist anarchy' in which human creativity is reduced to commodity status. It is to be the function of communism to restore the possibility of culture:

> Liberation from capitalism means liberation from the domination of economy. [. . .] Under capitalism there simply is no class which is called upon by virtue of its position to create culture. The destruction of capitalism, the construction of a communist society, takes hold of the problem precisely at this point. Communism aims at the creation of a social order in which each individual can participate in a way of life which, in the periods preceding capitalism, only the ruling classes could lead, but which under capitalism no class at all could enjoy.
> It is with communism that the history of mankind truly begins.[18]

There is a superficial resemblance here to the arguments of Trotsky in *Literature and Revolution* (as well as to portions of the *Communist Manifesto*): the dictatorship of the proletariat is conceived as a transitional phase in the progression towards a classless society and a socialist economic system, which alone are capable of furnishing the necessary preconditions for a new (socialist) culture. But Lukács's formulation is politically naive. It separates off the aim of the revolution from the precise economic conditions which make it possible (in Marxist terms) to pursue a revolutionary course, namely the growth of a proletarian labour force *within* the production system of capitalist society. Lukács's essay thus reflects the moral Utopianism which largely characterised the intellectual mood of Central

Europe as the terrible carnage of the First World War came to an end. It is unsurprising, therefore, that the Lukács of 1919–20 should have been criticised by Lenin in the context of his onslaught on the 'infantile disorder' of left-wing communism which was rife among the newly formed revolutionary parties of the post-war years. It is not specifically 'The Old Culture and the New', admittedly, which attracts Lenin's attention, but Lukács's role as the most active contributor to *Kommunismus,* the theoretical journal of the Third International for South-East Europe during the years 1920–1. In particular, Lukács's call for a Communist boycott of the parliamentary process as a matter of principle (and for the sake of conceptual clarity) is condemned by Lenin as 'purely verbal' Marxism, which makes artificial distinctions, lacks concrete analysis, and above all fails to take account of the need for revolutionaries to become involved in 'all fields of work and all institutions in which the bourgeoisie exerts its influence over the masses'.[19]

Lukács subsequently took care to emphasise the importance of political organisation on the Leninist model, but the terminology of his political writings remained essentially that of Hegel. In *History and Class Consciousness* (1923), the consciousness that Lukács sees as being 'ascribed' to the proletariat is emphatically not a collective psychological response to the social conditions in which they find themselves, but an intellectual apperception of the historical purpose which they are destined to fulfil by virtue of their very existence. In Hegelian terms, the proletariat is to fulfil the role of subject as well as object in the historical process, a role which Hegel himself had ascribed only to a transcendent World Spirit.[20] A Social Democrat reviewer of the time complained that Lukács was elevating social existence to the realm of metaphysics.[21] And in Moscow, too, the philosophical idealism of *History and Class Consciousness* was expressly denounced by Zinoviev at the Fifth World Congress of the Third International in 1924 in the course, again, of an attack on 'ultra-leftism'.[22] But in a recent study, the American scholars Andrew Arato and Paul Breines also note the irony that the very horror of 'alienation', which had earlier made Lukács adhere to absolute forms as the vehicles of sociological perception, now leads him to mythologise the Party as the perceiving subject of history. By envisaging the Communist Party as the organisational entity necessary to transcend individual subjectivity, Lukács effectively provides an intellectual justification for the process of bureaucratisation (and the 'Bolshevisation' of Communist parties outside the Soviet Union) which was to take place in the years that followed. By 1926 he had implicitly accepted the consolidation of Party organisation under Stalin's watchword of 'Socialism in One Country'.[23]

When Lukács turned his attention to Expressionism in an essay of 1934, 'Expressionism: its Significance and Decline', he acknowledged the opposi-tional role it had performed in Wilhelmine society, but he argued that that opposition had failed to rise ideologically above the political system it was criticising. Instead of exposing the war as a manifestation of imperialism (as Lenin had understood it), German writers and intellectuals had opposed 'war as such'. Instead of attacking the counter-revolutionary violence of the reactionary bourgeoisie, they had abominated 'violence as such'. And instead of identifying the proletariat as the component of society which is historically destined to overcome class antagonisms, Expressionists had rejected all social classes as equally 'bourgeois' in their mentality. This is what Lukács means when he calls the pacifism and the activism of the Expressionists 'abstract'. This is why he emphasises the bohemian and 'parasitic' character of their social existence. And it is their image of themselves as standing outside the entire structure of society, their merely intellectual striving for the transcendence of class conflict, that enable Lukács to argue that they stand in a direct lineage to the doctrines of fascism. Lukács is well able to find supporting evidence for his thesis among the ideological pronouncements of writers as varied in their outlooks as Kurt Hiller and Franz Werfel, Ludwig Rubiner and Wilhelm Worringer. But the underlying purpose of his argument is to identify Expressionism in all essential respects with the ideology of a specific political party which had been prominent during the brief period 1917–22, the Independent Social Democratic Party (USPD). Arising as a left-wing opposition to the war within the SPD (after the SPD had voted in favour of war credits in 1914), the USPD had been sustained for a while by revolutionary fervour as the war came to an end, but were ultimately unable to compete with the organisational strength of the Communists on the one hand and the Social Democrats on the other. In effect Lukács is equating Expressionism with that intellectual appeal for the moral regeneration of society which had characterised his own essays of the period 1918–20, and which he had subsequently subsumed within his philosophical justification of the Party machine.

When Ernst Bloch made his contribution to the Expressionism debate of 1938, it was not unnatural that he should have assumed that this essay by Lukács had fuelled the general assault on Expressionism (even if Kurella subsequently denied any such influence). At all events he framed his own essay as a refutation of Lukács as much as Kurella, pointedly giving it a plural title: 'Discussions about Expressionism'. Bloch was a decidedly unorthodox Marxist, a trained theologian, whose emphasis lay on the Utopian vision, the messianic impulse in the struggle of mankind to attain a higher social and cultural condition. His major work, recently published in English, carries the title *The Principle of Hope,* and traces the heritage of 'wishful thinking' in European philosophy from Plato to Marx. The close friendship he had enjoyed with Lukács since student days in 1910 was clearly based on an attraction of opposites, and Bloch subsequently assumed the role of Lukács's most loyal critic. He welcomed *History and Class Consciousness* when it first appeared, as an attempt to apply intellectual rigour to the issues of revolutionary politics, but Bloch was to reject Lukács's notion of a pure dichotomy between bourgeoisie and proletariat in capitalist society as one that had set the German Communist Party on the doomed path of factional politics in the period that led up to 1933.[24]

In certain respects, Bloch's lapidary commentaries on German politics anticipate the fusion of Marxist insights and Freudian psychology which is familiar from fuller studies of the origins of Fascism by Adorno and Horkheimer, Wilhelm Reich, Herbert Marcuse, and Alexander and Margarete Mitscherlich. Surveying the variety of social types – from first-generation office-workers and salesmen to long-established peasant-farmers – which cannot be accommodated within Lukács's scheme, Bloch observes that large sections of German society are not even living in the same century. He concludes from this essential non-contemporaneity (*Ungleichzeitigkeit*) that any effective political agitation must be based on a differentiated understanding of psychological motives, even if these appear archaic and irrational, rather than assuming that there is any automatic connection between economic circumstances and political consciousness.[25] It is his long acquaintance with Lukács's philosophical orientation, coupled with his concentrated analysis of its practical consequences, that enables Bloch to identify the intellectual assumptions which underpin the concerted attack on avant-garde art and literature in *Das Wort* in 1938. It is Bloch who recognises that the demands being made of the literary writer are predicated upon a conception of reality as a closed system, such as was cultivated by the classical German philosophical tradition. [*ED* 186] And in holding Lukács responsible for these arguments, Bloch acknowledges him to be the foremost contemporary exponent of a world-view which literary modernism consciously challenges and undermines.

Time has moved on since 1938: the positions of Seghers and Brecht are now preferred in the German Democratic Republic to those of Lukács, while the Western attempt to define a 'postmodernist' stance has incorporated a Hegelian transcendence of the entire Expressionism debate in its turn.[26] In both East and West, then, Lukács's position is recognised as having been superseded, and as unduly restrictive in its categorical opposition to modernism. His austere theory of Realism remains historically important, nevertheless, because it provides a rigorous intellectual testing ground for the political significance of the avant-garde. Moreover the cultural crisis which Lukács sought to resolve is one which continues to confront modernist writers and artists themselves.

Notes to chapter 3

1 Hans-Albert Walter, *Die deutsche Exilliteratur*, Vol. 4, Stuttgart, 1978, pp. 461ff.
2 Page references to *Die Expressionismusdebatte*, ed. Hans-Jürgen Schmitt, Frankfurt, 1973, are incorporated into the text as *ED*, followed by the page number.
3 Cf. Walter, *op. cit.*, Vol. 4, pp. 417–23, 480–4.
4 On Nazi attitudes to Expressionist art, see Chapter 15 of this volume.
5 Cf. Ernst Bloch *et al.*, *Aesthetics and Politics*, ed. Frederic Jameson, London, 1977, p. 48. See also Georg Lukács, *Essays on Realism*, London, 1980, pp. 137–8.
6 Helga Gallas, *Marxistische Literaturtheorie*, Neuwied, 1971, p. 27.
7 Gallas, *op. cit.*, pp. 64–71.
8 Lukács, 'Reportage or Portrayal?', *Essays on Realism*, pp. 45–75.
9 Walter, *op. cit.*, Vol. 4, pp. 484–7. On the substance of the recent controversy, see Lothar Baier, 'Vom Erhabenen der proletarischen Revolution', in *Der Streit mit Georg Lukács*, ed. Hans-Jürgen Schmitt, Frankfurt, 1978, pp. 55–76; also *Lehrstück Lukács*, ed. Jutta Matzner, Frankfurt, 1974.
10 Walter Benjamin, *Understanding Brecht*, London, 1977, p. 118.
11 *Ibid.*, p. 121.
12 Julius Hay, *Geboren 1900*, quoted in Alfred Kantorowicz, *Politik und Literatur im Exil*, Hamburg, 1978, p. 242.
13 Lukács, *Entwicklungsgeschichte des modernen Dramas* (*Werke*, Vol. 15), Darmstadt, 1981, p. 10.
14 On this early phase of Lukács's development, see György Márkus, 'Life and the Soul: the young Lukács and the Problem of Culture', in *Lukács Revalued*, ed. Agnes Heller, Oxford, 1983.
15 Lukács, *The Theory of the Novel*, London, 1971, p. 93.
16 Lukács, 'Der Bolschewismus als moralisches Problem', *Politische Aufsätze*, Vol. 1, Darmstadt, 1975, pp. 27–34.
17 Lukács, 'Die moralische Grundlage des Kommunismus', April 1919, *Politische Aufsätze*, Vol. 1, pp. 85–8.
18 Lukács, 'Alte Kultur und neue Kultur', *Politische Aufsätze*, Vol. 1, pp. 132–50 (134). An English translation of this essay is available in Georg Lukács, *Marxism and Human Liberation*, ed. E. San Juan, New York, 1973.
19 V. I. Lenin, *Collected Works*, London, 1925, Vol. 31, p. 165. Lukács' article 'The question of parliamentarianism' is contained in his *Political Writings*, pp. 53–63 (*Werke*, Vol. 2, pp. 95–104).
20 For an admirably concise exposition of the philosophical tradition within which Lukács is operating here, see G. H. R. Parkinson, *Georg Lukács*, London, 1977, pp. 40–7.
21 Siegfried Marck, 'Geschichte und Klassenbewußtsein', *Die Gesellschaft*, 1924, Vol. 1, pp. 573–8 (577).
22 A. Arato and P. Breines, *The Young Lukács and the Origins of Western Marxism*, New York, 1979, p. 180.
23 *Ibid.*, pp. 136, 155, 200.
24 For a detailed study of Communist policy in the closing years of the Weimar Republic,

see Eve Rosenhaft, *Beating the Fascists?*, Cambridge, 1983.
25   Ernst Bloch, *Erbschaft dieser Zeit* (*Gesamtausgabe,* Vol. 4), Frankfurt, 1977, pp. 104–60.
26   Hans Koch *et al., Zur Tradition des sozialistischen Realismus,* Berlin, 1975, pp. 181–3; Peter Bürger, *Theory of the Avant-Garde,* Manchester, 1984.

Bibliography

1   PRIMARY SOURCES

Ernst Bloch *et al., Aesthetics and Politics,* ed. Frederic Jameson, London, 1977
Georg Lukács, *Werke,* Neuwied, 1968—
Georg Lukács, *Politische Aufsätze,* Vol. 1, ed. J. Kammler and F. Benseler, Darmstadt, 1975
Georg Lukács, *Political Writings,* London, 1972
Georg Lukács, *Essays on Realism,* London, 1980
F. J. Raddatz (ed.), *Marxismus und Literatur,* Vol. 2, Reinbek, 1969
H.-J. Schmitt (ed.), *Die Expressionismusdebatte,* Frankfurt, 1973

2   SUGGESTED FURTHER READING

Andrew Arato and Paul Breines, *The Young Lukács and the Origins of Western Marxism,* New York, 1979
Ben Fowkes, *Communism in Germany under the Weimar Republic,* London, 1984
Helga Gallas, *Marxistische Literaturtheorie,* Neuwied, 1971
George Lichtheim, *Lukács* (Fontana Modern Masters), London, 1970
Michael Löwy, *Georg Lukács: from Romanticism to Bolshevism,* London, 1979
Eugene Lunn, *Marxism and Modernism,* Los Angeles, 1982
György Márkus, 'Life and the Soul: the Young Lukács and the Problem of Culture' in *Lukács Revalued,* ed. Agnes Heller, Oxford, 1983

Counterfactual artefacts: Walter Benjamin's philosophy of history

Throughout Benjamin's work between 1920 and 1940 there runs one major preoccupation: the sketching of a modernist theory of history. Closely linked to this are Benjamin's explorations of how human subjectivity might be reconstructed in a way which would meet the demands of cultural modernism without at the same time dissolving the capacity for political action. Thus his texts contain the basic elements for a new theory of the subject and a new theory of history; and, since history is itself a text, they also include a new hermeneutics of reading and writing.

As a modernist philosopher of history, Benjamin called into question such notions of traditional historical discourse as continuity, development, process, progress and organism. As a modernist theoretician of historiography, he was critical of traditional narrative with its rosary-like chain of cause-and-event stories. Inspired by the practice of the literary avant-garde, he developed his own theory of textual production or signification, which was based on the principle of fragmentation and montage: the central features of Benjamin's own texts are thus the quotation, the thesis, the fragment, the arrangement and the compilation.

It was the vision of nineteenth-century Paris, with its refracted and ruptured archaeology, which provided Benjamin with the material imagery out of which he strove to fashion his new conceptions. Paris was both the epitome of capitalism and a wellspring of the forces which opposed it, and as such it represented for him a mythological microcosm of modern times. Above all, Paris inspired Benjamin with its catalytic fusion of what he saw as the two most advanced developments in twentieth-century politics and culture: Marxism and Surrealism. In Benjamin's writing the two movements enrich and transform each other. The abstract language of Marxist theory becomes more concrete and sensually perceptible by being infused with the images of mythology (*Bilderschrift*). As Benjamin says:

> There is a central problem of historical materialism and it is about time it was recognized: that is, whether the Marxist understanding of history is only

possible at the cost of reducing the concrete presence of history before our eyes. Or: how is it possible to enhance this concrete presence of history and to combine it with the application of Marxist methods? The first stage will be to adapt the montage principle in history; that means to erect the large constructions from the smallest, precisely and pointedly manufactured units.[1]

At the same time the tendentially ahistorical mythologisation of Paris in avant-garde writing is revealed as a phantasm unless it is demystified by underpinning it with historical and political awareness. In this respect Benjamin explicitly sets his *Passagenwerk* apart from Aragon's *Paysan de Paris*:

> Whereas Aragon stays within the realm of dream, the aim in this case is to find the constellation of awakening. Whilst in Aragon there remains an element of impressionism – the mythology – and this impressionism is to be held responsible for the many formless philosophemes in the book, in this case it is a question of dissolving mythology into the realm of history. Of course, this can only happen by awakening an as yet unconscious knowledge of what has been.[2]

The concept of dream and awakening are of crucial importance in Benjamin's writing. Dream is the juncture of the imagery of physical concreteness and exuberant materialism with the structures of desire. But this dreamworld is furnished by objects which in capitalism are necessarily commodities, and consequently the structures of desire are made up of desire and fear (*Angst*) at once. In contrast, awakening is the moment where the spell or illusion of reconciling a desire for fulfilment with a structure of exploitation and alienation can be broken. In this dream, under the spell of capitalism, desire and objects of fulfilment are authentic and disorted at the same time. The task of the new historian is to set free the forces and drives of authentic liberation without giving up a materially better life and the more refined structures of desire which go with it.

Benjamin's starting point is to 'read' Paris. He says: 'The topos of Nature's book shows that it is possible to read reality like a text. So this will be done here with the reality of the nineteenth century.'[3] Benjamin's reading of nineteenth-century Paris constitutes the deciphering of the primal landscape (*Urlandschaft*) of twentieth-century capitalism and mass psychology. It is only better-informed later generations who will be able to look at the past in such a way as to produce a reading of it which illuminates the present like a flash of lightning. Conversely, Benjamin's specific reading of Paris can only come about at a historical moment where a fusion between Marxism and Surrealism is possible and where such an *idiosyncratic* reading is vital for the politics of Benjamin's own time.

It is not the case that the past sheds its light on the present or the present its light on the past, but the image is that in which, what has been, enters into a constellation with the 'Now' [*Jetzt*] in a sudden flash. In other words: the image is dialectics at a standstill [. . .]. The image read, i.e. the image in the 'Now' of the potential realization is most clearly marked by that critical and dangerous momentum, the basis of all reading.[4]

And, even more important: 'the historical index of the images not only tells us that they belong to a certain time, above all it tells us that only at a certain time do they become readable'.[5]

Thus we can detect two important implications for his philosophy of history. Firstly, to read the *world* in order to find out about history means that history becomes spatialised. The transformation of a temporal concept into a spatial one implies that a view of time as process or progression has been supplanted by a sense of time having stopped, of history having come to an end. This radical shift of perspective becomes a dominant theme of cultural production during the period opening around the turn of the century and culminating in the First World War and the proletarian revolutions which grew out of it. Secondly, to *read* the world assumes that history is seen as a text, as an artefact, as something constructed, the encoding and interpretation of which are always to be understood as socially and ideologically conditioned.

Both of these ideas, the spatialisation of time and history as text, emerged from the historical constellation from within which Benjamin began to write, and of which he was acutely aware from the beginning. With the First World War, history as *bourgeois* history, hitherto legitimised and sustained by the notion of 'progress', did indeed come to an end. Imperialism stood fully unmasked at last. At the same time an alternative force, whose political perspective opened up a whole new way of writing history, had seized power successfully in Russia. Nevertheless, after the defeat of the proletarian revolutions in Europe, the ruling classes reinforced their hegemony by satisfying certain demands for social and political reform. The Social Democrats increased their influence, but paid the high price of adapting themselves ever more to bourgeois modes of thought and action, a development facilitated by a deterministic interpretation of Marx's theory since the Second International.

Marx's analysis of capitalism had established on a theoretical level the proposition that capitalism necessarily produces the forces of its own destruction. But what he did not say was whether those counter-forces would inevitably triumph before capitalism had the chance to turn its own particular collapse into a universal catastrophe. It was on just such an assumption of inevitable triumph, however, that the social-democratic theory rested: the unconsidered supposition that the decline of capitalism would mean the ineluctable progress of socialism. This in turn made it possible to evolve the theory of the peaceful, because automatic, transformation of capitalism into socialism; a theory designed (not necessarily consciously) to still the desire to fight actively against bourgeois imperialism.

One social formation where this problem was perceived and tackled with increasing idiosyncrasy was the cultural avant-garde. Not only had bourgeois culture done nothing by 1914 to abolish ossified patterns of life, to eradicate social injustice and to prevent the First World War, but some artists had greeted and glorified that bloody spectacle in which a morally bankrupt capitalism flagrantly betrayed the humanist values to which it had hitherto claimed to subscribe. The reason for what looked like art's submission to the interests of the ruling class, and its function as a means of ideologically shoring up a crumbling society, was found in art's separation from life: by defining and institutionalising art as autonomous, bourgeois society had rendered it ineffectual. Thus the attempt to reintegrate art and life, to aestheticise life, in other words, was the common aim of avant-garde movements such as Dadaism, Futurism and Surrealism. It is the aim summed up in Breton's phrase 'pratiquer la poésie'. This reintegration was not, however, meant to take place within the existing society. Rather, the aesthetic way of perceiving and producing reality was seen as a means of changing society: a society dominated on all levels by abstraction, instrumentalism and technical rationality, and by an ideal of progress which concentrated wholly on the development of science and technology in order to maximise exploitation and profit.

Drastically oversimplified as it is, this outline of the situation around the time of the First World War needs to be borne in mind for a proper understanding of the historical and cultural trends which informed and shaped Benjamin's writings from 1920 to 1940. His whole *oeuvre* centres upon the same dominant issues, constantly weaving them together into the complex texture of his conception of history. Benjamin's idea of the pregnant or charged moment of historical recognition, whereby one can find condensed in a work a whole life, and in a life a whole epoch, applies equally to his own texts. Whichever of them we might select for closer analysis, and however remote it might seem at first sight from his main interests, it will turn out in the end to be one point in a magnetic field: a unit complete in its own specific thematic purpose, but directed at the same time towards a more fundamental and comprehensive concern which exists only in the total formation of its different units.

In this respect Benjamin's 'Theses on the Concept of History', written shortly before his death in 1940 and (significantly) not meant to be published, are only the very tip of the iceberg. This becomes clear when we recognise that the themes treated here recur in the *Passagenwerk*, his most ambitious intellectual project. Benjamin's 'Theses' are dictated by the drive to rewrite history from the perspective not of the victors of history, i.e. the ruling classes, but of their victims. Such an alternative reconstruction of the past does not mean, however, just another version of traditional historicism, a mere chronicle of past events and great figures supposedly unconnected with the present, though in fact, of course, shaped by the historian's conscious or unconscious alliance with the ruling class. On the contrary. The writing of an oppositional history is doubly rooted in the social formation of the writer's own time. On the one hand only an alliance with the victims of, and potential liberators from, social and political oppression in the present can provide the vanishing-point towards which the counter-history is projected. And on the other hand, this salvaged history, wrenched from the grasp of collective amnesia, is necessary for the abolition of the status quo, because, as Benjamin puts it, each generation has been vested with the messianic power to redeem all those who suffered in the past.[6]

This rewriting of history is not an easy task, and it is constantly threatened by failure. There are three main reasons for this. The first is that the witnesses of the other history are continually disappearing. They are only to be found in what the dominant process of history has secreted as waste, as the superseded and outmoded which can thus, by definition, have no function within the 'advancing' capitalist order. Once free of its use-value, this waste has once again the potential to indicate a counterfactual history. For what is left is a pure form – pure because it is defunct – into which new meaning can be deposited, an activity performed by the artist, the historian and the collector alike. 'Anything which you know won't be existing much longer becomes an image', says Benjamin with reference to Baudelaire's way of finding material for his urban poetry, and he draws the comparison between the artist of the capitalist city and the ragman:

> The poets find the refuse of society on their street and derive their heroic subject from this very refuse. This means that a common type is, as it were, superimposed upon their illustrious type. This new type is permeated by the features of the rag picker with whom Baudelaire repeatedly concerned himself. One year before he wrote 'Le vin des chiffoniers' he published a prose presentation of the figure: 'Here we have a man who has to gather the day's refuse in the capital city. Everything that the big city threw away, everything it lost, everything it despised, everything it crushed underfoot, he catalogues and collects. He collates the annals of intemperance, the stockpile of waste. He sorts things out and makes a wise choice; he collects, like a miser guarding

a treasure, the refuse which will assume the shape of useful or gratifying objects between the jaws of the goddess of Industry.'[7]

The loss of that which is outmoded is the loss of the dream material, the very stuff of mythological and symbolic resonance. For what is disappearing are those objects of our own past, in which the connection between technology and mythology had been created. Such a connection can only be achieved by children, says Benjamin.

> Task of childhood: to bring the new world into the realm of the symbolic. The child can do what an adult is totally incapable of doing: recognise the new once again. Railway engines already have the character of symbols for us because we saw them in our childhood. For our children cars – of which we ourselves see only the new, elegant, slick side – have this character [. . .] for every truly new natural formation [*Naturgestalt*] – and basically, technology is one such – there are corresponding new images. Each generation of children discovers these new images to incorporate them into mankind's treasury of images.[8]

So the second point is that this disappearance of the objective material of a counter-history is paralleled by an ever-increasing loss of experience on the part of the subject. Experience depends upon the capacity of personal memory to interrelate the biographical past and present. For Benjamin, biographical memory and historical memory are analogous procedures, and one cannot exist without the other. From this follows the third factor jeopardising the project. I have said that the medium in which the epistemological moment, the flash-like identity of subject and object, transpires, is for Benjamin no longer the language of theory but the language of images; but the mimetic powers are constantly being eroded and reduced by the demands of instrumental rationality, the philosophical backbone of capitalist technology.

These three points outline the material conditions for an alternative production of historical meaning. Benjamin's central stress on the mimetic and the imaginative as basic factors in changing the world of the status quo links him directly with surrealism and has also given rise to various attempts to claim him as a Judaic religious thinker. But what Benjamin found in the imagery of the Messiah or in the ecstatic moment of what he emphatically defines as '*profane illumination*', are precisely the emotional and pictorial foundations of sensuous perception, of an alternative way of seeing, in short: of creativity.

Until then the mimetic and imaginative faculties had not been made productive for scientific, political and historical practice, but had survived mainly in areas where inspiration, vision and revelation as elements of mystical discourse paraphrased the moment of recognition. As these fields of application were themselves concerned with the production of imaginative material, especially in religion or art, the general validity of the mimetic faculty for all kinds of epistemological activity had been overlooked. But if we recall, for instance, that Kekule, the founder of organic chemistry, had visualised the structure of the benzine ring while dreaming of a snake swallowing its own tail, it may not be altogether fanciful to consider whether the mimetic – the aesthetic – might indeed be the general organon in which theory and practice are linked.

Modern psychology still speaks of the 'desirable and proper mystery which surrounds the creative act', and adds modestly but significantly: 'the best that can be said is that certain uniformities do seem to characterise highly original scientists and artists'.[9] Even today we have only taken the very first steps towards establishing a psychology of the imagination, which neuro-physiologists do not hesitate to define as 'the highest level of mental experience', its processes inextricably bound up with those of 'the lower level of sensuous experience, imagery, hallucination and memory'.[10]

I am quoting this not least because it points up the remarkable insights of Benjamin and the Surrealists nearly forty years before the quoted essay was written. Imagination, hallucination and memory are the key categories deployed by them in order to grasp a framework of epistemological production which is by definition aesthetic because it is always mimetic. In the epistemological process correspondences are discovered between objects which hitherto had appeared unconnected. Benjamin's key witnesses on this point are Baudelaire, Proust, Aragon and Breton's *Nadja*. We develop these faculties only because nature itself is full of correspondences. Therefore the Surrealists, for instance, gave accounts of everyday life in the confidence that its aesthetic character made any artistic procedure superfluous. *Le hasard objectif* ('objectified chance') is an aesthetic feature of reality. It is only because correspondences exist between past and present that we can bring the two together, both on the personal biographical level and on the communal plane of history. Only in this way can true experience, that is, the investment of otherwise inert and isolated fragments with meaning, be achieved. It is precisely at this stage that Benjamin brings the philogenetic and the ontogenetic to the point of conflation. For authentic experience is always the salvaging of something in danger of being forgotten or repressed: the ever-vanishing traces of the historically defeated who did not write history, or the engrams of the unconscious described by Freud in *Beyond the Pleasure Principle* and by Proust as the content of the *mémoire involontaire*; especially when the chances of finding the right mimetic object for reactivating those fading traces are so slight and fleeting.

But for Benjamin it is not only the difficulty of still finding the right corresponding objects. The modern individual has also undergone a process of psychological reconstruction whereby unconscious engrams are increasingly less encoded. In mass society, especially in the cities, the main psychological stimulus is shock, but in order to avoid trauma the consciousness is continually on guard to protect itself against such an unforeseen flooding by high rates of impulse. According to Freud the psychic energy of conscious events disappears without trace. *Mémoire involontaire* and *mémoire volontaire* – memory and consciousness – are mutually exclusive. Thus Benjamin argues: 'Experience is indeed a matter of tradition, in collective existence as well as in private life. It is less the product of facts firmly anchored in memory than of a convergence in memory of accumulated and frequently unconscious data.'[11] But the more people are exposed to shocks, the less material is laid down in the *mémoire involontaire* as the reservoir of authentic emotional and sensuous experience. People in capitalist mass society find it more and more difficult to make sense of their own lives as a result of the impoverishment of their store of mimetic material and emotional energy. The shattering of the matter of memory into disconnected episodes and events, out of which the individual desperately strives to distil real experience, is epitomised in Baudelaire's notion of 'spleen'. Spleen is the condition produced by the running wild of isolated happenings which can find no place in the context of a personal – or social – history which would render them meaningful.[12]

Experience, understood as the reactivation of memory through its fusion with the present, is thus endangered by two factors. Firstly there is the diminishing possibility of accumulating unconscious data, which through correspondent structures would conflate and deepen the existing engrams or traces of memory in the cortex, as John Eccles has argued:

> The engram postulate accords well with the experience of remembered imagery. By far the most vivid memories are evoked by some closely similar experience. Here the new, evolving spatio-temporal pattern must tend to correspond closely to the old, congealed pattern: the impulses of the new pattern flow into a channel of the old and trigger its replaying.[13]

The second factor is the total randomness of the principle by which one finds the object or situation which might trigger the old memory. For Benjamin this, too, is due to radically changed patterns of perception in modern society. Through the separation of private and public interest and the consequent atomised existence of the individual, public matter can no longer be assimilated so readily to the personal life. As Benjamin observes:

> According to Proust, it is a matter of chance whether an individual forms an image of himself, whether he can take hold of his experience. It is by no means

inevitable to be dependent on chance in this matter. Man's inner concerns do
not have their inescapably private character by nature. They do so only when
he is increasingly unable to assimilate the data of the world around him by
way of experience.[14]

This is the reason for the disappearance of true story-telling, the oldest
form of communication. In contrast with the modern mass media, in
story-telling

> it is not the object of the story to convey a happening per se, which is the
> purpose of information; rather, it embeds it in the life of the storyteller in
> order to pass it on as experience to those listening. It thus bears the marks of
> the storyteller as much as the earthen vessel bears the marks of the potter's
> hand.[15]

What appears in the marks of the story-teller and the potter's hand is
Benjamin's concept of the aura. The aura is that emanation surrounding
something, in which the most subjective, that which can only be perceived
through an identification triggered by the senses, converges with the
factual. We really can speak of the *unio mystica*, the inextricable blending
of 'the nearest and the most remote': 'Experience of the aura thus rests on
the transposition of a response common in human relationships to the
relationship between the inanimate or natural object and man ... To
perceive the aura of an object we look at means to invest it with the ability to
look at us in turn.'[16]

It is the aura of Combray, the village which is so poignantly recalled by
Proust's narrator in *Du côté du chez Swann*, which appears in Proust's
mémoire involontaire, in contrast to the merely factual Combray of the
reflexive, discursive *mémoire volontaire*. From here we can see introspec-
tively the connection between the outmoded and the aura. But beyond the
utterly private acts of memory of the private gentleman Proust, the most
authentic experience, the strongest aura is evoked in the coincidence of
private and collective experience. The calendar, with its public feast-days,
provides a concept of time whereby such coincidences are socially
organised. But until such time as a new calendar might be conceptualised,
capable of really preserving individual memory through the collective
memory of a liberated society, it is necessary to sustain a memory of history
instilled with the desire for liberation. The struggle to conserve that alternative memory of history can be compared to the difficulty of evoking the
mémoire involontaire. The conscious, discursive memory of fact, void of
sensuous re-enactment and tending to stifle any experience truly pregnant
with subjectivity – that is, with unconscious, mimetic, imaginative material
– functions in the same way as the official bourgeois writing of history.

Furthermore, both the paradigm of historicism and the paradigm of progress are closed to the possibility of imparting meaning to the collective memory. For historicism there is no link between past and present. For progress neither past nor present really exists, because they are perceived highly selectively and always as transitional: time there is empty. But apart from that, in the official version of history the sheer facticity of things seems to acquire the self-evidence of the necessary and ineluctable. The once-existing possibility of alternative paths of collective action disappears.

But how can the repressed and the forgotten be restored? As regards the perceiving subject, new ways of seeing have to be activated. As regards the object, the refuse and detritus of history have to be examined for their alternative potential. Benjamin twice gives the same example of the kind of fresh historical vision that needs to be acquired and, significantly enough, they are spatial scenarios. It is not alien to the perceiving subject, but has been superseded by automatised, functional modes of perception. The non-automatised mode of vision existed in the past at the point of learning something. Once that process is finished, however, the attitude towards the object is almost fixed forever. Benjamin uses the image of the city in order to clarify these different ways of relating to history. In 'Städtebilder' he speaks about his experience of orientation in Moscow. At first the city was a phantasm created by the imagination around the names of streets, squares and buildings. This creation resists reality for a long time, unyielding. Then, in the clash between imagination and reality, the city becomes a labyrinth and the visitor falls victim to innumerable topographical traps. Now the city resists identification, it tries to mask itself, escapes and hatches plots. But finally the abstract schemes of maps will carry off the victory, and the vivid, sensuous encounter between man and city will be buried beneath a concept which is purely functional. And in *One-way Street* Benjamin says:

> What renders the very first sight of a village or town in the landscape so incomparable and irresistible is the fact that it combines distance in strong connection with closeness. Habit has not yet done its job. Once we start to get our bearings the landscape disappears all at once like the front of a house when we enter it. . . . Once we start to know the place that former image can never be restored.[17]

In order to reacquire that estranged vision, the mimetic and imaginative faculties must be developed and expanded through practice. The use of intoxicating drugs like opium or marijuana and the state of dreaming are only extreme forms of such practice, which can be pursued likewise in ordinary everyday activities such as reading, thinking, solitude or the strolling of the *flâneur* in the city. All these activities imply the discharge of consciousness. This intensified state of imaginative perception will then be able to recognise in certain outmoded objects and constellations those 'dialectical images' which can release material for an alternative, counterfactual history. The moment of recognition when the object 'opens its eyes beneath the gaze of the historian' is Benjamin's *profane Erleuchtung* ('profane illumination'). These moments are rare; they occur suddenly and fleetingly, like flashes of lightning.

The objects which are able to provide 'dialectical images' for an alternative historical signification are, on the one hand, the relics of an objectively scattered totality; and on the other, the fragments which the historian blasts out of what appears to be a coherent totality of historical meaning. What Benjamin recognises as the essence of modernist artistic production, the deconstruction of questionable totalities and the remounting of the fragments into artefacts, the meaning of which has no resemblance to their former function, is again fully applicable to the practice of the historian himself. The destruction of the organic artwork and its replacement by a form of art based on the montage principle is systematised in Benjamin's theory of allegory. The theory of allegory, the result of Benjamin's position as a modernist, but demonstrated fully in terms of the baroque drama, provides a general theory of the production of textual meaning.[18]

If we deconstruct Benjamin's concept of allegory we find the following determinants, which describe the main aspects of textual production and reception:

1. The allegorist breaks an element out of its normal context. By doing so he isolates it, deprives it of its original function and meaning. An allegory is therefore a fragment in contrast to the organic symbol. As Benjamin puts it: with allegory 'the false illusion of totality is extinguished'.
2. The allegorist re-assembles his fragments and creates a new meaning. This sort of meaning is constructed and derives in no way from the original context of the fragment.
3. Benjamin interprets the allegoric procedure as an expression of melancholy. Under the eyes of the melancholic (the one who turns his back on life and social activity, thus interrupting the coherence of his own totality of existence) objects are stunned. They lose the capacity to communicate meaning.

The relation between allegory and melancholy leads to a further point:

4. Allegory represents history as decay. It exposes the image of a fragmented, paralysed history in the form of a frozen primal landscape.

The comparison of the organic and non-organic text on the level of production shows the convergence between allegory and what is known as montage. While the 'classicist' (which I use as shorthand for the organically or symbolically producing artist) respects the traditional meaning of his material and tries to create a new totality in accordance with it, the avant-gardist kills off his material by blasting it out of its context, and mounts the fragments anew, regardless of their tradition. The classicist tries to cover the fact that his product is constructed, and wants to create a second nature. The avant-gardist exposes the materiality and technicality of his work, thus stressing its character as an artefact.

In so far as the avant-gardist assembles his work out of fragments, destroying the category of totality, montage can be seen as the basic principle of all modernist texts. This has consequences for the mode of reception too. In the organic work every part received its ultimate meaning through its relation to the whole. In contrast, the non-organic work releases its parts into utter freedom from the whole. They can be read individually or in groups and they make perfect sense in themselves.

The montage principle as a mode of alternative historiography exactly reflects the decline of bourgeois history. Historicism and the theory of progress are both organic concepts of history. The different epochs, which 'are all equally near to God', as the historicist Ranke put it, are seen as mature, fully developed totalities closed off against each other. The notion of progress underlies the concept of evolution, which is likewise based on the image of an organic body still developing towards its final mature state. But after the First World War the function of these concepts is concentrated exclusively on the affirmative aspect of ideological constructs. Objectively the history of the bourgeoisie has fallen apart into isolated fragments. The once totalising force of its signification as progressive, humane and ascendant over feudal society has turned openly into mechanisms of domination and exploitation at all costs. A whole mode of history has come to an end, and this is widely reflected in cultural production during the opening decades of the twentieth century.

History has been transformed into a space where all its fragments are stored in chaotic disorder. What finally lurks beneath the veneer of history as progress is history as continuous catastrophe. Hence Benjamin's famous angel of history:

> His face is turned towards the past. Where we perceive a chain of events, he sees one single catastrophe which keeps piling wreckage upon wreckage and hurls it in front of his feet. The angel would like to stay, awaken the dead, and make whole what had been smashed. But a storm is blowing from Paradise; it has got caught in his wings with such violence that the angel can no longer

close them. This storm irresistibly propels him into the future to which his back is turned, while the pile of debris before him grows skyward. This storm is what we call progress.[19]

In the angel we see the allegorist, the melancholic who is paralysed in the face of the catastrophic destruction of the world and its meaning. But for the dialectical historian and those who are interested with him in the reconstruction of an alternative world, it is precisely the wreckage, the debris out of which the new foundations can be constructed.

For Benjamin the treasure-house of such historical debris was the city: Berlin, where he grew up, but especially Paris, where he lived for a long time and which was for him the capital of the nineteenth century. We can see now that the centrepiece of his theory of textual production, the allegoresis, is completely determined by the ever-accelerating wastage of commodities and their contextual structures, which could best be experienced in the metropolis. But it is also to be found in that marginal literature and art which was never appropriated by the official canon of high culture; and indeed it can be discerned in high culture itself once the deconstruction of bourgeois modes of interpretation has opened up the possibility of alternative ways of reading. It is contained likewise in objects salvaged from oblivion by the collector – Benjamin himself being an avid collector of books, especially children's books. If we recall that the German word for 'to read' is *lesen*, which is directly related to the Latin word *legere*, meaning 'to collect', we can see the close connection between textual reception/production and the collecting of vanishing items. Benjamin's ultimate aim is 'lesen, was niemals geschrieben wurde' ('to read what has never been written').

In this paradox we find the essence of his methodology. Firstly there is the conflation of the two meanings of *lesen*. When Benjamin says 'History is a text of images', those images can be products of the imagination and they can be concrete objects, both not written in the strict sense of the word. And secondly, there is the endeavour to read in a way which destroys the text in question as a written document of its *own* time. To read a text from the past in the light of a present perspective, dissolves our notion of 'the original', of the 'genetic'. At the same time the idea of correspondences, which makes possible the charging of the past with a *Jetztzeit* constructed by the concern to emancipate society from repression, prevents such historiography from total arbitrariness or relativism. The concept of correspondences is at once the link between different periods and the avoidance of another powerful holistic and organic conception of history in the service of bourgeois society: Nietzsche's theory of eternal recurrence. In his collection of aphorisms entitled 'Central Park' Benjamin states:

As far as the idea of eternal recurrence is concerned, what is important is the fact that the bourgeoisie no longer dared to face the development of the productive relations which they themselves had initiated. The theory of Zarathustra and the motto embroidered on the cushion-cover – 'Rest but a quarter of an hour' – are complementary.[20]

Notes to chapter 4

1   Walter Benjamin, *Das Passagenwerk* in *Gesammelte Schriften*, Unter Mitwirkung von Th. W. Adorno and Gershom Scholem, ed. Rolf Thiedemann and Hermann Schwep-penhäuser, Vol. V.1, (Part 1), Frankfurt am Main, 1982, p. 575.
2   *Ibid.*, p. 571.
3   *Ibid.*, p. 580.
4   *Ibid.*, pp. 576–7.
5   *Ibid.*, p. 577.
6   See Walter Benjamin, 'Über den Begriff der Geschichte', in *Gesammelte Schriften*, Vol. I.2, pp. 693–4. Tr. as 'Theses on the Philosophy of History', in Benjamin, *Illuminations*, ed. Hannah Arendt, London, 1973.
7   Walter Benjamin, 'Charles Baudelaire. Ein Lyriker im Zeitalter des Hochkapitalismus', in *Gesammelte Schriften*, Vol. I.2, pp. 582–3.
8   Walter Benjamin, *Das Passagenwerk*, p. 493.
9   Frank Barron, 'The psychology of imagination', in *Scientific American*, 1958, Vol. 199, No. 3, p. 151.
10 John Eccles, 'The physiology of imagination', in *Scientific American*, 1958, Vol. 199, No. 3, p. 135.
11 Walter Benjamin, 'Charles Baudelaire', p. 608.
12 Benjamin, drawing heavily on Bergson's theory of memory, emphasises that Bergson never tried to analyse memory and experience as historically shaped phenomena. Benjamin himself seems to be very close to the theory of Maurice Halbwachs as developed in his study *Les cadres sociaux de la mémoire*, though his name is not mentioned in Benjamin's writings. Compare also my essay 'The Rhetoric of Forgetting. Brecht and the Historical Avant-garde' (together with Helmut Lethen), in *Convention and Innovation*, ed. Theo d'Haen, Rainer Grübel and Helmut Lethen, Amsterdam/Philadelphia, 1987.
13 John Eccles, *op. cit.*, p. 141.
14 Walter Benjamin, 'Charles Baudelaire', p. 610.
15 *Ibid.*, p. 611.
16 *Ibid.*, pp. 646–7.
17 Walter Benjamin, 'Einbahnstrasse', in *Gesammelte Schriften*, Vol. IV.1, ed. Tillman Rexroth, p. 119.
18 The relationship between the notions of modernism, montage and Benjamin's concept of allegory has been analysed by Peter Bürger, *Theory of the Avant-Garde*, Manchester, 1984.
19 Walter Benjamin, 'Über den Begriff der Geschichte', pp. 697–8.
20 Walter Benjamin, 'Zentralpark', in *Gesammelte Schriften*, Vol. I.2., p. 677.

PART II

MODERNISM AND POLITICS

The futures market: Marinetti and the Fascists of Milan

On the Fascist electoral list of November 1919 the name of Filippo Tommaso Marinetti appears after that of Benito Mussolini. From the distant vantage-point of today it looks as though the avant-garde group that prided itself on the notorious slogan, 'war – only hygiene of the world', had found a fitting outlet for its energies under the banner of a man who would take Italy into twenty years of right-wing dictatorship. The reality of the situation was a good deal more complex.

The first complexity involves Mussolini's early political career. For he began as a Marxist and came to occupy a prominent position within the Italian Socialist Party. Towards the end of 1914 Mussolini was ousted from the editorship of the socialist paper *Avanti!* and expelled from the Party, having gradually come to favour intervention on the *entente* side in the First World War. His concept of a 'revolutionary' war, capable of politicising the masses and preparing the way for fundamental changes in social organisation, was incompatible with the orthodox internationalist position of Socialist colleagues; but it was nonetheless still a notion fuelled by leftist ideology. Peculiarities of national history made the Italy of the new century a fertile terrain for 'aberrant' left-wing theorising; and in fact the early Fascism which evolved in Milan retained a left-wing character.

Here we encounter further difficulties. Futurism's insistence on Italian supremacy and its cult of youth and energy would lead one to assume that Marinetti and his friends were anything but responsive to the Left. Yet Lenin himself saw in the founder of Futurism a real power for revolution; and Gramsci, writing to Trotsky, expresses his approval, though admittedly he is referring to the cultural impact of the Movement in pre-war days.[1] But the supreme and awkward fact remains: Marinetti chose to part company with Fascism in May 1920. In later years, when the sphere of his activities had become more exclusively artistic, he repaired the damage, insisting that Futurism expressed the 'dynamic' spirit of Fascism. Yet following the 1920 Congress Marinetti remained aloof from the Fascists for some three years, just when the political movement was unequivocally emerging as Fascist in nature as well as name. Though Futurism wished to see society 'deregulated' and individual creativity released, its radicalism was so thoroughly interlaced with nationalist rhetoric and so patently disdainful of the real conditions of life in most of Italy that there seems little choice retrospectively but to class it as an extravagant, right-wing phenomenon. How then did Marinetti and his followers come to align themselves with a political movement whose original members came on the whole from a dissident or interventionist Left? And why did they remain within that movement only as long as its policies retained traces of a left-wing provenance?

In attempting to answer these questions, I shall begin by discussing Futurism's ideology as it emerges from the more imaginative pronouncements of the movement, and then outline its political policies. The two areas – 'vision' and 'blueprint' – are curiously mismatched in a good many respects. But first, by way of introduction, I offer a brief chronicle of some salient events surrounding the Marinetti–Mussolini alliance:[2]

February 1909   Marinetti publishes the Founding Manifesto of Futurism in *Le Figaro*. He includes the following 'articles':
   'Courage, audacity, and revolt will be essential elements of our poetry.'
   'Except in struggle there is no more beauty. No work without an aggressive character can be a masterpiece. Poetry must be conceived as a violent attack on unknown forces, to reduce and prostrate them before man.'
   'We will glorify war – the world's only hygiene – militarism, patriotism, the destructive gesture of the freedom-bringer, beautiful ideas worth dying for, and scorn for women.'[3]

January 1910   The first Futurist 'evening' takes place in Trieste (at that time under Austrian rule).

1909 and 1911   Futurist political manifestos for elections and one supporting Italy's colonial campaign in Libya. Mussolini is imprisoned for anti-war agitation.

September 1914   Anti-Austrian demonstration by the Futurists in Milan.

December 1914   Mussolini founds *Il Popolo d'Italia* and the Autonomous Fascio for Revolutionary Action.

Spring 1915   Mussolini is arrested with the Futurists Marinetti, Settimelli, and Carrà after interventionist speech-making. But the interventionist campaign succeeds, and Italy declares war on Germany and Austria–Hungary.

February 1918   First publication of the 'Manifesto of the Italian Futurist

Party'.

November 1918   The Futurist Mario Carli founds The Association for Italian Arditi (shock-troops). Futurist groups (*fasci*) are set up in various Italian cities.

January 1919   Marinetti and Mussolini involved in violent disruption at the Scala Theatre, Milan, while Bissolati (the reformist socialist and 1914 interventionist) attempts to expound a policy of reducing Italy's post-war territorial claims.

March 1919   Foundation of Fascism at Piazza San Sepolcro, Milan. Adherents include members of the Futurist *fasci*, of the Arditi Association, dissident or independent socialists, revolutionary and nationalist syndicalists, radical republicans.

April 1919   'The Battle of Via Mercanti'. Marinetti and Mussolini are present during anti-socialist incidents culminating in the destruction of offices of *Avanti!* (the paper Mussolini had formerly edited).

June 1919   *Il popolo d'Italia* publishes the Fascist programme.

October 1919   First Fascist Congress. Marinetti speaks on the necessity of removing the Papacy from Italy (*svaticanamento*). Electoral campaigning by Mussolini and Marinetti.

November 1919   Failure of Fascism at elections (4,567 votes out of a possible 270,000).[4] Arrest and imprisonment of Mussolini and Marinetti after arms are discovered at Fascist and Arditi headquarters.

May 1920   Futurists withdraw from Fascism.

It is on these early developments that I shall focus, leaving aside the events that followed Mussolini's rise to power and Marinetti's return to the fold. This denigrator of cultural institutions was eventually to become a member of the Fascist Academy, and he remained loyal to Mussolini for the rest of his life. He co-operated in the assimilation of Futurism by the regime; and in so doing he forfeited the movement's avant-garde status. If it is the case that true avant-gardes can exist only under liberal systems of government which permit plurality of opinion and freedom of expression, it is also the case that they cannot effectively survive the toleration of an authoritarian one, for conflict is their life-blood.

As the events listed above show, both Marinetti and Mussolini were prepared to take their battles on to the street, at risk of violence and illegality. The common ground on which these two Milanese residents first met was interventionism; and the Great War – a first-hand, front-line experience for their generation – remained a catalyst of action and a polariser of opinion in the circles they frequented. It was, for instance, the combatant associations founded by Carli, and shortly afterwards, in Milan, by Ferruccio Vecchi, that provided political Futurism with a 'shadow' organisation as well as potential adherents. As for the fairly heterogeneous group that met at Piazza San Sepolcro, it consisted of men who at the very least had welcomed Italy's intervention in the war, and now wished to see that participation pay off in political terms.

From the outset Futurism displays the activism and the agonism that Poggioli has seen as constitutive of avant-garde movements.[5] The Founding Manifesto sets the polemical, frenzied tone for all its successors. But all that passion for 'dynamic' technological society – for machines and factories, for 'multicoloured, polyphonic tides of revolution in modern capitals' (p. 10) – is accompanied by a readiness for self-immolation. In a land the Futurists see as fossilised by its cultural traditions and its scholarly mentality, the exuberant creativity that they seek seems locatable only in the instant which is *now,* and on the extreme periphery of experience. Futurism looks to a Dionysiac moment of heroism that releases the self from human limitations. Marinetti is willing to find it in ideas 'worth dying for', or in that murderous onslaught of even newer generations on the Futurists which he jubilantly predicts (p. 12). Futurism abolishes all notion of history as an ascending series. Reality for Marinetti involves an oscillating cycle of parricide and suicide; its 'perpetual becoming' is achieved by the unceasing struggle of the individual with himself. 'Overcome yourself, or cease to be', as he writes later (p. 402), in Nietzschean mood.

The first manifesto appeared in that phase of Italian life dominated by the pragmatic politics of the Liberal Prime Minister, Giovanni Giolitti. Beneath Futurism's calculated outrageousness, there are subtexts which betray something of the predicament of intellectuals in that period. Because of her late unification and economic backwardness, Italy was not a country that had been able to allow herself much in the way of cultural radicalism. But by 1909 things had changed. Where Italy had been predominantly an agricultural nation, she was belatedly industrialising, at least in the north, and had a fast-developing economy. But that prosperity was relative; her *per capita* income for 1911–13 was only just over half of Germany's, for instance, and less than one third of Britain's. It was a situation that at best made for fragile confidence. At worst Italians were caught between assertive desires and feelings of inferiority. Futurism lived out this conflict with particularly dramatic intensity.

It was of course clear, especially in a city like Milan, that the vitality of the nation lay with the creators of wealth, the industrial bourgeoisie. Futurism's machine aesthetic and its brave visions of a technological future represent a homage to industrial enterprise. The manifesto 'Destruction of

Syntax' (May 1913) takes stock of the 'complete renewal of human sensibility' brought about by scientific discoveries, and notes that modern patriotism is 'the heroic idealization of a people's commercial, industrial and artistic solidarity' (pp. 57, 59). The trouble, however, with the entrepreneur is not only that the value-system generated by his economic potency may tend in due course to become settled and stifling, but that it is a value-system in which men remain subject to individual exploitation while all glory goes to their artefacts. This ambiguous situation the Futurists nevertheless welcome in a spirit of 'willed optimism'.

This is only half the story. In reality the Futurist intellectual, who correctly pinpoints the true site of social change and its extraordinarily accelerated rhythms, also has to confront the possibility (and the fear) that art in these new circumstances is irrelevant. Thus when the Futurists abandoned the shadowy margins where artists had traditionally engaged in contemplation and took up a position in the neon glare of the marketplace, it was a move that was fundamentally defensive. All the quantifications and demystifications to be found in the 1914 Corradini–Settimelli manifesto, 'Weights, Measures and Prices of Artistic Genius', for example, are anti-bourgeois (and anti-art) in one sense; but in another they speak the language of bourgeois capitalism, and seek its shelter. Nor is this the Futurism's only ambivalence.

If one strategy for protecting the interests of artists in a new massproducing environment is to accommodate to it by treating artists as the makers of market products, another is to indulge in unashamed selfaggrandisement. Futurism publicly and persistently celebrates its own creative 'genius'; and in this it is hard to tell whether it viewed itself as audaciously bohemian or hardheadedly commercial. In any event it sees in what it calls genius not only the power to trigger energetic reactions between subject and object, text and context, but also that of determining the nature of the object itself. At one level, then, there is an orientation in Futurism to what is happening 'out there' in the real world; at another there is the flamboyant, theatrical narcissism which disguises a sense of vulnerability. Both factors are conducive to the artist's eruption into the 'real', political world. The activism of the movement works out on the formal plane in its lasting experimental verve. On the practical plane it translates first into those theatrical 'happenings', the Futurist *serate*, in which art is deemed to be created in the instant of confrontation. And the *serate,* always provocative as a phenomenon and seldom without some specific political content, easily become the pro-war rallies of 1914–15, such as that drawn by Cangiullo (Fig. 1). His *Milan-Demonstration* makes the crowds in the cathedral square spell out the names of Mussolini and

Marinetti in adjacent left-hand lines.

The notion of an instantaneous, ephemeral art is of course markedly anti-humanist; the radicalism of the rejection being reflected in the passage from free verse to free word-tables. Graphic elements, words, syllables, arithmetical and typographical signs explode in 'simultaneity' across the page, formal equivalents of an outlook that refuses history and reason (see Fig. 2). Futurism, like other avant-garde movements, tends to regard creativity as belonging to a primordial stratum of the psyche, one long mortified by cultural and moral prejudice. Its anti-humanist stance liberated what had been seen as anti-human, in particular the erotic and the aggressive. Yet in glorifying war as a hygiene, Marinetti at first tries to claim a mystical and apolitical stance. In a manifesto probably written in 1909 he insists that Futurist 'patriotism and love of war have nothing to do with ideology': without them there is quite simply 'nothing but decadence and death' (p. 247). He sees them as part of a heroic morality that seeks to potentiate the human, not to deny it. But of course his notion of heroism is inadequate all along – and precisely because it cannot be realised in strictly human terms.

The Futurists seem to have repressed a pessimism about modern living that was more openly acknowledged elsewhere – from the Expressionists to Eliot. Scientific advances and their industrial applications after all brought not only a sense of exhilaration but one of threat. New powers were available to men, but the whole configuration of their society was being changed: the individual was submerged in the anonymous urban mass, the realm of the natural was shrinking. In their 'artificial optimism' the Futurists, however, refuse all disquiet on this score. It is crucial that they choose instead to view human nature itself as incomplete: fulfilled only as far as it can be made to evolve towards 'a non-human and mechanical type', one 'constructed for omnipresent speed' and 'naturally cruel, omniscient and aggressive' (p. 256). This Machine-Man ideal offers the foundation for an aesthetic theory (requiring, for instance, the 'suppression of the I in literature' and a 'lyrical obsession with matter' (p. 44)); but also represents an ideological position. For if creativity and apotheosis in men comes about only through struggle against their own mortality, in the modern context that struggle can only mean war on an industrial scale.

All this may seem obvious when we consider the enthusiasm of Futurists for the wars of their time. But Marinetti's love-affair with notoriety on the one hand, and ordinary considerations of *realpolitik* on the other, may cloud the issue. The most telling observations can be made therefore, not in texts that deal directly with Tripoli, Adrianopolis or the Carso, but in areas more or less uncontaminated by activist rhetoric or political motive. In such an area lies a short Marinettian text of 1911: it is titled 'Electric War' and

subtitled 'Futurist Vision-Hypothesis'. The chaotic nihilism of a piece like 'Let's Kill the Moonlight' gives way here to a fantasy of control and efficiency. Electricity has turned the whole Italian countryside into an automated agricultural factory. Men in flying machines (which hardly ever touch down) regulate the accelerated processes of nature achieved in this controlled environment, watching while before their very eyes 'forests grow fantastically towards the moon' (p. 275). The humming landscape brings superproductivity. Hunger, poverty, social and economic problems, the drudgery of labour are at an end. This is the reign of intelligence. However, disputes over markets for the superabundance of products are the prelude to electric war. Machines with elephantine probosces suck vacuums in the air, bombarding the unbreathable emptiness with 'great tangles of irritated lightning' (p. 276).

The forecasts are far enough off target to let us enjoy the detail of these quaintly vigorous imaginings. But the fact remains that for Marinetti there is no earthly paradise without war. As Sanguineti comments, 'industrial war is not just the hygiene of the world, but its truth: the ultimate truth of nature and history'.[6]

'Electric War' reveals in allegory how fundamental to Marinetti is the

(*this page* 1) Cangiullo, *Milan Demonstration*; (*facing* 2) Marinetti, *Scrabrrrraanng* ('Lying in bed that evening, she reread the letter from her artilleryman at the front') (*and*|3) Depero, *Skyscrapers*

connection between productivity and bellicosity, or, to put it another way, between capitalist expansion and aggressive nationalism. The productivism of the movement bulks so large in its thinking that the image of the nation as factory survives into the post-war period. Later Futurist texts, like Depero's 'Skyscrapers' (Fig. 3), still celebrate what industry has created: the modern consumer city, built of iron and glass and crowded with restaurants, hotels, cinemas. And Marinetti, deeply observant of capitalist orthodoxy, writes: 'Patriotism for us is simply the sublimation of that respectful loyalty that good and prosperous businessmen inspire in their employees' (p. 357). The Futurist writer Volt identifies politics largely with economics, and wants union representation on his proposed legislative body determined not by size of membership, but by '*the importance of the economic function* the union exercises in the country' (p. 359).

After 1918, when Futurism was at its most 'democratic' and politically engaged, the political mileage in continuing to preach the joys of warfare was clearly limited (even though victory had brought Italy territorial gains). The other half of the productivity/bellicosity nexus was in trouble too, because of Italy's badly disrupted economy. Improvement in individual standards of living had in any case been a matter of deep indifference to Marinetti (who ploughed his own fortune into Futurism); and even he had had to concede that Italy, compared with other nations, was poor in natural resources. The result is that Marinetti becomes evasive on the key notion of imperialism. A certain sense of realism now causes him to advance the idea of Italy as representing, in relation to other nations, 'a super-brilliant minority composed entirely of individuals above the human average for their creative, innovative, improvisational powers'. The resultant 'democracy', he continues, 'will inevitably find itself in competition with the majority formed by the other nations, for whom numbers signify merely the more or less blind masses, that is to say, the democracy of the unaware' (p. 328). The once bellicose Marinetti has fallen back on the idea of a purely spiritual hegemony.

Now it is evident that Futurism's entry into the political arena and the mass participation it envisages in a Futurist Democracy are determined by the experience of war. 'It is the first time in history', Marinetti enthuses, 'that it has fallen to the lot of more than four million citizens of a single nation to have undergone in a mere four years a total, intensive education, learning by fire, by heroism and death. [. . .] Marvellous spectacle of a whole army leaving for war practically unaware and returning politicized and worthy to govern' (p. 330). Behind Futurism's political hopes lies the invigorating memory of everyday bravery in the trenches. But its optimism foundered badly. The goal of activating the masses, as the disastrous 1919 elections proved, was not so easily attained.

It seems likely that this moment of electoral defeat produced a further transformation in Marinetti's thinking, and ultimately caused him to withdraw from active politics. *Beyond Communism,* begun in prison a month after the elections of November 1919, is not an overtly dispirited work, though it has its pessimistic notes. But it is subtly reactionary, a work which in some respects points the way forward for Fascism.

Where *Futurist Democracy* of 1919 had been chiefly concerned to elaborate the policies of the party founded in 1918, and to stigmatise the attitudes of Italy's ruling classes, *Beyond Communism* retreats to Utopia and is often lyrical in tone. Its main impulse is to resuscitate the possibility of that disinterested heroism which belonged to early Futurism. Once again a modulation in attitude takes place, presumably because the magical transition from industrial plentitude to the heroic discharge of surfeit – such as was figured in 'Electric War' – is inconceivable in the context of post-war depression. Moreover the masses have refused to follow where Marinetti (and Mussolini) led; and so we return to the exaltation of a spiritual aristocracy. The 'heroic citizen' of *Beyond Communism* is in fact none other than the Futurist artist. The distinguishing features of the old pre-war movement reappear: pride in anarchic self-determination, a libertarianism now extended to the abolition of law-courts and police, the familiar horror of all levelling influences, with communism replacing socialism as target. Significant is the following: 'We hear all around shouts of "everyone will have enough to eat, everyone will be rich". We shout instead "everyone will be strong: a genius" ' (p. 415). When the material base shows its cracks, all that remains is the gratuitous heroism of the avant-garde.

In political terms, Marinetti is talking about leadership. He no longer really believes in *Futurist Democracy*'s 'race of geniuses', and this has a curious twofold effect. For the first time he acknowledges the waste lands of capitalism, the 'harsh, gloomy, stale and agitated rhythms of everyday living' (p. 422); and he ascribes to art the function of a counterbalance: 'We shall not have an earthly paradise, but the economic hell will be rejoiced and calmed by countless festivals of art' (p. 424). Even more important, in his re-emergent elitism, he distinguishes between those who have the 'right to create the Italian revolution and those who must submit to its conception and realization' (p. 417). Compare this with the assertion of *Futurist Democracy,* so short a time before, that Italy is made up of forty million individuals, 'all of them intelligent and capable of autonomy' (p. 329). And who now can be the artificers of the 'becoming-progress-revolution of the race' (p. 412)? Why, members of the *piccola borghesia,* that class caught between capital and labour which was eventually to be the backbone of Fascism. Marinetti writes:

> In all countries and particularly in Italy, the distinction between the proletariat and the bourgeoisie is a false one. [. . .] There are [. . .] so-called members of the rich bourgeoisie who work much harder than the working class; and workers who work as little as possible [. . .]. It is absurd to call that formidable mass of intelligent hard-working young men from the middle classes a rotten and moribund bourgeoisie [. . .]. They [. . .] are all anxious to outdo, by assiduous labour, the modest economic standing of their fathers. They went through war as lieutenants and captains, and to-day, not in the least exhausted, they are ready to take up their effort in life with heroism. (p. 415)

There is a marked similarity between this insistence of Marinetti's on economic striving and on the futility of class distinctions, and Mussolini's own vision of inter-class collaboration for the sake of national productivity, which he expressed at the Congress of May 1920: 'The bourgeoisie has technical and moral value: there are parasitical elements in the bourgeoisie just as there are in the proletariat. It will be a great step forward therefore to make the values of the proletariat and the bourgeoisie coincide. It is collaboration between the producing proletariat and the producing bourgeoisie alone that will take our civilization forward.'[7]

This parallel takes us back to the paradoxes of the Futurist–Fascist alliance, it being precisely at the 1920 Congress that Marinetti abandoned the Fascist Party. To understand this, we must look more closely at Futurist policies, and at the left-wing connotations of early Fascism into which they fed.

As far as those policies are concerned the war is a watershed. Though the few brief manifestos issued between 1909 and 1913 become gradually more specific, polemical generalities of a predictable kind remain the order of the day. More than once, for instance, the Futurists declare that 'the word ITALY must dominate the word LIBERTY'. The choice of Trieste as the venue for the first *serata futurista,* on the other hand, seems more focused. It meant that the movement espoused the cause of the *terre irredente,* those 'unredeemed lands' with their partly Italian-speaking population which at the time were part of the Austro–Hungarian Empire. Yet one can hardly avoid the thought that the Futurists may have been just as concerned to offer that challenge to the political establishment which is so vital to an avant-garde movement as with the unfinished business of the Risorgimento. The fact is that since the signing of the Triple Alliance with Austria and Germany in 1882, official Italy had been effectively muzzled on the question of this territory, so that Futurism was tapping a source of rebelliousness sufficiently widespread in northern Italy to give buoyancy to the movement, but able also to attract the equally desirable disapproval of the establishment.

In any case we are dealing with attitudes, not a coherent set of policies capable of enactment. The latter came only when the old supine Italy had become Italy-at-war, filling Marinetti's imagination with a new vision of his compatriots. The scale of participation must have seemed a fulfilment beyond every expectation of his activist dreams; and it is the resulting excitement and optimism that gives to the Manifesto of the Futurist Party of 1918 its unexpectedly democratic character. Much of this Manifesto found an echo in the two programmes of the *fasci di combattimento*, which appeared in *Il Popolo d'Italia* a few months after the San Sepolcro meeting and in necessary amplification of its generic statements.[8] For convenience I summarise the Futurist programme below, italicising elements which find some equivalent in the statements of the *fasci*:

> *Universal suffrage* and *proportional representation; a 'technical' parliament with strong representation by industry, agriculture, engineering and commerce; abolition of the Senate* (or its replacement by twenty young elected members to serve as an *eccitatorio* or stimulant to government). 'Socialization' of land, with *allocations to veterans, purchase or expropriation of underexploited areas, encouragement to co-operatives,* both *agricultural* and industrial. Land reclamation, *improved communications, systematic exploitation of natural resources.* Nationalization of waterways, waterworks and mines; modernization and industrialization of towns. *Progressive taxation, wealth tax, confiscation of two-thirds of war profits.* Elimination of conscription in favour of a small, professional army. Military skills and sport to be taught in schools; elimination of illiteracy, penal sanctions for non-attendance at *lay* elementary *schools.* Legal aid, elected judiciary, freedom to strike, of association, of press. *Eight-hour working day, minimum wages,* equal pay for men and women; *worker and veteran pension schemes,* collective wage bargaining, welfare benefits. *Radical reform of bureaucracy and its hierarchial career-structure, decentralization. Anticlericalism* and the introduction of divorce. (pp. 130–5)

On the evidence of summer 1919, there is no denying the radical and leftist orientation of Fascism at this early stage. But a certain truculence in tone, an insistence on the Italian character of the social revolution proposed (even more pronounced in the Futurist Party Manifesto), gives today's reader pause. Distinctions of left and right in fact do little to illuminate the complicated situation that obtained in Italy; and the wisdom of hindsight discerns with ease what the passions of the day made obscure. The curious vagaries of Mussolini's early career have often been interpreted superficially. Irritating contradictions can be all too conveniently dismissed as consonant with Mussolini's proven lack of integrity and his opportunism;

or else regarded as all of a piece with a political doctrine that prided itself on having burst free of rationalist constraint, and was not noted for the distinction of its intellectuals. Other commentators, in what is perhaps an effort to redress the balance, argue that Mussolini's early Fascism at least was an illegitimate offspring of Marxism itself, born at a time when odd liaisons were by no means rare.[9] The connections between Futurism and Fascism, as well as the oddnesses internal to the two movements, need to be seen against the background of their peculiarly hybrid theoretical ancestry. It was this that made the strange partnership possible.

To clarify this complex issue, we may consider their divergent reactions to the Libyan War of 1911. This colonial campaign found enthusiastic support among the Futurists, but was duly condemned by Mussolini and Italian Socialism, for whom it involved a reactionary strengthening of the military and the throne. Yet there were others of Marxist extraction – revolutionary socialists and syndicalists, expelled from the Party in 1906 during its more moderate, reformist phase – who supported the Libyan venture. Their support was based on the consideration that colonial expansion was acceptable where it was conducive to that maturing of the economic base which was an indispensable preliminary to the socialist revolution. It seemed to some, moreover, that the internationalism of socialist doctrine was likely to remain a chimera until all nations had reached the same stage of economic development. Syndicalists like Arturo Labriola, Olivetti and Orano believed that the masses could best be mobilised through a proletarian and revolutionary nationalism that would bring this economic advance. It was further argued that, since the Italian bourgeoisie still had its historic responsibility to discharge, the interests of its entrepreneurial sectors (as opposed to the landed gentry) temporarily coincided with those of the proletariat.

This was a distortion of Marxism, a 'Marxist heresy',[10] owing its existence to Italy's relative backwardness, and corresponding to a persecuted feeling among Italians that they needed to compress into the shortest possible span the hundred years during which the other nations had expanded and industrialised while Italy, as it seemed, had stood and watched: only then could she meet her neighbours on an equal footing. So it was that there existed in Italy by 1911 a left-wing rationale for imperialism.

These same expansionist views appear – much more predictably – in the nationalist thinking that also emerged in the first decade of the century.[11] This new 'revolutionary' nationalism eschewed old-style patriotic appeals. To talk of king and country where a people included so many labourers without stake of ownership was futile. Instead it was argued that radical economic regeneration alone could bring about a rebirth and a truly Italian way of life. Colonial possessions were desirable not only because they could staunch what one nationalist called the 'haemorrhage' of emigration, but precisely because of their regenerative potential.

So it was that while the aims of revolutionary socialists and syndicalists on the one hand and the 'new' nationalists on the other remained antagonistic, the two groupings nonetheless shared an emphasis on economic expansion. Both also believed in the role of an elite capable of articulating and focusing the stirrings of the masses; both based their strategies on an *anticipated* future rather than on existing material conditions; and both despised representative parliamentary democracy as a sham – which is less surprising when we reflect that until 1912 less than a quarter of the population was enfranchised.

These coincidences suggest something of the extraordinary blurring of political distinctions that occurs in the period. Futurism itself shares in the points of convergence I have outlined. Even if, for example, it always treated socialist doctrine disparagingly, calling it a recipe for 'belly-filling' cowardice, this does not preclude a debt to the theory of syndicalism. That theory supplemented the determinist view of economic history with the notion that ethical consciousness also plays its part in processes of change. Did Marinetti have Sorel's heroic 'mobilizing myths' in mind when he coined his slogan on war? It seems clear at any rate that Futurism's anti-parliamentarianism, its scorn for the traditional, opportunistic conduct of politics, its libertarianism are as much inspired by syndicalism as nationalism.

In an environment where strange debts are regularly contracted, where terms like 'proletarian nationalism' and 'nationalist syndicalism' have a meaning, no policy of Milanese Fascism can be said to derive simply or in line of direct descent from the Futurist Party. But if Marinetti's influence in the field of policy was probably less than is sometimes assumed, it seems to have exerted itself on the self-image of the *fasci*. Mussolini was willing to see them not as a party, but as a movement, an ideological avant-garde. And in that same summer of 1919, reading the following pronouncement by Mussolini, Marinetti must have been gratified to note the impact of artistic vision on political blueprint:

> Fascism is anti-academic. It refuses political deals. It has no statutes or rules [. . .] It does not tolerate endless speeches. [. . .] On the issue of workers' demands it is in line with nationalist syndicalism [. . .] Fascism is antipus [ie. anti-PSI – Italian Socialist Party], but because it is productivist it is not and cannot be antiproletarian.
>
> Fascism is [. . .] pragmatic, it has no preconceptions nor distant goals. It makes none of the usual promises of an ideal world, leaving that sort of

chatter to the herd of card-carriers. It doesn't presume to exist for ever, or even for long. [. . .] Once we decide that the solution to the fundamental problems troubling Italy to-day has been reached, Fascism won't cling to life [. . .] but will know how to die a glorious death, without protest or pomp. If Youth from the trenches, and students, flow into the Fasci [. . .] it's because there are no mouldering ideas in the Fasci, no venerable greybeards, no conventional scale of values: there is youth, energy and faith. Fascism will always be a movement that belongs to a minority. It cannot spread outside the cities, but soon [. . .] the forthcoming national rally will draw together in concord and libertarian unity of action this formidable grouping of new energies.[12]

Fascism is here closer to a revolutionary Left than to the so-called revolutionary nationalist Right; and in its agonism, its heroic irrationalism, its urban elitism, its insistence on youth and energy, it speaks the purist avant-garde idiom. Mussolini could allow himself such recklessness precisely because the *Fasci* represented to him no more than a temporary anchorage that kept him in the political swim. A bloc moulded from the official interventionalist left was what he really wished to lead. After the defeat of Milanese Fascism in November 1919 (arguably caused in part by a too great overlap of some of its policies with those of socialism),[13] and after Mussolini failed to engineer his bloc, the movement found that its new adherents tended to come from the provinces, and that its best chances of survival lay in more 'realistic' directions. This was no longer the moment to speak of abolishing senate, monarchy or papacy. 'Unpatriotic', socialist-inspired strikes proliferated and the *Fasci* no longer talked of going out to meet Labour, but of rigorously opposing those confrontations 'in which purely economic motivation has become subject to the mystifications of calculating demagogues'.[14]

At the May Congress of 1920 Marinetti resisted this turn of events, apparently criticising the current position on strike action,[15] as well as deploring the conciliatory stance now being adopted by Fascism in relation to monarch and Pope. When he came to record the schism between the two movements in *Futurism and Fascism* (1924), he made no mention, however, of having espoused the workers' cause. Any reference to conflict provoked by Futurist attitudes which looked left-wing, even if they might more accurately be described as anarchic and libertarian,[16] would have been totally inappropriate: for by this time Marinetti had come to heel, and was anxious to demonstrate that Futurism was Fascism's precursor. In explaining the break with Fascism, he therefore mentioned only the issues of the monarchy and the Vatican. It may also have been the impulse to defend the movement he had founded that caused him to tell the story as he did, for it permitted him, even as he claimed that as yet Fascism had only realised Futurism's 'minimalist programme' (p. 430), to make a last-ditch bid for that front-line territory of the avant-garde which in reality was well and truly lost.

Perhaps there is more to that moment of defection and Marinetti's explanation of it. If the really coercive reason for his bowing out was indeed the desire to see Italy free of monarch and Pope, he had certainly picked issues that were politically suicidal. In so doing he offered an oblique indication that at the heart of his dissent lay the failure of Fascism to embrace a radicalism that was total and uncompromising. In later years there would no longer be any doubt about the subordination of Marinetti the visionary to Mussolini the dictator. But in 1920, when Fascism ceased to be an *eccitatorio,* a thorn in the flesh of the old body politic, and looked to its future, Futurism briefly acted out the old agonistic ideal.

Notes to chapter 5

1   See *Futurismo e fascismo,* ed. A. Schiavo, Rome 1981, p. 5; and Antonio Gramsci, *Socialismo e fascismo,* Turin, 1966, pp. 527–8. (In English, see *Antonio Gramsci: Selections from Cultural Writings,* tr. William Boelhower, ed. Geoffrey Nowell-Smith and David Forgacs, London, 1985, pp. 52–4.)

2   For a detailed factual account see James Joll, *Intellectuals in Politics,* London, 1960, pp. 131–84. Also Julie R. Dashwood, 'Futurism and Fascism', *Italian Studies,* 27, 1972, pp. 91–103.

3   For the full text see *Teoria e invenzione futurista,* pp. 7–13, Vol. II of *Opere di F. T. Marinetti,* ed. Luciano De Maria, 4 vols., Milan, 1968. Page references to this source are henceforward given in the text. For English translations of a selection of manifestos, see *Futurist Manifestos,* ed. Umbro Apollonio, London, 1973.

4   Figures given in Renzo De Felice's fundamental *Mussolini il rivoluzionario,* Turin, 1965, p. 572.

5   See Renato Poggioli, Chs 2 and 4, in *Theory of the Avant-Garde,* Cambridge, Mass., 1968, pp. 16–40, 60–77.

6   Edoardo Sanguineti, *Ideologia e linguaggio,* Milan, 1970, p. 43.

7   *Opera omnia di Benito Mussolini,* ed. Edoardo and Duilio Susmel, 44 vols., Florence and Rome, 1951–80, Vol. XIV, p. 469.

8   See Appendices in De Felice, *op. cit.,* pp. 742–5.

9   See, for instance, A. James Gregor, *Young Mussolini and the Intellectual Origins of Fascism,* Berkeley–Los Angeles–London, 1979.

10 I borrow the expression from *ibid.,* p. xi.

11 See, for example, 'Giovanni Papini: A Nationalist Programme', in *Italian Fascisms,* ed. Adrian Lyttelton, London, 1973, pp. 99–119. (Papini was also a Futurist, editor of the important Futurist organ *Lacerba,* published in Florence before the war.)

12 *Opera omnia di Benito Mussolini,* Vol. XIII, pp. 219–20.

13 See Paolo Alatri, *Origini del fascismo,* 5th ed., Rome, 1971, p. 44.

14 See 'Postulati del programma fascista (maggio 1920)', in Renzo De Felice, *op. cit.,* p. 746.

15 *Ibid.,* p. 596. No source given, but see *Opera omnia,* Vol. XIV, p. 470.

16 A similar problem of terminology is perhaps present when Caroline Tisdall and Angelo Bozzolla state that Marinetti had tried unsuccessfully 'to force a left-wing position' on the Fascist Party. (See their *Futurism,* London, 1977, p. 207.)

The politics of English Modernism: Eliot, Pound, Joyce

An intriguing, and sometimes exasperating problem of English Modernist literature is its connection with the politics of the extreme right. Eliot and Pound are the principal writers involved, with Wyndham Lewis in the wings. They held political views which it is now difficult to countenance, and they elaborated wider social and cultural theories which, though sometimes challenging in their radical conservatism, frequently constitute an impediment to the reading and enjoyment of their arts. Is the reader of poetry and novels inevitably bound to engage with the writers' political opinions? How far did their politics influence their poetic and fictional writing, and how far has the reception of their work as a whole taken proper account of political issues? If we find their political opinions rebarbative, or unworthy of such apparently major writers, are we thereby shut out to some degree from the literary work itself?

It can sometimes seem, reading Eliot's verse, that his anti-Semitism and his contempt for tolerance (for example) are marginal matters in comparison with the profound imaginative vision which his verse communicates; but at other times this conviction is far less strong. His political opinions were expressed repeatedly over a long period, but the connections between them and the verse remain elusive. It is perilously easy to overstate the importance of the politics, yet too simple to ignore them. The political vision is there, and it seems altogether narrower, more dated, and far less accessible to imaginative assent than the vision of the verse. Yet the politics and the verse also seem to relate and overlap in ways which defy such a simplistic division. This makes response to the verse itself a complex and problematic business.

Eliot is the greatest of the English-language writers to present this sort of difficulty, and he will thus require the most sustained attention. We may then give some thought to the tragic but perhaps simpler case of Pound, whose political opinions are far less sophisticated than Eliot's, far more brutal, and far more widely and loudly expressed in his poetry itself. These two writers give us cause to consider some of the difficulties involved in reading the literature of the great modernist 'reactionaries'. We may then turn briefly to Joyce, the other great presence in English literary modernism, who is, however, completely different, remote from the politics of the extreme Right, and who provides a salutary point of contrasting reference.

During his first year in Europe, in 1910–11, Eliot slowly put together both 'The Love Song of J. Alfred Prufrock' and 'Portrait of a Lady'. He was twenty-two, caught uncertainly between the conflicting claims of poetry and philosophy, and hesitating between Europe and America. He copied the two great poems into a notebook and left them there for four years.

Slowly poetry gained the upper hand over philosophy and Europe over America; and in 1915, back in Europe, with his career as a philosopher tailing off during a Fellowship year in Oxford, with poetry taking up more and more of his attention, and with Pound hustling and encouraging, he published the two poems in magazine form. 'Prufrock' appeared in June 1915; 'Portrait of a Lady' in September. In between had come the 'Preludes' and Rhapsody on a Windy Night'. His contributions to Pound's *Catholic Anthology* in November completed the first year of his literary career.[1]

Two years later there was enough for a book, and in 1917 *Prufrock and Other Observations* appeared, a tiny volume containing only twelve poems. Most reviewers thought it slight. Only the inner circle of the modernist literati thought that this was work of sustained genius. Pound called it 'the best thing in poetry since . . .' and left out the date 'for the sake of peace'. He said it was 'complete art', that there was 'nothing better'. He heard Eliot's 'personal rhythm' and liked his 'cold gray-green tones'. 'I should like the reader to note how complete is Mr Eliot's depiction of our contemporary condition', he said; and 'I would praise the work for its fine tone, its humanity, and its realism.'[2]

The 'fine tone' and 'humanity' of the book are in its pathos and comedy, its ear for the sudden terror and panic of things, and its wistful, fragile moments of longing. The title poem is a marvellous example of what became the characteristic Eliot music, attaching phantasmagoric mists and whispers to banal, solid things like drains, stairs, chimneys, and

> one-night cheap hotels
> And sawdust restaurants with oyster-shells.

Its dominant note of tenderness and comedy might come from Chekhov; but there are also sudden horrors which could be Kafka (Prufrock 'pinned and wriggling', his head on a platter, his nerves exposed on a screen). The hero is one of the classic anti-heroes of modern literature, a descendant of Flaubert's unheroic protagonists and a cousin of Joyce's Mr Bloom. His

voice is unfitted for sonorous utterance (for 'how should I presume'),
though he remains subject to occasional quixotic temptations:

> 'I am Lazarus, come from the dead,
> Come back to tell you all, I shall tell you all' —.

His dreams are fitful, if intense, and they come sadly attended by self-mis-
trust ('do I dare to eat a peach?'), and by famous images of an ordinary life's
fretful decline:

> I grow old . . . I grow old
> I shall wear the bottoms of my trousers rolled.

Tone shades into tone to build up, in a brief poem, as much detail of voice,
character, and world as one might get from a drama or novel. Such writing
connects with the small-scale, tragic worlds of Joyce, Chekhov, and Kafka.
Their short stories are perhaps the nearest literary relatives of this moving,
unheroically tragic verse.

'Portrait of a Lady' shares this mastery of the unheroic, with its use of
genteel cliché to provoke now comedy, now poignancy, now both. The
clichés of sensitivity ('so intimate, this Chopin'), of anguish ('you do not
know'), of hope ('across the gulf you reach your hand'), and of resignation
('we must leave it now to fate') coalesce in something which again sends one
back to Flaubert as the ever-present precursor of the modernists. There is a
good deal of Emma Bovary in this lady whose portrait Eliot paints. Eliot's
tones are more subdued than Flaubert's, but they are just as subtly mixed,
with occasional horrors and grotesqueries disrupting the flow of tragi-
comic gentility as tom-toms hammer, bears dance, and parrots cry in
dissonant interruptions of the poem's normally 'attenuated tones'.

After these two great poems come the wonderfully dingy 'Preludes', and
the Kafkaesque 'Rhapsody on a Windy Night', where pain, madness, and
revulsion compete for dominance in a mind which is a mere 'crowd of
twisted things'. The 'Rhapsody' is far from rhapsodic, the 'Preludes' much
less lyrical than Chopin's. Prufrock's 'Love Song' was likewise only fitfully
amorous. Eliot has a genius for pitching his own distinctive music against
more familiar, lyrical expectations.[3]

Then come the tiny urban dramas; 'Morning at the Window', with the
anguish of the 'Rhapsody' in it, but with comedy too ('damp souls . . . /
Sprouting despondently' like underfed pot-plants), and the superbly
economical Bostonian poems, each one a family comedy full of melancholy
shadows. These Boston poems paint, without animus, spite, or contempt, a
world of evening papers, pet dogs, ticking clocks, and maiden aunts, in
which the occasional eccentric cousin brings no lasting disruption to the
discreet order of things.

The brilliant laughter of 'Mr Apollinax' follows, a tiny carnival of a poem featuring a Priapus–Centaur with seaweed in his hair loosed improbably amidst nervous tea and cakes; then the mixed comedy and anguish of 'Hysteria' where another edgy tea suffers embarrassing disruptions; then 'Conversation Galante', witty, self-rebuking, and self-knowing. Finally there is 'La Figlia che Piange', portraying another weeping woman, whose beautiful poem is pitched between frail beauty and tired lyric cliché. The tenderness, ardour, and longing of this closing poem, together with its mistrust of such things, bring the volume to a perfect conclusion. It is the last of the book's sub-tragic miniatures, the last of its tiny, searching dramas of distress.

Fitfully comic, fitfully aspirant, with a constant undercurrent of pain, these poems are full of generosity and dramatic empathy. *Prufrock and Other Observations* is the slimmest of volumes, yet it is packed with scene and circumstance, with the dramatic presence of the human everywhere in it, and with never a diagnostic, dismissive note of impatience or foreclosure. Everywhere there is humour, with its disabused intelligence; but nowhere is there scorn or contempt. No wonder Pound was struck by its 'humanity'. Empathy is balanced by detachment, solidarity by reserve. The delicate balances involved are judged beautifully.

No poet ever started better, but there are, alas, changes in store. 'Humanity', 'empathy', and 'solidarity' will never again be such easy words to use of Eliot's writing. It will seldom be so easy to talk of the multiplicity of lives and stories patiently respected in his verse, or to say that his humour is free from contempt. There is no abrupt switch anywhere in the development of his verse, but in so far as a change of register can be detected, it is after *Prufrock* that it comes.

Many readers of Eliot have responded strongly to the force of his poetic genius but still felt some disappointment at the range of human things to which that genius was given. Some of the reasons for disappointment and bafflement become apparent with this early change of register, and Eliot's politics would seem to be involved. Signalling the change, his next volume opens, in 1920, with two examples of anti-Semitism. The prejudice takes the feline form of an unreadiness to waste capital letters on Jews, as Gerontion grumbles that 'the jew squats on the windowsill', and Eliot agrees, vehemently: 'The jew is underneath the lot' ('Burbank with a Baedeker'). Such habits of mind were widespread in the European culture of the time, as Ritchie Robertson shows in Chapter 12. But the fact that a prejudice is commonplace does not mean that it does no damage, nor that it can easily be overlooked. Anti-Semitism is not nearly so central and ugly a thing in Eliot as it is in Pound, but it is nonetheless there, and it retains its power to surprise us, as an unexpected vulgarity, in the mind that created *Prufrock*.

Less immediately nasty but probably more deep-seated is the aggressive-defensive literariness of the volume. With its original Provençal title, the six-part, crossword-puzzle, Venetian epigraph to 'Burbank with a Baedeker',[4] and the inward-turned referentiality of the poems, the volume seems deliberately less open to access than *Prufrock*. This too is a widespread phenomenon, by no means unique to Eliot. Moderism regularly displays a literary self-consciousness which is not simply to be diagnosed as a sign of some elitist refusal of common humanity. But Modernist literariness and obscurity are always worth reconsidering, and it is not impossible to feel that, by contrast with the 'solidarity' which Pound saw in *Prufrock*, this next volume makes a display of gnomic inaccessibility, with impenetrable obscurities calculated to confound the lubberly. Such uncongeniality too has its disappointing aspects.

This must not be exaggerated. Eliot's music is still there, heard, for example, when Hakagawa bows among the Titians or 'vacant shuttles/ Weave the wind' in 'Gerontion', and heard in the more fanciful of the French pieces ('Le directeur', 'Mélange adultère de tout') whose manner is less astringent than that of the quatrain poems. There are still the evocative whispers of waste, the sudden terrors, the fine verse intelligence. But the register has changed. There is more volition in Eliot's voice, less impersonality. There is more judgemental drive in the verse, more contempt in its humour. His characters are allowed less humanity, and some receive (as nobody did in *Prufrock*) a mauling. Wormwood and vinegar are on the increase. The foul-mouthed Gerontion is privileged as the significant witness of decay.

It does not of course mean that everything is different. But after *Prufrock* it is disturbing to come upon this increased acidity and tightening of grip; and as we read through the poetry which Eliot wrote in the twenties and thirties we may wonder what has happened to some of the best qualities of his first volume. In *The Waste Land* itself, then in the unfinished *Sweeney Agonistes*, the grim sketches of *The Hollow Men*, and the unfinished 'Coriolan' suite, the great verse, which is still manifestly there, comes accompanied by a morose, relentless drive, which gives it a different feel from the poetry of the early years. The hesitations of the earlier tragicomedy, leaving the dramatic representation of life free from judgemental and diagnostic foreclosure, have gone. The verse shows the same drive towards an overarching vision and explication of the demise of Christian Europe's traditional culture as can be found in the critical/philosophical projects of this period. Eliot repeatedly aspired to the writing of books and suites of books which would fix the great vision of moral decline once and for all. The projects were not realised, just as some of the poems were left unfinished. But the will towards them was ever-present, and it is a simpler, more partisan thing than the 'humanity' of *Prufrock*.

There must have been many factors involved in turning Eliot's genius towards this new and different manner. The painful circumstances of his personal life, very sensitively and sympathetically explored in Peter Ackroyd's biography, must account for much of the element of arrest which one can feel in the unfolding of his genius. Beyond purely personal matters the horror of the Great War was clearly the biggest factor, for Eliot as for Pound, in driving the creative mind on to the defensive as it strove with the diagnosis of waste. Such historical pressure may have made the open patience of *Prufrock* seem like an unaffordable generosity, perhaps even like a sentimental avoidance.

As this new volition entered the verse, so his politics formed themselves into a regular system. He began to formulate a political thesis within whose tight stockade he was to keep his sensibility withheld from empathies which had once fed his dramatic imagination. The politics are part of a perceptible shut-down in sensibility. Something closed in him, and a sign of the closing is his gradual, steady development of a rather arcane system of political/moral diagnosis which treated modern culture very widely and very negatively, hankering after the presumed coherences of a Christian past which had prevailed before the slackness of the modern world began eating at the roots of life.

Sifting and summarising the not inconsiderable mass of Eliot's political writings of two decades, we can arrive at a brief summary of its main points. 'Order' and 'orthodoxy' were the key positive terms of this political thesis, the prime desiderata. 'Original sin' was his fundamental presupposition. Eliot believed that, without the bracing recognition of this concept, his contemporaries were floundering in the euphoria of reform and philosophical slackness. 'Romanticism', 'liberalism', 'tolerance', and 'democracy' were the major enemies or, as Eliot liked to call them, 'heresies', evolved by the erring modern mind as it lost its sense of sin and succumbed to vacuousness. Social mobility had made the traditional edifice of order precarious. Now the great secular, individualist, free-thinking heresies of a socially mobile world, thriving in its shifting soil, threatened to bring things to their final ruin.[5]

Looking back now, one is surprised that so great a mind should have been content to box itself into such quaint circumscriptions. Eliot was, of course, by no means alone in the promulgation of a radical conservative system of moral and political values, but there is reason to be more baffled than impressed by his unbending adoption of so simplistic a political philosophy. There is also room to wonder how an analysis of cultural decline made in these arcane terms was, in English literary–critical circles, widely felt to constitute a challenging intellectual vision.

While Eliot the great poet is rigorous and self-demanding, the author of these political ideas is loose and slack. In the political prose, he never put his ideas to proper tests of history and practice. He asked few questions about the cost of the repression of individual opinion which he proposed, or the means that might be needed to secure it. He never wondered how social immobility might feel to those thus immobilised, how an industrial society could function without mobility, what liberalism liberated people from, what abuses democracy secured them from. He never seriously investigated the actual historical performance of such closed elites and theocracies as he was advocating, nor how such elites were created, nor how they might need to defend themselves. He does not seem to have thought seriously about the nature of power, or about how power, in actual history, had been used and abused by its various wielders.

He always underestimated how much of Europe's traditional culture had been created outside the terms of his tight orthodoxy, or in active opposition to it; and he paid little attention to the manifold resistances to creative expression of which his orthodoxy had, in actual history, been guilty. He never thought responsibly about the wealth of achievement which would have to be sacrificed if even one of his swingeing dismissals ('romanticism', say) were to be taken seriously.

He did not remark how original sin, for him the *sine qua non* of intellectual respectability, has been, under other names, very widely assented to as a simple acknowledgement of human imperfection; nor how one could concede imperfectibility without feeling syllogistically constrained to retreat, to fall back on fortified Anglo-Catholicism as the only antidote to it. There was truth, which lived in tradition, and there was heresy, for truth to resist: such a perception of the varieties of creativity and intelligence is pitifully thin and primly formulated. It is as if Eliot were bent at all costs on saving what he took to be the mind of humanity from contamination by mere human minds.

In the political prose he never thought very cogently about order as a socio-economic reality. He did not see how one might concede the imperative value of order without equating it with orthodoxy or homogeneity, and without thinking that the maintenance of order requires the unremitting application of a little bundle of values which exclude most of the ways of being human. As far as such values go Eliot believed in discipline, humility, obedience, and chastity; but we will look in vain in these writings for any proper recognition of (say) love, friendship, courage, kindness, patience, empathy, or generosity as virtues which might be worth consideration. The moral vision is severely attenuated, the accompanying political thought unexamined and amateurish.

Two things about this writing throw its characteristic weaknesses into sharp relief. The first is its provincialism, the second its attitude to Shakespeare.

As regards provincialism, Eliot's concern was ostensibly for the traditions and well-being of Christendom and of Latin Europe. These sound like big provinces; but Eliot contrived to make them seem very small. Most forms even of Christianity were anathema to him, and he made Latin Europe sound like a huddled little place whose few true minds clung defensively together against much that Latin Europe has been, in actual historical practice. He never welcomed difference for its own rich sake, or even conceded the variety of Europe's traditions.

As regards Shakespeare, Eliot shared with Pound a desire to cut him down to size on the map of English and European culture. His attempt to make *Hamlet* sound like an artistic failure sounds a major warning, as does his attribution of Shakespeare's apparent shortcomings to the laxness of his non-Christian and non-medieval philosophy.[6] Eliot was wrong-footed by the tremendous plenum of Shakespeare's human world, the diversity of flesh-and-blood people represented and respected there, just as he was wrong-footed by the profusion of European traditions. The immense variety of human beings in Shakespearean drama unsettled him. Like Pound he preferred Dante, finding there an articulated moral and intellectual coherence, more seamless and austere (so he thought) than Shakespeare's heretically tolerant mess.

It is difficult to reconcile the fixity and unrealism of such political and intellectual ideas with the openness of response which Eliot's great verse embodies. The world of his political ideas never has the viciousness of Pound or Lewis, but it is often hard to draw breath in it. The intellectual stockade of his political mind was shut tight. It may be that in the end even a great poetic genius will begin to starve in such circumstances, and that what the young Pound had called its 'humanity' will be in some peril.

Traces of slow starvation can in fact be found throughout the poetry of the two decades after *Prufrock* and before *Four Quartets*; and then again, after the *Quartets,* when Eliot was no longer the great writer he had been. He seems to have come precariously close to being a great poet who was gradually wasted and silenced by, amongst other things, his retreat into the corral of his political vision. The late flowering of the *Quartets* interrupts an otherwise ominously direct though not steeply inclined line, down the slope of which one can trace the waning of some of his earliest and finest qualities.

After the increased foreclosure of the 1920 *Poems, The Waste Land* recovers the *Prufrock* music in all sorts of ways. It begins with it indeed, with that cruel April, with fear in a handful of dust, with the haunting cityscape; and it sustains it in the great *Anthony and Cleopatra* parody of section II, the passage on the typist in section III, the drowning of Phlebas in section IV, and the dry, rocky landscape of section V. This is wonderful poetry of sterility, wasted desire, and unfulfilment, interwoven with poignant memories of childhood, youth, and romance.

But the wormwood spirit of the 1920 *Poems* is detectable too. There is a relentlessly inclement diagnosis in the poem, an irritable reaching after fact and reason which threatens always to thin characters into exempla and to sour humour into routine detraction. There is a noble, grieving sense of waste, but there is also a whiff of contempt for many of the people who drift by, as desolation follows desolation, down to the chanted withdrawal of the poem's end. There is less magnanimity than in *Prufrock,* and less curiosity about life. The poem is haunted by a conviction that the truly perceptive mind has already 'foresuffered all' (243), so that nothing remains but to record the tired vanities of small, urban lives which are all essentially similar.

In *Prufrock* no two lives were the same. No two people suffered alike, so nobody could presume to have 'foresuffered all'. If it was then disconcerting to see Eliot adopt the calumniating Gerontion as significant witness to corruption, it is disconcerting again to find the imperious Tiresias given so privileged a voice in the diagnosis of waste. The Tiresian air of foreknowledge and fatigue tends to reduce the individual lives it contemplates to dusty fragments in a predictable desert.

The Waste Land cannot be other than a great poem. Its verse texture is of such richness and resource as to make all but the greatest writers seem clumsy by comparison. But there is still an impoverishment of human response compared with the earliest poems. The steady *misérabilisme* of its stance and manner is not always exacting and exploratory. Its imperious wisdom of despair is sometimes routine. As such the great poem leads on to *Sweeney Agonistes* and *The Hollow Men* where even the verse textures begin to thin as response declines.

Apart from the *Four Quartets,* which left the outer, political world largely alone and turned inwards in intense and patient meditation, the erosion was fairly steady. The *Quartets* tower over everything else in the later Eliot. Their resourceful and finally radiant contemplation make them the crown of his career. But they are surrounded by a great deal of emptiness. Without them, it would be difficult to survey his career without becoming aware of a gradual decline, running down to the later years of weary drama where a tiny derivative of the Tiresian voice is the dulling keynote of the verse.

In the end we may be able to set aside many of these doubts and bafflements as of relatively little 'interest in comparison with what Eliot undoubtedly achieved. It is also possible to decide that, even if there is some sense of decline or wasting in his verse development, the causes of it are more personal than political. The poetry as it stands is perhaps so fine as to make these reservations seem of small consequence. But Eliot himself would not have thought that his cultural–political enterprise, embodied in the grey prose about modern heresy, could simply be shuffled off as of no concern to the reader of poetry. Response to him is therefore a complex and difficult matter, requiring much minute discrimination.

The truth about his work and his opinions is not only complex but also in many ways tragic. One part of the truth cannot but concern the gradual loss of what Pound had greeted excitedly as the young Eliot's 'humanity', and the demise of Eliot's genius after the *Quartets*. Cause and effect are impossible to determine with any certainty, but the politics would look to have played a damaging role in this development. During the twenties and thirties, Eliot looked at a world where Fascism and Stalinism were consuming Europe and decided that the principal social and cultural enemies were liberalism, democracy, and tolerance. That should be regarded as a very curious, very flawed, and now very dated judgement, which may well have had a profoundly adverse effect on the growth of his imagination, and which certainly cannot simply be ignored.

As with Eliot, so with Pound, the political opinions are closely bound up with the trials and harassments of his personality. Cause and effect are again hard to determine. In Pound's case the personality looks most gravely injured, and from the injuries come political views of an extremity, violence, and vulgarity unequalled in any other writer of comparable stature. He published his *Cantos* in ten volumes, between 1925 and 1969, and as the huge incremental poem grew through the central period of European Fascism so his hatreds and prejudices grew with it. In the *Cantos* of the 1930s his obsessions know no bounds; later they smoulder on, with fitful but frequent bursts of flame. The progressive damage done to the verse is enormous.

Eliot was apt to be feline in his antipathies ('a spirit of excessive tolerance is to be deprecated';[7] 'it would appear to be for.the best that the great majority of human beings should go on living in the place in which they were born'[8]) and guardedly insinuating about his few concrete commitments ('the developments of fascism in Italy may produce very interesting results in ten or twenty years';[9] 'I believe that the fascist form of unreason is less remote from my own than is that of the communists'[10]). He favoured lofty imprecision when promulgating his general theories ('a thorough reorganization of industry and of agriculture is essential'[11]) and, as if fearing attack for the audacity of such thoughts, he took refuge in affectations of sybilline unconcern ('it does not so much matter at present whether any measures put forward are practical . . .'[12]). Such prose has the air of having been written for utterance in evening dress on some not very demanding occasion.

The sartorial tenor of Pound's political writing is, by contrast, aggressively suggestive of belts and toe-caps. Some of it, in prose and verse, seems to have been written with a knuckle-duster. His language often smells of the gang and the gutter. When he disagreed with someone he was not above simply dismissing his opponent as a Jew, yid, or kike. There was no need actually to be Jewish to come in for this treatment. There were non-Jewish kikes too, like Roosevelt. He even suspected Eliot's Christianity as being a Jewish infection, and indeed Milton's too.

When he turned to Chinese history, where Jews could hardly be blamed for everything, he was quickly able to identify their local surrogates. These were apt to be either religious offenders ('bhuds', 'hochang', 'foes', 'shave-heads', etc.[13]), or else sexually intolerable people such as palace women, eunuchs, effeminate fops, frequenters of night-clubs, and wearers of 'arab cosmetics'.[14] Phobias and prejudices riot in profusion in the *Cantos* of Chinese history. The vulgarity of the poetry's human and political content is in stark, hardly believable contrast with the sophistication of rhythm and melody of which the accomplished verse is still capable.

Race and religion apart, the rest of his language for the expression of angry prejudice is not lovely. One hears much of the barbarians, imbeciles, dullards, suet-heads, and blockheads who irk him. That is when he is feeling quite polite. Otherwise it is a matter of slobs, buggers, bastards, eunuchs, wops, snot, crap, excrement, and stinks. The language of his politics is such as one normally associates with people who put things through letter-boxes. Recipients of Pound's postal attentions go as far back as Pindar ('wind-bag'[15]), Plato ('purple swine'[16]), Aristotle ('dhirty greek'[17]), and Virgil ('second-rater'[18]), for, as he gloomily says in the *Cantos,* history has been little else but 'wrong never ending'.[19]

The sort of spelling he favoured when expressing these ludicrous and horrible opinions was doubtless supposed to indicate that he was so urgently engaged at the cutting edge of cultural effort as to leave no time for the niceties; but in reality his talk of 'kulchur' and 'licherchoor' is just further evidence of aggressive philistinism.

To save him from the hordes of filthy things that he feared, he looked to Mussolini, the modern world's guardian against 'pus-sacks and destroyers',[20] and occasionally to Hitler as well. Mussolini gradually crystallised as the super-hero in what had always been a hero-worshipping mind, occupying the place which, in Pound's ingrained romanticism of the isolate self, had earlier, in better days, been occupied by high-singing troubadours, the high-hearted Malatesta, or lonely indomitables like the speaker of 'The Seafarer'.[21]

All this presents far fewer difficulties than do the political opinions of Eliot, for Pound put these Iagoesque notions uncensored into his verse and the damage they did there was ruinous. From the early thirties onwards the catch-all, scapegoating idea of usury came to dominate the *Cantos*. Usury, almost always hailed in Latin as *Usura* as if that were the name of some arcane monster he was called upon to slay, was regarded by Pound as a master key, capable of unlocking all history and exposing all fraud. It gave him an instant understanding of capitalism, imperialism, and international finance, and enabled him to unmask their primarily Jewish masters. It also enabled him to understand at a glance how all the arts of Europe had been in steady decline since the Middle Ages, and how the decline was directly attributable to excessive rates of interest. It is dreadful quackery, and it makes over more and more of the verse to sterility.

It is appalling to think of the talents and generosities of the young Pound, and then to see what he became once he let himself be consumed by the most vulgar commonplace of racial and sexual bigotry. The decline set in when he was in his thirties, littering the poetry with long phobia-ridden jeremiads and with the bits and scraps of rancid hatred. After the age of forty-five the most valuable thing left for him to do in verse was to confess, in the *Pisan Cantos* and the *Drafts and Fragments*, how far astray he had gone. The confessional poetry is sometimes of wonderful power, but to have been brought to it is a terrible fate, involving a terrible decline. In Pound's case there can be no pretending that his hooligan opinions do not matter. They matter terribly. Confessions apart, they destroyed him, as man and poet, destroying thereby one of the finest verse talents of our century.

Astonishing as it may be to see a mind of such exceptional literary sensitivity and magnanimity overtaken by such crassness, the internal logic of the personality involved in the process is, at any rate with hindsight, not hard to trace. Certain features of Pound's personality laid him open to this fate. Firstly there is his endemic hero-worship, which gives evidence both of weakness and of a kind of arrogance, since the hero-worshipper is not only a man who needs a stronger man to adore but also a talent-spotter who knows, as others do not, how to identify the great masters. Secondly, there is his sexism. He liked to worship goddesses, but ordinary women, lacking the goddess credentials, came in for displays of machismo. Many of the women in *Hugh Selwyn Mauberley* are jeered at for their aesthetic and sexual limitations. Looking back, we can see them as among the first to be subjected to the aggressions which, later, were offered to most of humanity. Thirdly, there is a personal gift which went horribly sour on him. With his brilliant talent as translator, Pound could project himself superbly into other men's beings and styles. But the gift was cruelly flawed, partly because there was always an element of appropriation in the act, but chiefly because there was a kind of substitution in it, as if Pound, hollow himself, were trying to conceal that fact by dressing up as other people. One of the most tragic centres of his personality is the point at which the great translator shades into the sad mimic and the personality that could dissolve itself into the beings of other poets dissolves itself instead in silly mimes and a fondness for exotic nicknames.

Pound's politics can only be read in this diagnostic way. It is scarcely possible to feel that there may be some sustained merit, as vision, in his sweepingly unnuanced denunciations of the ravages of Usura; and quite impossible to imagine that the human and artistic objects of his hatred are not serving him as scapegoats. His phobias flowed unchecked into his political antipathies, coarsening enthusiasms into manias and stiffening hostilities into venomous hatreds.

One thing only remained to him once the rage of his opinions had made away with the middle part of his life. That was, in old age, the capacity to confess. It is dreadfully moving, indeed awesome, to hear him weep out his hatreds, at Pisa and then in the *Drafts and Fragments* with which the *Cantos* come to a dying fall. His surviving qualities both as man and as poet are never better shown than in those confessions:

> That I lost my centre
> > fighting the world.
> The dreams clash
> > and are shattered.
> > (*Drafts and Fragments,* Notes for CXVII *et seq.*)

That is beautiful and terrible. It weighs very heavy in the balance. But account must also be fairly taken of the long deserts of sterility and vehemence which take up hundreds of pages in the *Cantos* as a whole. They too have to count when we try to assess what Pound was, what he achieved, and what became of his talent.

To turn to Joyce after Pound is to rediscover the commonplace decencies; but to turn to him even after Eliot is to move out into wider air. There is, to one's relief, none of Pound's brittle scapegoating, nor of Eliot's elaboration of the ideological defences which he employed to shore himself against his ruins. There is no racism and no Mussolini, either embraced with Pound's hideous enthusiasm or irresponsibly toyed with in Eliot's manner. There is none of Pound's blackguarding commitment to the merest handful of human beings with the rest written off as trash; nor of the 'sad way that Eliot, with the air of one engaged in the higher discriminations, showed his austere intolerance of the diversity of ways of being human. There is no fear, no hate, no contempt, no foulness of mouth, no felinity of manner; and clearly, with the Jewish (or quasi-Jewish) Mr Bloom as the hero of *Ulysses,* no possibility of any truck with anti-Semitic prejudice.

Joyce published no credo, but his writing is implicitly liberal, democratic, and tolerant in exactly the senses which brought out Eliot's distaste and Pound's virulence. The development of his prose, from the early *Dubliners* and *A Portrait of the Artist as a Young Man* to the comic masterpiece of *Ulysses* (1922), and thence to the formidable linguistic experiments of *Finnegans Wake* (1940), reveals his continuous pursuit of an ever more open and pluralistic medium. Hospitable to all the world's words, myths, styles, and stories; voraciously curious and instinctively generous about the varieties of people; faithful to experience and sense-impressions, to the itemisation of objects grand and banal; erudite without display; inhabiting a world of flux, flow, and movement without any impulse to arrest it and bring it to simplified ordonnance: Joyce is the saving humanist of English-language modernism, redeeming the tradition as a whole from the disappointing sense of narrowness which, even at its most brilliant, it is otherwise apt to convey.

Notes to chapter 6

1   For these and other details of the composition and publication of Eliot's early work see Peter Ackroyd, *T. S. Eliot,* London, 1984.
2   Review of *Prufrock and Other Observations, Poetry,* 1917; reprinted in *Literary Essays of Ezra Pound,* London, 1954, pp. 418–22.
3   On this musical theme, unpublished poems include 'Caprices in North Cambridge', 'Opera', and 'Interlude in London'. Later of course there will be 'Five-Finger Exercises' and *Four Quartets.*
4   Consisting of six brief quotations from different sources whose common denominator is some connection with Venice.
5   The terms in quotation marks appear throughout the prose works on political themes. These include the *Criterion* articles of the twenties and thirties and the three substantial essays, *After Strange Gods: A Primer of Modern Hersy* (1933), *The Idea of a Christian Society* (1939), and *Notes Towards the Definition of Culture* (1948). A particularly

useful discussion of these is William Chace, *The Political Identies of Ezra Pound and T. S. Eliot,* Stanford, 1973.

6   '*Hamlet*' (1920); 'Shakespeare and the Stoicism of Seneca' (1927).
7   *ASG,* 20.
8   *NTDC,* 125.
9   'The Literature of Fascism', quoted in Chace, *op. cit.,* p. 144.
10   *Criterion,* July 1929, quoted in Chace, *op. cit.,* p. 146.
11   *Criterion,* April 1931.
12   *ASG,* 18.
13   Cantos LII–LXI, *passim.* Canto LVI contains a phrase which fairly sums up the tenor of this anti-religious bent: 'shit and religion always stinking in concord'.
14   Canto LVI.
15   Letter to Iris Barry, July 1916, in *The Selected Letters of Ezra Pound 1907–41,* ed. D. D. Paige, revised edn, London, 1974, p. 87.
16   *Guide to Kulchur* (1938), p. 327.
17   *Ibid.,* p. 327.
18   *Letters, ed. cit.,* p. 87 (to Iris Barry, July 1916).
19   Canto LVIII.
20   *Letters, ed. cit.,* p. 239 (to John Drummond, 18 February 1932).
21   Sigismundo Malatesta (1417–68) is celebrated in Cantos VIII–XI. The Anglo-Saxon poem 'The Seafarer' was translated in 1911 and published in *Ripostes* the following year. Both, famously, present the kind of isolated, pagan, physically and spiritually courageous hero with whom Pound was always taken.

Left Review, New Writing and the broad alliance against Fascism

It is often assumed now that young intellectuals in the thirties were drawn towards communism and Marxism for emotional reasons, in search of a vision or a faith. But as I recall it the process was rather the opposite, and the half-forgotten poem of my own which (somewhat to my surprise) provides the title of this book confirms this:

> For seeing visions on the evening sky
> I can do tolerably well: but I
> Can read no blue prints and erect no schemes.[1]

Those of us who came from liberal, Labour or religious backgrounds were not short of visions, high ideals of a future without poverty or war. What we lacked and were searching for was a reasoned analysis of the actual terrifying world in which we were living and a rational plan of practical action to change it: 'blueprints' and 'schemes' based on concrete material facts, rather than 'sapphire dreams'.

This was what made two new periodicals particularly attractive – *Left Review* (1934–8) for its firm intellectual commitment and rational hope, and *New Writing* (1935–40) because it grounded this in the lived experience of ordinary people all over the world. These two literary organs of the British Left articulated some of the crucial discussion, and between them introduced much of the seminal writing of these years. To study them provides a context for the most characteristic thirties writing.

The impact of Hitler's coming to power on European intellectuals was immediate and profound. Some writers were fascinated or even attracted by this radical solution for what they saw as a corrupt, decadent civilisation. But far more were repelled, angry or frightened, especially after the ceremonial burning of books (in 1933), the onslaught on 'decadent' avant-garde art, and the victimisation of Jewish and progressive intellectuals, all in what was supposed to be one of the most advanced countries. Mussolini's Fascism had provoked much less widespread antagonism and fear.

E

The self-image of the writer and artist as proudly 'non-political', detached, concerned only with the individual, had been especially strong in Britain. For many it was now severely shaken; and this led briefly to an outburst of radical art politics, unique at least for this country, which has become something of a landmark for later generations, even if often misunderstood or mythologised. The moment still looks a crucial one, and not only to those (like myself) whose youth it was. For many writers it is their work of the thirties that has proved the most enduring, and all the many attempts to rewrite history and edit it out – as Auden later tried to do in successive versions of his thirties poems – have scarcely altered this.

The international context

For Marxists Hitler's victory meant a painful reappraisal. In the period 1927–32 European Communists had thought in terms of a final capitalist collapse and imminent proletarian revolution on the lines of the October Revolution in Russia. As the economic crisis deepened, and appeared insoluble within capitalist society, it was confidently assumed that the workers would *inevitably* become convinced of the necessity for revolution – especially in Germany, where the economic debacle was most extreme and the Communist Party largest. Hence the main enemy tended to be seen by Communist writers as non-revolutionary middle-class 'liberalism' and social democracy (whose leaders had aborted German revolutions after the First World War and recently ordered police to fire on demonstrating workers). Art and writing should be directly revolutionary and produced, as far as possible, by, for and about the working class. Even Barbusse was attacked in *International Literature* (Moscow) for opening the columns of his paper to social democrats and 'enemy' writers: and there was deep hostility to most avant-garde writing as morbid, diversionary and, in any case, of no interest to the workers.

Ilya Ehrenburg, then *Izvestia* correspondent in Western Europe, recalls in his memoirs a tragically typical conversation he had in Berlin in 1931 with one Rudolf, a *Rote Fahne* activist, who confidently forecast that 'healthy instinct' would win back to socialism the millions of working-class voters who 'vote for the Nazis because they hate capitalism'.[2] As we know now, events falsified such over-confident predictions. Divisions on the Left, and the social democratic leaders' obsessive fear of Communist violence, allowed the Nazis to be brought to power legally and crush all opposition, without the anti-Fascist forces being able to mobilise effective resistance. And the conviction that this regime would be only a brief interlude, leading to revolution once the workers had time to see through Nazi promises, proved illusory. Fascist ideology, irrational though it might be, successfully appealed not only to the *petit-bourgeois* and the totally dispossessed, but to many intellectuals and workers. A broad alliance of all groups and individuals who were prepared to oppose Fascism and defend existing liberties, whatever their other differences, seemed to offer the only hope of stemming its advance. And that required an ideological counter-campaign in which writers and intellectuals would have a crucial part to play.

The pervasive movement towards a broad alliance of all writers opposed to Fascism made itself felt first in France, where the leading spirits included Henri Barbusse, André Malraux, Jean-Richard Bloch, Romain Rolland and Louis Aragon. It was briefly symbolised in the International Congress of Writers for the Defence of Culture, rapidly organised by Bloch, Malraux, Ehrenburg and a group of French writers in Paris in June 1935, which brought together about two hundred writers from fifteen different countries. This event was broadly in line with the policy officially adopted a few weeks later by the Seventh World Congress of the Comintern, where Georgi Dimitrov, already famous for his defiance of Goering at the Reichstag fire trial in 1933, called for a united front of the working class and all peace-loving people against Fascism and war.

This People's Front strategy necessarily involved a far broader and more tolerant approach to writers and intellectuals than had been evident before the Communist movement. It is interesting that both Bloch and Ehrenburg at the Soviet Writers' Congress in 1934 had protested against sectarian attacks by the main speakers on liberal, pacifist or avant-garde writers like Joyce and Remarque, and had defended the writer's freedom to experiment and to address a minority audience. But Bloch in his speech at Paris qualified this argument:

> At Moscow, I felt it incumbent upon me to stress the need for safeguarding the margin of freedom which the artist must enjoy, and I was heard with far more sympathy than I expected. Here in Paris, the writer must guard against his inclination to demand unrestricted independence of the claims of society ... What we hope to achieve is a strong and permanent alliance, a civilising understanding between the creator and the masses.[3]

That international Communist support could be given to a meeting organised on this basis indicates the real strength of the forces for a 'broad alliance' strategy at this critical moment. The organisers were indeed able to get Babel and Pasternak included at the last moment in the Soviet writers' delegation to address the Congress.

The importance of this Congress of Writers in Defence of Culture, as of later ones in London (1936) and Madrid (1937), was that it established international solidarity across frontiers and created a climate for informal discussions and practical contacts among writers, editors and publishers, among other things providing *Left Review* and later *New Writing* with international contributors. Above all it represented a challenge to set habits of arrogant sectarianism or liberal apathy.

For Brecht, as for other left-wing writers, the 'broad alliance' strategy involved some drastic rethinking. In his speech at Paris he was still arguing that it was futile for writers to describe and denounce Fascist brutality unless they also explained that the only alternative was a Communist revolution:

> Many writers who learn of the horrors of Fascism and are appalled by them
> . . . have still not discovered the roots of the brutality that appals them . . .
> They stick to existing property relations because they think the cruelties of
> Fascism are not essential to their defence. But to maintain existing property
> relations these cruelties are essential.[4]

It follows, he adds in a note after the congress (*ibid.*, p. 247), that writers who are not prepared to work to end capitalism cannot be reliable fighters against Fascism, and may even succumb to it.

Later, however, he attached more importance to fighting the *effects* of Fascism, and criticised his own past contempt for non-revolutionary movements such as pacifism or the League for Human Rights. His experience since the Nazi take-over in Germany had made him respect the practical work such 'weak' organisations did to save victims and expose injustice:

> So we see that injustice has to be fought not only in the ultimate sense which
> includes its causes, but in the widest way, with all means including the
> weakest. For much more disastrous than the illusion that the results of
> unnecessary suffering can be removed without removing the causes is the
> illusion that the causes can be fought without fighting the results, and
> separately from the results, and ignoring the 'weak' means.[5]

For Brecht, as for many anti-Fascists, the Spanish war further clarified the issue: for here the 'liberal' defence of democracy and culture, which he had criticised as an abstract intellectuals' slogan, became a practical reality: 'Culture, which for too long has been defended only with spiritual weapons but attached with material weapons, is itself not only a spiritual but a material affair, and must be defended with material weapons.'[6]

Thus Marxists like Brecht found common ground with liberals like E. M. Forster, who were also rethinking their positions in response to the threat of Fascism. Forster, president of the newly-founded National Council for Civil Liberties, was chairman of the British delegation to the

1935 Paris Congress. He was to play a crucial role in the anti-Fascist movement among British writers, on many of whom he was a powerful influence (notably on Isherwood, Day Lewis and Lehmann). And he himself was to contribute to *New Writing*.

Forster's speech to the Congress (reported at the time in *Left Review* and reprinted in *Abinger Harvest,* 1936) dealt with 'Liberty in England', which he agrees is strictly race-bound and class-bound. 'It means freedom for the Englishman, but not for the subject races of his empire'. General Smuts, in a magnificent recent speech about freedom, 'never suggested that the blessings he praised so eloquently might be applicable to the coloured people of South Africa'. As to class, 'freedom in England is only enjoyed by people who are fairly well off. For the down-and-out it is not worth a plate of fish and chips.' But in spite of this the British form may still be worth defending as a basis for further advance:

> As for my politics, you will have guessed that I am not a Fascist. Fascism does evil that evil may come. And I am not a Communist, though perhaps I might be one if I was a younger and braver man, for in Communism I see hope. It does many things which I think evil, but I know that it intends good.[7]

In England, where people at least still have to *pretend* to care about freedom, the immediate danger comes from 'the dictator spirit working away behind the façade of Government forms' – passing a Sedition Act here, endorsing a departmental tyranny there, emphasising the national need for secrecy, controlling broadcasting so that 'the opposition is tamed and gulled', and imposing a censorship whereby, in England more than elsewhere, the writer's work is hampered because he cannot write freely about sex. (He instanced the banning of *Boy* and *The Well of Loneliness,* which dealt with homosexuality.)

International Literature (1935, No. 8) was dismissive about Forster's speech. 'Because his programme included chiefly a defence of English liberties it implied more waiting than action.' But Forster's ironic, modest tone was misleading. He did a good deal personally to organise action, through the NCCL and elsewhere, against the Sedition Act and the censorship, in defence of hunger marchers and anti-Fascist demonstrators attacked by the police. He wrote persuasively urging non-Communist writers like J. B. Priestley to join the movement, and angrily to those like Edmund Blunden and Hugh Walpole who he thought were giving countenance to the Nazis. And soon after the outbreak of the war in Spain (22 August 1936) he headed a long list of eminent writers, scientists and artists in signing a public letter supporting the Republican Government.

Origins of the periodicals

Diverse currents of oppositional writing in Britain found their most effective channels in the periodicals *Left Review* (1934–8) and *New Writing* (1935–41), although in the mid-thirties left-wing journalism and publishing in Britain were operating on a shoestring, as the publishing history of both journals demonstrates.[8] The origins and control of the radical politics in the two periodicals were quite distinct, yet in practice they largely reinforced and complemented one another.

Left Review, under mainly Communist and Marxist editorship, was a sixpenny monthly review of all the arts, as well as a popular campaigning magazine. During its four years of life it did much to define the beginnings of a more, open, historically-minded kind of Marxism – what we might now call 'Gramscian'. This was concerned with ideas as an active force in history rather than simply a reflection of economic conditions, and with culture as a central aspect of social change.

The paper started as the organ of the British section of the Writers' International (later the Association of Writers for the Defence of Culture). The founding group included Edgell Rickword and Douglas Garman, both formerly of the 1920's *Calendar of Modern Letters* and noted for their work on English and French modernism; Ralph Fox, Tom Wintringham and T. A. Jackson, the Communist Party's most established writers; Amabel Williams-Ellis and John Strachey (from the disillusioned ex-Labour left), Montagu Slater, Sylvia Townsend Warner, Christina Stead, Hugh MacDiarmid, A. L. Morton, Randall Swingler and A. L. Lloyd. Despite the paper's Marxist editorship it involved a wide range of left-of-centre writers, for example Winifred Holtby, Naomi Mitchison and Storm Jameson (all left–Labour), James Hanley, Arthur Calder-Marshall, Herbert Read, Eric Gill, Auden, Lehmann, Spender and Day Lewis.

Although the Writers' International as an organisation rather faded out of the picture as far as the journal was concerned, the very existence of *Left Review* was a sign that the British Communist Party was beginning to take cultural politics more seriously. And open and heated discussions on what and how to write flourished in the pages of the magazine and at contributors' conferences.

New Writing (1935–41), published bi-annually as a bound volume, aimed to provide an outlet for broadly anti-Fascist writers while declaring itself 'independent of any political party'. It concentrated to start with exclusively on imaginative writing as distinct from criticism or literary theory, assembling on the one hand the young writers who had contributed to Michael Roberts's anthology *New Country* in 1933 (Auden, Spender,

Day Lewis, Edward Upward, among them), and on the other work from international authors, many of them appearing in English for the first time.

Unlike the *Left Review* group, most of whom were connected with some part of the organised left wing and thought in terms of collective action, the *New Country* writers were as yet unattached individuals, in revolt against the insecurity and decay of the Oxbridge and public-school culture they came from, and looking to some kind of revolutionary change, though without any agreed view as to what that meant or how it might come about. *New Writing* was still an independent, individualist enterprise, but more consciously linked with a wider movement. John Lehmann, the young Bloomsbury writer who edited it and found the finance, had spent much time in pre-Hitler Berlin and pre-Dollfuss Austria, and urgently wanted to do something practical against Fascism. In Paris in 1934 he made contact with the Amsterdam–Pleyel movement 'against War and Fascism' (founded in 1932), with its chairman Barbusse, and with the French anti-Fascist writers and German and Italian exiles who formed its literary side. Attracted by its paper, *Vendredi,* where the politics were interspersed with stories and reportage by André Chamson, Paul Nizan, Louis Guilloux, André Malraux, Luc Durtain and others, he determined to create a periodical in which 'literature would come first, with the politics as an undertone'. He became himself practically involved with the anti-war movement; for a time ran an undercover news service for it in Vienna, thus assuaging his 'rentier-guilt, the characteristic malady of my class and generation'; and with the help of Ralph Fox also made contact with Russian and Chinese contributors. All this gave him the contacts and credibility on which the success of *New Writing* so largely depended. It became for a period virtually a paper reflecting the international anti-Fascist movement.

Exposing Fascism

The first function of both periodicals was to keep the meaning and actions of the 'new barbarism' concretely present to their readers – especially as the British Government and the Establishment were increasingly concerned to play it down and to argue that after all the Nazis were doing a lot for Germany.

Thus *Left Review* articles documented the Nazis' purge of the universities, their racial theories, their anti-feminist drive to reduce women to producers and servants of Aryan warriors. At home, not only the posturing of Mosley's blackshirts, but the creeping 'Fabio-fascism' of which Forster had warned in his Paris speech was strongly imaged in cartoons and stories on the censorship, the Sedition Act, the Special Branch, the policing of demonstrations.

In *New Writing* first-hand reportage and stories from the Fascist countries put things in a much sharper perspective than the earlier *New Country* had done. Anna Seghers, in the first number, set the tone with 'The Lord's Prayer', a painful story of the arrest and beating-up of Communist militants in the early days of Hitler. In later issues Lehmann's friend Jura Soyfer ('Georg Anders') contributed a tense incident from the Austrian underground movement; P. Montech the portrait of a German family disintegrating through political hatreds; Ignazio Silone a fantasy about a dispossessed Italian peasant vainly trying to escape his native poverty by emigrating and finally coming full circle in his own village; Brecht a scene from *Fear and Misery of the Third Reich* showing respectable parents in abject terror that their schoolboy son has informed on them. This kind of work was the cement of the whole movement and a powerful influence on the imaginative works produced by British writers.

These contributions were perhaps the more effective for being placed alongside others where the political content appeared indirectly or not at all – stories of French peasant life from André Chamson and Jean Giono, V. S. Pritchett's ironic small-town anecdote 'Sense of Humour', Soviet fantasy and love-poetry from Yuri Olyesha and Tizian Tabidze. Auden's great lyric 'Lay your sleeping head, my love' took on additional meaning in this context. Its effect here was not to vindicate the possibility of real love between men, but to evoke the value of sexual love itself, even in a world menaced by destruction (the issue in which it appeared was the first to include prose and poetry from the Spanish front). And this was important too, balancing the horror with human rather than mystical ecstasy.

The transforming impact of European reality on the English avant-garde is felt above all in Isherwood's stories of pre-Hitler Berlin, several of which appeared in *New Writing*. The author's oft-cited phrase 'I am a camera' is misleading, unless indeed one recognises how selective film and television cameras are. For Isherwood, who regarded these stories as his 'tiny contribution' to the anti-Fascist cause, did not simply record in documentary fashion everything that came before the unwinking lens. His method is based on carefully selected camera angles, cutting and montage, to bring out grotesque ironies and contrasts between rich and poor, demoralised *petit-bourgeois* and deprived slum-dwellers. Underlying the tragi-comic treatment of 'decadence' is an understanding clearly owing much to his many left-wing contacts, among whom Claud Cockburn perhaps impressed him most.[9] In the conclusion, the superior English detachment of the observer–narrator (more or less the author) in face of the exploding disaster is itself ironically mocked. After the Nazi take-over the weather is beautiful. 'I am horrified to find that I am smiling . . . Even now I can't altogether believe that any of this has really happened.' It was a note that was to recur in Auden's 'Musée des Beaux Arts' (*NW*, Spring 1939) which portrays the apathy of bystanders to martyrdoms, as figured in Breughel's *Fall of Icarus*:

> the expensive delicate ship that must have seen
> Something amazing, a boy falling out of the sky,
> Had somewhere to get to and sailed calmly on.

Socialist realism and literary theory

The aesthetic and literary judgements of *Left Review* critics like Rickword, Slater and Lloyd are quite clearly independent, embodying their own understanding of Marxist politics as well as literature and art. Indeed, despite its general support for Soviet policy, and the great prestige of the Soviet example, *Left Review* was far from trying to impose an approved standard of 'socialist realism' or 'proletarian culture' on English writers. Editorially it largely ignored such slogans, taking from Soviet and international discussions mainly what was felt to be useful and relevant to conditions in Britain.[10]

The main *Left Review* writers evidently welcomed what they saw as a turning-away from RAPP hard-line policies. For them the new, broader approach was confirmed by the Seventh Comintern Congress and the Paris Congress of Writers. Later, when the magazine's central attention was on Spain, they were apparently unable or unwilling to see or admit that the situation of Soviet writers had really changed for the worse.[11] By the time of the show trial and execution of Bukharin early in 1938, which was followed by the secret arrests of 'cosmopolitans' and 'formalists' like Meyerhold, Babel, Pilnyak and Koltsov, *Left Review* had ceased publication. In any case, Lehmann and other *New Writing* Utopian Socialists tended to be more idealistic about the Soviet Union than hard-headed *Left Review* Communists like Tom Wintringham who had lived there, and who defended vital Soviet achievements whilst privately regretting errors and excesses, which they attributed partly to backwardness inherited from the Tsarist regime, but mainly to pressures from a hostile capitalist world.

Discussion on *Left Review*'s aims in the early issues showed that underlying questions of literary style there was still deep hostility among some left-wing writers to the whole developing strategy of a broad alliance. Thus the novelist Alec Brown declared that 'the vast jellyfish of the petty middle class' was not worth bothering about, except to organise 'destructive criticism of their morals, their religion and their rachitic ethics'. Brown argued that the aim should be to create a completely new proletarian literature, based on spoken English and understood by every worker on sight: 'Literary English from Caxton to us is an artificial dialect of the ruling class. Written English begins with us.'[12] This approach was strongly rejected by the editors, supported by Hugh MacDiarmid, who called it 'talking down to the people' and 'stereotyping the cultural disabilities forced upon the working class under capitalism'.[13] They argued that the past and its culture had to be reappropriated and reworked by the socialist movement, not buried. As for the 'vast jellyfish', it was, as Slater pointed out, the class to which all professional writers belonged; to treat it with contempt was arrogant and stupid.

The critique of Modernism and the quest for a revolutionary tradition

It is evident from *Left Review* itself that there was no wholesale rejection by British Communist intellectuals of the experiments and achievements of the avant-garde, though this had indeed been a feature of the Russian and international discussions of 1927–32 and was still to the fore at the Soviet Writers' Congress in 1934. A total condemnation (on the lines of Radek's notorious description of Joyce's work as 'a heap of dung crawling with worms, photographed by a cinema apparatus through a microscope') would have been unacceptable to writers many of whom had been deeply influenced by the avant-garde and valued much of its destructive attack on bourgeois certainties.[14]

When *Left Review* criticised the English modernists, it was not simply rejecting Eliot or Pound because they were difficult or 'intellectual'. Who, after all, could be more aggressively 'intellectual' than MacDiarmid, insisting in Scots dialect verse that the workers were entitled to be given the full complexity of Lenin's thought, specialist language and all?[15] The real danger in modernism was seen rather in the trend towards obscurantism and irrationalism.

An acute essay by Edgell Rickword in the first issue of *Left Review* (October 1934, 'Straws for the Wary: Antecedents to Fascism') defines a critical stance towards some major modernist writers and relates them to currents of thought which have elsewhere led intellectuals towards Fascism. After the 1919 war, he argues,

Side by side with the literature expressing maladjustment between the writer and his social environment (Lawrence, Eliot, Joyce, Huxley, etc.) there grew up a clinical literature attempting to diagnose and prescribe for the pathological condition which, in many cases, the writers recognised in themselves. In his creative work, Lawrence tried to depict the 'primitive' sort of life in which he would have been able to function normally, and Eliot poultices his poetic malaise with dreams of a world of catholic, classic tradition which would restore the human dignity the loss of which he has so consistently exploited as the subject-matter of his poems.[16]

The war had led to an 'anti-rationalist revival' which naturally flourished in the soil provided by the slaughter of so many generous and humanitarian illusions. His characterisation of much contemporary avant-garde writing (including early Auden) as 'sinking-ship psychology' leads on into a terrifying factual analysis, illustrated by quotation, of anti-rational Fascist attitudes in Germany and Italy, and the Mosley movement in Britain.

Though some sectarianism still lived on, the magazine's main critics did not indulge in sweeping dismissals of all modernist writing as worthless (they wrote appreciatively, though not uncritically, on D. H. Lawrence and Joyce). And Spender and Day Lewis, though sharply criticised in *Left Review*'s reviews, became regular contributors.

However, Rickword's main argument stood. His essay was published in the same year (1934) as Eliot's *After Strange Gods,* the most right-wing of all his writings, its social project verging on racism and anti-Semitism (it was caustically reviewed by Garman in *Left Review,* No. 1). As in the related case of Pound, it was not simply the 'disdainful obscurantism' that the *Review* attacked, but the underlying social attitudes. Rickword cites Eliot's first religious play, performed in the same year:

'None of you is without an 'ome', the serio-comic workman exhorted us in Eliot's *The Rock,* 'but God 'as no 'ome. Build 'im one.' And this was at Sadler's Wells, within two minutes' walk of some of the most abominable slums.[17]

By 1936, Eliot in *The Criterion* was publicly denouncing all the anti-Fascist movements then gathering strength among writers and intellectuals. For the avant-garde he came to represent the counter-tendency not only to the Marxism of *Left Review,* but to the liberal-democratic anti-Fascism of Forster, Priestley, Aldous Huxley and the *New Writing* authors. Pound, as Michael Long shows in Chapter 6, did worse.

From the outset, *Left Review* was concerned to recover the democratic, popular traditions of English literature and history, taking hold of the idea of 'English freedom' (of which right-wing ideologues then as now made use) and showing it as something fought for and in part achieved only by popular and (in later times) working-class struggle. Thus the very first issue started a series, 'The Revolutionist's Handbook' with a piece on 'Dick Overton, Leveller'; and 'Flint and Steel English' praised the language of Radical and Chartist pamphlets of the early nineteenth century.

The stress on the 'cultural heritage' laid great emphasis on recovering episodes of struggle in which the common people had played an active role: *Left Review* returns frequently to the Peasants' Revolt, the Levellers and Diggers, the radicals of the Industrial Revolution, the Chartists. The great authors to whom attention is paid are those around whom an alternative popular-democratic tradition can be constructed – Langland, Milton, Bunyan, Shakespeare, Swift, Blake, Dickens, Burns, Owen, Morris and Shaw. And there is also discussion of more complex cases like More and Erasmus. To give them back to the people was seen as a real contribution to the anti-Fascist struggle. Alick West, criticising D. Mirsky's recently-published *The Intelligentsia of Great Britain* for its narrow-minded attack on almost all intellectuals, past and present, says:

> In reality we have allies everywhere – if we know how to bring them in. But we cannot do so by asking them to line up with us in an intellectual desert, which is the result of making Darwin into a mere servant of capitalism. On the contrary, we have to show the past in the richest light, for we need the past to fight the present and the past.[18]

This was a statement of some political importance, since Mirsky's book was being recommended in some quarters as the last word in uncompromising Marxist analysis. A great tradition was reasserted, but it was not much like that of Eliot or Leavis; nor did it centre (as Lukács's did) on the realist novelists of the nineteenth century. It provided an inspiration and a sense of historical process, rather than a model of how to write. In this it foreshadowed much modern Marxist cultural writing, notably by Christopher Hill (a collaborator of Rickword in the late thirties) and Edward Thompson.

Working-class writers and intellectuals

The isolation of most literary production from the language and experience of ordinary people (at a time when seventy-five per cent of the population were manual workers) was seen as a crucial problem. Indeed, a main object of *Left Review* was to get workers writing directly about their own lives. One of the strengths of both magazines lay in the effort made to tap these voices, which was more difficult then than it is now, in the absence of tape recorders, with most workers leaving school at fourteen and those employed working very long hours. The magazines could at least offer encouragement, the chance to get into print, and some help with technique. *Left Review* devoted much of its space to competition for reports and stories by workers, and both papers also spent much editorial time on help to new writers.

In the early days there had been some argument as to whether *all* left-wing authors should write about working-class life, or only those who had some first-hand experience. *Left Review* seems to have firmly assumed the latter, and though taken to task by some contributors, Rickword and the leading group continued to be scornful of the idea that middle-class writers *ought* to write either about communism or about anything else which they knew only superficially. Michael Roberts, in his editorial introduction to *New Country* (1933), had looked for 'the evolution of a style which, coming partly from the "shirtsleeves" worker and partly from the "intellectual", will make the revolutionary movement articulate'. No one, of course, could write successfully in such a hybrid non-language. But the very presence of pieces from British working-class writers alongside Isherwood's Berlin stories or Auden's poems did something to reinforce the sense of broad alliance without falsity.

The unity sought and partly achieved was a unity of anti-Fascist sympathy and solidarity, not of literary styles. The urgent need felt by many avant-garde writers to reach a wider audience did, however, lead to experiments with direct colloquial language and accessible forms. Lehmann indeed saw this as one of the fundamental things the foreign contributors to *New Writing* had in common:

> They were interested, first of all, in the *people* . . . rather than in the world of the select few to whom the advantages of life have fallen; they were attempting, consciously or unconsciously, to create a new kind of realism . . . which in the case of most of them involved a concentration on simplicity of style and a rejection of the elaboration and abstruse experimenting which had been characteristic of the main literary trends of the previous period.[19]

As Rickword came to terms with political experience, he found 'a transition from the metaphysical to the satiric' taking place in his own poetry: 'a naturalistic idiom became more appropriate, through necessarily with ironic overtones'. And Auden felt with great regret that 'personally the kind of poetry I should like to write, but can't', would be 'the thoughts of a wise man in the speech of the common people'.[20] The novelist Edward Upward said later that his own change of style was only partly due to the Soviet promotion of socialist realism. 'I was just as much influenced by my own recognition that an allusive, modernist style, such as that of *The Railway Accident* or even *Journey to the Border*, would make my work difficult for an intelligent working-class man or women to read.'[21]

From another angle Louis MacNeice, a *New Writing* contributor, never a Communist and certainly not a romantic 'workerist', argued polemically in *Modern Poetry* (1938) that a break in *style* with the old avant-garde had become essential for younger poets. His book makes a case for 'impure poetry, that is, for poetry conditioned by the poet's life and the world around him'. Eliot's contemplation of a heap of fragments from various cultures has become boring, he says, and so has the surrealists' attempt to be 'fortuitous' by dispensing with syntax and punctuation. 'The poet, like the practical man, must presuppose a scale of values.' On the whole modern poetry 'is becoming more lucid, and that because its subject is less esoteric'. The poets are 'working back from luxury writing and trying once more to become functional'. He instances the recent work of Auden, who has been taking hints from mummers' plays, broadsheets, American cowboy poetry, nonsense verse and jazz songs, and lately has been writing 'light lyrics for music (a healthy occupation) and a series of straightforward, satirical contemporary ballads' (of which 'Victor' and 'Miss Gee' first appeared in *New Writing*).[22]

MacNeice's argument, with its caution against writing from 'beliefs one hasn't quite grown into', sums up a general feeling among anti-Fascist writers. The sceptical, colloquial tone of *Autumn Journal* and the dry clarity of his later lyrics in *New Writing* are responses to the urgency of the times. And here, as for Auden, the example of Brecht's songs was probably as influential as any 'socialist realist' theory. Clarity of style did not of course have to entail over-simplification of meaning. Indeed *Autumn Journal* itself is one of the most keenly observed studies of political and psychological contradiction in the period.[23]

Beyond the spatially-limited format of the periodicals themselves, left-wing writers were turning to popular forms like the thriller (Day Lewis, Graham Greene), or adapting to the new media (Auden working with Grierson's documentary film unit, Isherwood filming with Berthold Viertel). The pages of *Left Review* reflect their work outside the recognised literary culture, in collecting, translating or reviving anti-Fascist and working-class songs, writing plays for left-wing theatres about the miners' strike and collaborating on 'living newspapers', helping to produce historical pageants for the co-operative movement or the miners' union, or writing poetry for mass declamation – something which, as Rickword said later, could have come off only at a time of great emotional intensity, but was highly effective at Aid Spain meetings. For Jack Lindsay this was 'the initial and primary form of our new poetry. For there we get the most direct contact with the new audience.'[24]

Sexual politics

What we might now call sexual politics was an important side of the anti-Fascist movement, but obscured and partly distorted by censorship (*Lady Chatterley's Lover* and *Ulysses* were still banned books). The Nazis clamped down on women's rights, and brutally repressed sexual (as well as political) dissent. In Britain working women were exploited economically, their wages were lower than men's, poverty forced them into abortion (then illegal) and prostitution. These issues are to the fore in stories, articles and books reviewed in *Left Review* which, unlike *New Writing,* had many women contributors. Several of these, such as Naomi Mitchison and Philippa Polson, challenged the complacency of contemporary bourgeois feminism. However, the treatment of sexual morality and the choice of subjects was inhibited both because of the obscenity laws, which made homosexual acts illegal, and probably also because of actual or expected prejudice among readers.

Revolt against the repression of homosexuals worked both for and against involvement in politics. For some writers, indeed, it was the beginning of their rebellion against upper-class values ('At school I lived in a Fascist state', Auden wrote).[25] It helped to make Forster a critic of imperialism as well as a determined opponent of censorship. And a number of the most gifted young writers based their lives in Berlin and Vienna in search of greater sexual freedom, thus coming into contact with left-wing avant-garde culture and experiencing the shock of Hitler's victory as a threatening first-hand reality. Without this, Isherwood's *Goodbye to Berlin* stories in *New Writing,* Auden's 'A Bride in the Thirties', Lehmann's long poem 'The Noise of History' – among the most memorable work of anti-Fascist writers – would never have come into being, nor, probably, would *New Writing* itself.

On the other hand, since the law made discussion and campaigning for the rights of homosexuals almost impossible, the problem was often seen on the Left, and even by homosexuals themselves, as a private rather than a social and political matter, a case for toleration or treatment rather than a cause for protest – unlike the oppression of women. And this intensified the split between the material, objective remedies for the world's evils proposed by Marxists and the inward-looking personal ones offered by the new psychology, between collective action and private 'healing' or change of heart, which underlies so much thirties writing. The sense of the poet as alienated from ordinary people even when most involved in their cause, the awkward attempts to synthesise Marxism and psychoanalysis, derive in part from this situation, leading to the alternative endings of *The Ascent of*

F6 and the curiously inhibited commitment to political action at the end of Auden's *Spain,* which jarred on Communist sensibilities at the time. Edgell Rickword, for instance, diagnoses the 'psychological' approach of Auden and Isherwood (in their verse plays and in *Spain*) as a neurotic evasion of social struggle, and does not relate the problem to their situation in a sexually repressive culture, where there *is* no social struggle on an issue that so deeply concerns them.[26]

Pluralism

Characteristic of this moment of unity was a measure of openness and pluralism, with sharp contradictions of philosophy and artistic method coexisting within a single movement for common aims. Both periodicals were indeed criticised by more dogmatic Marxists at the time for being 'too much a miscellany', lacking in a single clear aesthetic and ideological direction. In that, perhaps, lay part of their orginality and importance. There was more in this pluralism than unprincipled eclecticism or opportunism. The alliance was open and conscious, the differences clearly articulated. Criticism of surrealists or abstract artists did not prevent appreciation of their practical work in the fight against Fascism. And this meant that controversy – on religious art, pacifism, freedom for the writer – could be conducted rationally rather than by abuse or suppression.

Thus in *Left Review* the Catholic sculptor Eric Gill and the scientist Joseph Needham (using the pen-name Henry Holorenshaw) wrote on the progressive potential of Christian religious art, as did the Marxist art historian Francis Klingender. Herbert Read, anarchist and surrealist, reviewed the Communist T. A. Jackson's *Dialectics,* and Jackson no less courteously reviewed Read. Admiration and praise for Soviet achievement in building and planning (notably from Sidney Webb and Sir Ernest Simon) did not exclude criticisms of grandiose current fashions in architecture. Thus Clough Williams-Ellis described the new Palace of the Soviets as:

> rather like a gigantic Gothic wedding-cake with Lenin taking the place of the usual cupid on top. This colossal statue of chromium steel is to be so large – well I forget the statistics, but I know one could play badminton in its boots. It is a magnificent gesture of reverence and affection, but I doubt if it is architecture.[27]

An outstanding example was the extended discussion of surrealism in *Left Review* in 1936–7, initiated by Herbert Read (in a special supplement with illustrations from Miro and Magritte, July 1936). Read described it as 'the only all-embracing aesthetic which opposes the aesthetic conventions of the capitalist epoch' and attacked the Soviet doctrine of socialist realism for its 'flirtation with the ideology of capitalism' and its 'pious respect for the pictorial conventions of the Royal Academy'. On the other side, Anthony Blunt and Alick West argued that although 'the rational investigation of the irrational' by surrealists might have been therapeutic in destroying false standards, in every other way surrealism was irrational, negative, a sidetrack, 'a liberation of words, an empty gesture'. Later (January 1937) A. L. Lloyd, in a long review of Read's book *Surrealism* (which included an article by Breton), discussed seriously the surrealists' claim to be revolutionary artists: 'We all know how sad it is to see politically left artists preoccupied with painting academic pictures of muscle-bound workers with a hammer and sickle in the sky above them.' Nevertheless, the surrealists' form of anti-rationalism, even in Picasso or Max Ernst, 'does not lead fantasy into any action of real social significance' – it is 'a particularly subtle form of fake revolution'.

Openness and pluralism, however, given the general political context, could only be limited and relative. Because of the ban on Labour people co-operating with Communists, specifically Labour views were under-represented. And the toleration accorded to anarchists, pacifists and liberals did not extend to those regarded as Trotskyists, who were treated as political enemies to be exposed rather than argued with.[28]

Spain

The outbreak of the Spanish Civil War in July 1936 presented the broad alliance with its greatest challenge. For here for the first time a democratic government and people, faced with a revolt led by right-wing generals and backed from the start by German and Italian troops and arms, were standing up and resisting the advance of Fascism, and this inspired new hope in anti-Fascists everywhere. The reviews and advertisements in *Left Review* alone show the unprecedented extent to which writers became involved in practical action and the campaign for solidarity, despite the British Government's policy of so-called non-intervention – which in practice amounted to helping Franco to strangle the Republic. The flood of poetry, documentary writing and fiction about the war, much of it by writers who fought for the Republic, should not be seen merely as a romantic emotional response. It was the outcome of some years of political rethinking, explanation and exposure. The 'pull' of Spain (Lehmann's phrase) was not, for most writers, a blind flight into action, but a lucidly

Design by Pablo Picasso (1937) dedicated to the mothers and children of Spain

ROYAL ALBERT HALL

(MANAGER: C. B. COCHRAN)

SPAIN & CULTURE

JUNE 24th

1937

Spain and Culture: (4) design by Pablo Picasso for the programme of the Grand International Meeting of 1937; and (5, *facing*) programme for the Meeting, listing participants and supporters

GRAND INTERNATIONAL MEETING

Under the Auspices of the National Joint Committee for Spanish Relief

IN AID OF THE BASQUE REFUGEE CHILDREN

" Science and Art belong to the whole world and the barriers of nationality vanish before them." GOETHE

1 *At the Organ :* DR. OSBORNE H. PEASGOOD

2 *In the Chair :* Her Grace THE DUCHESS OF ATHOLL, D.B.E., M.P.

3 PICASSO

4 *Professor* PAUL LANGEVIN

5 HEINRICH MANN

6 *Professor* W. G. CONSTABLE

7 ISABEL BROWN *will appeal for funds for the support of the Basque children*

8 *Auction of Pictures*

9 *Basque children singing Folk Songs*
(*by special arrangement with The Gramophone Co., Ltd.*)

10 BROADCAST FROM MOSCOW BY PAUL ROBESON

11 *Professor* J. B. S. HALDANE, F.R.S.

Supported by

Lascelles Abercrombie
Frederick Ashton
W. H. Auden
Sir Arnold Bax
Vanessa Bell
J. D. Bernal, F.R.S.
Professor P. M. S. Blackett, F.R.S.
Henry Brinton
   (*Commandant, Basque Children's Camp*)
Professor W. E. Le Gros Clark, F.R.S.
Sean O'Casey
Dr. Stella Churchill
Havelock Ellis
Jacob Epstein
E. M. Forster
Gwen Ffrangçon-Davies
Duncan Grant
Viscount Hastings
Barbara Hepworth

Professor Julian Huxley
Parry Jones
Edmond Kapp
E. McKnight Kauffer
John Langdon-Davies
Rupert Lee
David Low
C. Day Lewis
Rose Macaulay
Desmond McCarthy
Professor John MacMurray
Henry Moore
Naomi Mitchison
Professor Enrique Moreno
Paul Nash
H. W. Nevinson
Algernon Newton, A.R.A.
Ben Nicholson
Hon. Harold Nicolson, M.P.

Philip Noel-Baker, M.P.
Sir John Boyd Orr
Amédée Ozenfant
D. N. Pritt, K.C., M.P.
Professor J. A. Ryle
John Robertson Scott
Hugh de Selincourt
Evelyn Sharp
Professor Charles Singer
Stephen Spender
Rev. Dr. Stewart
Dame Sybil Thorndike
Professor J. B. Trend
Edward Wadsworth
Sylvia Townsend Warner
H. G. Wells
Rebecca West
Dr. R. Vaughan Williams
Virginia Woolf

and other distinguished guests

accepted chance to save European civilisation and culture.[29]

Many of the writers on both periodicals fought in Spain or served in the medical units.[30] The casualties (as in the Republican forces generally) were terribly high. In successive issues *Left Review* had to report the deaths of Ralph Fox, John Cornford, Charles Donnelly and Christopher Caudwell. Others went on visits to report (Auden, Spender, MacNeice) or as delegates to the International Writers' Congress in Madrid in July 1937 (Rickword, Spender, Sylvia Townsend Warner, Valentine Ackland). Many more were involved in solidarity work at home – medical aid, food-ships, homes for refugee children, campaigns for the Republic's right to buy arms (C. Day Lewis, J. Bronowski, E. M. Forster, Naomi Mitchison, Sean O'Casey among them). Their writing was seen as another contribution – not that they were all to turn into political propagandists, but because, as Edgell Rickword wrote on his return from Madrid: 'The writers must fulfil their function, which is to write books. They have to enrich the human spirit as well as defend the achievements of the past . . . The power of the creative word is incalculable – and proportionately feared by the reactionaries.'[31] In this climate differences of artistic style seemed of minor importance – witness the programme of the great 'Spain and Culture' meeting in the Albert Hall in June 1937, whose programme cover design was one of Picasso's *Guernica* drawings (see Figs. 4 and 5).[32]

The most memorable anti-Fascist writing came at this point. The high quality of documentary reportage was especially important owing to the lack of adequate films, due to capitalist control of the industry and right-wing censorship. A handful of documentary films were made with finance from the Republican government. The most famous, Ivens's *Spanish Earth* (scripted mainly by Hemingway), was licensed in Britain for public showing only on condition that all references to Germany and Italy were removed. Reports of brutality and suffering, as from Cuthbert Worsley driving an ambulance on the road from Malaga, where defenceless refugees were machine-gunned from the air, brought home what 'non-intervention' really entailed. Other pieces laid bare the specific human complexities of the struggle. Thus Ralph Bates and Sylvia Townsend Warner wrote revealingly on the anarchist burning of churches for readers with no experience of mass anti-clericalism. Ilya Ehrenburg talked sympathetically with Italian cons-cript prisoners. Spender recorded conversations with José Bergamín explaining why he, as a Catholic writer, supported the Republic. And the poverty, oppression and resistance of the people – the fundamental meaning of the war – came to life above all through the Spanish writers, as in C. M. Arconada's pre-war story 'Children of Estremadura'.

One of the earliest first-hand accounts of the fighting came from John

Sommerfield, a member of the small English group which had fought in the University City in defence of Madrid in November–December 1936. He had already written an experimental 'collective' novel, *May Day*; and his reportage too, parts of which were printed in both *Left Review* and *New Writing*, is the record of a group action, rather than simply personal autobiography.[33] There were reports from Wintringham commanding on the Jarama front; and from Wogan Philipps in a mixed Spanish–International battalion, driving an ambulance sent from a Midlands town, with two Chinese stretcher-bearers and a Jewish-Canadian mate – an account doubly moving for the internationalist spirit it records.

In the midst of war, the writing was indeed intensely international in feeling as well as in practice, linking the sufferings of the Spanish people with those already endured by their like in Germany and Italy, and clearly awaiting Britain too if the war was lost. The *Song Book of the International Brigades*, published in Barcelona in 1938, was a striking testimony to this, a 136-page booklet, edited by Brecht's friend, the actor–singer Ernst Busch, giving texts and music in fifteen languages.

English poets, too, expressed this solidarity in memorable forms. The extreme experience and the intensity of commitment gave rise to a powerful and varied poetry, in crucial ways different from most First World War English poetry, where the mood of the most sensitive was so often passive and helpless. Indeed, so much impressive verse was produced that it overflowed the space of *Left Review* and *New Writing*, leading Lehmann and Spender to edit an anthology, *Poems for Spain*.[34]

The horror and squalor, the hideous waste of war, are given with a revulsion and anger as painful as anything in Owen or Sassoon. Reports of the bombing of civilians and undefended towns on this scale, press photographs of dead children killed at play, were something new and shattering then, though too easily taken for granted now. Witness Herbert Read's terrible 'Bombing casualties in Spain', Wintringham's 'Barcelona Nerves', Spender's 'Fall of a City'.

Yet as well as the agony and sorrow, the poetry speaks of the determination of the 'army of anti-militarists' to see this struggle through to the end. Not mysterious forces but ruthless class hatreds had unloosed the carnage. This was as clear to the British working-class volunteers and German exiles in the International Brigade,[35] who had fought Fascism on their own streets, as it was to Edgell Rickword in his furious satire 'To the wife of any Non-intervention Statesman':

> From small beginnings mighty ends.
> From calling rebel generals friends,
> From being taught at public schools

> To think the common people fools,
> Spain bleeds, and England wildly gambles
> To bribe the butcher in the shambles.[36]

And with this understanding, much of the poetry embodies also the vision of a people's unity that could yet transform the threatened world – the work of writers like Rafael Alberti, Miguel Hernández, Pablo Neruda, poignant even in translation, or of British poets like Clive Branson, George Barker and John Cornford.

Changes in the political situation and a growing sense of defeat were to break up the moment of unity. The great decisions were of course taken by politicians, not writers. But after the betrayal of Munich, which led directly to the fall of the Spanish Republic, many felt that the last chance had been missed and that war and reaction were now inevitable. As hope began to fade, differences which had always existed within the anti-Fascist movement sharpened: if nothing could now be done, it was no longer worth while subordinating reservations or personal fears to common action – better perhaps (like Auden and Isherwood) to escape altogether. Forster wrote sadly to Day Lewis (30 October 1938):

> I can see no way out of our dilemma. Either we yield to the Nazis and they subdue us. Or we stand up to them, come to resemble them in the process, and are subdued to them that way . . . Since I spoke up for Communism at Paris three years ago, I have disillusionments which don't altogether proceed from my own weakness. Russia, perhaps through no fault of her own, seems to be going in the wrong direction: too much uniformity and too much bloodshed. Perhaps – and under another name – Communism will restart after the next European catastrophe and do better. Indeed, a vision sometimes comes to me that it will start again and again, always more strongly, and in the end be too strong for the catastrophes. But that won't be in our time, nor perhaps in Europe's. If *that* is the way, I think my own job is to fall out and die by the wayside.[37]

Yet despite divisions and disillusion the fight went on, as it had to; and the influence of the thirties movement contributed to the anti-Fascist understanding with which it was fought. Forster himself, characteristically, after war broke out became an effective anti-Nazi broadcaster, at the same time organising successful protests against the BBC's bans on other left-wing artists and writers. In a longer historical perspective, the trend in the 1930s towards a broader, less dogmatic, more open conception of Marxism united with popular democratic forces emerges more clearly, though unevenly, anticipating the concerns of many writers on the left today who face even greater dangers with some measure of hope.[38]

Notes to chapter 7

1 'For R. J. C. (summer 1936)', *New Writing*, Autumn 1937, reprinted in V. Cunningham (ed.), *Spanish Front*, Oxford, 1986, pp. 335–6.

2 I. Ehrenburg, *Men, Years, Life*, Vol. 3., London, 1963, p. 202.

3 J.-R. Bloch, *Left Review*, August 1935, p. 466.

4 B. Brecht, *Gesammelte Werke*, Vol. 18, Frankfurt, 1967, p. 245, tr. M. H.

5 B. Brecht, undated note, 'Man muss das Unrecht auch mit schwachen Mitteln bekämpfen', *Gesammelte Werke*, Vol. 20, Frankfurt, 1967, pp. 229–30, tr. M. H.

6 Speech sent to Second International Conference of Writers in Defence of Culture, Madrid, July 1937, *Gesammelte Werke*, Vol. 18, p. 247, tr. M. H.

7 E. M. Forster, 'Liberty in England', *Abinger Harvest*, London, 1936, pp. 62–8 (p. 63).

8 On *Left Review* the editors as well as the contributors were unpaid and part-time. John Lehmann, editor of *New Writing*, had great difficulty in securing a publisher after the Bodley Head withdrew. The journal was saved on Rickword's initiative by Lawrence and Wishart, the small publisher recently established by the Communist Party, who agreed to publish it temporarily without interfering with editorial policy. From 1938 the Woolfs were persuaded to publish it at their Hogarth Press. Information about the origins and publishing history of the journal is based on John Lehmann, *The Whispering Gallery*, 1955, and *Thrown to the Woolfs*, 1978.

9 Cockburn had been in Berlin as a foreign correspondent, and was for a time married to the original 'Sally Bowles', Jean Ross, who later became an active CP member in England and remained a lifelong friend of Isherwood.

10 Thus the report of the 1934 Soviet Writers' Congress by Amabel Williams-Ellis, the only British delegate (*LR*, November 1934, pp. 17–28), praising the interest shown by thousands of Soviet workers and peasants, does not mention Zhdanov's subsequently notorious speech at all. And a year later, when the Congress proceedings appeared in book form, Montagu Slater's review article ('The Turning Point', *LR*, October 1935, pp. 15–23) praises Bukharin and Gorky, criticises Radek for sectarianism, and again omits Zhdanov, which must represent a deliberate choice.

11 See John Lehmann's *Left Review* article on 'Epic and the future of the Soviet arts', which defends the situation of Soviet writers and artists (against the criticisms of Kurt London) as late as November 1937 (*LR*, November 1937, pp. 580–3).

12 A. Brown, 'Controversy', *Left Review*, December 1934, pp. 76–7.

13 H. MacDiarmid, 'Controversy', *Left Review*, February 1935, pp. 182.

14 The impact of Eliot's *Waste Land* in the twenties, for example, is appreciated in A. L. Morton's essay on Eliot in *The Matter of Britain*, London, 1966.

15 'Second Hymn to Lenin', 1935, *Collected Poems of Hugh MacDiarmid*, London, 1962, pp. 298–303.

16 *Left Review*, 1, October 1934, pp. 19–25.

17 *Left Review*, 1, October 1934, p. 22.

18 A. West, 'Mirsky's one-sided picture', *Left Review*, May 1935, pp. 324–8.

19 J. Lehmann, *New Writing in Europe*, London, 1940, p. 102.

20 *The English Auden*, ed. E. Mendelson, London, 1977, p. 360.

21 Paper by Edward Upward in F. Barker (ed.), *Practices of Literature and Politics*, Essex, 1978.

22 L. MacNeice, *Modern Poetry*, London, 1938, esp. Ch. 1: 'A Change of Attitude'.

23 See L. MacNeice, *Autumn Journal*, London, 1939. See also Margot Heinemann, 'Three Left-wing Poets', in *Culture and Crisis in Britain in the Thirties*, ed. J. Clark *et al.*, London, 1979.

24 J. Lindsay, 'A plea for Mass Declamation', *Left Review*, October 1937, p. 516. And see Lindsay's 'On guard for Spain' in *The Penguin Book of Spanish Civil War Verse*, ed. V. Cunningham, London, 1980, pp. 253–63.

25 In *The Old School*, ed. Graham Greene, 1934. Reprinted in *The English Auden*, p. 325.

26 See Rickword, 'Auden and politics', *New Verse*, November 1937, pp. 00.

27 C. William-Ellis, 'Soviet architecture', *Left Review*, November 1937, p. 592.

28 On Trotsky and attitudes to Trotskyism in this period, see Monty Johnstone, 'Trotsky and the People's Front', in J. Fyrth ed., *Britain, Fascism and the People's Front*, London, 1985.

29 See also *The Signal was Spain*, by J. Fyrth, London, 1986, the first full study of the solidarity movements in Britain.

30 They included Tom Wintringham, Clive Branson, Ralph Bates, George Orwell, Miles Tomalin, John Sommerfield, T. C. Worsley, Wogan Philipps; and among foreign contributors, André Malraux, Gustav Regler, Ludwig Renn.

31 E. Rickword, 'In defence of culture, Madrid, July 1937', *Left Review*, August 1937, p. 383.

32 Note also the famous questionnaire *Writers take sides*, the results of which were published as a pamphlet by *Left Review*, showing that British writers answered overwhelmingly on the side of the Spanish Republic. The questionnaire was sent out over the signatures of Aragon, Auden, José Bergamín, J. R. Bloch, Nancy Cunard, Brian Howard, Heinrich Mann, Ivor Montagu, Pablo Neruda, Ramon Sender, Stephen Spender and Tristan Tzara – a remarkable line-up of the avant-garde and radical politics. (See *Spanish Front*, ed. V. Cunningham, Oxford, 1986, pp. 51–7).

33 See John Sommerfield, *Volunteer in Spain*, London, 1937.

34 For further discussion see my articles in *Culture and Crisis in Britain in the 1930's* (ed. J. Clark *et al.*, London, 1979) and the forthcoming symposium on the war edited by Stephen Hart (forthcoming, 1987).

35 See Hywel Francis, *Miners against Fascism: Wales and the Spanish Civil War*, London, 1984, quoting letters from miner volunteers, pp. 269–93.

36 *Left Review*, March 1938, pp. 834–6.

37 E. M. Forster, *Selected Letters*, ed. M. Lago and P. N. Furbank, London, 1985.

38 Peter Weiss's monumental attempt to reexamine the total experience of the thirties in his long novel *Aesthetik des Widerstands*, Frankfurt, 1975–81, illustrates this point.

The poetry of protest:
Auden, Aragon and Eluard

By focusing on three major poems, which were inspired by moments of great crisis in the thirties (Auden's 'Spain', Aragon's 'Front rouge' and Eluard's 'La Victoire de Guernica'), this chapter hopes to explore a range of rhetorical response by avant-garde writers to political crisis. Aragon uses a flamboyantly modernist style. His chaotic verse overruns divisions between visionary imagery and militant reportage. Auden, on the other hand, tries to provide a structured cultural and historical argument, to impose a clear moral and visual image in traditional verse. Eluard's Surrealist inspiration and Communist sympathies merge in a strangely ambiguous and muted text, where outraged humanism and lyrical irony uneasily mingle.

The poems arose from divergent occasions. Aragon's was a brazen call for revolution, inspired by his conversion in 1930 (at the International Writers' Congress at Kharkov) to orthodox Soviet interpretations of revolution, as opposed to private Surrealist experimentation. Despite its self-consciously avant-garde style, its incitement to mutiny and murder caused Aragon to be threatened with imprisonment. Auden's poem was also inspired by a Marxist interpretation of history, and also urged solidarity. But his poem, sold or declaimed in order to raise funds for medical aid in Spain in 1936, was a more reflective, generalised statement of intent. Eluard's reaction to the Fascist bombing of Guernica in 1937 was a more private reflection, his overt condemnation being disturbed by intuitions of the universality of violence.

W. H. Auden: the road to 'Spain'

In 1927 in their preface to the anthology *Oxford Poetry,* which can be seen in retrospect as the founding statement of the 'Auden group', W. H. Auden and C. Day Lewis defined all genuine poetry as 'the formation of private spheres out of public chaos'.[1] This was not an invitation to retreat into the ivory tower, for in recognising public chaos as the source of the poet's self-expression, they pointed out that 'it is environment which conditions values'. They defined three areas of debate for modern poetry – the psychological, the ethical and the logical. Freud is no doubt behind their identification of a 'psychological conflict between self as subject and self as object'; Marx may be in their minds when they announce: 'a struggle to reconcile the notion of Pure Art [. . .] with those experiences which its conditions of existence as a product of a human mind and culture must involve'; and perhaps Saussure and Jakobson are responsible for their identification of a dichotomy 'between the denotatory and the connotatory sense of words' [RC 25–6].

With hindsight, this debate still seems absolutely crucial. The new insights of psychoanalysis and linguistics made the dialectic between aesthetic form and social forum more complex than ever. This complexity was fully acknowledged in the twenties in the fiction of James Joyce or Virginia Woolf, but it had not really been integrated into the early modernist poetry of T. S. Eliot or that of Pound and his *Imagistes*.

Yet a decade later (a decade which saw Hitler rise to power and start to persecute all free cultural enquiry), Auden and political poetry had become the dominant voices. Louis MacNeice, in an open 'Letter to W. H. Auden' (1937),[2] declared: 'I take it that you are important and, before that, that poetry itself is important. Poets are not legislators [. . .] but they put facts and feelings in italics, which makes people think about them and such thinking may in the end have an outcome in action' [RC 57]. MacNeice continued to plead for 'impure poetry'.[3] But the politics still had to be secondary. Poetry was not propaganda: 'the poet [. . .] is not the loudspeaker of society, but something much more like its still, small voice. At his highest he can be its conscience, its critical faculty' [RC 34].

It is not that the earlier modernists had not reintroduced a poetry of ideas, but Auden is now praised for being partisan, for making the ideas of poetry politically effective: 'Mr Eliot brought back ideas into poetry but he uses the ideas, say, of anthropology more academically and less humanely than you use Marx or Groddeck. This is because you are always taking sides [. . .] You go to extremes, of course, but that is all to the good' [RC 57, 58].

The problem which Auden and Day Lewis had announced in 1927 remained, however, that these ideas could lead back to private psychological hermeneutics, or to linguistic self-indulgence, and that Auden's poetic ambitions as a leading member of an experimental *cultural* vanguard could cut his ideas off from the *political* vanguard. Thus Auden increasingly experimented with a variety of traditional popular styles, and looked beyond the format of the slim volume of verse to lend his voice to such media as documentary film and group theatre. Again MacNeice defines the dangers: 'Your return to a versification in more regular stanzas and rhymes is, I think, a very good thing [. . .] But I hope you will not start writing down to the crowd for, if you write down far enough, you will have to be careful to give them nothing that they don't know already and then your own end will be defeated' [RC 58–9].

Margot Heinemann suggests in Chapter 7 that Auden's expression of his political commitment was probably inhibited by self-consciousness over his homosexuality. What seems even more likely is that (unlike MacNeice, who turns his intellectual and moral scruples over political commitment into the virtuoso verse of his *Autumn Journal*, 1938), Auden never quite got right the balancing of his intellectual insights, political beliefs and social loyalties.

The English Auden allows us to trace Auden's political progress.[4] 'Consider this' (1930) warns financiers, but particularly lecturers and clergymen, that 'the game is up . . . it is later than you think'. The more complex 'Get there if you can' (1930) regrets the demise of a long list of spiritual masters from Blake and Baudelaire to Lawrence and Freud, and paints a vivid picture of class privilege and industrial decay. But finally it seems most eager to attack supermarkets and intellectuals, who might equally well be bombed to smithereens or miraculously changed from within:

> Engine-drivers with their oil-cans, factory girls in overalls
> Blowing sky-high monster stores, destroying intellectuals?
> [. . .]
>
> If we really want to live, we'd better start at once to try;
> If we don't it doesn't matter, but we'd better start to die.

'Roar Gloucestershire' (1931) is as hostile to the middle as to the upper classes:

> As for our upper class:
> Let's be frank a moment, fellows – they won't pass.
> Majors, Vicars, Lawyers, Doctors, Advertisers, Maiden Aunts,
> They're all in a funk but they daren't do a bunk.

This poem, too, focuses on writers and intellectuals as most symptomatic of upper-class funk, irrelevance and extremism, lumping them together with Liberals, Fascists and leftists:

> Where is Lewis? Under the sofa.
> Where is Eliot? Dreaming of nuns.
> Their day is over, they shall decorate the Zoo
> With Professor Jeans and Bishop Barnes at 2d a view,

> Or be ducked in a gletcher, as they ought to be,
> With the Simonites, the Mosleyites and the I.L.P.

Auden seems to suggest that education and intellectual activity should be largely replaced by manual labour:

> The few shall be taught who want to understand,
> Most of the rest shall live upon the land;
> Living in one place with a satisfied face
> All of the women and most of the men
> Shall work with their hands and not think again.

The targets of 'Brothers who when the sirens roar', (August 1932, alternatively entitled 'A Communist to Others'), are those who fail to protest at the unjust privileges of Cambridge, and the economists who:

> [. . .] show the poor by mathematics
> In their defence
> That wealth and poverty are merely
> Mental pictures.

In 'September 1932' the well-meaning liberal, who has 'been to a great public school' and has 'a little money invested', but who would like to talk to the workers, or write 'A book that will cause a furore / About a world that has had its day', has to be warned:

> Remember you'd be no use at all
> Behind the barricade
> You belong to a world that has had its day.

Auden's ironic denunciations of upper-class intellectuals, public schools, Cambridge and Liberals constantly involve self-irony and guilt (perhaps inevitable in a middle-class Oxford graduate teaching in a prep school). His sweeping denunciations of liberal intellectuals as somehow exemplary of the corrupt, decaying society they wish to reform are typical of the writers of the thirties. George Orwell's *The Road to Wigan Pier* (1937) is particularly virulent. But Orwell, after Eton and the British police force in India, had made a clean break with the Establishment. A popular novel like Graham Greene's *It's a Battlefield* (1934) shows utter contempt both for upper-class privilege and for smug left-wing intellectuals (there is a searing portrait of a fastidious, wealthy Communist, Mr Surrogate). But Richard Hoggart has noted Auden's particularly uncertain tone and attitude, the difficulty of ascertaining how much ironic distance lies between Auden and his various poetic personae, and he notes the concentration on guilt in *Look Stranger* of 1936 [*RC* 98–9].

'Out on the lawn I lie in bed' (June 1933), where the moon looks down and sees through those who

> [. . .] do not care to know
> Where Poland draws her Eastern bow,
> What violence is done;
> Nor ask what doubtful act allows
> Our freedom in this English house,
> Our picnics in the sun, [. . .]

is an example of Auden's acute and sensitive insight into this complicity. And yet his nocturnal insight dissolves into a violent but vague vision:

> Soon through the dykes of our content
> The crumpling flood will force a rent
> [. . .]

> After discharges of alarm,
> All unpredicted may it calm
> The pulse of nervous nations;
> Forgive the murderer in his glass
> Tough in his patience to surpass
> The tigress her swift motions.

Another example of uncertain focus is 'Easily my dear' (November 1934), where Hitler and Churchill cancel each other out to form an almost neutral background to unhappy love.

It is difficult to avoid feeling that, during the early thirties, the truest expression of Auden's political vision lies in the Surrealistic scenarios of 'The Orators' (1930), where his comic revolution is to start with 'a preliminary bombardment of obscene telephone messages' and to culminate ('After Victory'), in 'few executions except for newspaper peers' [EA 91, 92]. Typically, it is hard to tell who or what are the real targets of this satirical extravaganza, and whether they mask any serious beliefs or proposals – not a criticism one would make of Rabelais, Swift or Voltaire (nor of Huxley or Orwell). It is an impressively modernist patchwork of styles – formal and free verse, dream, diary, conversation, broadcast, political oration. Somehow, however, this avant-garde collage is *not* kaleidoscopic. It keeps collapsing into private, prep-school jokes. Auden later expressed surprise that it was not seen as an ironic satire of Fascist feelings [EA xv], but this statement itself is probably yet another product of his usual defensive second-degree irony.

But at the end of the thirties Auden produced some fine political verse. 'Spain', particularly, caught the public imagination in 1937, and it still now seems Auden's most dignified, moving and persuasive political poem. Its power is achieved, however, at the expense of any avant-garde stylistic pretensions that Auden may previously have harboured.

Current views of the importance of Auden as a political poet have been distorted by Auden's – and some critics' – decision to discount 'Spain',[5] which Auden revised in 1939 as 'Spain 1937', and later excluded from his *Collected Verse*. Indeed, Auden retained trivial ballads, like 'Victor' and 'Miss Gee', in his *Selected Verse,* whilst excluding the more biting 'James Honeyman' (where an irresponsible scientist, who invents a high explosive, is blasted by bombers using his own invention). But despite Auden's later retractions, 'Spain' was ultimately retrieved for the British public, with Auden's very reluctant consent.[6]

In 'Spain' Auden finds a style which expresses a clear political and philosophical view in terms comprehensible to the general public, without resorting to his irritatingly folksy style of the early thirties. 'Spain' is also a political act – it was sold, and read in public, in aid of the Spanish Republic. The poem also expresses Auden's most precise commitment to some clear political future, as opposed to generalised lyrical laments, or apocalyptic dismissals of the upper classes, and naive condemnations of writers and intellectuals.

Arnold Kettle argues that the poem's power – and Auden's reason for later denouncing it – lies in its mixture of private fears with public events.[7] But this statement seems to apply rather better to his *earlier* political poems. 'Spain' at last strikes a confident note, free of introspection. It is untypically cogent and consistent – lacking the usual self-ironies and petty hatreds. It is no doubt helped by being destined for public sale and performance, rather than for the Oxbridge literati who so appreciated the ironies Auden had aimed at them.

Auden includes in his illustrations of the radiant socialist future images drawn from working-class experience. But he does not simply paint a 'workerist' picture of life after the revolution. He also includes a vision of a newly responsible applied science, and a rediscovery of literature and leisure (the latter had also been important ideals for the French Popular Front Government elected in 1936). At one and the same time he opens up his visions to something both more joyful and more precise than his previous vague floods and explosions:

> To-morrow, perhaps, the future: the research on fatigue
> And the movements of packers; the gradual exploration of all the
>> Octaves of radiation;
>> Tomorrow the enlarging of consciousness by diet and breathing.
>
> To-morrow the rediscovery of romantic love;
> The photographing of ravens; all the fun under
>> Liberty's masterful shadow;

> To-morrow the hour of the pageant-master and the musician.
>
> To-morrow for the young the poets exploding like bombs,
> The walks by the lake, the winter of perfect communion;
>   To-morrow the bicycle races
> Through the suburbs on summer evenings: but to-day the struggle.

Auden implicitly supports a Leninist road to this idyllic future. He alludes approvingly to some of the less subtle points of Bolshevik practice and Marxist theory. His vision of a moment of dramatic choice for Europe also entailed an acceptance of revolutionary violence:

> Today the deliberate increase in the chances of death;
> The conscious acceptance of guilt in the necessary murder

although in 1939 he commuted this into something less wilful:

> Today the inevitable increase in the chances of death;
> The conscious acceptance of guilt in the fact of murder.

In 1939 he also omitted a whole stanza which linked overtones of Red Army choirs, proletarian back yards and a kind of direct Soviet people's democracy:

> The beautiful roar of the chorus under the dome;
> Tomorrow the exchanging of tips on the breeding of terriers,
>   The eager election of chairmen
> By the sudden forest of hands. But to-day the struggle.

Simultaneously, and perhaps not entirely consciously, Auden shows an intellectual's distaste for the political process in his mention of the tedious stages on the way to the milennium: 'the pamphlet and the boring meeting', relieved by occasional 'masculine jokes'.

On the historical plane, however, Auden achieves a magnificent overview, running through the developments of various civilisations and technologies in a series of metaphors which are concise and comprehensible, without sacrificing suggestiveness or complexity:

> Yesterday all the past. The language of size
> Spreading to China along the trade-routes; the diffusion
>   Of the counting-frame and the cromlech;
> Yesterday the shadow-reckoning in the sunny climates.

This imagery may occasionally wield a distinctly erudite allusiveness, as in Auden's desire to move beyond Darwinism (perhaps guilty of fostering the socially regressive doctrines of social Darwinism?):

> Yesterday the classic lecture
> On the origin of mankind. But to-day the struggle

or in his attack on private and public attempts to appeal to God for some
transcendental solution to the Spanish crisis:

> And the nations combine each cry, invoking the life
> That shapes the individual belly and orders
>   The private nocturnal terror:
> 'Did you not found once the city state of the sponge,
>
> 'Raise the vast military empires of the shark
> And the tiger, establish the robin's plucky canton?
>   Intervene, O descend as a dove or
> A furious papa or a mild engineer: but descend.'

(Is he suggesting that there is a misguided historical interpretation of
different state organisations as natural, rather than man-made?). At all
events, the repetitions, modulations and crescendos of 'Spain' make its
main thrust clear, with the rejections of 'Yesterday' and the appeals to
'To-morrow' organising the argument symphonically, however sophisticated its historical connotations.

Where it is not sophisticated is in its political argument – it merely
suggests the cessation of all past civilisation (rather beautifully evoked), in
the name of a socialism seen as inevitable in some unexplained, non-conflic-
tual way. Indeed, the historical overview and the political simplification go
together, since Auden adopts a sweeping Marxist vision of 'History' as an
inevitable and amoral progression towards socialism:

> History to the defeated
> May say Alas but cannot help or pardon.

Morally, however, it is much more subtle, with its dramatisation of the
moment of the Spanish Civil War as a case of conscience, even a metaphysical challenge, for every reader:

> 'What's your proposal? To build the Just City? I will.
> I agree. Or is it the suicide pact, the romantic
>   Death? Very well, I accept, for
> I am your choice, your decision: yes, I am Spain.'

This dramatisation of Spain as destiny, as moment of choice and commitment, is rather loosely connected to the Marxist philosophy involved. But it
is tremendously forceful, and expresses what many people felt at the time,
as well as what has become clear in retrospect.

Yet in 1939 Auden omitted lines which linked the Spanish crusade very
powerfully to disgust with European capitalism, whose collapse had provoked a desperate last stand at Madrid, intended to halt its overthrow:

> And our faces, the institute-face, the chain-store, the ruin
>
> Are projecting their greed as the firing-squad and the bomb.
> Madrid is the heart. Our moments of tenderness blossom
>   As the ambulance and the sandbag;
> Our hours of friendship into a people's army.

This moving conjunction of armed fraternity and embattled love, against a background of destruction, brilliantly expresses the way the 'public chaos' of Spain invaded the 'private spheres' of Auden and many others. He later excluded the whole poem from the canon of his collected verse.[8] But its enduring fascination lies in the ambiguity of the balance between past, present and future: 'to-day the struggle. To-morrow, perhaps, the future.' Auden may not always succeed in reconciling the discourses of history, Marxism, working-class culture and poetic vision, but his poem is a triumphal vision of politics as a vital force affecting our lives.

'Spain' is an occasional poem in the best sense of the term. The occasion is a turning-point in modern history, with enormous moral and political consequences for Britain and the rest of Europe, as well as for Spain. The poem rises to the occasion. It addresses the general public as well as the militant, and it looks forward to a new social harmony beyond the anti-Fascist struggle. It records a pivotal moment in European history, when Fascism suddenly appeared dangerously exportable, and commitment an urgent imperative rather than an intellectual luxury. It also incites to action in order to shape that history.

Auden wrote at least two more major political poems before his retreat to an apolitical life on emigrating to America in 1939. 'Commentary', inspired by a visit to China in 1938, is an impressive extended poem. Its long succession of unrhymed but rhythmically perfect tercets (nearly one hundred stanzas) wields moral and political debate with the assurance of a Dante:

> North of the Alps where dark hair turns to blonde,
> In Germany now loudest, land without a centre
> Where the sad plains are like a sounding rostrum,
>
> And on these tidy and volcanic summits near us now,
> From which the Black Stream hides the Tuscarora Deep,
> The voice is quieter but the more inhuman and triumphant.
>
> By wire and wireless, in a score of bad translations,
> They give their simple message to the world of man:
> *Man can have Unity if Man will give up Freedom.*
>
> *The State is real, the Individual is wicked;*
> *Violence shall synchronise your movements like a tune,*
> *And terror like a frost shall halt the flood of thinking.*

F

[. . .]

Night falls on China; the great arc of travelling shadow
Moves over land and ocean, altering life:
Thibet already silent, the packed Indias cooling,

Inert in the paralysis of caste.

This confident verse already starts to defend a socialist humanism compatible with individual liberty. It sounds likely to be as hostile to state communism as it was intended to be to Fascism.

It was certainly not the poetic muse which failed Auden's political message. 'Spain' and 'Commentary' show that he found a confident poetic rhetoric adequate for his politics. The retreat of 1939 is a political retreat. The fine verse and the sadness of 'September 1, 1939' go deeper than the oft-quoted opening lines:

I am in one of the dives
On Fifty-Second Street
Uncertain and afraid
As the clever hopes expire
Of a low dishonest decade.

The poem expresses Auden's despair at the violence that has engulfed Europe, and still brings an intelligent cultural sensibility, informed by psychoanalysis and Marxism, to bear on both his private anguish and the public collapse of Europe:

Accurate scholarship can
Unearth the whole offence
From Luther until now
That has driven a culture mad,
Find what occured at Linz,
What huge imago made
A psychopathic god:
I and the public know
What all schoolchildren learn,
Those to whom evil is done
Do evil in return.
[. . .]

Into this neutral air
Where blind skyscrapers use
Their full height to proclaim
The strength of Collective Man,
Each language pours its vain
Competitive excuse:
But who can live for long

In an euphoric dream;
Out of the mirror they stare,
Imperialism's face
And the international wrong.

The ruin of Auden's 'euphoric dream' was the more tragic for having been more intensely felt. After naively countenancing revolutionary violence, his rediscovery of the virtues of democracy and peace at the moment they were being destroyed all over Europe was not unique. But it made it impossible for him to continue to write political verse. 'Spain' records that extraordinary moment when a Marxist philosophy of history, underpinning personal disgust with the English intelligentsia and upper classes, seemed to sanction guiltless intervention against a monstrous foe. The elegiac dignity, rich associations and restrained assonance of 'Commentary' and 'September 1, 1939' make us regret all the more Auden's later political silence.

Louis Aragon: 'Front rouge'

The imagery of Aragon's early Surrealist poetry, 'Feu de joie', ('Bonfire', 1920) and 'Une vague de rêves' ('A Wave of Dreams', 1924), is so fragmented and irrational that no connection with politics is to be discovered. His blistering attack in *Traité du style* ('Treatise on Style', 1928) on all literature from Goethe, Ronsard and Rimbaud to Freud, Benda and Gide suggests that no creative writing could be politically relevant. His peripatetic novel, *Le Paysan de Paris* ('Paris Peasant', 1926), explores erotic liberation, but makes only peripherally unfavourable remarks about capitalist institutions and bourgeois morality. The clandestine *Le Con d'Irène* (1929) was genuine pornography. Yet in the thirties Aragon became a decisively committed poet, and later, under the German occupation, a brave and effective resistance worker who wrote inspiring, lyrical underground poetry.

Aragon joined the French Communist Party in 1927 with Breton and Eluard, and he had his share in the iconoclastic orientation of the Surrealist reviews *La Révolution surréaliste* and *Le surréalisme au service de la révolution*. A typical personal political act was his punitive expedition to chastise a journalist who had suggested that Mayakovsky's suicide was provoked by despair at persecution by the Soviet authorities, rather than by his unhappy love for Lili Brik (Aragon was already living with Lili's sister Elsa Triolet at this period). When Aragon left Paris with Georges Sadoul to represent revolutionary left-wing French literature at the 1930 Kharkov International Congress of Writers, it is doubtful whether anyone, apart from the other Surrealists, ascribed much importance to this irrational poet and amateur activist. Like Breton, Aragon had always seemed to separate political support for the Communist Party, expressed in journalism or demonstrations, from an apolitical, artistic cult of inner liberation.

Breton had stated a carefully balanced position in his *Second Manifesto* of 1929, praising the philosophy of dialectical materialism but calling for individual artistic freedom; supporting Communist revolution but as a subordinate part of a wider vision of individual liberation; quoting Trotsky on the inanity of 'proletarian' literature, but considering his dispute with Stalin as a mere debate between rival revolutionary tactitians. This position was untenable for Aragon and Sadoul when they arrived in the Soviet Union. They had to sign a statement denouncing Trotsky and Freud – a flagrant betrayal of Breton's two luminaries – declaring unstinting support for organised Marxist Communism, and denouncing the Surrealists' previous non-Party activities. Back in France Aragon recanted, but not before revealing, through the publication in Paris in November 1931 of his poem 'Front rouge', the extent of his conversion to the official Communist Party version of revolution.[9]

'Front rouge', written for *La Littérature de la révolution mondiale*, published by the International Union of Revolutionary Writers, was an inflammatory poem, calling on comrades to 'gun down the cops' and 'open fire on the dancing bears of social democracy', among other acts of revolutionary violence. (At that time the Social Democratic parties of Europe were still treated as 'Social Fascists' by Moscow.) Aragon was indicted by the public prosecutor in January 1932 for demoralisation of the army and the nation. Breton hastened to produce a petition signed by Braque, Brecht, Le Corbusier, Léger, Lorca, Thomas Mann, Matisse and Picasso, in favour of his disculpation, on the grounds that poetry is not answerable to the law. He did this despite his anger at Aragon committing the Surrealists to inflexible and dogmatic positions behind his back, and despite his lack of enthusiasm for political poetry. In a complementary pamphlet, entitled *Misère de la poésie*, Breton rather lamely argued that poetry is politically irrelevant, since the scope and meaning of a poem are different from the sum of its separate elements, and the poet is not himself responsible for his unconscious associations. Although Aragon was perhaps spared five years in prison through the intervention of his Surrealist friends, he could hardly be enchanted by Breton's argument, which denied his poem all political relevance. He rejected the terms of Breton's defence, left the Surrealist group for good, and went on to become one of the French Communist Party's most faithful intellectuals and cultural supporters.

Breton was surely wrong to deny this poem any political importance. It does constitute a powerful irruption of history and politics into verse. As in Auden's poem, there is an attempt to integrate historical motifs into the political vision. But in Aragon's, rather than a seamless progression from the cromlech, via the sundial, to the end of capitalism, there are very specific allusions to revolutionary heroes – Babeuf, a tragic anarchist victim of the 1789 Revolution's Jacobin centralisation; Jaurès, the French socialist leader assassinated in 1914; Sacco and Vanzetti, the American anarchists executed in 1927 for a murder they probably did not commit. There is in fact a systematic network of political and historical allusions, which creates a considerable depth of analysis through suggestion – reference to Babeuf, for instance, links the Soviet revolution with the pre-Marxist French leftist tradition. In one concise image Aragon refers to a massively left-wing working-class Parisian suburb, St Denis, in whose cathedral the kings of France lie buried, suggesting the power of modern workers to overthrow the most powerful traditions and tyrannies:

> St. Denis
> where the kings are prisoners of the reds.

The poem is politically extremist, rather than simply radical. Aragon calls for a flood of revolutionary workers to 'bend the lamp-posts like wheat-stalks, knock over the news-stands' and 'kill the cops'; to raze the *Elysée* (the Presidential palace) to the ground and 'blow up the Arc de Triomphe'. On his list of people to be shot are the French Socialist leader Léon Blum, and 'saboteurs of the Quinquennial Plan'. Mothers, families, and religion are also to be swept aside by the Communist Youth, although their fate is less specific. His ideal revolutionary monument is, he says, 'easily produced with a church and some dynamite'. He describes White Russian *émigrés* in terms of bodily excreta. The capital letters 'URSS' and 'SSRR' (the French and Russian versions of 'USSR') recur as a kind of refrain.

There are specific references to Marxist theory and Soviet practice:

> Glory to dialectical materialism
> and glory to its incarnation
> the Red
> Army.
> [. . .]
>
> we can't use machine guns as freely as we'd like
> against routine and obstinacy
> but already 80% of this year's bread
> has been produced by the Marxist wheat from the Kolkhozy.[10]

Slogans from Marx like 'workers of the world unite' are repeated verbatim, 'the panther History' is led on a lead by the Third International, and 'the five-year plan will be accomplished in four years'.

Aragon's dogmatic diatribe has its visionary thrust. It is rooted in an ironic vision of an intolerable capitalist present:

> We are at Maxim's in the year one thousand
> Nine hundred and thirty
> They put mats under the bottles
> So their aristocratic bottoms
> avoid meeting life's problems.

This anticipates an imminent revolutionary ferment which will overthrow the old world:

> Paris your crossroads are still quivering with every nostril
> Your cobbles poised to hurtle through the air
> [. . .]
>
> In a crumbling of plaster
> among the withered blooms of antique decorations
> the last doilies and display shelves
> underline the strange life of trinkets
> The worm of the bourgeoisie
> tries in vain to join up its scattered segments
> Here dying in convulsions lies a class.

Aragon looks forward like Auden to the revolutionary future, but in more violent, less leisurely terms. His fantastic future, to be hastened by the Red Army and the Young Communists, is hustled along by the repeated image of the Russian Revolution as an express train hissing 'USSR' as it hurtles inexorably round the world. It is also imaged in fantasies of the wind singing 'USSR', the stars coming 'casually down to earth', and more prosiac utopias of hills flowering with communal crèches, clubs and kitchens (no doubt to replace the redundant mothers and families).

Aragon's poem is fully avant-garde in its style. Not only is there no regular rhyme or metre, but there is an aggressively self-conscious deflation of any claim to rhetorical consistency or artistic status. Aragon even provides clear proof that it is not a Symbolist poem or even a capitalist advertisement – 'for those who claim that this is not a poem / for those who prefer lilies or Palmolive soap' – by inserting into the text a longish prose section reporting Western plots to subvert the USSR.

Aragon's poem can be compared to the stream-of-consciousness writing of Joyce, with its collage of different layers of time and consciousness. But Aragon's associative process, unlike Joyce's, is governed by history and politics rather than the private libido. The text is perhaps more

like the Cubist painters' collages – or the textual collages of Eliot's *Waste
Land* and Apollinaire's 'Lundi rue Christine' – in its juxtaposition of
diverse linguistic material. The registers of language are wildly disparate, as
Aragon satirises upper-class diction, speaks with working-class slang, or
uses slogan, song, propaganda, prose reportage, apostrophe and incantation. Above all there is the alliterative refrain 'USSR', its letters constantly
disrupted, modulated, rearranged – the poem's only punctuation, providing phonetic dynamism and syllablic fragmentation, enacting with its
syncopated rhythms the movement of a train forging ahead:

> The past dies time changes gear
> SSSR SSSR
> the wheels lunge the rails heat SSSR
> The train hurtles towards tomorrow
> SSSR quicker and quicker SSSR.

This also enhances the sense of urgency, with the telegraphic capitals eliding
slower and staider propositions:

> The noise of the hammer and the noise of the sickle
> rise from the ground S it
> the sickle R S
> it the hamm R the air is full of crickets
> rattles and caress S
> USSR.

At times there is the epic chant of a Leninist Virgil or Whitman: 'I sing
the violent domination of the bourgeoisie by the Proletariat.' And from time
to time a lyrical symbol intrudes. In the Soviet fields

> The poppies have become red flags
> and novel monsters munch the wheat-stalks;

whilst at a workers' demonstration in Paris the crowd, forming a 'black
flood',

> [. . .] took shape like a fist closing
> the shops put shutters over their eyes
> so not to see the lightning pass.

Indeed, there is so much word play and switching of register that the text
becomes a self-conscious artefact, constantly listening to its own
production of voices. Its intertextual layering suggests from allusion to
allusion and quotation to quotation a myriad of intersecting viewpoints
and voices, some reported, some parodied, some admired, some reviled. To
a considerable extent this fragmentation of discourse is a gauge of its
pressure and urgency. The poem appears governed by an overall strategy of

rhetorical denunciation and appeal. The whole cacophony of voices, styles and images re-enacts with bravado a 'public chaos'. The lack of formal control, and the visceral violence which spill over into the diction, are part of the performance.

This 1931 poem was not a historical record or a moral meditation. As well as a vivid fantasy of a revolution, it was a violent appeal to revolutionary action, an appeal which was taken seriously by the public prosecutor. Certainly its fragmented, self-conscious, ludic form and its centripetal allusiveness would make it immediately accessible to only an erudite minority of progressive militants. But its violence, its political and imaginative vigour, its satirical verve, its polemical immediacy, even its extraordinary formal transgression of poetic norms, carrying political crisis and debate into the public arena through the medium of a 400-line poem, could help create a *new* audience.

Deteriorating political circumstances accelerated Aragon's change from a style of oneiric association to that of an enactment of more public desires. Aragon's underground protest against the German occupation, and his desire to reach a mass audience, led him later into the more simple and regular lyrical style of his *Le crève-coeur* ('Heartbreak', 1941). But Aragon's avant-garde fireworks in 'Front rouge' form a dazzling, outrageous tribute to one of the great moments in the twentieth century, when it seemed possible to fuse optimistic revolutionary fervour with advanced literary experiment.

Paul Eluard: 'La Victoire de Guernica'

Eluard's early Surrealist poetry, like that of Aragon, had little political relevance. Throughout the twenties and the first half of the thirties his political comments, activities and attitudes, like those of Breton, were expressed through journalism, demonstration and Party membership, rather than in verse. Eluard's major poetic collection *Capitale de la douleur* ('Capital of Suffering', 1926), is essentially motivated by the imagery of dreams, death and desire, and constructed according to the principle of free association, with its unexplained, unconscious Freudian associations linking the irrational images:

> On the ceiling of the dragonfly
> A mad child hanged himself.[11]

Even the flamboyant *L'Immaculée conception* ('The Immaculate Conception', 1930), written in collaboration with André Breton, which reconstructs the various languages of madness, is at best tangentially anarchic, and by definition could not claim to sustain a reasoned political argument. Eluard's membership of the Communist Party from 1927 to 1933 seems not to have affected his verse. It was the Spanish Civil War and the Second World War which brought about a transformation. Eluard himself (like Aragon, Char, Camus and Malraux), was active in the Resistance, printing, among other things, the underground paper *Les Lettres françaises*.

Eluard's 'La Victoire de Guernica'[12] was produced in 1937 in direct response to the bombing of the historic Basque town on 27 April 1937 by German aircraft supporting Franco's rebellion.[13] The poem is a sad record rather than a political programme, although, in its way, it too could constitute an appeal to action. Eluard was by now as much the leading lyric poet in France as Auden was in England. And just as Auden tried to temper the eccentricity of his verse, so Eluard progressively abandoned the extreme avant-gardism of *Capitale de la Douleur* and *L'Immaculée conception*.

Like Auden, Eluard in 'La Victoire de Guernica' uses a clear rhetorical structure, but limited more baldly to a repetitive series of simple phrases. The poem is a series of seemingly flat statements and bare descriptions, portraying an apparently simple moral universe:

> Lovely world of farms
> Of mines and fields
> [...]
>
> They made you pay for the bread
> The sky the earth the water the sleep
> And the misery
> Of your life.

The syntax is minimal, with its lack of analytic argument or subordinate clauses. Its collocation of short, paratactical, verbless clauses perhaps enacts such sentiments as resignation, incomprehension, shock, horror, paralysis. The stanza structure, unlike Auden's regular elegy form, is also skeletal. (The first three stanzas have two, two and three lines respectively, the fourth has only one, and the fifth has four.) There is no system of rhyme or metre, only this ebb and flow, dispersal and regrouping of brief lines into fragile stanzas. Even the imagery lacks complexity. Rather than Auden's cultural kaleidoscope, or Aragon's historical allusions, Eluard relies on a simple string of natural objects, based on the human form and the simplest natural environment, no doubt because his topic is not a historical or political programme, but a simple human outrage. There is no explicit political message, nor even any specific identification of aggressors and victims.

Eluard thus emphasises the fact that the razing to the ground of a complete community in Guernica is a crime against humanity, rather than some specifically Fascist or anti-Republican crime. The poem is in fact a statement of natural ethics, like Picasso's painting on the same theme, whose timeless imagery of horse and bull, light and fist, sword and child aspires to mythical rather than local status.

Eluard's series of brief, asymmetrical, dislocated stanzas recalls Picasso's jagged images, and his controlled litotes recalls Picasso's ghastly monocrome (likened by Spender to that of a newspaper photograph or a cinema newsreel).[14] But behind the superficial avoidance of rhetoric is a strategy of irony and ambiguity, masked by the sheer simplicity of the grammar, vocabulary and argument. At first the few images seem almost banal:

> Death so difficult and so facile
> [. . .]
>
> The women the children have the same treasure
> In their eyes
> All show their blood.

But this langauge of stark paradox may reveal important ambiguities: 'Death so difficult and so facile' is perhaps not 'difficult' and 'facile' for the same people; the blood that informs the flesh with life and beauty appeals to the thirst of the aggressor, who makes it flow in death. These tragically empty eyes were anticipated early in the poem:

> Visages bons à tout
> Voici le vide qui vous fixe
> Votre mort va servir d'exemple.

The dual meaning is direct and profound:

> Faces good for anything
> Here the void transfixes you
> Your death will be an example.

The simpleness of the faces makes them disposable, yet their goodness challenges death. And instead of the vacant dead eyes staring at the void, there is a vacancy (thoughtlessness, meaninglessness, inhumanity – of the public, of Britain and France refusing intervention, of the blank reader?) which stares at, 'fixes', frames and mounts the faces for ever in an unforgettable, unforgiving photographic image.

Moreover, the lesson which the Fascists wanted the destruction of Guernica to teach others, 'Your death will be an example', is simultaneously a lesson to others of the brutality of Fascism. Likewise in an earlier image the faces were apparently in harmony with nature: 'Visages bons au feu bons au froid' – 'Faces good in firelight good in cold weather' – but were treated by the Fascists as 'Faces good for burning good for freezing'.

This allusion to fire is as close as Eluard gets to the reality of the bombing, and his image – 'Real men for whom despair / Feeds the consuming fire of hope' – is a covert reminder that the Fascist milennium is designed for an unrealistically theoretical Man. The blaze of the bombed city will ignite rather than incinerate the will to resist.

Traces of Eluard's Surrealist imagery based on free association remain, but the process is less arcane. The succession of disarmingly simple and lyrical images – roses, cheeks, firesides – is subverted now through syntax (the inversion of 'le vide qui vous fixe'), now through surrealistic juxtaposition (in the miniature stanza IV: 'La mort coeur renversé' ('death upset heart'). The latter is a graphic, childish image of the ace of spades pictured as an inverted ace of hearts, yet in addition to this plain symbol, there is also the literal vision of the vital organ overturned in death, with its real spilling of blood, not to mention the metaphorical upsetting and revulsion of our emotions, as well as of life and love themselves transformed into death. There is a very complex structure of connotations built into the superficially laconic image. Similarly, a homely image is powerfully renewed towards the end of the poem: 'Let us open together the last bud of the future' reminds us that the flower of life has been savagely and prematurely ripped open by the inhuman aggressor, rather than its buds allowed to ripen – and yet the 'last bud' warns that this is also a 'last chance' for mankind.

Overall it is a profoundly ambiguous and allusive poem, which would mean little to the reader unaware of the circumstances of the bombing of Guernica. Line after line could refer to the victims as well as the aggressors. 'Ils saluaient les cadavres' ('They greeted [saluted] corpses') suggests the peasants' paying their fraternal respects to the dead, but also the formal military salute of the soldier or the dive bomber to their victims. 'Ils persévèrent ils exagèrent ils ne sont pas de notre monde' ('They preserve they exaggerate they are not of our world') could be said ironically of the heroic victims ('They persisted, they held out too long, they have left our world'), or disgustedly of the aggressors ('They refuse to stop, they have gone too far, they are no longer human').

The latter reading, with its nonetheless ironic condemnation of the aggressor for placing himself beyond the pale, would square with the more limpid 'Novembre 1936', Eluard's previous poem of protest against the Spanish Fascists:

> Watch the builders of ruins at work
> They are rich patient orderly sombre and stupid
> But they are doing their best to be the only survivors
> They are on the fringe of humanity flinging their filth
> They flatten brainless palaces to the ground.[15]

But in 'La Victoire de Guernica' it is precisely the bizarre verbal overlap of sympathy for the victims and condemnation of the aggressor which releases an ironic, but somewhat unnerving insight: disturbingly, the black disaster has the colour of our own darkest night; it reminds us of the tediously eternal beast within us all:

> Pariahs death the earth and the hideousness
> of our enemies have the monotonous
> colour of our night.

The important question is whether this ironic, ambiguous verse does 'put facts and feelings in italics', as Auden's verse did, or whether it leaves them uneasily bracketed out. At least the poem finishes with a powerful cry of protest: 'Nous en aurons raison!' – this line, which means idiomatically 'we shall overcome', retains some of its etymological aura, suggesting that reason will triumph. Yet with post-Freudian insight Eluard realises that he and his audience are not merely fighting some unspeakable alien – both aggression and suffering have the colour of 'our night' – we are fighting the dark underside of the collective European unconscious, in which we all participate.

The dominant strategy being ambiguity and irony, this poem presupposes a sophisticated literary reader, alert to the avant-garde tendency to juxtapose images based on unexplained associations, alert to the political situation and able to interpret the whole in an anti-Fascist optic. It is ultimately perhaps an over-private poem, projecting an honourable numbness, suggesting bravery and defiance as well as sorrow and disgust, but not suggesting any specific reading of history or politics except in its very general condemnation of excess. It is a journey to a private world from the domain of public chaos, but is seems to have lost almost all specific denotation.

Later, in 'Liberté' (1942), Eluard returned to an insistent, regular rhythmical and stanzaic structure.[16] The need to convey a memorable message and inspire an urge to resist was more desperate. The diction remained entirely general, with no reference to identifiable time, place, or people. But then the theme of 'Liberté', freedom, needed no specific reference in a country occupied by the Nazis. This beautiful poem was recited secretly all over France; it was an inspirational act, a spiritual propaganda victory.

The three poems show a wide range of response among committed avant-garde writers to moments of great crisis – joining a revolutionary movement, supporting intervention in Spain, reacting to the terrifying tragedy of Guernica. In each case the style adopted represents a modification of the author's modernist rhetoric. The stylistic options – a violent dramatisation of discourse in Aragon, a tightly-structured and limpid return to regular prosody in Auden, a discreet post-Surrealist allusiveness in Eluard – all have their distinctive power to interpret and to move. They show that divergent stylistic responses may have different but equally valid strategic merit in different situations. Correlatively, they suggest that the same style may be adapted for different political ends: Aragon's expressionist enactment uses the intertextual echoes and linguistic fragmentation which, in other contexts, could reflect Eliot's passive refraction of the experience of a decaying culture, or perform Pound's disgusted rage. Auden's traditional stylisation was a solution increasingly adopted by British left-wing poets in the thirties, who wanted their work to reach a large number of people in the *political* vanguard, yet it was this formal harmony which the avant-garde of the twenties had violently rejected for its conservative connotations. Eluard's retreat from Freudian association again seems a stylistic regression, although he maintains a generally modernist rejection of regular formal pattern.

At all events, these poems warn us to be prepared to look beyond the contours of the critical labels of the period – 'Socialist Realism', 'Surrealism', and 'Expressionism'. They also suggest how politically ambiguous such modernist categories as 'fragmentation', 'self-consciousness' and 'enactment' may be. But above all, they show us that the relation between the two poles of the avant-garde – its experimental writing and its search for popular communication – is a complex, shifting process, which has to be perpetually redefined by each new writer in each new situation.

Notes to chapter 8

1 In R. Carter (ed.), *Thirties Poets: The Auden Group*, London, 1984 (abbreviated as *RC*, followed by page number).
2 *New Verse*, 'Auden Double Number', Nos. 26–7, November 1937, pp. 11–13.
3 'Statement', *New Verse*, Autumn 1938, p. 7.
4 E. Mendelson (ed.), *The English Auden*, London, 1978, 1986 (abbreviated as *EA*).
5 A. Bold (ed.), *Auden, The Far Interior*, London, 1985, is a good example. It contains two chapters on Auden's politics (W. Perrie on 'Auden's Political Vision' and J. Montefiore on 'Goebbels and Goblins. Politics and the Fairytale in Auden's Political Poems'), neither of which mentions 'Spain'.
6 The original (1937) version of 'Spain' is available in the following anthologies: V.

Cunningham (ed.), *Spanish Front*, London, 1986, pp. 1–4; V. Cunningham (ed.), *The Penguin Book of Spanish Civil War Verse*, London, 1980, pp. 97–100; R. Skelton (ed.), *Poetry of the Thirties*, London, 1985, pp. 133–6.

7   A. Kettle, 'W. H. Auden: Poetry and Politics in the Thirties', in *Culture and Crisis in Britain in the Thirties*, ed. J. Clark *et al.*, London, 1979, pp. 83–101.

8   The 1939 version of 'Spain 1937' is published in Mendelson, *ed. cit.*, pp. 210–12. Mendelson reports that Auden revised the poem a month *before* Orwell's hostile criticism (of the irresponsible intellectual advocating murder) appeared (*EA* 425). See G. Orwell, 'Inside the Whale' (1940), in *Selected Essays*, London, 1957, pp. 36–7.

9   The complete text of 'Front rouge' is reproduced in M. Nadeau, *Documents surréalistes*, Paris, 1948.

10 A *Kolkhoz* (plural *Kolkhozy*) is a collective farm. Stalin's massive collectivisation of agriculture had recently started.

11 'Le plus jeune', in V. J. Daniel (ed.), P. Eluard, *Capitale de la Douleur*, Oxford, 1985, p. 68; or P. Eluard, *Oeuvres completes*, Vol. I, Paris, 1968, p. 188 (my translation).

12 First published in *Cahiers d'Art*, 1937, 1–3, p. 36, and (with an English translation by Roland Penrose and George Reavey and a photograph of Picasso's *Guernica*) in *London Bulletin*, 1938, October, No. 6, pp. 7–8, reprinted in *Cours naturel*, Paris, 1938. Now in *Oeuvres complètes*, Vol. I, pp. 812–14 (my translation).

13 See H. Thomas, *The Spanish Civil War*, London, 1986, pp. 624–9.

14 S. Spender, 'Guernica', in *The Penguin Book of Spanish Civil War Verse*, pp. 418–20.

15 'Novembre 1936', first published in the Communist daily *L'Humanité*, on 17 December 1936. Reprinted in *Cours naturel*, Paris, 1938. Now in *Oeuvres complètes*, Vol. I, pp. 801–2.

16 'Liberté' was distributed and performed all over occupied France, and copies were even dropped by the RAF. It was reprinted in *Poésie et vérité*, 1942. Now in *Oeuvres complètes*, Vol. I, pp. 1105–7.

André Malraux
and the radical dilemma

André Malraux was a man of deep contradictions. As a very young man, his appetite for artistic innovation had led him to form an acquaintance with the leading light of Cubism, Daniel-Henry Kahnweiler. When, at the age of nineteen, Malraux's first book appeared, it contained illustrations by Juan Gris, Georges Braque and Fernand Léger. Pursuing political objectives with no less enthusiasm, Malraux declared himself a convert to the Communist world-view[1] and put his convictions into practice by commanding a squadron of fighter planes on the side of the Republicans during the Spanish Civil War, as well as playing a prominent role in the resistance of the Free French to Fascism, during the Second World War. Yet in spite of his pro-Communist assertions, Malraux's artistic sensibilities could never be fully subsumed within a political dogma.[2] The boundaries of his creative vision (as this chapter will show) encompassed both an admiration for Communist ideals – especially those of Trotsky – and a susceptibility to the temptations of the radical Right; exemplified by Barrès, Maurras, Drieu and Céline.

Revolution

In the initial flowering of his left-wing sympathies, Malraux developed a high regard for Leon Trotsky, one of the architects of the Bolshevik Revolution, who was forced into exile by Stalin. In a sense, Trotsky inhabited Malraux psychologically. Trotsky was one of the great figures from Malraux's pantheon of myth-inspiring characters like Saint-Just and Nietzsche. The mystique surrounding Trotsky seduced Malraux, and in an account of a meeting they had in 1934, Malraux referred to Trotsky as being one of a breed of 'superior men', deferring to Trotsky's intellectual stature by describing him as a man who considered 'thought as something to be mastered and not recited'.[3]

The transformation of the human condition through revolution is a key feature of Malraux's novels and the matrix of Trotsky's thought. Both appeared to follow the established Marxist belief that revolution was indispensable if the workers were to be transformed into a proletarian class imbued with a Socialist consciousness, and if that class was to succeed in 'ridding itself of all the muck of ages and become fitted to found society anew.'[4] However, criticising Malraux's first novel, Trotsky identified a certain ambiguity in his attitude to revolution. *Les Conquérants*, published in 1928, unfolds against a background of events provided by the revolutionary strikes in Canton in 1925. Though deeply involved in the organisation of the workers against the forces of the Right and foreign capital, Garine, the hero, maintains a curious sense of remove from the people for whom he fights, as if embodying Malraux's observation that 'at the heart of European man, dominating the great developments in his life, lies an essential absurdity.[5] In his criticism of *The Conquerors*, Trotsky perceived in Garine a contempt for revolutionary theory which undermined his action: 'the revolutionary who "despises" revolutionary doctrine is no better than the healer who despises medical doctrine'.[6] But Trotsky's criticism of the character was a facet of his general criticism of its creator: 'what is lacking in the novel is a natural affinity between the writer . . . and his heroine, the Revolution'.[7]

Trotsky's criticism of the novel focused on what he perceived to be Malraux's inability to illuminate a revolutionary way forward for the uprising in Canton. In *Stalin*,[8] Trotsky's own blueprint for revolution, he identified three approaches to the accomplishment of the Revolution. In the first, the Menshevik approach, the establishment of a liberal bourgeois democracy was regarded as the crucial prerequisite for the effective pursuit of socialism by the proletariat, because it would allow the proletariat to develop its full potential, to the point where it could successfully replace the bourgeois Revolution with its own. In the second approach, propounded by the Leninists, it was believed that the bourgeoisie could not accomplish its own revolution, and that this task had to be completed by the proletariat and the peasantry. The revolutionary masses, however, could not accomplish their historical mission immediately, as before so doing they still needed the bourgeoisie to propel Russia from a stage of virtually feudal backwardness into one of American-style capitalism. Finally, in his own approach to the problem of accomplishing the Revolution, Trotsky rejected the need for any class collaboration or intervening phase after the overthrow of the old order by the masses.

The nub of the distinction between Trotsky's view of the Revolution and the views of the Mensheviks and the Leninists has its roots in a contradiction underlined by Marx. Though exploitative, capitalism also has civilising effects in laying the ground for socialism. A high level of industrial capitalism and the emergence of a modern, strong proletariat would, with the advent of revolution, enable society to liberate men and women for an important part of their working time from the need to produce directly their own material existence, thus eliminating the basic social division of labour between direct producers and administrators. Consequently, the precondition for socialism would be achieved with the emergence of a social class which would be prepared to substitute general-ised co-operation and solidarity for the forms of behaviour associated with private property and competition.

There was, however, no reason for the masses in an economically underdeveloped country to hand power back to the bourgeoisie or those representing it, once they had captured power. Though the individual nations of the world had reached an uneven level of development, Trotsky believed that they were combined in their revolutionary potential. To the organic unity of the capitalist world market, Trotsky counterposed the organic unity of 'national' class struggles. The transnational development of productive forces and the operation of capital was accompanied by the internationalisation of the class struggle. To abort the Revolution in one country, because of the shortcomings of the 'national' struggle, would be to abort the general struggle for socialism.

In his reading of *The Conquerors*, Trotsky saw the emergence of a distinguishably Menshevik line. The leader of the moderate wing of the Kuomingtang, Tcheng-Dai, and the Nationalist Government, are charac-terised by the impotence which was the hallmark of Kerensky's assumption of power in revolutionary Russia. They are reluctant to promulgate the decree called for by Garine, that would prohibit entry to the harbour of Canton to any ship having called at Hong Kong, thereby, according to Garine, paralysing Hong Kong and dealing a severe blow to the British Empire. Only, in the Canton depicted by Malraux, Trotsky found that those who are most Menshevik in their attitude are the 'pseudo-Bolshevik' delegates of the Communist International. The victims of this compromise are, inevitably, the masses. Instead of preparing the workers for the con-quest of power, the bureaucracy of the Communist International has 'incul-cated the masses with the notion of the necessity of submitting themselves to the bourgeoisie'.[9] Malraux had failed to produce an authentic novel of revolution, Trotsky believed, because he viewed the events he described from on high, as an indifferent observer – an uncommitted writer. In criticising *The Conquerors*, Trotsky sought to criticise an imagination which floated on a revolutionary *élan* that could dip in any direction; for this kind of revolutionary fervour was not sustained by a properly defined theory of revolution. Examining his motives for fighting, Garine admits: "I don't even like the poor, the people, in fact those for whom I fight.'[10]

Trotsky's criticism of *The Conquerors* was based on a naive premiss. Whereas Malraux conveyed in fictionalised terms the situation as he knew it to be, Trotsky wanted a novel that conformed to his normative prescriptions for the proper resolution of the revolutionary situation depicted. As Malraux pointed out in his reply to Trotsky,[11] the strikes in Canton were undermined to a significant extent by the fact that many skilled workers, notably the Union of Mechanics, were affiliated to the right wing of the Kuomintang, i.e. the Nationalist Party. This was the party which was to sever its anti-imperialist alliance with the Communists in 1927 and drive them underground.

In contrast to his attack on *The Conquerors*, Trotsky's reaction to Malraux's most famous novel, *La Condition Humaine (Man's Estate)*, was one of fulsome praise. He hailed its author as a great and original talent, declaring the novel free from philosophical didacticism and from beginning to end a work of art.[12] It would not have escaped Trotsky that implicit in the novel is a critique, similar to his own, regarding the reasons for the failure of the Chinese Revolution.

Man's Estate was first serialised, then published as a book in 1933, and the framework for the novel is provided by the events which took place in Shanghai during the spring of 1927. The city was on the point of falling into the hands of the southern Nationalist army of the Kuomintang, and with the fall of Shanghai the whole of China would be under their control. At that time an alliance still existed between the Kuomintang and the Communists. But the Kuomintang, led by Chang Kai Shek, decided to break with the Communists, and the heart of the novel focuses on the point when, in April 1927, they attempted to suppress the Communists by force. *Man's Estate* depicts the unravelling of three strands of action: the uprising in Shanghai, timed to coincide with the arrival of the army from the south, in which three chief protagonists, Kyo, Tchen and Katow are involved; the anti-Communist activities of Western capitalists and some members of the Kuomintang; and the elimination of the Communist Party, during the course of which Katow and Kyo meet their deaths.

The conflicts portrayed in Malraux's novel need to be seen in historical context. Though the Communists had gained power in the Soviet Union, Stalin had in 1927 not yet fully consolidated his position. In November of that year he succeeded in forcing Trotsky into exile, but his position was still threatened by a difficult domestic situation. Soviet industry had to be reconstructed, but without the help of foreign capital, and a section of the rural population, having seized ownership of the land in 1917–18, was becoming a non-Socialist force interested principally in obtaining higher prices for the food it produced. For the Soviet Union to make a major material commitment to the Chinese Revolution, in pursuit of Trotsky's belief that for Socialist revolution to be successful it had to occur on a world scale, could, from Stalin's point of view, only exacerbate the contentious domestic problems he faced. Stalin therefore inclined to Bukharin's belief that 'Socialism in one country' was possible, as long as it proceeded 'at the speed of the peasant nag'. The repercussions of this policy on the attitude of the Communist International in China during 1927 was to result, in Trotsky's opinion, in a certain ambiguity. Moscow's representatives in China found themselves walking a tightrope. While on the one hand professing a desire to advance the Communist cause, they were, on the other hand, reluctant to allow their Chinese fellow-Communists to proceed too far too fast, for fear of jeopardising their tactical alliance with the powerful Kuomintang. Trotsky, however, regarded this alliance less a compromise than as a betrayal of the class interests of the peasants and the proletariat. For throughout the duration of that alliance, he argued, the Chinese Communist Party had not been in alliance with the revolutionary petty-bourgeois section of the Kuomintang, but in subordination to the whole Kuomintang.[13]

In *Man's Estate*, Kyo advances an identical analysis when he goes to see Vologuine, Moscow's Stalinist representative in Hankow. Kyo proposes that the Chinese Communist Party should build on the *de facto* Sovieti-sation of the workers in Shanghai to challenge Chang Kai Shek and the domination of the Kuomintang, in order to prevent the Revolution from being stifled. Vologuine's instruction to Kyo, however, is that the workers in Shanghai must be disarmed in order to appease their Nationalist allies. Vologuine is an inflexible conduit for the dictates of the hierarchy, and his sommnabulist features mirror his function. He justifies Moscow's decision by arguing that the alliance with the Kuomintang has served as a vehicle for Communist ambitions for over two years. To which Kyo retorts with the conclusion also articulated by Trotsky: 'as long as you accepted their aims'.[14] A similar confrontation occurs in *The Conquerors*, between the maverick revolutionary dynamism of Garine and the bureaucratic obses-sions of the professional Bolshevik organiser, represented by Borodine. There also, Garine warns of the potentially counter-revolutionary conse-quences of an apparently useful alliance with the Kuomintang.

The irrational *élan*

Trotsky's dismissive reaction to the political content of *The Conquerors*, and his warm approval of *Man's Estate*, are indicative of his failure to realise that Malraux's fiction was animated by neither a Stalinist nor a Trotskyist conception of revolution, but by something less susceptible to reason. Malraux was not only an admirer of Trotsky. He was also fascinated by the intellectual vitality and action of some of the most radical reactionary members of France's literary establishment. In his preface to *Mlle Monk* (*Miss Monk*) by Charles Maurras, the leading ideologue of the right-wing organisation *Action Française*, Malraux declared him to be 'one of the most powerful intellectual figures of today'.[15] And at the base of Maurice Barrès's Nationalist politics, Malraux discerned a commendable generosity of emotion and vision.[16] As for Drieu La Rochelle, no charge of treason brought against him at the end of the Second World War, due to his Fascist sympathies, could outweigh Malraux's understanding of his motives.[17] What the young Malraux shared with Drieu and Barrès was a preference for action over intellectualism. All three had a vision of the state of being to which man should progress, and however dubious the path to it, what mattered was that it be trod with *élan*, by a protagonist who defined himself through his action.

In his trilogy of novels entitled *Le Culte du Moi* (*The Worship of Self*), Barrès depicts a hero, Philippe, engaged in a search for an authentic sense of identity and a satisfying place in the world. In a transparently weighted argument between Barrès's hero and a philosopher, Barrès underlines his belief that Reason is a hindrance to the fulfilment of the self, and personifies it ironically as 'the glorious old man whose authority is accepted everywhere'.[18]

In the *Histoire Secrète*, written towards the end of his life, Drieu revealed the logically intractable, dark disposition which coloured his view of man's estate. The individual was born on a path leading to personal decline and the nation was destined to decadence. Surveying France, Drieu imagined he saw the agents of capitalism, radicals, Jews and freemasons, picking over the body politic in their endeavour to precipitate its disintegration. What Drieu perceived as the objective reason for his commitment to the philosophy of force, as embodied in German Fascism, was the rising spectre of Russian Communism. But the mainspring for the 'commitment' of the artist was identified by Drieu as an intuitive impulse. It was only this intuitive identification of 'artistic temperaments with an aspect of their epoch' which gave any value to political commitment.[19]

The intellectual climate in which the Fascist creed – and its reflection in

Drieu's ideas – was shaped, was significantly influenced by the belief of the philosopher Bergson in the primacy of instinct over reason. The appeal of one of Bergson's most well-known concepts, the *élan vital*, to the reductionist mentality supporting a philosophy of force, was that it could be used to reduce reality to a single principle that could not be verified because it was immaterial, and could not be elucidated by further enquiry because it transcended the world of facts. It nourished and justified a need to act, in a manner that would cleave through attendant intellectual and moral ambiguities. In fairness to Bergson, however, this was the interpretation imposed upon his ideas by others, whereas the philosopher himself inclined, ultimately, more to the mystical than the violently irrational.

Malraux's speeches and articles during the mid-thirties convey a sense of conviction in communism as first and foremost a vital force that could cut through political equivocation and rescue mankind from the grip of nature and a destiny of suffering. At a conference held by the International Association of Writers for the Defence of Culture, in London in 1936, Malraux argued that there was a fundamental compatibility between Marxism and democracy, as both mobilised man's energy against destiny.[20] Drieu was also drawn to communism for a period, for equally non-rational reasons. As the hero argues in his novel, *Une femme à sa fenêtre*, in their hearts the Communists are as corrupt as the capitalists, but at least they have a spark of virility, a will to fight.[21] The shared assumptions of Fascism and communism lay in the prospect of vital action, and this irrational need for momentum, for fear that stasis entails a loss of self, invites a comparison with Garine in *The Conquerors*. Before going to China, Garine insists that his principal motivation is not sympathy with its oppressed masses, but the search for a vehicle in which to convey his action as forcefully as possible. He says: 'I want . . . a certain kind of power', and if the chosen vehicle is deficient, 'I'll start again, here or elsewhere.'[22]

Maurras's irrational *élan* towards a redemptive methaphysic for his countrymen did spring from an accurate surmise. France's loss of vigour was dramatically evident in comparison to the ubiquitous manifestations of British power and the remarkable transformation of imperial Germany in the late nineteenth century. Maurras's proposed solution, however, was based on the assumption that since Britain and Germany enjoyed rising national fortunes and France did not, and since those two countries had in common the institution of monarchy, of which France had been dispossessed, it followed therefore that the restitution of the monarchy would restore France to the paths of national glory. The nineteenth-century tradition of republicanism was to be spurned, in favour of the new metaphysic which Maurras's deduction had illuminated; royalism was the cloak of light draped around a faith in 'comprehensive nationalism'. Thus royalism provided an ostensibly rational system for the realization of the essentially irrational.

In his preface to *Miss Monk*, Malraux remarked on Maurras's ability to make 'order admirable because all order represents beauty and strength'. This is indicative, however, not of a political conviction shared by the two writers but a common sensibility. For Maurras, order was indispensable for the fulfilment of the self, as the self 'disintegrates for want of order to sustain it.[23] The redemption of the essentially human is the end towards which Malraux's heroes journey. Maurras, Barrès and Drieu were engaged in an instinctive endeavour to transform the qualities of man in individual and collective terms, rather than attempting to comprehend in scientific terms the motor of history. It was to this irrational impulse that Malraux was attuned. The sense of the 'Self' strained increasingly within the limitations of conventional definitions, which Barrès in particular clearly found stifling and obsolete. A need to renew the self emerges from Barrès's fiction and finds a notable reflection in Malraux's novels.

The self

The hero in Barrès *The Worship of Self*, like Malraux's conquering heroes, particularly Claude Vannec and Perken, the two protagonists in *La Voie royale* (*The Royal Way*, 1930), share a motivation that is virtually identical; the need to recast and possess the self through the liberation of the will. Barrès's hero, Philippe, instead of adapting to the world, attempts to order the world around him. It is in the nature of Philippe's quest that he detaches himself from his fellows for he seeks to construct 'a personal vision of the universe . . . where I can take refuge, just me, a free man'.[24] For Malraux's adventurer Perken, too, the universe which frames his existence is simply something on which to impose his will and fashion his inner liberation: 'life is just matter, the question is, what to do with it'.[25] Barrès's and Malraux's heroes pursue ambitions that provide them with a passion, a dynamic without which life would be intolerable. At the centre of these ambitions is the self, in search of a justification for its existence. Barrès declared that his hero reflected his endeavour to find a reason for living, a discipline.[26] The response of Malraux's heroes to this challenge is depicted in *The Royal Way*.

Outwardly, Claude Vannec's purpose in journeying to the Cambodian interior is to acquire antiquities from the temples that line *The Royal Way*, the trail from Angkor to the lakes of Menam. He engages Perken, a man familiar with the region, to be his guide. (Vannec may resemble the adventurous young Malraux himself, who smuggled art treasures out of Indo-China, as much as the official Malraux, who called for justice and reform in these French territories. But it seems likely that the defeat of Perken's individualistic empire-building reveals Malraux's critique of the Western exploitation of the Colonies.)[27] Their journey into the heart of the jungle, however, mirrors an equally harrowing journey into the depths of the self. Claude and Perken are outsiders to the conventional game played by society and they place their 'last bet' on a game of their own devising. Barrès's hero, too, moves through the world as an outsider. He is in the world but not of it, and in common with the conquering heroes of Malraux's novels, his reflections are self-regarding. There is virtue in a turning in on oneself, for only through this can man truly find 'where his instinct leads'. The self is enhanced not by projection but by introversion. As the individual defines himself in contradistinction to the world, he must strive against it to establish his own dominion, and this entails a process of rejection. In a far more dramatic way than Barrès's hero, however, Claude and Perken pursue their ambitions in the face of hostile 'barbarians', that is, in essence, everything that is non-self. The self is tested in every respect, by hostile tribesmen and by the alien immensity of the jungle through which Claude and Perken must journey. Yet the more it is threatened, the more tenaciously Perken clings to what Barrès called 'the only reality', the self; a tenacity most desperately expressed in the shadow of his creeping but inevitable death from poisoning at the close of the novel.

Action and energy are currents that pass through these figures and are indispensable for the gratification of their sense of being. In the product of Malraux's more mature literary talent, *Man's Estate*, the theme of man's confrontation with death and destiny, and his attempt to rescue an abiding sense of self, is once more delineated, but in a much more complex and explicitly political way. In *La tentation de l'Occident*, a short book of philosophical reflections published by Malraux in 1926 in the form of an exchange of letters between a Westerner and an Oriental, the Oriental observes that formerly the absolute reality for Westerners had been religion, later succeeded by Man. Now, however, the notion of Man is dead. In *Man's Estate*, Malraux explores the social and political avenues whereby new life may be given to that notion. The case for a new, less individually self-obsessed vision of Man is established through a number of contrasts and parallels. The need of a figure like Kyo for energy and action, is, as with Malraux's earlier heroes, of fundamental importance. Kyo's father, Gisors, is a highly percipient academic, an intellectual observer of the human condition who attempts to support Kyo's endeavour to change it by arguing for the active virtues of Marxism with his students. But his attitude, in comparison with Kyo's, is like that of the scholastic compared with that of the humanist. Kyo chooses *negotium*: attempting to forge an organic link between an idea of man, and life, through action. Gisors prefers *otium*: retreating into a life of contemplation, diffusing the consciousness of his solitude through the wisps of opium smoke.

In flagrant contrast to Gisors, the terrorist Tchen shares Kyo's commitment to ideologically determined action, but the crucial distinction between the two is that the revolutionary political dimension of Tchen's action is undermined, and its socially beneficial effects negated, by his utterly individualistic pursuit of the mythical sense of redemption through violence. Tchen's fellow-terrorists eventually recognise that his determination to detonate a bomb under Chang Kai Shek's car is an expression of his capitulation before a voracious sense of self. Tchen will pursue his 'inverted ecstasy', if necessary, at the expense of the wider political struggle. His is the kind of sensibility which in another context would have been susceptible to the appeal of Fascism. In contrast, when Kyo dies, it does not mark the extinction of a forlorn political endeavour, but the apotheosis of a new spirit of brotherhood. For Kyo embodies the motivation which underlies the commitment to left-wing political struggle in Malraux's life and work; a belief in the possibility of that struggle advancing the ethical value that redeems mankind from humiliating indignity: fraternity.

The appeal of Fascism

There was, paradoxically, a fundamental flexibility in Fascism which enabled it to appeal across frontiers and political persuasions. Whereas communism was an international doctrine, elaborated in theoretical terms before being adjusted to differing national circumstances, one may argue that Fascism was quite the opposite: essentially a series of opportunistic, non-intellectual national reactions projected as an international doctrine due to the common social and economic conditions that prevailed in Europe during the 1920s and 1930s – uncontrolled inflation, mass unemployment, economic collapse.[28] By the beginning of the 1930s, arguments for the defence of collective rights against private interests, a rejection of the ability of the liberal democracy to meet the needs of the people, and the discounting of the existing property system as the legitimate foundation of social order, were being formulated by both Left and Right. Ultimately, the traditional groupings of Left and Right would no longer be able to contain the increasingly strident antiphony of voices emerging from their ranks,

from which many Fascist leaders would break away: like Mosley from
Labour, Degrelle from the Belgian Catholic Movement, and in France,
Doriot from communism and Déat from socialism. All of whom were
preceded most notably by Mussolini, the former Italian Socialist.

It has been argued that Fascism was intrinsically alien to the traditions
of the French Right,[29] since it attacked economic liberalism, proposed state
control and praised the plebiscitary heritage of 1789. However, it is beyond
doubt that it did secure a place in the hearts and minds of a significant
section of the French literati. For what it offered them was a new sense of
being, a sense of style. In contrast with emotionally flaccid, objective values,
Fascism provided the creative spirit with new afflatus, comprising a subjective vision of the world and above all an aesthetic. Many of the young
writers who were seduced by Fascism were the heirs of Maurras's metaphysic, who had allowed their vision of society's needs to be influenced by
Fascism's trenchant analysis of the failures of the liberal economic system.
Robert Brasillach, a vocal mouthpiece for the writers of the radical Right,
perceived a need in Malraux which he experienced himself, for action and
renewal, which made them both inheritors of Maurras's legacy. He believed
that Malraux did not pursue in revolution an economic or social doctrine,
so much as a form of action and a new image of man.[30] But Brasillach was in
the van of those who fastened that legacy to a brutally styled, spurious form
of virility.

In their testaments on youth, published in 1927, both Drieu and Malraux expressed the desire for a new style of self-definition. In his essay,
D'une jeunesse européenne, Malraux described Man as limited, both in his
social being and in his inner life, to a radius of action that transforms his
efforts into the impotent postures of a trapped creature. The question then
is: 'What rebellions are possible?'[31] Faced with his 'defunct deities', Man
has to rescue a complete sense of himself if he is to overcome the feeling of
cosmic isolation from living in a godless universe. A similar need for a new,
reviving definition of Man is expressed in Drieu's *Le jeune Européen*, a
figure who laments the non-realisation of the 'idea of the complete man.'[32]
That completeness was something which Malraux, the committed writer,
seemed to have achieved. In an article published in 1930, Drieu made clear
his admiration for the posture Malraux had struck in balancing literary and
human commitments. Malraux's apparent resolution of the intellectual's
dilemma, by engaging his life and art in action, incarnated something to
which Drieu's fascist sensibility inclined – the myth of action.[33]

Myth was central to the ideology of Fascism because its very unreality
made it possible to keep up a violent, intransigent and doctrinaire position.
The dynamic of Fascism resulted from the primary importance attached to

fervent action and the secondary importance ascribed to its direction. The non-rational nature of this faith made it incontrovertible and thus more compelling to minds like Drieu's. He looked forward to a new breed of men who would regenerate the national community through the practice of 'virile virtues'. The new man envisioned by Drieu would believe only in action and order his actions according to a myth.

The motivation which engendered an adherence to the myth of action was common to the creative vision of Malraux and Drieu. In Drieu's universe, there were no barriers separating literary and political life. Action in the former sphere implied action in the latter. Authentic literature was crucially dependent on lived experience, therefore his quest as a writer was indissociable from his quest as a man: to leave a mark on the world. Drieu's praise for Malraux as the 'new man', was heaped on one whom he believed to share the same ambition as himself. Drieu had found substance for this belief in the heroes created in Malraux's first two novels, who echoed in fictional terms the desire he had articulated. As Perken says: 'I want to leave a scar on the map'.[34] Malraux's conquering heroes wager on action to solve the contradictions in their lives. Like an imaginary forerunner announcing Drieu's fatal ambition, Garine exposed the motivation that could express itself through a cult of force. As his illness gains ground against his resistance and obliges him to leave Canton, Garine clutches at the idea that force will restore his link with the essence of life, and that the quarter from which that force originates is irrelevant. Asked where he would like to go on departing from Canton, Garine replies: 'to England. Now I know what Empire means; a tenacious, unyielding violence. . . . That's where life is.'[35]

Forceful action is an absolute necessity for the fulfilment of Fascist aspirations; it complements a world-view in which history awaits its maker. But the sensibility which responds to the challenge of life in this manner is politically ambivalent. The response of the young Malraux to the challenge facing man was not disciplined, according to Socialist doctrine, but emotive. It is the spontaneity of Malraux's desire for the redefinition of man's estate that makes the myth of action appealing because, as an instinctive desire, it does not need an explicit explanation, nor could it be contained by one. The myth of action is reflected in the conquering hero of Malraux's literary creation. In his praise of force, Garine expresses a will to power similar to the one which motivated Drieu in reality. However, Garine's forceful but pragmatic exploitation of events in pursuit of political change also owes something to Malraux's assimilation of the ideas of the nineteenth-century Parisian revolutionary, Auguste Blanqui, leading to that form of vitalism which has been called the 'Fascism of the Left'. Drieu's approach was more black and white, resulting in an excessive regard for the totality in which the individual was to be subsumed. His anti-Semitism stemmed from a clear desire to expel 'impure elements' from the race. Whereas, for Malraux, the role of the individual *vis-à-vis* his society or the political movement he served was often agonisingly difficult to resolve, as is illustrated by his fictional heroes (Garine, for instance, is racked by scruples when he finds himself obliged to order the execution of rebels who have poisoned his men's water supply).

An even purer distillation of the fatal allure of force is found in the figure of Tchen in *Man's Estate*. Beneath the right-wing bravado of Drieu's outlook and the reckless revolutionary courage of Tchen when he attempts to assassinate Chang Kai Shek, lies the same tension. The unique sense of liberation that results from resurrecting man's primitive, amoral combativeness is transient, and the prospect it offers of lasting self-affirmation is illusory. As Drieu knew and as is depicted in Tchen's fate, individualistic action is irrelevant in the wider context of conflicts between classes or states. Tchen fails in his bid to blow up Chang Kai Shek's car, and his failure is doubly underlined by the discovery that Chang Kai Shek is not even in the vehicle. The attempt to define the self through such action is doomed to failure, but this is the very impasse which motivates Tchen's tragic attempt to overcome his destiny, through the release of a primordial instinct for violence.

Unfettered vitality as the touchstone of faith in the process of self-affirmation tends to operate against the affirmation of mankind as a whole, since it functions as an amoral law unto itself. As Tchen and Garine show in their attitudes to the political causes they serve, when action becomes absolute, good and evil become relative values which can slide to the bottom of the scale of priorities in extreme situations, ultimately diminishing the dignity of man's existence. To reach that point, the conquering hero must succumb to the appeal of the idea that a life purely invested with action is the only remedy for the vertigo drawing man into the abyss of death. But the heroes of Malraux's fiction progress to a broader and more redeeming vision of man's destiny, whereas Drieu's vision became stubbornly tragic, a fatal absolute.

Moral commitment

At a particular juncture in the development of his ideas, Malraux offered similarities with those right-wing writers discussed above. But in his overarching moral commitment to mankind, he could not follow their steps down an absolute path that was fatal to the individual human sensibility.

Royalism was an integral part of Maurras's *Action Française* because it provided a rational criterion by which authoritarianism could be made to appear palatable. It defined a locus of power and described a hierarchy which made parliament redundant, and it negated the rights which had accrued to the individual after 1789. The thrust of Maurras's ambition for his society undermined the role of the individual and his prerogatives. For the notion of good to which man was supposed to aspire resided with society, the national community, and not the individual. Ultimately, the 'individual self' was sacrificed for the benefit of the 'national self'.

Barrès's hero at the end of *The Worship of Self* experiences a need that would find a sympathetic echo in Malraux's literary creation. He wants to emerge from a sterile egoism into a fuller and more rewarding form of consciousness. But in his progression from *The Worship of the Self* to *The Novel of National Energy*, Barrès performs what in reality is an about-face. Whereas in the former trilogy national energy is regarded as consequent upon the expansion of the individual, in the latter it is the strengthening of one's sense of belonging to the nation which is portrayed as the essential precondition for the expansion of the self. The 'individual self' is sacrificed for the 'social self'.

In Malraux's moral universe, the need to redefine the 'self' does not become so absolute as to exclude an account of the moral cost in individual terms. Paradoxically, Brasillach provided unwitting proof of this when he wrote that in Malraux's fictional world heroism was never depicted without a distastefully indulgent portrayal of suffering and death.[36] Brasillach's rejection of Malraux's vision of the human condition is indicative of the fact that though Malraux was susceptible to the temptation of the Right, it was not deep enough to prejudice his moral perception and thus diminish the broad nature of his humanist commitment. Malraux does not show heroism without horror, sacrifice without suffering, or the heady wine of violence without the moral hangover it entails. By contrast, Drieu pursues his vision of man with a narrowness that excludes contradictory details. Drieu viewed the 'self' as merely an accident on the permanent substratum of life which constitutes the 'whole'. This vision is not only fatal in its consequences for the individual but also for humanity, for it has roots in a morbid fascination. Drieu eventually became obsessed with death as a means for Man's return journey to a fundamental continuity, an organic essence.

As Drieu La Rochelle approached the vortex of human self-destructiveness from the Right, so it was approached by Louis-Ferdinand Céline from the Left. Céline provides an instructive contrast with Malraux, as an apparently left-wing writer whose desire to hew a new foundation for mankind's self-regard is not attenuated by humane scruples. It thus becomes an amoral quest, similar to the right-wing cult of force. When Céline's *Voyage au bout de la nuit* appeared in 1932, the description it contained of the Ford assembly plant in Detroit was acclaimed by some Communists as a cogent observation on the exploitative nature of capitalism. Yet on his return from a visit to the Soviet Union in 1936, Céline castigated the Soviet system as a vast prison camp designed to put the worker systematically in chains. What motivated Céline's transgression of bourgeois received wisdom was not a reasoned commitment to a political alternative, but a rejection of reason itself. The ascendancy of reason threatened to vitiate man's ability to feel a part of the whole, to experience the pulse of the universe. To escape the dead hand of reason, Céline discerned the need for the espousal of the opposite: the unreasoned or 'gratuitous'. Céline's powerfully satirical treatment of war, colonialism, education, medicine, psychiatry and the other major props of the Establishment was engendered by an anarchic energy that refused to accept the lunacies imposed by official rationality and morality. Implicit in his daemonic urge was the assumption that insanity was in itself politically subversive. The complex of irrational motives which engendered Céline's implicit criticism of the alienation caused by capitalism also engendered his anti-Semitism and eventual support of Hitler. Whereas, although Malraux was attracted to the idea of transcending reason, he never succumbed to the lure of pure unreason.

An opposition of 'self' and 'whole' is discernible in Malraux's vision as well as in Drieu's and Céline's, but the 'whole' is living and enhances the human quality of the 'self'. In *Man's Estate* Kyo dies in a political conflict, but his triumph is spiritual, pointing to how the human spirit may be redeemed by the sacrifice of the self for the fraternal collectivity. *L'Espoir* (*Days of Hope*) published in 1937, confirms Malraux's commitment. It expresses immediate commitment to a contemporary struggle, in Spain, as opposed to a historical reconstruction of events in a far-off country like China. It ends not with the fragile hope of *The Conquerors* and *Man's Estate*, but on a note of triumph for the politics of the Left. It covers the period of the Civil War in Spain which begins with the battle of Barcelona on 19 July 1936 and ends with the great Republican victory at Guadalajara on 18 March 1937. Like other members of the left-wing intelligentsia of Europe, Malraux was shaken by the events of July 1936, when a number of Spanish generals, led by General Sanjurjo and General Franco, rose against the Popular Front government and thereby sparked off a three-year-long civil war. It was a struggle passionately engaged on both sides, and in the minds of many on the Left, particularly in France, it represented the last of the great revolutions, following in the traces of 1848 and the Commune of 1871. It was especially crucial as it seemed to threaten the viability of France's vulnerable new Popular Front Government, elected in June 1936.

In form as well as in content, Malraux goes further than he did in *Man's Estate* to express a revolutionary sensibility. In *Man's Estate* Malraux exchews the seamless continuity achieved by a conventional omniscient narrator, and instead portrays the action in a sequence of scenes that are dated and timed, underlining the historicity and revolutionary tension of the situation depicted. In *Days of Hope*, Malraux draws on a number of techniques to achieve a particularly supple kind of narrative form, which enables him to explore the revolutionary consciousness both of the individual and the group.[37] The viewpoint, focus and plot in *Days of Hope* are fragmented, in order to give the idea of a collective novel. Furthermore, the suppleness of Malraux's technique enables the reader to grasp the significance of the Civil War on different levels: as the struggle to establish certain political beliefs, but also as the struggle for human values that transcend any historical context, to touch the realm of the epic and the eternal. The climax of the novel occurs when a Republican war plane crashes on a mountainside on the return from a mission, and Magnin, the crew's commanding officer, has to organise their rescue. The scene depicting the descent of the survivors from the mountainside is a lyrical evocation of fraternal values, and its revolutionary significance is mirrored in the faces of the peasants who witness the rescue, fists raised, in an expression of hope that marries their human aspirations with their political allegiances. In this scene we have a synthesis of the conflicting impulses analysed in this chapter: the claims of revolutionary action and the myth of redemption through vital affirmation of the self.

Notes to chapter 9

1   Malraux described himself as 'a revolutionary who is unable to depart from a dictatorial view of life or from the honest application of historical materialism', in an interview given to Ernesto Madero for *El Nacional*, 8 March 1937. Reproduced in the *New York Literary Forum*, 3, 1979, pp. 219–23 (p. 221).
2   See Malraux's defence of artistic independence in 'L'attitude de l'artiste', *Commune*, 15, 1934, pp. 166–74 (p. 166).
3   Jean Lacouture, *Malraux, une vie dans le siècle*, Paris, 1976, p. 202.
4   K. Marx and F. Engels, *The German Ideology*, Moscow, 1968, p. 87.
5   André Malraux, 'Lettres d'un Chinois', *Nouvelle Revue Française*, 151, 1926, pp. 409–20 (p. 416).
6   L. Trotsky, 'La Révolution étranglée', *Nouvelle Revue Française*, CCXI, 1931, pp. 488–500 (p. 493).
7   *Ibid.*, p. 489.

8   L. Trotsky, *Stalin*, tr. C. Malamuth, London, 1968.
9   Trotsky, 'La Révolution Etranglée', p. 496.
10 A. Malraux, *Les Conquérants*, in *Romans*, Paris, 1959, p. 51.
11 A. Malraux, 'Réponse à Trotsky', *Nouvelle Revue Française*, CCXI, 1931, pp. 501–7.
12 L. Trotsky in a letter to Simon and Schuster, in I. Deutscher, *The Prophet Outcast*, London, 1963, p. 269, n. 1.
13 L. Trotsky, *Problems of the Chinese Revolution*, trans. M. Shachtman, Ann Arbor, 1967.
14 A. Malraux, *La Condition Humaine*, in *Romans*, Paris, 1959, p. 285.
15 C. Maurras, *Mlle Monk*, Paris, 1923.
16 Discours prononcé aux assises nationales du RPF (Nancy), 25 November 1951.
17 G. Picon, *Malraux par lui-même*, Paris, 1961, p. 90.
18 M. Barrès, *Sous l'oeil des barbares*, Paris, 1922, p. 195.
19 P. Drieu La Rochelle, *Genève ou Moscou*, Paris, 1928, p. 15.
20 Picon, *op. cit.*, p. 92.
21 P. Drieu La Rochelle, *Une femme à sa fenêtre*, Paris, 1930, p. 279.
22 *Les Conquérants*, p. 51.
23 C. Maurras, *Mes idées politiques*, Paris, 1937, p. 36.
24 M. Barrès, *Un homme libre*, Paris, 1922, p. 13.
25 A. Malraux, 'La Voie Royale', *Cahiers Verts*, 4, Paris, 1930, p. 159.
26 Barrès, *op. cit.*, p. vii.
27 See A. Malraux, 'S.O.S.', *Marianne*, 11 October 1933, and his preface to A. Vollis, *Indochine S.O.S.*, Paris, 1935, p. x.
28 See *Fascism in Europe*, ed. S. J. Woolf, London, 1981.
29 See R. Rémond, *Les Droites en France*, Paris, 1982.
30 R. Brasillach, *Portraits*, Paris, 1935, p. 219.
31 A. Malraux, 'D'une jeunesse européenne', in *Cahiers Verts*, 70, Paris, 1927, pp. 133–53 (p. 149).
32 P. Drieu La Rochelle, *Le jeune Européen*, Paris, 1927, p. 90.
33 P. Drieu La Rochelle, 'Malraux, l'homme nouveau', *Nouvelle Revue Francaise*, 207, 1930, pp. 879–85 (p. 881).
34 *La Voie Royale*, p. 87.
35 *Les Conquérants*, p. 161.
36 Brasillach, *op. cit.*, p. 223.
37 See P. Carrard, 'Malraux ou le récit hybride', *Situation*, 36, Paris, 1976.

Further reading

On Malraux:

L. Goldmann, *Pour une sociologie du roman*, Paris, 1975
J. Hoffman, *L'humanisme de Malraux*, Paris, 1963
P. H. Simon, *L'homme en procès*, Paris, 1965
R. Stéphane, *André Malraux, entretiens et précisions*, Paris, 1984

On the revolutions in China and Spain:

B. Bolloten, *The Grand Camouflage*, London, 1961
E. Snow, *Red Star over China*. London, 1978
H. Thomas, *The Spanish Civil War*, London, 1977

On the literary radical Right in France:

R. Griffiths, *The Reactionary Revolution: The Catholic Revival in French Literature 1870–1914*, London, 1965
T. Kunnas, *Drieu La Rochelle, Céline, Brasillach et la tentation fasciste*, Paris, 1972
J. Plumyène and L. La Sierra, *Les Fascimes Français 1923–1963*, Paris, 1963
P. Sérant, *Le Romantisme Fasciste*, Paris, 1969

Nâzım Hikmet:
poetry and politics
in Kemalist Turkey

To live like tree, unique and free,
like a forest in harmony.

The humanist vision of Nâzım Hikmet (1902–63), one of the greatest poets of modern Turkey, is summed up in these lines.[1] But this vision proved so difficult to achieve that the poet spent the greater part of his adult life either in prison or in exile. Hikmet was a poet, playwright and political activist who even in prison remained a free man (the lines quoted above were written in 1947 in Bursa Prison). He lived through the period of revolutionary upheaval which followed the collapse of the Ottoman Empire. Initially he was an admirer of Kemal Atatürk, the military leader who founded the Turkish Republic and introduced a programme of Westernisation. But four years spent in the Soviet Union during the early 1920s provided Hikmet with more radical models: Lenin's blueprint for a communist society and Mayakovsky's vision of the poet as spokesman for the aspirations of the common people.

The poetry which Hikmet wrote during the 1920s and 1930s brought him into conflict with increasingly authoritarian tendencies of the Kemalist regime. After shorter periods of imprisonment he was sentenced in 1938 to a total of twenty-eight years on charges of subversion. He was released under a general amnesty in 1950 and escaped to the Soviet Union, where he died in 1963. His poetry is still subject to censorship in Turkey, twenty-five years after his death. And a line used as the title for a book devoted to Hikmet, recently published in Berlin, provides his most fitting epitaph: 'They are frightened of our songs.'[2]

Nâzım Hikmet's career exemplifies the dilemma of a politically committed poet in a developing country during a period of social transformation. The question faced by the Turkish elite was how to transform a traditional Islamic society based on an agrarian peasant economy into a modern secular state. Kemal Atatürk's solution was to introduce sweeping reforms based on Western models. He abolished the Caliphate, secularised the state, substituted the Latin for the Arabic alphabet, introduced Western-style surnames, banned the veil and the fez, introduced Western clothing, and initiated literacy programmes and educational reforms. Although he also set up state-owed industries and marketing organisations, Atatürk's reforms were essentially superstructural changes, unsupported by any radical transformation of the economy. Turkey remained an agrarian peasant society, dominated by large landowners and by a military and bureaucratic elite.[3]

The ensuing historical contradictions form the substance of Hikmet's poetry. Formally as well as thematically, his work marks a radical break with Ottoman traditions.[4] Combining a new freedom of form with a strong sense of rhythm, his poetry conveys the urgent need for political commitment. This is exemplified by the famous lines from his early poem 'Kerem gibi' ('Like Kerem', 1930), inspired by the legend of a folk hero. In the legend, Kerem, unbuttoning the dress of his beloved Shirin on their wedding night, fails to undo all the buttons within the allotted time and is consumed by fire. In Hikmet's poem this becomes an image of political passion:

Ben yanmasam	(If I don't burn
sen yanmasan,	if you don't burn
biz yanmasak,	if we don't burn,
nasıl	how will
çıkar	the darkness
karanlıklar	change to
aydınlığa . . .	light?)[5]

Turkish is a highly inflected language whose extended verbal forms acquire, through subtle modulations, a cumulative power. It is also governed by patterns of vowel harmony which endow spoken verse with elements of incantation (some of Hikmet's poems have been popularised by musical settings). Such vocalic and syntactic modulations are hard to convey in a largely non-inflected language like English. But even in translation the suggestive power of Hikmet's image of 'burning' is clear, conveying a passionate commitment which may also involve anguished suffering – as the price to be paid for illumination.

Though the rhythmic qualities of Hikmet's poetry elude the translator, his political vision can be made accessible in any language. The paradoxes of personal experience convey the contradictions of the modern world, as in the late poem 'Autobiography' (1961):

I was born in 1902
I never once went back to my birthplace
I don't like to turn back
at three I served as a pasha's grandson in Aleppo

at nineteen as a student at Moscow Communist University
at forty-nine I was back in Moscow as a guest of the Tcheka Party
and I've been a poet since I was fourteen
some people know all about plants some about fish
                                        I know separation
some people know the names of stars by heart
                                        I recite absenses
I've slept in prisons and in grand hotels
I've known hunger even a hunger strike and there's almost no
                                        food I haven't tasted
at thirty they wanted to hang me
at forty-eight to give me the Peace Medal
                        which they did
at thirty-six I covered four square meters of concrete in half a year
at fifty-nine I flew from Prague to Havana in eighteen hours
I never saw Lenin I stood watch at his coffin in '24
in '61 the tomb that I visit is his books
[. . .]
my writings are published in thirty forty languages
        in my Turkey in my Turkish they're banned[6]

Like Brecht, he endows his experience of revolutionary conflict and political persecution with an exemplary quality. Indeed, as the prison walls
closed in around him, his writing acquired an exceptional radiance. He was
able to celebrate the consoling objects of prison routine – a stub of pencil, a
mulberry tree in the exercise yard – because he was aware that his longing
for liberation was shared by oppressed people throughout the world.

The 'birthplace' to which the poet never returned was Salonika (Thessaloniki), a cosmopolitan city which at that time formed the western outpost
of the Ottoman Empire.[7] In addition to its large Greek and Turkish
communities, Salonika had traditionally been a place of refuge for Jews.
Each of these flourishing communities took pride in its own culture and
traditions, crafts and skills. And its geographical position, as well as its
cosmopolitan population, made the city particularly accessible to ideas
from Western Europe. It can scarcely be a coincidence that Salonika was
also the birthplace of Kemal Atatürk (1881–1938). Hikmet's mother was
partly of Polish and Huguenot descent, and the poet was later to take pride
in his international ancestry. His grandfather was a member of the Turkish
military elite – a pasha who became governor of Aleppo (where Hikmet
spent part of his childhood).

It was through Salonika that revolutionary ideas entered the Ottoman
Empire. In 1908 the city provided the Young Turks with the base from
which they made their bid for power.[8] The success of this military coup by a
group of nationalistic officers led to the deposition of the despotic Sultan

Abdul Hamid. But their policies became repressive as the position of the Empire became increasingly unstable. The Balkan Wars of 1911–13 led to further losses of territory (Salonika had to be ceded to Greece). And as other minorities also pressed for independence, the Young Turks sought to prop up the ramshackle Empire by means of a military alliance with Germany. In 1914 they entered the Great War on the German side. And it was during the Gallipoli campaign that Kemal Atatürk first rose to prominence, as commander of the army which successfully repulsed the British invasion. However the defeat of Germany and Austria–Hungary in 1918 also brought about the collapse of the Ottoman Empire.

The weakness of the Ottoman Government, which was unable to oppose the occupation and proposed partition of Turkey by the victorious Western allies, provoked a patriotic reaction among the Turkish people. Under the Treaty of Sèvres some of the richest provinces of Anatolia were to be ceded to Greece and Italy. But Kemal Atatürk, hero of Gallipoli, secretly left Istanbul and began to organise an army of national resistance in central Anatolia, with its headquarters at Ankara. Declaring the Treaty of Sèvres invalid, he launched a war of independence which lasted for over two years (1920–2). It ended in complete victory for the Turks. The Western powers were forced to recognise the independence and territorial integrity of Turkey, which was declared a republic with its capital in Ankara. Atatürk became the first President and embarked on his sweeping programme of reforms.[9]

Atatürk had spent his formative years as a military envoy in Germany, and his reform programme was essentially based on Western models. But during the war of independence he had enjoyed a measure of support from the revolutionary government of the Soviet Union, which saw in Kemalist Turkey a possible ally against Western imperialism. A treaty of friendship was signed with the Soviet Union in March 1921. And there were progressive groups in Turkey which looked to Moscow rather than to Berlin for their model of a revolutionary society. A Turkish Communist Party was founded in 1920, only to be banned two years later. But although communism was prevented from becoming an organised political party, it remained a potent ideological force. And Nâzım Hikmet, who joined the party in 1923 and remained a member until the end of his life, was to prove its most eloquent spokesman.[10]

Like Atatürk before him, Hikmet owed his educational opportunities to the Ottoman military academies which had been reorganised along Western lines. When the war ended in 1918, he was a sixteen-year-old serving on the destroyer *Hamidiye*. He joined the protest movement against the Western occupation of Istanbul and, after being discharged from the navy, set out with a group of friends to join Atatürk in Ankara. The last nine days of their arduous journey had to be completed on foot. During this period Hikmet experienced at first hand the courage and endurance of the people of Anatolia. He also met members of the resistance movement who had been influenced by the ideas of the German Spartacists. This was his first encounter with Marxism.

When Hikmet and a fellow-poet were introduced to Atatürk, the Turkish leader is recorded as saying: 'I recommend you to write poems with a purpose.'[11] He can hardly have guessed the direction which Hikmet's talents were soon to take:

> I am a poet
> I've written as many poems as it rains in a year
> But to start the real
> the best work of mine [. . .]
> I shall have to wait
> till I know *Das Kapital* by heart.[12]

That 'real work' (the poem suggests) would be a blend of Marxist theory with the techniques of the Russian Constructivists.

Instead of joining the army of national resistance, Hikmet was sent to serve as a teacher in Bolu. Then, during 1921, benefiting from the cordial relations between Kemalist Turkey and the Soviet Union, he made the journey overland via Trebizond, Tiflis and Batum to Moscow, where he arrived early in 1922. His experience while travelling through areas between Batum and Moscow which were suffering from famine made an indelible impression on his mind. Attempting to write a poem about the famine, he became aware how incongrous it would be to use the closed form of conventional rhymed verse for such a subject. But in Batum his eye was caught by a poem in *Pravda* (possibly by Mayakovsky), using an experimental typography which scattered short lines across the page. Although he could hardly understand a word of Russian, he intuitively grasped the principle of free verse, in which (as he put it) 'the poet's thought is like the waves of the sea'. The ensuing poem is characteristic of his evolving style:

> Hungry lines hungry!
> Not men, not women, not boys or girls,
>   bent twisted trees
>   with skinny thin
>   bent twisted branches![13]

As a student in Moscow Hikmet took courses in French, physics and chemistry. But his political education was even more significant. The inspiring example of Lenin remained with him until the end of his life. Hikmet was in Moscow in 1924 at the time of Lenin's death and participated in the vigil at his coffin. Artistically, too, his mind was enriched by the efflorescence of experimental art and poetry during the first years of the Soviet Republic. He was introduced to Mayakovsky, Selvinsky and Meyerhold. From the theatre of Meyerhold he learnt the art of combining revolutionary political themes with elements from popular tradition and folklore.[14] He followed the debates between the Futurists and the Constructivists, and was so impressed by Mayakovsky that he started calling himself a 'Futurist', until a friend with a sophisticated knowledge of Russian told him that the Futurists 'denied lyricism'. 'Then I am not a Futurist!', Hikmet declared. There is a tongue-in-cheek quality about this remark; for later in life he was to recall with pride that he had shared a platform with Mayakovsky at a poetry reading.[15]

He shared with the Futurists an enthusiasm for mechanisation, experimenting with new sounds and rhythms to convey the dynamism of modern technology:

> trrrrum,
> > trrrrum,
> > > trrrrum!
> trak tiki tak
> I want to be
> > mechanised!
> I will find a solution to this
> and only then will I be happy,
> the day when I have a turbine in my belly
> and a couple of wings on my tail!
> trrrrum,
> > trrrrum,
> > > trrrrum![16]

And like the Futurists he gained inspiration from a polemical confrontation with the bourgeois culture of the past. The romantic lure of the Orient had always appealed to sentimentally inclined tourists, including the French poet and naval officer Pierre Loti. Taking issue with this tradition in the poem 'East-West' (1926), Hikmet creates a memorable sequence of juxtapositions:

> Opium!
> Submission!
> Kismet!
> Lattice-work, caravanserai
> > fountains
> a sultan dancing on a silver tray!
> Maharajah, rajah

a thousand-year-old shah!
Waving from minarets
clogs made of mother-of-pearl;
women with henna-stained noses
working their looms with their feet.
In the wind, green-turbaned imams
                              calling people to prayer;

This is the Orient the French poet sees.

[. . .]
Orient!
The soil on which
              naked slaves
                         die of hunger.
The common property of everyone
except those born on it.
The land where hunger itself
                    perishes with famine!
But the silos are full to the brim,
full of grain—
              only for Europe.[17]

After reading Lenin's *Materialism and Empiricism*, Hikmet was inspired to incorporate philosophical themes into poetry. His diatribe against the solipsism of Bishop Berkeley, who had argued that material objects have no reality beyond the sphere of subjective perception, illustrates this extension of his imaginative range:

Heeey
Berkeley,
the frocked gallant of tavern maids,
              the Knight of the King,
              the golden sound of capital—
              and God's bishop!
The smell of the incense of your philosophy
              is to make our heads dizzy
              to make our knees drag us
              in this struggle to live.

[. . .]
This is what you think:
the apple
          you hold in your hand
                    round
                              bright
          you call
          a 'compound of ideas'

[. . .]
      only you
         and God are real . . .
oh, but you the drunk bishop of dark taverns:
wasn't the publican's young daughter
who kept wriggling in your hairy arms
         outside your own filthy body?
Or, should we assume that you slept
      with Bishop Berkeley?[18]

Hikmet himself was a Materialist in the best sense, with a poet's respect for the texture of social experience. Taking issue at a later date with more abstract forms of dialectical materialism, he insisted that a Marxist is not a 'mechanical man', but a person with 'flesh, blood, nerves, head, and heart'.[19]

After his return to Turkey in 1925, Hikmet's gift for coining vivid images to convey a revolutionary message soon brought him into conflict with the authorities. By the end of the year he had to return to the Soviet Union in order to escape imprisonment. In his absence he was sentenced to fifteen years for writing a poem in which the redness of the sun figures as an image of revolution:

Here, in this fire
    fallen
    from the sun
    burn millions of red hearts . . .
        ('The Song of One who Drinks the Sun')[20]

During his second period in Moscow (1925–8) he began to write plays and stories, as well as poetry. Meanwhile, his style was becoming more lyrical as he wrote poems which express the longing of the exile for his homeland. And in his political poetry, too, he was increasingly aware of the need for oblique modes of expression. Like Mayakovsky, he was concerned to give his poetry an oral impact that would appeal to pre-literate audiences. But Mayakovsky, the master of poetry for public declamation, was no longer an adequate model for a poet who had to operate under conditions of political repression. This point is made in one of Hikmet's own self-commentaries: 'Mayakovsky is my master, but [. . .] I don't write like him. When I read poems in Moscow, I read to large audiences and I have to shout. But in Turkey I have to whisper my poems to the ears of my audiences. Thus I have to choose softer words.'[21]

Those softer words appeal even to readers who abhor Hikmet's politics. He had a gift for poetry of contemplation, as in the gentle cadences of his 'Fable' about the cat and the plane tree, which an abbreviated translation can only imperfectly convey:

> Resting by the water-side,
> the plane tree, I, the cat and the sun.
> Our reflections are thrown on the water
> the plane tree's, mine, the cat's and the sun's.
> The sparkle of the water hits us
> the plane tree, me, the cat and the sun.
>
> [. . .]
> Resting by the water-side.
>
> First the cat will go
> its reflection will be lost on the water.
> Then I will go
> my reflection will be lost on the water.
> Then the plane tree will go
> its reflection will be lost on the water.
> Then the water will go
> the sun will remain
> [. . .][22]

He also had great gifts as a love-poet (he was married several times and there is ample evidence of his gifts for the expression of tenderness). But like Brecht he felt that the pressures of political life imposed other priorities. His lyric poetry can never be divorced from this political commitment, since he saw poetry as a means of articulating political contradictions at every level of experience.

He returned to Turkey in 1928 after the announcement of an amnesty. He was promptly imprisoned for eight months and then released, and imprisoned again briefly in 1931 after the publication of 'The City that Lost its Voice' (1931), written against the background of a taxi drivers' strike in Istanbul. But he continued to write both poetry and plays. In one extended poem he debated the social responsibilities of the artist, in another (perhaps provoked by the suicide of Mayakovsky in 1930) he explored the conflicting imperatives of socialism, individualism and love.[23] He was aware of the Soviet debate about Socialist Realism. But artistically he retained the freedom to experiment, just as politically his allegiance was to the radicalism of Lenin.

During a further period of imprisonment (1932–5) he wrote the epic poem 'Sheik Bedreddin', which portrays a fifteenth-century peasant uprising against political and economic oppression. The scholar and mystic Bedreddin is seen as a folk hero who advocates socialism, equality and the abolition of private property; and the rebellion as a combined attempt by Turks, Greeks and Jews to take over the land of feudal lords. A blend of poetry and prose, of realistic narrative with lyrical interludes, makes these themes accessible in a popular style. Atatürk's introduction of the Latin alphabet, together with language reforms aimed at 'purifying' Turkish of Arabic and Persian elements, had broken the continuity of literary discourse. Hikmet's 'Sheik Bedreddin' re-establishes contact with more primitive folk myths:

> Do not sigh my friends, do not weep,
> connect yesterday to today,
> today to tomorrow.[24]

The repeated experience of imprisonment, under arduous conditions which did permanent damage to his health, failed to crush Hikmet's spirit. During these periods of confinement his poetic range was indeed enlarged as he incorporated the wider world of international politics into his work. The rise of Fascism is dealt with in 'Letters to Taranta-Babu' (1935), which interprets the triumph of Mussolini in a wider historical context.[25] The passages dealing with the role of bourgeois intellectuals in Italy constitute also an oblique attack on authoritarian tendencies in Turkey. The parallels were indeed only too close. In 1936 the repressive penal code of Fascist Italy was incorporated into the constitution of the Turkish state. Its notorious paragraphs 141 and 142, which prohibit radical Socialist publications, remain in force to the present day. In an atmosphere of increasing political repression Hikmet was arrested again in 1938 and sentenced to fifteen years on the trumped-up charge that he had incited cadets from the military academy to mutiny. After the death of Atatürk at the end of 1938, a second sentence was passed extending Hikmet's term of imprisonment to a total of twenty-eight years.

The curbs on his physical freedom never weakened his commitment to communism. His resilience, both as a person and as a poet, had a number of different sources. First, despite several periods of solitary confinement, he was never really alone. He was by no means the only Turkish writer to find himself in jail. And sharing a cell first with the novelists Orhan Kemal and Kemal Tahir, later with the painter Ibrahim Balaban, he was sustained by a sense of common purpose. There were moments when Bursa Prison became a kind of academy for revolutionary Turkish art. Above all, Hikmet was able to write. Under the pressures of prison censorship, which precluded political writing, he developed more oblique strategies which extended his expressive range. Between 9 and 10 pm at night he wrote poems in the form of letters to his wife Piraye.[26] His 'Letters from Prison' to Kemal Tahir have also become well known.[27] But the main work of the day, when the manual tasks of prison routine (like weaving) had been completed, was to write his most ambitious epic poem.

Under Atatürk's successor Ismet Inönü, Turkey contrived to remain neutral during the Second World War. But Hikmet followed the political news with a profound sense of the world–historical issues that were at stake. The news of the German invasion of the Soviet Union in 1942 inspired him to embark on a grandiose panorama of twentieth-century events, richly interwoven with the experiences of ordinary people. By the time he was released from prison he had written over 60,000 lines, but he was unable to take the manuscript with him when he finally left Turkey for the Soviet Union in 1951 (substantial sections of the poem were subsequently confiscated or destroyed). The sections which survived, totalling 17,000 lines, were not published in Turkey until 1966.

This poem, *Human Landscapes* (published in an English version in 1982), uses a railway journey across Anatolia as a means of showing how historical events impinge on ordinary men and women. For Hikmet, as for Brecht, it is not 'great men' who make history. The real heroes are the working people. Using flexible 'montage' techniques, Hikmet juxtaposes a wide variety of voices and perspectives. One of the most striking features of the poem is the prominence it gives to the experience of Anatolian women, so long the prisoners of multiple forms of oppression. During the Turkish War of Independence women had helped to produce munitions and to guide the ox carts which transported them to the front. This forms the theme of a remarkable poetic reminiscence:

> The ox carts rolled beyond Akshehir toward Afyon.
> [. . .]
> The night was bright and warm,
> and in their wooden beds on the ox carts
> the dark-blue bombshells were stark-naked.
> And the women
> hid their glances from each other
> as they eyed the dead oxen
> and wheels from past convoys . . .
> And the women,
> our women
> with their awesome, sacred hands,
>   pointed little chins, and big eyes,
>   our mothers, lovers, wives,
> who die without ever having lived,
> who get fed at our tables
>   after the oxen,
> who we abduct and carry off to the hills
>   and go to prison for,
> who harvest grain, cut tobacco, chop wood, and barter in the markets,

who we harness to our plows,
and who with their bells and undulant heavy hips
surrender to us in sheepfolds
in the gleam of knives stuck in the ground—

>   the women,
>   our women,

walked under the moon now
behind the ox carts and shells
with the same ease
and accustomed weariness of women
hauling amber-eared sheaves to the threshing place.
And scrawny-necked children
        slept on the steel of 15-cm. shrapnel shells.
And the ox carts advanced under the moon
beyond Akshehir toward Afyon.[28]

The passage has a certain epic grandeur and yet abounds in critical irony. The erotic undercurrent subverts the easy equation of modern weaponry with male sexual conquest. In Hikmet's poem the protest against centuries of oppression implies that women are capable of taking power into their own hands. This impression is reinforced by the illustration for this passage provided by Hikmet's fellow political exile, Abidin Dino (Fig. 6).

(6) Dino, *Women with Munitions*

Despite the power of his epic vision, Hikmet's most poignant prison poems are written in a personal voice. The poet's resilience expresses itself in subtle variations of tone. The opening stanzas of 'Since I Was Thrown Into This Hole' (1947) have a wry humour:

> Since I was thrown into this hole
> the Earth has gone round the sun ten times.
> If you ask the Earth, it will say,
>   'Doesn't deserve mention
>   such a microscopic amount of time.'
> If you ask me, I'll say,
>   'Ten years off my life.'
>
> The day I was imprisoned
>   I had a small pencil
> which I used up within a week.
> If you ask the pencil, it will say,
>   'My whole lifetime.'
> If you ask me, I'll say,
>   'So what? Only a week.' [. . .]²⁹

But there are also moments of exhilaration, as in 'That's How It Goes' (written in Bursa Prison the following summer):

> Am in the middle of a spreading light,
> my hands inspired, the world beautiful.
>   Cannot stop looking at trees:
> they're so hopeful and so green.
> A sunny pathway stretches beyond the mulberries,
> I stand before the window in the prison hospital,
>   cannot smell the smell of medicine:
>   somewhere carnations must be in bloom.
> That's how it goes, my friend.
> The problem is not falling a captive,
> it's how to avoid surrender.³⁰

Nâzim Hikmet never surrendered either to self-pity or despair. In prison he experienced extremes of hardship and illness, but he never lost his capacity for imaginative self-identification with the sufferings of others, for example, the Japanese fishermen whose boat strayed into waters contaminated by American nuclear tests (the subject of a powerful late poem).³¹ He was also strengthened by his faith in the cause of revolution. The news of Mao's victory in China in 1949, coming at a time when he was acutely ill, is synthesised in one of his final prison poems into a visionary blend of the political and the personal:

The Armies of China Saved Me Too

I'm serving the twelfth year of my sentence;
for three months past I've been
                    just like a corpse.

I was the corpse
                    stretched on a narrow bed,
the living I was looking at him
                    warned by his deadness;
and the living I could do nothing, nothing else.
That corpse had consumed himself for nothing,
he was alone like every other corpse . . .

An old woman came and stood in the doorway,
she was my mother, she and the living I together
lifted the corpse, mother and son together.
I held him by the feet, she held him by the head,
slowly and slowly we brought him down
and threw him into the river Yangtse.

And from the North bright armies will come down.[32]

By showing that Communist revolution was possible in an agrarian peasant society, Mao's victory vindicated the cause which had inspired Hikmet's poetic vision.

Hikmet's ordeal ended in 1950, when he was released from prison after a hunger-strike and an intensive campaign by leading left-wing writers abroad. Aragon, Tzara, Sartre, Neruda and Brecht were among those who petitioned for his freedom.[33] He was released under a political amnesty, after a general election which brought Adnan Menderes to power. But within a year the political persecution of the left was renewed, and Hikmet's freedom was threatened once again. However, although he was under constant police surveillance, he was able to slip away at night from his flat in Istanbul and escape in a small boat along the Black Sea coast. He was picked up by the steamer *Plekhanov* (named after the famous Marxist theoretician) and later received a hero's welcome in Moscow. The last twelve years of his life, which fall outside the scope of this book, were spent in exile.[34] He became a prominent figure in the International Peace Movement, while remaining productive as poet and playwright. His writings were widely translated, and an edition of his collected works was issued by a Turkish-language press in Bulgaria. In Turkey itself his works have been published intermittently during periods of liberalisation in the 1960s and 1970s. Musical settings have transformed some of his poems into popular political songs, and Hikmet has become a folk hero of the left. But the subsequent crack-down by military regimes has made it at times an

arrestable offence to have books by Nâzım Hikmet on your shelf. It is a
tribute to his revolutionary commitment that the greatest poet of modern
Turkey is still feared by the authorities twenty-five years after his death. But
Nâzım Hikmet was not only the poet of the Turkish people. His poetry
expresses a more universal struggle against oppression. Hikmet himself
summed up his achievement when he wrote (in the introduction to his
collected poems):

> The roots of my poetry are in the soil of my country.
> But the branches extend to the whole world.[35]

Notes to chapter 10

1 From the poem 'Davet' in Nâzım Hikmet, *Bütün Eserleri*, ed. Ekber Babayef, 8 vols.,
   Sofia, 1967–72, Vol. 1, p. 351. Subsequent references to this edition are identified by
   BE, followed by volume and page number. Translations are by Saime Göksu, unless
   otherwise indicated. We are grateful to Taner Baybars, Richard McKane, Randy
   Blasing and Mutlu Konuk for permission to quote from the translations listed below.

2 *Nâzım Hikmet – 'Sie haben Angst vor unseren Liedern'*, ed. Mehmet Aksoy *et al.*,
   Berlin, 1977 (with parallel texts in German and Turkish).

3 See Bernard Lewis, *The Emergence of Modern Turkey*, 2nd edn, London, 1968.

4 See *The Penguin Book of Turkish Verse*, ed. Nermin Menemencioğlu, Harmondsworth, 1978, esp. Introduction.

5 'Kerem gibi', *BE*, 1, 193. For an English version of the complete poem see Nâzım
   Hikmet, *The Moscow Symphony and other poems*, tr. Taner Baybars, London, 1970,
   pp. 46–7.

6 'Otobiyografi', *BE*, 2, 327–8; English version from *Things I Didn't Know I Loved*, tr.
   Randy Blasing and Mutlu Konuk, New York, 1975, pp. 77–8.

7 See Apostolos E. Vacalopoulos, *A History of Thessaloniki*, tr. T. F. Carney, Thessaloniki, 1972.

8 See Serif Mardin, *The Genesis of Young Ottoman Thought: A Study in the Moderniz-
   ation of Turkish Political Ideas*, Princeton, 1962.

9 See Lord Kinross, *Atatürk: The Rebirth of a Nation*, London, 1964.

10 For a detailed chronology, which charts Hikmet's career against contemporary political developments, see Aksoy, *et al., ed. cit.*, pp. 10–26.

11 Quoted in Müjdat Gezen and Savaş Dinçel, *Çizgilerle Nâzım Hikmet*, Istanbul, 1978,
   p. 23.

12 'Gözlerimiz', *BE*, 1, 62.

13 'Açların Gözbebekleri', *BE*, 1, 55.

14 Nâzım Hikmet, 'Erinnerungen an Meyerhold', in Aksoy, *et al., ed. cit.*, pp. 138–40.

15 See *ibid.*, p. 92; and Ehrenburg, *Men – Years – Life*, Vol. VI, London, 1966, p. 272.

16 'Makinalaşmak', *BE*, 1, 85.

17 'Şark-Garp', *BE*, 1, 116–18; English version from Nazim Hikmet, *Selected Poems*, tr.
   Taner Baybars, London, 1967, pp. 19–20.

18 'Berkeley', *BE*, 1, 132–7; English version from *Selected Poems*, tr. Taner Baybars, pp.
   24–6.

19 Nâzım Hikmet, *The Epic of Sheik Bedreddin and other poems*, tr. Randy Blasing and
   Mutlu Konuk, New York, p. 48 (footnote).

20 'Güneşi Icenlerin Türküsü, *BE*, 1, 109–12.

21 Quoted in Gezen and Dinçel, *op. cit.*, p. 26.
22 *BE*, 2, 155–56; English version from *Penguin Book of Turkish Verse*, pp. 214–15 (tr. Richard McKane).
23 'Benerci Kendini Niçin Öldürdü', *BE*, 3, 45–143.
24 'Şeyh Bedreddin Destanı', *BE*, 3, 193–253 (p. 253); English version in *The Epic of Sheik Bedreddin and other poems*, op. cit.
25 'Taranta-Babu'ya Mektuplar', *BE*, 3, 147–92; for an English version see *Selected Poems*, tr. Taner Baybars, pp. 47–65.
26 Nâzım Hikmet, *Saat 21–22 Şiirleri*, Istanbul, 1965. A short selection of 'Poems for Piraye' is included in Nâzım Hikmet, *The Day Before Tomorrow*, tr. Taner Baybars, Oxford, 1972, pp. 40–4.
27 Nâzım Hikmet, *Kemal Tahir'e Mahpusaneden Mektuplar*, Ankara, 1968.
28 'Insan Manzaraları', *BE*, 4, 5–574 (pp. 253–6); English version from Hikmet, *Human Landscapes*, tr. Randy Blasing and Mutlu Konuk, New York, 1982, pp. 131–2.
29 'Ben Içeri Düstüğümden Beri', *BE*, 1, 353–5; English version from *Selected Poems*, tr. Taner Baybars, p. 78.
30 'Işte Böyle Laz Ismail', *BE*, 1, 378; English version from *Selected Poems*, tr. Taner Baybars, p. 82.
31 'Japon Balıkcısı', *BE*, 2, 94–6.
32 'Çin Halk Orduları Bir Gün Beni De Kurtardı', *BE*, 1, 391; English version from *Selected Poems*, tr. Taner Baybars, p. 83.
33 Tributes to Nâzım Hikmet by Louis Aragon, Pablo Neruda, Jean-Paul Sartre, Tristan Tzara and others are included in Aksoy *et al.*, ed. cit., pp. 176–99.
34 For a vivid picture of Hikmet's final years in exile, see Ehrenburg, *op. cit.*, vol. VI, pp. 270–5.
35 *BE*, 1, 5.

PART III

MASSES
AND MINORITIES

Freud
and the crowd

A new type of revolutionary crowd emerged in the course of the nineteenth century. It made its appearance first in France and Britain. In France 1848 saw the first great armed collision between workers and bourgeoisie, and the emergence of wage-earners, now organised in their own political clubs and imbued with the new ideas of socialism, as the predominant element in revolutionary crowds. In Britain the advent of Chartism marked the completion of a process in which strikes began to eclipse food riots as the typical form of social protest, and in which direct conflicts between wage-earners and employers became a common feature of urban communities. With the advance of capitalist industry this new element of civil unrest was to recur, and to spread beyond Western Europe. In France the days of the Commune in 1871 were echoed in the Syndicalist agitation that raged between 1906 and 1910. In Russia the Revolution of 1905 prefigured that of 1917. In Britain the eve of the First World War saw the ruling class threatened by industrial unrest. At the end of the War a series of left-wing uprisings shook the Central Powers. In Germany there were the Spartakist risings in Berlin in January 1919 and the month-long episode of a workers' republic in Bavaria. In Italy the years 1919–21 were a period of strikes and virtual civil war. And in the Habsburg Empire there were national and social revolutions combined; with the break-up of the Austro–Hungarian army into its component elements each of them rushed back to its separate national home, there to promote the social revolution in Vienna and Budapest, or the national revolution in Prague and Agram.

In response to these developments there began to flourish a new genre of conservative political analysis which sought to understand the workings of political life by studying the collective emotions of the masses.[1] The threat of crowd violence was not always perceived to be posed by a social group precisely identifiable as this new class of wage-earners; that apprehension was given a narrative form also by the memory of the French Revolution. Represented as a 'vile multitude' by Burke and as *la canaille* by Taine, the revolutionary crowd was treated as a disembodied abstraction and the personification of evil; it remained a shaping imaginative force in all subsequent discussion of crowd behaviour.[2] Both Taine in *Les Origines de la France contemporaine* ('The Origins of Contemporary France', 1876) and Le Bon in *La Psychologie des foules* ('The Psychology of Crowds', 1895) regarded the French Revolution as the most obvious source for investigating the rise of political irrationality, and considered the Commune to be the beginning of a return to a state of barbarism. Taine contrasted the kind of people who make up 'mobs' with the rational elite, themselves extremely few, who by implication, because they are capable of reasoning, do not take part in this kind of political activity; and he drew an ironic contrast between the *philosophes* themselves and the barbarity of the people to whom they thought their rational ideals would apply. Le Bon saw in the founding of the *Syndicats,* with their intention of totally remodelling society according to the precepts of a primitive communism, the threat of a regression to a pre-civilised state; and he went beyond Taine when he argued that the ruled have a pathological desire to submit to slavery, that this is what, in the depths of their unconscious, they actually desire. In other writers, notably in Tarde's two papers on 'The Crimes of Crowds' and 'Crowds and Sects from the Criminal Point of View', delivered to the Third Congress of 'criminal anthropologists' at Brussels in 1893, the two themes of fear of revolution and the image of the criminal were completely interwoven. In his *Instincts of the Herd in Peace and War* (1916) Trotter proposed the view that man is a 'herd animal'. And in *The Group Mind* (1920) McDougall re-echoed Le Bon when he sought to explain away politics as an instinct of submission, the satisfaction of which alone can make man happy. Part analysis and part polemic, this genre of writing studied not the anatomy of institutions but the pathology of sentiments.

Freud's *Massenpsychologie und Ich-Analyse* (1921) carries this tradition of inquiry one step further. In doing so its achievement is a paradoxical one. Freud displays no great interest in politics and never devoted himself to the study of contemporary social developments. He produced an explanation of collective phenomena deliberately conceived in terms of individual psychology; he is saying that what individuals have in common is the same set of mental characteristics, but that these characteristics are all potentially in existence, and therefore potentially discoverable, before the phenomenon of the crowd brings them into action. Yet within the terms of his purely psychological categories, he clearly foresaw the nature of Fascist mass movements and the fascination dictators exercise over their followers. His analysis is a singular blend of myopia and clairvoyance.

Freud asks the following questions: What is a mass? How does it

acquire the capacity for exercising such a decisive influence over the mental life of the individual? And what is the nature of the mental change which it forces upon the individual?[3] Two remarks of a general nature need to be made about the way in which Freud sets up the problem.

First, Freud's approach to his subject is completely mentalistic. He alerts us to this by two of his questions, one of which refers to the 'mental life', the other to the 'mental change', of the individual who forms a member of a crowd. His description of mass behaviour remains consistent with this approach. When an individual becomes part of a mass, 'his liability to affect becomes extraordinarily intensified, while his intellectual ability is markedly reduced'.[4] Since the 'feelings of the mass are always very simple and very exaggerated', it 'knows neither doubt nor uncertainty'.[5] 'If a suspicion is expressed, it is instantly changed into an incontrovertible certainty; a trace of antipathy is turned into furious hatred.'[6] A crowd is 'extraordinarily credulous', it 'has no critical faculty', and 'the improbable does not exist for it'.[7] Masses 'demand illusions', they 'constantly give what is unreal precedence over what is real; they are almost as strongly influenced by what is untrue as by what is true'.[8] A mass 'thinks in images' 'whose agreement with reality is never checked by any reasonable agency'.[9] All these remarks – which we need not dispute – are characterisations of mental states and dispositions.

Secondly, Freud's subject is the behaviour of masses. He uses the German word *Massen*; the rendering of this in the Standard Edition as 'group', and the new title *Group Psychology and the Analysis of the Ego*, are fundamentally misleading. Strachey offers an explanation for this mistranslation in a footnote. 'Group', he writes, 'is used throughout the translations as equivalent to the rather more comprehensive German "Masse". The author uses this latter word to render both McDougall's "group" and also Le Bon's "foule", which would be more naturally translated "crowd" in English'; 'for the sake of uniformity', however, ' "group" has been preferred in this case as well, and has been substituted for "crowd" even in the extracts from the English translation of Le Bon.'[10] But no real justification is given by Strachey for considering 'group' and 'mass' as equivalent terms: which in fact they are not, whether we follow common usage or dictionary definitions. The term 'mass' is defined in *Webster's* as a 'quantity of matter forming a body of indefinite shape and size, usually of relatively large size'; and we have no reason to suppose that a 'group', as distinct from a 'mass', is either of indefinite shape or of relatively large size. The German text makes it clear that Freud is talking about the phenomena which he sees as underlying the formation of large masses.[11]

It is by no means unproblematic to subsume a set of phenomena under the category of 'mass behaviour', and Freud acknowledges this. He begins with the capacious characterisation of mass psychology as concerned with 'the individual man as a member of a race, of a nation, of a caste, of a profession, of an institution, or as a component part of a crowd of people who have been organized into a mass at some particular time for some definite purpose'.[12] But he then goes on to admit that 'a number of very different structures have probably been merged under the term "mass" and may require to be distinguished'. Some descriptions of mass behaviour refer to 'masses of a short-lived character, which some passing interest has hastily agglomerated out of various sorts of individuals'; these are 'the characteristics of revolutionary masses'. Other descriptions of revolutionary behaviour refer to 'those stable masses or associations in which mankind pass their lives'; these are 'embodied in the institutions of society'.[13] This distinction, however, is one that Freud mentions without insisting upon it. What he lays special stress on, rather, is the contrast between leaderless masses and masses with leaders.[14] 'Many equals', he concludes, 'who can identify themselves with one another, and a single person superior to them all – that is the situation that we find realized in masses which are capable of subsisting.'[15] Freud's interest in this relationship is asymmetrical; he does not examine leaders as such but offers a psychology of the ruled. What he offers – and this is his originality – is an explanation of how it comes about the that men will submit willingly to the kind of rule which can only be described as totalitarian, in the specific sense of submission in the inmost recesses of the mind.

Freud belives that the bond which integrates individuals into a mass is of a libidinal nature. Earlier psychologists, McDougall, for instance, had noted the fact that men's emotions are stirred in a large group to a pitch which they never or seldom reach under other conditions, that it is a pleasurable experience for those concerned to surrender themselves unreservedly to their passions, to become merged in the group and to lose the sense of the limits of their own individuality. Freud seizes upon the most explicit and fundamental element in this observation. In both the church and the army, he says, 'the same illusion' prevails, according to which there is 'a head – in the Catholic Church Christ, in an army its Commander-in-Chief – who loves all the individuals in the mass with an equal love. Everything', he concludes, 'depends upon this illusion; if it were to be dropped, then both Church and army would dissolve, so far as the external force permitted them to.'[16] It is true that in organised social formations such as the army and the church there is either no mention of love at all between the members, or at most it is expressed in a sublimated and indirect way, through the mediation of some religious image in the love of whom the members unite and whose all-embracing love they are enjoined to imitate in their attitude towards each other. But this does not contradict the thesis Freud is advancing. For he insists just as much upon the concealed nature of the libidinal bond as upon the fact of its existence.

Since the libidinal bond between the members who make up masses is obviously not of an uninhibited sexual nature, the problem arises as to what psychological mechanisms transform primary sexual energy into feelings which hold masses together. Freud proposes that we view a mass as held together by two emotional components: the followers are bound to the leader, and they are bound to each other. They are bound to the leader because they love the leader but cannot possess him; hence they have a relationship to a leader similar to the emotional structure of unrequited love, where the loved object is identified with the ego ideal. They are bound to each other because they share a common love for a leader and a common realisation of this bond; hence they identify in their ego with the other members of the group. Thus the mechanism which transforms libido into the double bond between followers and the leader, and between the followers themselves, is the process of identification. A primary mass of the kind Freud is considering '*is a number of individuals who have put one and the same object in the place of their ego ideal and have consequently identified themselves with one another in their ego*'.[17]

This is a way of explaining what happens when whole masses of people act in concert in terms of individual as well as collective psychology. It sees leadership as a form of social contract, an erotic contract, between the leader and his following. It is a contract in that the seduced are the accomplices of the seducer as well as his victims. But Freud wants to link this explanation to a logically distinct claim about the history of the human species. According to this second claim, the relation to the leader is to be understood not just as a social contract but as a historical survival. On this view, the coerciveness and suggestibility characteristic of mass formations may 'be traced back to the fact of their origin from the primal horde'.[18] Any form of mass behaviour, therefore, is said to reactivate very early parts of humanity's 'archaic heritage'. It is a 'revival' of the behaviour characteristic of relatively small groups of people ruled over by a powerful despotic male, orginally the father. 'The leader of the mass is still the dreaded primal father; the mass still wishes to be governed by unrestricted force.'[19] Even the means by which 'artificial masses', like the church and the army, are held together is said to betray their ultimate origins in the constitution of the primal horde; the illusion in the church and the army that the leader loves all of the individuals equally and justly 'is simply an idealist remodelling of the state of affairs in the primal horde, where all of the sons knew that they were equally *persecuted* by the primal father, and *feared* him equally'.[20] Far from being a peculiarly modern phenomenon, the contract between the leader and the led is a continuing and always ineradicable possibility based on primal events.

To say of modern mass movements that they reactivate an archaic heritage is to invoke a concept of regression. But that is a potentially confusing concept. Regression as a political term may be used in two separate ways, and it is in the confusion of these two distinguishable usages that its polemical value lies. In the first instance, the implication of the term is merely that of a return to a more 'primitive' or 'barbaric' stage of development. Its opposite is 'civilised' or 'advanced'. This is the ordinary use of the term, and it implies no more than disapproval or distaste. The second sense is technical. Thus in Freud as in Le Bon, when they describe the psychology of masses as 'markedly reduced in intellectual ability', as having an 'extraordinarily intensified liability to affect', as 'extraordinarily credulous', or as 'demanding illusions', there is a new, technical appreciation of what regression is, which can be explained in psychological terms. To confuse these two senses is in the interests of conservative polemic. It is quite legitimate for Freud and Le Bon to attempt to show that in a crowd or mass certain new mental characteristics arise which can be studied scientifically. It is quite another thing to say with Le Bon that communism is a regression to a primitive form of social organisation, or with Freud that the primal horde may arise once more out of any random collection, and to assume for those statements the aura of positive proof which emanates from their technical appreciation of the primitivism which crowds display.

There is a further feature of Freud's analysis which lends itself to a more covert kind of polemic. In explaining the working of mass psychology Freud cites two examples: the Catholic Church and the army. It is undeniable that in both cases we encounter large numbers of people who do not necessarily know each other and whose behaviour together derives its cohesion from their common acceptance of ideas and leaders. But neither the church nor the army can justly be considered as instances of mass behaviour.

The army is not a mass but a hierarchically organised social group. It is an assembly of people held together by a definite structure of command and obedience: a structure which can at any time be divided into the units out of which it is built up and recombined in an orderly manner. It is of the essence of a military structure that, by means of a military command, two soliders can be separated off from a group of ten or three hundred and be inserted at some other point in the structure, without the cohesion of the whole being impaired. Sometimes this pattern of organisation disintegrates. Under the impact of a particularly vehement and sustained attack, an army may turn to flight, and it is then that we may say that it becomes a mass, a fleeing mass; in *Sword of Honour* Evelyn Waugh vividly describes such a transformation in his account of the British army's retreat from Crete. But it is precisely at such moments of disintegration that the essence of military structure is lost.

The Catholic Church, also, is not a mass but a hierarchically organised social group. It is bound together not simply by a shared love of the figure of Christ but by the behaviour of Christ's embodied representatives, his bishops and priests. Freud gives far too much weight to the mental element, the belief in Christ, and far too little to the social element, the activities of those who work within the institutions of the church. It is through the operation of their pastoral power, for instance in the sacraments of confession and communion, that bonds are forged between the community of believers and what we may call these 'secondary leaders'. The behaviour of such secondary leaders is typically quite different from that of a political mass leader. The secular politician seeks to give his followers faith in the absolute reality of the concrete, immediate moment; there are no standards of reference outside the quality of his performance, which may at its most impressive exert a narcotic effect on an audience. But the priest, however charismatically gifted, is always tied to his role as an explicit representative of a transcendent power; he may be considered to embody divine grace, but he can never claim to own or monopolise it.

There is, then, a peculiar inappropriateness about the examples cited by Freud in support of his analysis. Yet we cannot simply say that he is unaware of the distinction between the formation of masses and the organisation of hierarchical groups; indeed, he came close to making precisely such a distinction when he contrasted 'masses of a short-lived character' such as revolutionary masses, with 'stable masses' such as are embodied in 'the institutions of society'. It is not accidental that he failed to press this distinction any further, for these two different types of social cohesion are to a significant extent established by aspects of behaviour which Freud's analytical approach is neither designed nor apt to bring out into the open. Part of what constitutes the church and the army as hierarchically organised social groups is what we may call their politics of the body.

This is obviously so in the case of the army. Foucault has taught us to see the formation of modern armies as part of a wider story in which an increasingly efficient process of invigilation established a new disciplining of societies in Europe since the eighteenth century, a new 'micro-physics' of power in schools, hospitals, factories and prisons.[21] By the late eighteenth century the soldier has become something that can be made. Posture is gradually corrected and a calculated restraint runs through each part of the body, making it pliable and training it in the automatisms of habit. Recruits become accustomed to holding their heads erect; to standing upright, without bending the back; to throwing out the chest and throwing back the shoulders. A whole ensemble of regulated communications – drills, coded signs of obedience, differentiation marks of the 'value' of each person – are combined with a whole series of power processes – enclosures, surveillances, punishments. The body is manipulated, shaped, trained; it responds, obeys, becomes skilful. Discipline increases the forces of the body (in terms of their utility) while at the same time diminishing these same forces (in terms of obedience). Disciplinary coercion establishes in the body the link between an increased aptitude and an increased domination. It produces bodies that are at once practised and subjected – 'docile bodies'.

The pastoral power of the Catholic Chruch requires its own politics of the body.[22] This is provided by ritual, with its quality of sustained deliberation and solemn repetition. Whatever is liturgically performed is enacted calmly and slowly. The movements of the priests in their robes, their measured steps, the slowness of their utterances, the quiet kneeling of the congregation – all this is as it were spread out in an even and sustained way, so that, even when the rites commemoratively lament the Passion of Christ, hardly anything remains in the rite itself of the violence of grief. Then, too, communication between worshippers is strictly moderated. They do not preach to each other; and those waiting to receive communion are occupied in silent contemplation, the other communicants in front or behind or beside them being attended to less at such moments than fellow human beings in ordinary life. It is a peculiarity of the way in which the liturgy links the individual believer with the visible and invisible church that it in a sense detaches him from those actually present. This spaciousness and calm is utterly unlike, and entirely inimical to, the violent and noisy eruptions of crowd behaviour.

The politics of the body specific to the modern urban crowd is designed not to sustain but to challenge group hierarchy.[23] The primary features of its bodily composition and behaviour mark it out as an oppositional practice against a structure of social life in which hierarchy is expressed by being laid out in distances. These distances were constructed around property and occupation. Such a hierarchy prevented people from touching anyone more exalted or descending, except in appearance, to anyone lower. But in the literal closeness of the crowd, in its density, scarcely any space between bodies remains, each one is almost as close to the other as to itself, and no one is greater or better than another. This is not a quiet but a noisy closeness, and its noise expresses and is perceived as a symbolic threat. It signalled a pointed interruption in that public silence among workers which was taken by the bourgeoisie to be a sign that the urban worker was, if not content, than at least submissive; for if workers were allowed to congregate together, they might compare injustices, they might conspire and foment revolutionary intrigues. The crowd's urge to eliminate both real and symbolic distances ultimately culminates in destructiveness. But the destructiveness of the crowd is unlike that of the army, which aims at the instrumental defeat of the enemy. It is a fundamentally expressive action. It attacks privileged social spaces like houses, breaking down their vulnerable exterior of doors and windows so that anyone may enter and no one can remain protected. This destruction is an attack on social boundaries, a violation of generally acknowledged and visible distances.

Nor should we forget that the threat posed by the crowd's sudden and potentially destructive cohesion has a special urgency within the structure of the nineteenth-century and early twentieth-century city. The most recent urban spaces – all those that have been developed since the end of the Second World War, including all newer urban neighbourhoods and new towns – present an aspect quite different from the scenes which witnessed the crowd eruptions of the period 1848–1920. For most of our century, urban spaces have been systematically designed and organised to ensure that collisions and confrontations will not take place there. The characteristic feature of twentieth-century urbanism has been the highway, which is a means of keeping people apart. But the distinctive sign of nineteenth-century urbanism was the boulevard, which was a medium for bringing human forces together.[24]

The questions which, as we have seen, Freud poses at the beginning of *Massenpsychologie und Ich-Analyse* may now be reformulated as follows: What is the body of a mass like? How does it acquire the capacity for exercising such a decisive influence over the bodily life of the individual? And what is the nature of the bodily change which it forces upon the individual? What Freud tends to eliminate, from his questions, his descriptions and his explanation, is the body politics of mass psychology.

This is in some ways rather surprising. When he turned to examine the problem of mass psychology Freud was dependent neither on the reports of other theorists like Le Bon (whom he quotes at length) nor on the image of the French Revolution (which he predictably cites). The behaviour of the crowd was not and never could be an academic matter for him. Living in Vienna, he was in a position to experience both the imaginative proximity and the reality of social revolution.[25] He grew up at a time when the lower social strata were beginning to contest the power of the old elites there: out of the working class there arose socialism, out of the lower middle class and peasantry there developed Nationalist and Christian Social Parties, both virulently anti-Semitic. He witnessed the challenge issued to the liberal hegemony from the 1880s onwards by newly formed mass parties and by a wide range of popular movements such as Czech Nationalism, Pan-Germanism, and Zionism. He was able to observe at work two of the leading virtuosi of the new style of mass politics – Karl Lueger, the Christian Social Mayor of Vienna, and Georg von Schönerer, the leader of the Pan-Germans – who were the inspirers and political models of Hitler.

None of this is explicitly mentioned in *Massenpsychologie und Ich-Analyse*. But it is the landscape of experience which that work tacitly assumes. Freud belonged by conviction, by family background and by ethnic affiliation to the social group most threatened by the new mass politics: Viennese liberal Jewry. That he was conscious of this threat is made clear beyond doubt by his correspondence. This awareness took the form partly of a general apprehension regarding the behaviour of what he called 'the mob', and partly of a more particular sense of the threat posed by the anti-Semitic crowd.

Freud had a growing awareness of the brutalistic and precarious nature of social existence. In a letter to his fiancée, Martha Bernays, in August 1883, he writes that 'the mob gives vent to its appetites and we' – that is, the middle class – 'deprive ourselves. We deprive ourselves in over to maintain our integrity, we economize in our health, our capacity for enjoyment, our emotions . . . and this habit of constant suppression of natural instincts gives us our quality of refinement'. He contrasts this with the different psychological make-up of the lower classes. 'The poor people, the masses, could not survive without their thick skins and their easygoing ways . . . why should they scorn the pleasures of the moment when no other awaits them? The poor are too helpless, too exposed, to behave like us . . . "the people" judge, think and work in a manner utterly different from ourselves.' He concludes that 'there is a psychology of the common man which differs considerably from ours'.[26] In other letters from Paris dating from the period 1885–6 Freud sees a correlation between lower-class political radicalism and libidinal freedom;[27] and he was later to use the metaphor of a revolutionary mob being kept in place by a prudent upper class to illustrate the psychoanalytic view of the mind. Our mind, he suggests, might be compared with a modern state in which a mob, eager for destruction, has to be held down forcibly by a prudent and superior class. This vision of the masses as 'lower orders' living close to an archiac heritage, a heritage which all people possess but which civilised people conquer and control at great personal cost, was powerfully reanimated by events in Austria after 1918.

The civil disturbances, combined with the pessimism which the Great War had engendered, left Freud with a profound feeling of the insecurity of social existence. His son Martin, writing of this period, summarised the mood of the time thus: 'This inflation, so devastating to the foundations of middle-class life, was bad enough; but the sense of insecurity, caused by an absence of discipline which permitted the mob to get out of hand, was hardest to bear.'[28]

Although Freud's correspondence shows no detailed grasp of politics and indeed displays no great interest in politics, there is one major exception: political anti-Semitism. His very general sense of the brutalism of the 'mob' was sharpened by a more specific apprehension of the anti-Semitic crowd. In explaining his fantasy about Hannibal, he tells us that even in his schooldays

> when in the higher classes I began to understand for the first time what it meant to belong to an alien race, and anti-semitic feelings among the other boys warned me that I must take up a definite position, the figure of the semitic general rose still higher in my esteem. To my youthful mind Hannibal and Rome symbolized the conflict between the tenacity of Jewry and the organization of the Catholic church. And the increasing importance of the effects of the anti-semitic movement upon our emotional life helped to fix the thoughts and feelings of those early days.[29]

Elsewhere he tells us how in later life he watched anxiously the rise of anti-Semitism both in Austria and abroad, and how he viewed Zola, the champion of Dreyfus, as his political hero, and the anti-Semite Lueger as his *bête noire*.[30] His correspondence makes it clear that he was involved personally in the effects of Austrian anti-Semitism. In a letter from Leipzig in 1883 he describes an encounter with anti-Semitism during a train journey. Although he tries to minimise the importance of the incident, calling it a 'silly story', it is evident that he takes great pride in his refusal to be browbeaten. 'I was not in the least frightened by that mob', he writes, 'for I felt ready for a fight. I do think I held my own quite well, and used the means at my disposal quite courageously, in any case I didn't fall to their level . . . they must have noticed that I wasn't afraid.'[31] Martin Freud describes a similar incident which occurred when the Freud family was on holiday. Freud was returning to the hotel with his children, and when he was confronted by a crowd shouting anti-Semitic slogans and blocking the way, he deliberately walked towards the middle of the mob, swinging his stick, at which they dispersed and let him through.[32] Freud's courage when faced with the invasion of his home in Vienna by Nazis – Jones describes the circumstances of his departure from Vienna in detail[33] – has become proverbial. We are surely entitled, then, to consider the phenomenon of political anti-Semitism central to an understanding of Freud's political psychology.

We have seen that Freud knew directly about the behaviour of masses in at least two tangible ways, in the form of Socialist and anti-Semitic crowds. We may be permitted to suspect, on the evidence of the comparison between what is made explicit in his correspondence and what is obscured if not entirely omitted from the *Massenpsychologie,* that there is at work an element of repression when he proposes an explanation of mass psychology. In this sense Strachey's rendering of *Masse* as 'group' is not wholly untrue to the spirit of Freud's text. Although Strachey's translation of *Masse* as 'group' is not justified by the literal meaning of *Masse* in German, this mistranslation takes its cue from a break in Freud's own text and retraces the path of that break. The gap in Freud's text occurs between his description of mass psychology, where in characterising the mental disposition of masses he quotes extensively from Le Bon's discussion of crowd behaviour, and his explanation of mass psychology, where he cites the examples of two hierarchically organised social groups, the church and the army, in support of his own theory of identification. The rather uneasy coexistence of these two textual components may, I suggest, be seen as the expression of a repressive move by the author. On the analogy of his own analysis of the textual strategies typically employed in dream-work, we may see the citation of the church and the army in *Massenpsychologie* as secondary elaborations which are designed to displace attention from the behaviour of the urban crowd. The belief which we have seen Freud express to his fiancée, that the middle classes were obliged to subjugate their natural instincts by a bodily discipline unknown to the 'lower orders', doubtless helps to explain why the cardinal examples of mass movements which he singled out should be precisely those forms of social organisation in which the body is most severely disciplined. It is not in spite of his knowledge of the threat to middle-class order posed by the eruptions of the crowd, but because of that knowledge, that the threat is thus backgrounded.

The backgrounding of the urban crowd and of its characteristic politics of the body is significant less for its symptomatic autobiographical features than for more general procedural reasons. For there is at least one sense in which its mode of approach, and more particularly its unspoken strategy of exclusion, is not peculiar to Freud but is more widely encountered in a good deal of modern social thought. There is a sense in which we may read it as representative of a marked tendency within social history towards the disappearance of the human body from its object–domain.[34] This disappearance results from what may be called a strategy of etherealisation. In the case of certain more recent conceptions of social theory, for instance, the object–domain for social theory is defined in terms of what is taken to be the distinctive feature of the human species, language: this itself in turn being conceptualised by the various Wittgensteinian, hermeneutic, Structuralist and post-Structuralist schools as a set of social rules, or a text, or a system of signs, or a powerful discourse. The human body cannot be included in a domain defined in these ways, at least not when it is regarded as a material thing. It can be included only by assuming an etherealised form, as the arbitrary carrier of linguistic or quasi-linguistic meanings. For instance, elements of bodily behaviour can perform or be entailed as the signifiers of a Saussurean sign, as in Lévi-Strauss's codes of food categories or in Barthes's taxonomies of clothing codes; or, in a hermeneutic account of psychoanalysis of the kind offered by Habermas, bodily processes may function as hysterical symptoms to be deciphered like the distorted texts of the dream. In one sense it is of course particularly unjust to charge Freud with a similar analytical exclusion. For in a number of his writings he brought us to see how from earliest infancy the ego in conceptualising its activities employs mental representations that are modelled upon bodily processes and activities.[35] When he spoke of the ego as being 'first and foremost a bodily ego' one of the things he had in mind was the way in which the most basic mental acts in the infant's repertoire – acceptance, denial, and interrogation – are entertained under crude corporeal fantasies of ingestion, expulsion and penetration. But if the etherealisation of the body is at play only in a minor key when Freud insists on the presence of elementary bodily processes in mental representation, it becomes the dominant note when, in *Massenpsychologie*, he views mass behaviour as describable in terms of mental dispositions and explicable in terms of mental identification.

Notes to chapter 11

I wish to thank Ritchie Robertson for his comments on an earlier draft of this paper.

1   On this tradition see P. Rieff, 'The origins of Freud's political philosophy', *Journal of the History of Ideas*, 17, 1956, pp. 235ff., and 'Psychology and politics: the Freudian connection', *World Politics*, 7, 1954, pp. 293ff. See also the unpublished Cambridge dissertation by J. S. McClelland, 'Aspects of a political theory of mass behaviour in the work of H. Taine, G. Le Bon and S. Freud, 1870–1930'.

2   On the distinction between the French Revolutionary crowd and the nineteenth-century crowd see G. Rudé, *The Crowd in the French Revolution*, Oxford, 1959, and *The Crowd in History*, London, 1964.

3   S. Freud, *Group Psychology and the Analysis of the Ego*, Standard Edition (hereafter referred to as SE followed by volume and page number), XVIII, 72.

4   SE, XVIII, 88.

5   SE, XVIII, 78. Here and elsewhere I have substituted 'mass' for 'group', Strachey's translation of the German *Masse*.
6   SE, XVIII, 78.
7   SE, XVIII, 78.
8   SE, XVIII, 80.
9   SE, XVIII, 78.
10 SE, XVIII, 69.
11 For a discussion of mistranslation in the Standard Edition, see B. Bettelheim, *Freud and Man's Soul*, London, 1983.
12 SE, XVIII, 70
13 SE, XVIII, 83.
14 SE, XVIII, 93.
15 SE, XVIII, 121.
16 SE, XVIII, 94.
17 SE, XVIII, 116. Original emphasis.
18 SE, XVIII, 127.
19 SE, XVIII, 127.
20 SE, XVIII, 124–5. Original emphasis.
21 See M. Foucault, *Discipline and Punish*, tr. A. Sheridan, London, 1977, pp. 135ff.
22 For a suggestive comparison of ritual behaviour in Catholicism and Islam, see E. Canetti, *Crowds and Power*, tr. C. Stewart, London, 1962, pp. 168–84.
23 For many interesting remarks on bodily aspects of crowd behaviour, see Canetti, *op. cit.*
24 For a discussion of the contrast between nineteenth and twentieth-century urban spaces, see M. Berman, *All That Is Solid Melts Into Air*, New York, 1982.
25 See C. Schorske, *Fin-de-Siècle Vienna*, Cambridge, 1981, especially pp.. 116–201.
26 Quoted in W. J. McGrath, 'Freud as Hannibal: politics of the brother band', *Central European History*, 7, 1974, pp. 33–4.
27 *Ibid.*, pp. 34, 43.
28 See M. Freud, *Sigmund*, New York, 1958, p. 188.
29 S. Freud, *The Interpretation of Dreams*, SE, V, 196–7.
30 See Schorske, *op. cit.*, p. 185.
31 S. Freud, *Letters*, London, 1964, pp. 78–9.
32 M. Freud, *op. cit.*, pp. 70–1.
33 See E. Jones, *Sigmund Freud: Life and Work*, 3 vols., London, 1953–7, III, pp. 233–4, and M. Freud, *op. cit.*, pp. 205ff.
34 For an important recent critique of this aspect of social theory, with particular reference to the work of Reich and Foucault, see R. Keat, 'The human body and social theory', *Radical Philosophy*, 42, 1986, pp. 24–33.
35 Attention is drawn to this aspect of Freud's work by R. Wollheim in *The Sheep and the Ceremony*, Cambridge, 1979, and *The Thread of Life*, Cambridge, 1984, pp. 183–4, 259–61.

Nationalism and modernity: German–Jewish writers and the Zionist movement

'The idea that I am possessed with is that of restoring a political existence to my people, making them a nation again, giving them a national centre.'[1] In 1876, the year in which George Eliot published *Daniel Deronda,* these words spoken by her Jewish hero seemed merely visionary. Yet only twenty years later Theodor Herzl initiated the Zionist movement by presenting a detailed blueprint for such a national centre in *Der Judenstaat* ('The Jewish State'); in 1917 the British Government announced its support for 'the establishment in Palestine of a national home for the Jewish people'; and on 14 May 1948 the State of Israel was proclaimed.[2]

Zionism provides a dramatic instance of the success of nationalism, which is arguably one of the most widespread and influential political principles in the modern world. A person without a nationality is as inconceivable now as a person without a religion was before the Enlightenment; even someone unfortunate enough to be legally stateless retains a sense of national identity. Nationalism has inherited much of the emotional power formerly possessed by religion. While millions have died for their countries during this century's innumerable wars, international bodies like the European Community or the United Nations do not inspire such sacrifices. This became apparent in August 1914, when the various socialist parties forming the Second International responded to the outbreak of war by discarding their commitment to the world proletariat and lining up behind their respective governments.

Until recently nationalism embarrassed social theorists by refusing to fit into either liberal or Marxist schemes. Two books, however, both published in 1983, Ernest Gellner's *Nations and Nationalism* and Benedict Anderson's *Imagined Communities,* converge from different political directions on broadly the same theory.[3] In this view, the pervasiveness of nationalism can be ascribed largely to modernisation. This process could be called the transition from the village to the city, from the plough to the factory, from traditional to modern society, or, in the language of the nineteenth-century sociologist Ferdinand Tönnies, from *Gemeinschaft to Gesellschaft*.[4] By *Gemeinschaft* Tönnies means a type of society which is small-scale, close-knit, co-operative, governed by tradition, and often unified by shared religious practices. *Gesellschaft* denotes the opposite type: large-scale, urban, anonymous, competitive, and bureaucratic, in which problems are solved not by consulting tradition but by rationally working out an efficient solution, and religion has become a private matter while society as a whole is secular. Living as we do in *Gesellschaft,* we can regard it more positively than did Tönnies, who viewed with dismay the rapid industrialisation of Germany and tended to idealise the rural communities whose inhabitants were in such a hurry to leave them for Kiel or Berlin. While the size and anonymity of *Gesellschaft* can, notoriously, produce extreme loneliness, they can also offer freedoms unthinkable in the small, tightly-knit communities where everyone knows everyone else's business. Still, because of its size, *Gesellschaft* needs to furnish its members with a group identity, and since religion no longer fulfils this purpose, group identity most often comes from an officially sponsored nationalism. However the inhabitants of New York or New Delhi may differ in race and language, they can all feel themselves to be Americans or Indians.

In Germany and Austria modernisation took place with disruptive swiftness. At mid-century, Berlin and Vienna had populations of some 400,000; in 1910 and 1914 respectively, they reached two million. The anomic effects of industrialisation had to be countered by emphatic assertions of national identity, supplied in Austria by the Habsburg myth and in Germany by the official nationalism whose most prominent spokesman was the Prussian historian Heinrich von Treitschke. Modernisation met with criticism from within its heartlands, notably in the widely-read book *Rembrandt als Erzieher* ('Rembrandt as Educator', 1890) by Julius Langbehn, who complained that industrialism had degraded the Germans into a *Pöbel* (rabble) and advocated an agrarian, organic society, composed of nobility and peasantry, in which they could again become a *Volk*. Meanwhile, on the periphery of modernity, the non-German peoples belonging to the Austrian Empire were asserting their identities: both historic nations like the Poles and the Hungarians, and newly-conscious nationalities like the Slovaks and the Southern Slavs. The policy of gradually raising the subject peoples to full political participation was abandoned with the fall of the last liberal government in 1879. The conservative Count Taaffe, Prime Minister from 1879 to 1893, was credited with remarking that government in Austria consisted in keeping all national groups in a state of well-tempered dissatisfaction, and he and his successors made large concessions to the Poles and Czechs which, instead of holding the Empire

H

together, hastened its dissolution. In reaction there arose a German nationalist movement, led by Georg von Schönerer, which demanded the union of German-speaking Austria with the German Empire. Though noisy and ineffectual, Schönerer provided an inspiration for the young Hitler, who was later to carry out the Pan-German programme with a vengeance.

The decline of liberalism and the growth of conflicting nationalisms created an uncomfortable situation for German and Austrian Jews. The historian Salo Baron has argued that they owed their legal emancipation to the tendency of a modernising society to promote homogeneity among its citizens by means of liberal forms of nationalism.[5] Jews in Germany were first admitted to civil rights in 1812, and attained full emancipation throughout the Empire on its proclamation in 1871, while in Austria–Hungary they were finally freed from legal disabilities in 1867. Since liberalism allowed them to share in an expanding commercial and industrial society, and since they had no territory or language of their own, it was with liberal *Gesellschaft* that they identified and that they were identified by the illiberal nationalists who also condemned them as an alien racial group. In Germany, 1879 saw a brief but alarming outbreak of anti-Semitic agitation, in which Treitschke thundered against the 'crowd of ambitious trouser-selling youths' supposedly entering Germany from Eastern Europe, 'whose children and grandchildren', he continued, 'will one day control Germany's stock-markets and newspapers'.[6] More sustained anti-Semitism, strengthened by new radical doctrines, set in from the 1890s onwards. In Austria, Jews were especially prominent in professions such as law, medicine and journalism, and thus supplied a ready scapegoat for lower-middle-class discontent. Carefully managed anti-Semitism contributed to the appeal of the populist Mayor of Vienna, Karl Lueger, while elsewhere in the Empire Jews were identified with the German-speaking elite and thus aroused the hostility of the emergent nations.

Yet despite vulgar abuse and polemic, and even occasional trumped-up charges of ritual murder, German and Austrian anti-Semitism was hardly comparable to the continuous oppression and occasional massacres of Jews that formed official policy in Russia. After the murder of Tsar Alexander II in 1881, fanatical mobs in Kiev, Odessa and other cities killed and injured Jews and looted their property with the connivance of the police. In the Kishinev pogrom of 1903, forty-five Jews were killed, and 810 perished in twelve days of rioting in October 1905. These massacres horrified a world which had not yet conceived the possibility of genocide.

Although anti-Semitism in the German-speaking world was largely verbal, it was perceptibly increasing, and the ironies of assimilation made it almost impossible for the Jews to reply. A century earlier, Moses Mendelssohn had enabled Jews to participate in the Enlightenment by redefining them not as a nation (i.e. a self-governing theocratic community) but as practitioners of a religion which, being a private matter, need not hinder their assimilation into a basically secular society. His followers often styled themselves 'Israelites' instead of 'Jews', and called Judaism the 'Mosaic religion'. An organised response to anti-Semitic agitation therefore risked undoing Mendelssohn's work by implying that the Jews did after all constitute an unassimilated national group. The *Centralverein deutscher Staatsbürger jüdischen Glaubens* ('Union of German Citizens of the Jewish Faith'), founded in 1893 to resist anti-Semitic libels, took this risk by urging Jews to assert their Jewish identity. It never went so far as to sympathise with Zionism, and yet the logic of its position implied that ultimately the Jews could only respond effectively to nationalist hostility by developing a nationalism of their own.[7]

This conclusion was drawn by the Viennese journalist Theodor Herzl, though not directly in response to Austrian anti-Semitism. As Paris correspondent for the *Neue Freie Presse,* Herzl found in France a widespread and vocal anti-Semitism, illustrated by the popularity of Edouard Drumont's polemic *La France juive* (1885) and later by the Dreyfus trial, which he feared could spread to comparatively tolerant countries like Austria and Germany. He also felt it necessary to provide a refuge for Jews threatened by Russian pogroms. Thus Herzl was impelled into Zionism by practical considerations, and accordingly *The Jewish State* is a level-headed and far from visionary document, full of detail about capital investment, the mechanisation of agriculture, and the seven-hour working day.

Some of the impulses behind Herzl's Zionism, however, were less rational. His French experiences had convinced him that liberal democracy was being undermined by class warfare and parliamentary corruption. He expected it to be replaced by some form of monarchy, and enjoyed envisaging himself as a charismatic leader. 'I shall be the Parnell of the Jews', he told his diary.[8] His political forebodings were complemented by the cultural despair of his friend and fellow-Zionist Max Nordau, whose book *Entartung* ('Degeneration', 1893) denounced such examples of modern art as Ibsen, Wagner, and Impressionism, attributing their shortcomings to declining vitality and morbid over-refinement. Yet Nordau was deeply influenced by the *fin de siècle* pessimism which he attacked, and both he and Herzl became Zionists from the conviction that the values of European civilisation could be preserved only by founding a new society overseas.

Herzl described such a society in his novel *Altneuland* ('Old–New Land', 1902), set twenty years in the future. Although his doubts about democracy had earlier made him imagine the Jewish state as an oligarchic republic like Venice, the 'New Society', as it is called in the novel, is a democracy where the liberal values threatened in Herzl's Europe survive unimpaired. The national question which was making the Austrian Empire ungovernable has here been solved, for a Palestinian Arab, Reschid Bei, enjoys full citizenship and complete harmony with his Jewish neighbours. Herzl's vision was to be belied by events. Though Jews and Arabs did sometimes live on good terms, even before the founding of Israel the Arabs so much resented the presence of the Jewish settlers that, after violent clashes in 1921 and 1929, in 1936 they began an armed insurrection which lasted for three years.

Although the Temple at Jerusalem has been rebuilt, the 'New Society' seems otherwise to lack a distinctively Jewish culture. Herzl scorned the notion that inhabitants of the Jewish State should speak Hebrew, and thought that all the major European languages would be used, with German predominating. He was even prepared to consider establishing a provisional state on land donated by the British Government in Uganda, until territory in Palestine should become available. When the 'Uganda project' was discussed at the 1903 Zionist Congress, however, it almost split the movement. Nor is this surprising, for Zionism could never have succeeded if it had been merely a practical and philanthropical scheme. As a national movement, it had to acquire a territory and a language which linked the Jewish people to a half-historical, half-mythical past. Every society requires a myth of origin, as Régis Debray has said: society cannot 'derive from an infinite regression of cause and effect' but must have an origin which allows 'ritual repetition, the ritualization of memory, celebration, commemoration'.[9] National solidarity could only be created among such a widely-scattered people by the 'return' to Palestine and the adoption of Hebrew. In 1882 an immigrant from Russia called Eliezer Perlmann had arrived in Palestine, changed his name to Ben Yehuda, and begun reviving the Hebrew language. He made his family use it exclusively, and did not hesitate to coin new words when modern conditions required them. Among his first neologisms was the word *leumiut*, 'nationalism'.

The cultural pessimism of Herzl and Nordau illustrates yet another response to modernisation, and one shared by many writers who felt that it was relentlessly destroying the cultural and social values inherited from the past. Some distrusted political escape-routes and felt this process to be irremediable. Such global pessimism seemed confirmed by the First World War and left its most impressive monument in Spengler's *Der Untergang des Abendlandes* ('The Decline of the West', 1918–22). Literary counterparts to such jeremiads can be found in the fiction written during and after the War by Franz Kafka and Joseph Roth. Both Kafka, a Western Jew from

Prague, and Roth, an Eastern Jew from Brody near Austria's Russian frontier, felt the Jews to be out of place in modern society, but while Kafka attained a cautious sympathy with Zionism, Roth rejected it, along with every other possible substitute for the religious culture of traditional Jewish communities.

In Kafka's wartime fiction, a heroic or religious past is repeatedly contrasted with a mediocre, secular present. The penal settlement of *In der Strafkolonie* (1914) is governed by a Commandant who professes a hypocritical humanitarianism but is mainly interested in technical projects for extending the harbour, whereas his predecessor, the Old Commandant, ruled a community which found its symbolic focus in ceremonial executions where the sufferer was at last rewarded with spiritual insight. *Der neue Advokat* ('The New Advocate', 1917) shows the war-horse of Alexander the Great surviving into a banal present devoid of political leadership or spiritual guidance, and finding a niche in a lawyer's office as 'Dr Bucephalus'. *Ein altes Blatt* ('An Old Manuscript', 1917), set in a semi-mythical China, further explores the decline of authority. Bestial nomads have invaded the capital, and the Emperor has withdrawn into the interior of his palace, leaving only small shopkeepers and tradesmen to assume the impossible task of defending their country. The country doctor of *Ein Landarzt* (1917) is likewise faced with a task beyond his powers. Now that not only his patients but even their priest have lost faith in religion, the doctor is called upon to heal the wound which seems spiritual rather than medical. Being merely an overworked GP without supernatural powers, he makes an inglorious escape, only to find himself trapped in 'the frost of this most unhappy of ages'.[10]

Though set realistically in an industrial town based on Lódź, Roth's *Hotel Savoy* (1924) is also a symbolic vision of the modern world. As the poor are crowded into its upper storeys, while the rich live in comfort below, the hotel represents an unjust, hierarchical society. Its mysterious, unseen owner Kaleguropulos finally proves to be identical with the lift-attendant Ignatz, who perishes when the hotel is burnt down amid revolutionary chaos. Like Kafka's Emperor, he suggests both a discredited ruling class and an absconded God. The shallow materialism Roth attributes to the West is embodied in the brainless Jewish playboy Alexander Böhlaug, who, like Kafka's new advocate, is explicitly contrasted with Alexander the Great. Roth's favourite character is the millionaire Henry Bloomfield (originally Blumenfeld) who is not ashamed of being an Eastern Jew and returns annually from America to visit his father's grave. Against the vacuity of modern Europe, Roth sets a nostalgic piety which becomes more intense and more uncompromising as his work develops.

For Roth, the Jew was essentially a religious being, and the most genuine Jews were the orthodox Jews of Eastern Europe, who showed their intimacy with God by smoking pipes and discussing politics in the synagogue. In his long essay *Juden auf Wanderschaft* ('Jews on their Travels', 1927) Roth argued that assimilation to the secular society of the West deprived them of their distinctively religious nature and reduced them to standard modern Europeans, indistinguishable from any others. The most abject surrender to Western values had been made by the Zionists, who profaned the essence of Jewishness by building roads on the Sabbath. Their nationalism was merely a regression to a primitive level of politics which the Jews of the Diaspora had long since transcended. A Jewish state would be just another European state: 'We may have our own country, but no Jews.'[11]

Other writers shared Roth's attachment to the Eastern Jews but not his pessimism. Rejecting Herzl's notion of transplanting liberal *Gesellschaft* overseas, they thought that Eastern Jewish communities represented a form of *Gemeinschaft* which could help to provide a model for a distinctively Jewish society and culture. The restoration of *Gemeinschaft* was advocated most influentially by Martin Buber, who had been impressed by early contact with Eastern Jews. Westerners like Herzl knew little about the millions of Yiddish-speaking Jews who inhabited communities dominated by orthodox religious tradition in German-occupied Poland, in the Austrian province of Galicia, and in the Pale of Settlement, an area stretching from the Baltic to the Black Sea, to which Russian Jews had been confined by a decree of 1791. As a boy, Buber spent his summers in Galicia, where he encountered Hasidism, the eighteenth-century spiritual movement still widespread among Eastern Jews. Hasidic religious leaders were credited with miraculous powers; their office was hereditary, and some maintained courts thronged with adherents and petitioners. To the young Buber, such a figure and his court seemed to embody authority and communal feeling. 'As I saw the Rabbi stride through the ranks of waiting people', he later recalled, 'I had the feeling: "Leader" [*Führer*], and when I saw the Hasidim dancing with the Torah, I had the feeling: "Community" [*Gemeinschaft*].'[12]

Buber made a close study of Hasidism and published several collections of tales and parables by Hasidic masters, retold in flowery German, which he thought attested the creativity that the Jews had possessed before assimilation to Western society had degraded them into superficial imitators of its rationalism and commercialism. Modern Western Jews had to rediscover their roots by acknowledging the ties of blood linking them spiritually to their people. In 1902 Buber declared: 'A people [*Volk*] is held together by primary elements: its blood, its fate – in so far as it rests on the development of the blood – and the power that creates culture – in so far as this is determined by the unique character arising from the blood.'[13] To become a *Volk*, the Jews would need to recover their ancient language and regain contact with the soil of Palestine, where Jewish creativity had flourished in Old Testament times.

Buber's version of nationalism, which appealed to many young Zionists in Central Europe before and during the First World War, owed its popularity to having taken over the radical critique of modernity from German nationalism and substituting a Jewish *Volk* for Langbehn's Germanic *Volk*. More generally, Buber's romantic view of the Eastern Jews, and his exaltation of irrational blood-consciousness, make him a representative of modern primitivism – i.e. the nostalgia of highly cultivated denizens of modernity for the vital energy and warm community life which they attribute to the social and/or racial groups least affected by modernisation. (Delacroix's Arabs, Melville's and Gauguin's Polynesians, and Lawrence's Mexicans come to mind as examples.) Nor was he alone in calling modern Jews' attention to their Old Testament heritage. In her *Hebräische Balladen* ('Hebrew Ballads', 1913) Else Lasker-Schüler deplored the degeneracy of modern Jews ('Der Fels wird morsch, / Dem ich entspringe / Und meine Gotteslieder singe'[14] – 'The rock is crumbling from which I spring and sing my songs of God') and conjured up a noble, warlike past populated by Abraham and Isaac, Moses and Joshua. Like Mendelssohn's followers a century earlier, she was in search of an alternative image of the Jew; but whereas they called themselves 'Israelites', she once declared that the word 'Jew' should be abolished and replaced by 'Hebrew'.

Roth likewise wanted to reject Western stereotypes of the Jew, and, though an opponent of Zionism, he resembled Buber in idealising the Eastern Jews. He does this most blatantly in his novel *Hiob* (1930), where the modern Job, a Russian Jew named Mendel Singer, has his faith tested by a succession of misfortunes, including the insanity of his daughter, the death of his wife, and the loss of two sons fighting on opposite sides in the First World War; but finally Mendel's faith is restored by the reappearance of his third son, supposedly a congenital idiot, as an adult who is not only cured but famous as a conductor. The suspicious ease with which Roth's initial realism modulates into the fairytale manner of the conclusion indicates how far that realism was already blurred by nostalgia. While in his best novel, *Radetzkymarsch* ('The Radetzky March', 1932), Roth's nostalgia for the Habsburg Empire is laced with sceptical insight into its hollowness, no such perceptions are allowed to qualify the Jewish idyll of *Hiob*.

At the outbreak of the First World War many German and Austrian Zionists, under Buber's influence, were more concerned with theories of *Gemeinschaft* than with the practicalities of building a new society. But the war made them look to the present and future instead of to the past, by forcing them into contact with Eastern Jews in the flesh instead of on paper. The Russian offensives compelled thousands of Galician Jews to flee to Vienna, Prague and Berlin, where the local Zionists had to look after them. Other Zionists encountered traditional Jewish communities while serving on the Eastern front. The Berlin Zionist Sammy Gronemann, whose military service introduced him to the great Jewish community of Vilna (now Vilnius), responded by juxtaposing Eastern and Western Jews in his excellent and unjustly forgotten novel *Tohuwabohu* ('Topsy-Turvydom', 1920). Here Heinz Lehnsen (formerly Levysohn), a Berlin Jew whose family is as assimilated as the snobbery of their Gentile neighbours will permit, is first embarrassed and then intrigued by discovering that his first cousin, Jossel Schlenker, is an Eastern Jew from Russia. Cut off from Europeans by his Jewishness and from Eastern Jews by his baptism, Heinz is finally left wondering whether to follow his cousin into the Zionist movement, with its aim of constructing a community embracing all Jews.

Meanwhile, the settlers in Palestine had already proved that such a community was possible. The second *aliya* ('ascent', i.e. immigration), comprising some six thousand people, arrived there between 1905 and 1914. Farming in swampy, malarial land with an uncongenial climate was desperately hard, and many were disheartened enough to leave, but the remainder showed by their example that the Jew need not be a trader or an intellectual. One of them, A. D. Gordon, developed a Tolstoyan doctrine of self-realisation through physical labour, which also appealed to Zionists busy caring for refugees in Central Europe. Buber's romantic nationalism gave way to a Socialist concern for building a co-operative society which would incorporate the communal spirit Zionists had found among Eastern Jews.

This new mood attracted Kafka to Zionism. Before the war he had been repelled by the bookish rhetoric of the Prague Zionists, but had responded warmly to the Galician actors who performed Yiddish plays in an obscure Prague café. For some time afterwards his interest in Jewish matters was so much eclipsed by personal concerns that in 1913, after Max Brod had tried to convert him to Zionism, he wrote in his diary: 'What have I in common with Jews? I have hardly anything in common with myself.'[15] But when Zionists assumed practical responsibilities, he warmed to them and urged his fiancée, Felice Bauer, to help in a Zionist-run home for Jewish refugees in Berlin, though he also told her cryptically: 'Zionism is only the entry to something more important.'[16] The meaning of this utterance can be inferred from his story *Beim Bau der chinesischen Mauer* ('Building the Great Wall of China', 1917). The newly completed wall is a *Volkswerk,* the work of the people, built by 'two great armies of labour, the eastern and the western'[17] – an evident allusion to the co-operation of Eastern and Western Jews in Zionism. This task has created among them a solidarity that Kafka describes in terms reminiscent of Buber: 'Unity! Unity! Shoulder to shoulder, a ring of brothers, a current of blood no longer confined within the narrow circulation of one body, but sweetly rolling and yet ever returning throughout the endless leagues of China' (*ibid.,* p. 142). When, however, the narrator inquires about the purpose of the wall, he finds no adequate practical explanation: the supposed enemy, the Northern nomads, are too remote to threaten most of China, while the system of piecemeal building means that the wall is wholly useless until it is complete. He concludes that the building of the wall corresponds less to a practical imperative than to a timeless, supernatural reality: 'the high command has existed from all eternity, and the decision to build the wall likewise'. Kafka is implying that a nation's solidarity needs a religious, not merely a utilitarian basis.

Gordon's doctrine of labour, combined with Buber's nationalism, appealed still more strongly to the young Arnold Zweig. Like Gronemann, he encountered traditional Jewish communities in German-occupied Lithuania in 1917–18, and in *Das ostjüdische Antlitz* ('The Face of the Eastern Jew', 1920) he celebrates their simplicity and religiosity in language that sometimes anticipates Joseph Roth. But while evoking their medieval heritage, and contrasting them with the materialistic Western Jew, Zweig asks whether they are really doomed to be swept away by the tide of Western civilisation. Practical Zionism, he suggests, can satisfy the Socialist idealism of younger Eastern Jews while preserving the best features of their fathers' way of life in a close-knit *Volksgemeinschaft* relying on manual labour rather than commerce. In the essay *Das neue Kanaan* ('The New Canaan', 1924), Zweig speculates on how the return to Palestine will change the Jewish character. He foresees a new form of democracy, based on the primacy of labour, with no need for the doctrinaire application of what he calls 'Marx's universal medicine'.[18] Even more grandiose anticipations are worked into Zweig's first and best novel, *Der Streit um den Sergeanten Grischa* ('The Dispute over Sergeant Grisha', 1927), where the Russian prisoner-of-war Grischa is unjustly executed on 2 November 1917, the day of the Balfour Declaration. A conversation among Grischa's would-be rescuers on Germany's increasing power and declining morality is juxtaposed with a scene in which pious Eastern Jews, who have just finished studying their way through the entire Talmud, discuss the apocalyptic significance of the Declaration and speculate that the sixth world-empire, that of the Germans and Russians, is about to give place to a seventh and last, in which a Jew will again reign in Jerusalem.

Zweig first visited Palestine in the spring of 1932 and collected material for his novel *De Vriendt kehrt heim* ('De Vriendt Comes Home', 1932), which examines in precise and prescient detail the effect of Palestinian conditions on the Jewish character. It is based on recent events, including the murder of an orthodox anti-Zionist, de Haan, in 1924, and the week-long riots occasioned in August 1929 by the Arabs' reluctance to let Jews pray at the Wailing Wall. Zweig's democratic humanism is apparent in the very form of the novel. Though the main centre of consciousness is an English police officer (testimony to Zweig's lifelong Anglophilia), the narrative enters the minds of all parties – Arabs, Jewish anti-Zionists, and Zionists of diverse factions – to give each a hearing. Two oppositions illuminate Zweig's conception of the changing Jewish character. The main one is between two extremists: the anti-Zionist de Vriendt, who is criticised for ignoring reality, and his assassin, Mendel Glass, a settler newly arrived from Russia, who admires the militarist Vladimir Jabotinsky (the mentor, in reality, of Menachem Begin). But two minor characters are also significantly contrasted: the intellectual, over-sensitive German Jew, Heinrich Klopfer, and the Russian Jew, Eli Saamen, who is described as full of vital energy. Both Glass and Saamen have learnt from their Russian oppressors how to fight. Glass witnessed pogroms as a child in the Ukraine, while in Minsk, at the age of thirteen, Saamen saved the lives of some fellow-Jews by shooting a pogromist at close range. What Zweig condemns in Glass is not violence as such, but wanton terrorism; and as Glass (somewhat implausibly) repents of his crime and decides to expiate it by working in a potash plant on the Dead Sea, he will clearly continue to serve Zionism. The aptly-named Saamen ('seed') stands for organised self-defence, and his Russian experience proves its worth in the 1929 riots, during which, according to Zweig, the 133 Jews killed were mostly defenceless old people, while the 116 Arab victims died fighting against superior opponents. 'The victims, these Jews, have changed completely. They strike back, and their blows have an impact.'[19] Since Zweig died in 1968, his lifetime included three of the four wars (1948, 1956, 1967 and 1973) in which a vastly outnumbered Israel has fought for its very existence; but as early as 1932 he had realised that, for better or worse, a new type of Jew, cultivating toughness and efficiency, was coming into existence to defend the new Jewish community.

Ironically, these changes in the Jewish character helped to make Zweig unhappy in Palestine when he emigrated there after Hitler's seizure of power in 1933. Middle-class professional people found it hard enough to make a living in a small, impoverished country where the bulk of the population were manual workers. Moreover, his failure to learn Hebrew made it almost impossible for Zweig to publish or to become part of the community. In any case, German Jews like himself could not discard their ingrained allegiance to the German language and culture. But because of this, and because they had come to Palestine more from necessity than commitment, they were regarded by the settlers with some derision. It is perhaps not surprising that Zweig, surrounded by Jews of a disturbingly new type, left Israel in July 1948 and took up a dignified though solitary life as the grand old man of East German literature. Else Lasker-Schüler, obliged to stay in Palestine from 1939 till her death in 1945, felt similarly out of place. German poetry about ancient Israel had few readers in Hebrew-speaking modern Palestine. Poor, frail and neglected, she wrote in her poem 'Jerusalem': 'Ich wandele wie durch Mausoleen – / Versteint ist unsere Heilige Stadt' ('I walk as though through mausoleums – our Holy City is turned to stone', *Sämtliche Gedichte*, p. 196).

Zweig's and Lasker-Schüler's discomfort in Palestine shows how rapidly Zionism was creating a new society. But this achievement has always been exposed to internal as well as external threats. The founding of Israel can serve to mark a change in the character of Zionism as a nationalist movement: having begun as a reaction against aspects of modernisation, it has gradually become an instrument of modernisation, cultivating the desert, creating modern cities, and enabling Jews from diverse backgrounds (North Africa, the Middle East, the Soviet Union, Ethiopia) to be absorbed into a modern *Gesellschaft*. The danger still exists that this absorption may be too successful and transform the Jewish state, as Roth feared, into just another Western society with a homogeneous and characterless population. But there is a much more pressing danger that this absorptive process may stop short of the Palestinian Arabs who form a substantial (around fifteen per cent) and increasing minority of the population of Israel. Nationalism contains a fatal dialectic whereby the oppressed become oppressors in their turn. To escape from this trap will require an exceptional outlay of such rare qualities as goodwill, far-sightedness, and enlightened self-interest.

Notes to chapter 12

I should like to thank Professor J. B. Segal for his detailed and helpful comments on a draft of this paper.

1   George Eliot, *Daniel Deronda*, Harmondsworth, 1967, p. 875.
2   See Walter Laqueur, *A History of Zionism*, London, 1972.
3   See Benedict Anderson, *Imagined Communities*, London, 1983; Ernest Gellner, *Nations and Nationalism*, Oxford, 1983, and *Thought and Change*, London, 1964; Elie Kedourie, *Nationalism*, 3rd edn., London, 1966; Hugh Seton-Watson, *Nations and States*, London, 1977; Anthony D. Smith, *Theories of Nationalism*, 2nd edn., London, 1983.
4   See Ferdinand Tönnies, *Community and Society (Gemeinschaft und Gesellschaft)*, tr. Charles P. Loomis, East Lansing, Mich., 1957; first published 1887.
5   Salo W. Baron, 'Newer approaches to Jewish emancipation', *Diogenes*, 29, spring 1960, pp. 56–81.
6   Heinrich von Treitschke, 'Unsere Aussichten', *Preußische Jahrbücher*, 44, 1879, pp. 559–76 (pp. 572–3). Cf. Fritz Stern, *The Politics of Cultural Despair*, Berkeley and Los Angeles, 1961; P. G. J. Pulzer, *The Rise of Political Anti-Semitism in Germany and Austria*, New York, 1964.
7   See Michael A. Meyer, *The Origins of the Modern Jew*, Detroit, 1967; Ismar Schorsch, *Jewish Reactions to German Anti-Semitism, 1870–1914*, New York, 1972. For literary surveys, see Klara P. Carmely, *Das Identitätsproblem jüdischer Autoren im deutschen Sprachraum von der Jahrhundertwende bis zu Hitler*, Königstein/Ts., 1981; Gunter E. Grimm and Hans-Peter Bayerdörfer (eds.), *Im Zeichen Hiobs: Jüdische Schriftsteller und deutsche Literatur im 20. Jahrhundert*, Königstein/Ts., 1985.
8   *The Complete Diaries of Theodor Herzl*, tr. Harry Zohn, 5 vols., New York, 1960, I, p. 248. Cf. Carl E. Schorske, *Fin-de-siècle Vienna*, Cambridge, 1981, pp. 146–75.
9   Régis Debray, 'Marxism and the national question', *New Left Review*, 105, September–October 1977, pp. 25–41 (p. 27). Cf. Eric Hobsbawm and Terence Ranger (eds.), *The Invention of Tradition*, Cambridge, 1983.
10 Franz Kafka, *In the Penal Settlement*, tr. Willa and Edwin Muir, London, 1949, p. 139. Cf. Giuliano Baioni, *Kafka: letteratura ed ebraismo*, Turin, 1984; Ritchie Robertson, *Kafka: Judaism, Politics, and Literature*, Oxford, 1985.
11 'Juden auf Wanderschaft' in Joseph Roth, *Werke*, ed. Hermann Kesten, 2nd edn., 4 vols., Cologne, 1975–6, III, pp. 291–369 (p. 309). Cf. David Bronsen, *Joseph Roth: Eine Biographie*, Cologne, 1974; Claudio Magris, *Weit von wo: Verlorene Welt des Ostjudentums*, tr. Jutta Prasse, Vienna, 1974.
12 'Mein Weg zum Chassidismus' in Martin Buber, *Werke*, 3 vols., Munich, 1962–4, III, pp. 959–73 (p. 964). Cf. Steven E. Aschheim, *Brothers and Strangers: The East European Jew in German and German Jewish Consciousness, 1800–1923*, Madison, Wis., 1982, esp. pp. 121–38.
13 Buber, *Die jüdische Bewegung*, 2 vols., Berlin, 1920, I, pp. 68–9.
14 'Mein Volk', in Else Lasker-Schüler, *Sämtliche Gedichte*, Munich, 1977, p. 171. Cf. Sigrid Bauschinger, *Else Lasker-Schüler: Ihr Werk und ihre Zeit*, Heidelberg, 1980.
15 Kafka, *Tagebücher 1910–1923*, ed. Max Brod, Frankfurt, 1951, p. 350.
16 Kafka, *Briefe an Felice*, ed. Erich Heller and Jürgen Born, Frankfurt, 1967, p. 675.
17 Kafka, *The Great Wall of China*, tr. Willa and Edwin Muir, London, 1933, p. 136.
18 'Das neue Kanaan' in Arnold Zweig, *Herkunft und Zukunft*, Vienna, 1929, pp. 165–224 (p. 209).
19 Zweig, *De Vriendt kehrt heim*, Berlin, 1960, p. 217. Cf. David R. Midgley, *Arnold Zweig: Zu Werk und Wandlung 1927–1948*, Königstein/Ts., 1980; Manuel Wiznitzer, *Arnold Zweig: Das Leben eines deutsch-jüdischen Schriftstellers*, Königstein/Ts., 1983.

Elitism and the cult
of the popular in Spain

The Spanish Civil War rivals the First World War for the impact it had on literature, particularly in the English-speaking world. One consequence of this is that the culture of Spain in the early twentieth century tends to be viewed rather externally. What follows is an account of the intellectual debates among Spanish authors during the years which led up to the Civil War.

In the 1920s and early 1930s Spanish avant-garde activity was at its most intense and, artistically speaking, at its best. Earlier than 1920 we can find manifestos of the *vanguardia*. They are local, such as Alomar's Futurist manifesto of 1909[1] or Ramón Gómez de la Serna's *Proclama futurista a los españoles* (1910),[2] and they are international, such as Marinetti's 1910 *Proclama futurista a los españoles*.[3] The beginnings of *ultraísmo* and *creacionismo* are there from 1917 onwards, and European avant-garde activity is echoed and presaged in the work of *modernistas* and *ultraístas,* in Diego, Huidobro, Larrea, Guillermo de Torre. But one has to wait until well into the 1920s to find those works which now stand as the major achievements of the Spanish avant-garde, namely the works of the Generation of '27.[4]

When compared with the avant-garde in other European countries, the Generation of '27 are notable for being what their label suggests: a generation, not a closed group or a school, but a collection of individuals with pronounced literary talents, friends, mutual critics, who adopted the new modes of expression as and when they found them most appropriate to their own artistic or personal needs. At the same time as the Spanish avant-garde is marked by a lack of emphasis on ideological 'correctness' in art, it is marked equally by the high level of individualism. There is also a pronounced awareness of Hispanic literary and artistic traditions of previous centuries.

While individualism and nonconformism coupled with individual respect for tradition characterise the avant-garde in its artistic manifestations, on the theoretical front there is a further *doble vertiente* which is equally pronounced: a duality so pronounced that it appears to constitute a paradox. For the major theorist of the decade, Ortega, is profoundly aristocratic and elitist. Yet, while many of the works of the Spanish avant-garde can be found to be consistent with his principles, there is another line of aesthetic (and eventually social and political) theory, which is apparently non-elitist: the valuation of popular literary forms and traditions.

Ortega's essay, *La deshumanización del arte* (1925) argues strongly for purity of form, for absolute standards, for a view of aesthetic enjoyment which is separate from, not dependent on, any process of emotional identification with the content of a work of art. Most important of all for Ortega is the question of how the 'new art' functions: modern art is divisive, and it divides people along a sociological line:

> The new art has the masses against it, and will always have them against it. It is essentially unpopular: more than this: it is anti-popular . . . It divides [the public] into two sections, one of them extremely small, made up of the small number of people who are favourable towards it; the other, the hostile majority, of the countless people who are against it.[5]

The new art has the function it does because of an underlying intention, that it should seek out only those who are able to understand or appreciate it. When Ortega refers to the masses who dislike the new art, he has in mind not the lower classes, not an urban proletariat (a concept which is of reduced relevance given the predominantly rural nature of Spain even in the 1920s), but the bourgeoisie, as he goes on to reveal: 'The art of the young, no sooner is it seen than it obliges the average citizen to feel himself to be just what he is: Mr Average Citizen, a being unfitted for receiving the sacrament of art, blind and deaf to all pure beauty.'[6] Within this essay Ortega does something which is confusing for our purpose. He interchanges, rather indiscriminately, the terms *masas, pueblo* (people) and bourgeoisie, always using them to indicate the section of modern society which, in its reaction of dislike to modern art, shows itself to be philistine. This failure to categorise and differentiate is unhelpful in an argument which purports to be sociological. As we shall see below, however, the sociological distinctions are not always easy to preserve in the face of a tendency to linguistic blurring within the Spanish language.

The nature of this art which is so alienating to the bourgeoisie is, briefly, one in which form has primacy over content to an almost absolute degree. Ortega conveys this by the simple example of a garden viewed through a window. If we look through the window we will see the garden, and not the glass of the window-pane. But if we make an effort, we can disregard the garden and concentrate on the pane. The two operations are separate and incompatible. And for Ortega, the majority of onlookers or spectators are those who cannot focus on the glass (the form) but pass through it to 'wallow in the human reality alluded to in the work of art'.[7] Ortega offers a list of seven tendencies as delimitations of the new art. They emphasise the aristocratic appeal, the non-committed (non-transcendental) nature of the art, and define it as the property of the leisured and educated elite. New art tends:

> (1) to the dehumanization of art (2) to the avoidance of living forms (3) to ensuring that the work of art is nothing but a work of art (4) to considering art as a game, and nothing more (5) to an essential irony (6) to avoiding all falsity, and thus aspiring to scrupulous realization, and (7) to considering art as an object which has no transcendence.[8]

In retrospect, we can see that Ortega's delineation of the norms of the new art is remarkably accurate in relation to Spanish art (and in particular, poetry) as it was in 1924, and as it was to be in the poetry produced by the Generation of '27. The status of the essay was, however, prophetic rather than prescriptive.

The elitism at the heart of Ortega's ideas in the *Deshumanización* is not restricted to this essay on aesthetics, but is a constant factor in his work, and has its place in a more general European context. The valuation of those individuals in a society who are exacting in the standards they set themselves, and who became the core of a sort of existential elite, is part of a general valuation of the aspiration to individual excellence. Effort is at the base of the *razón vital* which Ortega had outlined in *El tema de nuestro tiempo* ('The theme of our time', 1923), and personal effort combined with a sense of responsibility is what distinguishes the members of the 'natural' nobility, as opposed to the masses whose rising was to be posited as a tremendous threat to a healthy and developing society in *La rebelión de las masas* ('The Revolt of the Masses', 1930). Here the concept of 'nobility' is defined: 'the select man is not a petulant being who believes himself to be superior to others, but one who requires more of himself than others do'.[9] The prime threat of the masses for Ortega is not on the political level of the acquisition and inappropriate exercise of power. It is, significantly, the threat that is posed to the individual's realisation of his own potential.[10]

Ortega's intended audience for these elitist ideas was a relatively catholic one. *La rebelión de las masas,* which appeared in book form in 1930, had orginally been published in article form in 1926 in *El Sol,* a leading Madrid daily paper.[11] *La deshumanización del arte* itself was published orginally in *El Sol* in January and February of 1924. Ortega was attempting to disseminate the concept of elitism, and his was a voice that was unlikely to be ignored: he was recognised as an intellectual leader in Spain even in the 1920s.

Within intellectual life in Spain in this period, Ortega's status as an individual was paralleled by that of an academic insitution, the *Institución Libre de Enseñanza*. Founded in 1875 by Giner de los Ríos, the aims of the *Institución* were extremely liberal and progressive. To assert, however, that it was different from Ortega in essential philosophy, is to pass over the fact that Ortega's aims were to contribute to social advance, and equally, to pass over some of the elitist beliefs that lay behind the liberal aims of the *Institución*.

In a speech to open the 1880–1 session at the Institución by Giner de los Ríos, there is a prefiguration of Ortega's belief in the need for exceptional individuals to combat the spread of mediocrity. The need to form such individuals was necessary in the face of spiritual, moral and physical degeneration in Spain. The education of individuals was to be realised in a context where 'the idolatry of the levelling out of the "great" masses has reached its height'.[12]

That the individual is valued, and must be formed, in the face of the threat of the masses, was clear to the Director of the *Institución* in 1880, and fifty years later, to Ortega. It is not fortuitous, perhaps, that these statements of the Director of the Institución should have been collected and re-published in 1926, the year in which the *Rebelión* began public appearance.

The more one looks at the stated aims of the *Institución,* the more pronounced this sense of an elite-forming body becomes. And yet it is an elite with the same good intentions that could be imputed to Ortega's *minoría*: educating others, spearheading the diffusion of culture. The *Institución* and Ortega are not promoting ivory-tower elitist views, but are full of a sense of responsibility to the more general social context from which they spring. Where they part company with later 'committed' writers of the 1930s is in their refusal to compromise their own standards, ideals, language, artistic values, in order to overcome practical issues of politics and communication with the masses. The extent of their influence both then and now suggests that it is not necessary to do so. The high standards of personal culture are those of Leavis and Eliot,[13] but Ortega is a good example of how high standards need not result in unintelligibility. His prose is stretching, lucid and imaginative, but is neither opaque nor full of obvious condescension to the reader.

While *La deshumanización* provided a central resumé of belief for the Spanish avant-garde (a resumé which spoke of what was happening in art, and not of what should happen), a similarly central contribution to avant-garde activity came via the *Institución*. In 1910 it had founded an elitist offshoot at university level, the *Residencia de Estudiantes,* and in the 1920s this came to provide an intellectual forum for the most prominent writers, thinkers and artists of the avant-garde in Spain, and was a means of establishing vital cultural contacts between Spain and the rest of Europe.[14] In a declaration outlining the aims of the Residencia, we can see a practical response to Ortega's concern with the *minoría*. Interestingly, the word *vanguardia,* which we have tended to consider so far only in its artistic context, now appears as an intellectual, and perhaps even a spiritual or moral or even civic vanguard, which would be heir to the Generation of 1898:

> The Residencia believes, in the way one believes in life itself, in a future spiritual mission of Spain, and desires to cultivate within it, by a process of mutual exaltation, those individual and civic virtues necessary to achieve with dignity the historic destiny of the race. The sight of the miseries of our country created a generation of pessimists who, although they lived amid negation and scepticism, had the courage to denounce all the false activities that ordered Spanish life. This same generation now continues its manly activity, rising – energetic and united – impelled by faith which will lead it to recover what is lost, whatever the effort necessary to do so may be. In the vanguard of this group of believers and fighters we want to take our place . . .[15]

If we look briefly at the ethos implied in this statement, we can begin to see how it is that political attitudes of the avant-garde are puzzling. They are puzzling because of apparently contradictory attitudes within the body of those proposing revolutionary alternatives in art and politics. They are united, or one could argue, they are blurred, by a common belief in excellence, and by the definition of those qualities which are necessary to the attainment of that excellence. The reference to 'manly activity' is, in a serious vein, not far from *machista* or right-wing proclamations such as those of the Futurists, but at the same time the millenarial tone is one which will be characteristic of writers of left-wing periodicals in the 1930s. This ambiguity can, however, be resolved. The characteristic which unites members of the avant-garde, whether they are of the 1920s or 1930s, whether they are propounders of an elite that will lead because of its excellence, or of a revolution that will overthrow a stale and complacent bourgeois order, is their sense of being leaders.

   In Spain there is a transition: from elitism in the 1920s, to an increasing democratism or fraternalism in the 1930s. It is partly this transition which resolves the paradox of the *doble vertiente* and diminishes some of the contradictions within the Spanish avant-garde. The political factor responsible for the shift is the change from Primo de Rivera's eccentric right-wing dictatorship of 1923–30 to the more open politics of the Second Republic of 1931–6 and the Civil War (1936–9). The Generation of '27, from which the best-known Spanish *vanguardistas* come, is also known as the 'generation of the dictatorship', and produced works which combined artistic experimentation with a vital rediscovery of strong cultural traditions. With the coming of the Second Republic, it became possible to write with greater freedom, but what is curious is that, with the exception of works such as *El público* (1931) by Lorca, the result was not a significant increase in artistic experimentation.

One of the constants in *vanguardista* interest, the *pueblo*, is partly responsible for the transition to committed and less experimental writing. Furthermore, the double meaning of the word *pueblo* allows us to see how it was of value to the elite, and then championed by the Republicans. In political contexts, where questions of class arise, *pueblo* may well be used to signify 'lower classes', although with distinctly more favourable connotations than the term *clase baja,* or *clase obrera* ('lower class' or 'working class'). But *pueblo* is also used for 'nation' and with connotations of warmth and humanity, as in 'people' or the German *Volk*. The definitions offered by María Moliner in the *Diccionario del uso del español* (Madrid, 1967) express in both cases a warm, if paternalistic, view of the *pueblo*: 'group of people of the same race, who form a community, whether their occupation of a country is stable or not' and 'those people who live modestly by their labour, generally physical labour'. The patronisation implicit in 'modestly' recurs in the definition offered by the dictionary of the Spanish Royal Academy, 'gente común y humilde de una población' ('the common and humble people of a population').

In the 1920s, in the wake of Unamuno and his desire to find the 'soul' of Spain, the spiritual and cultural connotations of the *pueblo* were emphasised and political ones were reduced. Unamuno, by positing the value of *intrahistoria* in contrast to the shallow political values of *historia,* had disassociated the *pueblo* from the dirty business of practical politics.[16] History, for Unamuno, was the surface level of dates and political events, whereas *intrahistoria* provided depth. It was the complete life of the nation which continued despite and throughout those events, and was contained within the *pueblo*. In literary terms, his view of the *pueblo* could be considered to be expressed in the Spanish phenomenon of *poesía popular,* a distinct poetic trend which occurred alongside the more obvious avant-garde movements of *poesía pura* and Surrealism.

Poesía popular is not a simple imitation of the poetic forms deemed to belong to the *pueblo*, but a use of those forms with all the sophistication of the twentieth century. Bécquer had championed the notion of the *pueblo* as the best source of poetry in his introduction to *La Soledad* by Ferrán. He contrasted a polished and decorative poetry with another, the 'popular': 'another which is natural, brief, dry, that springs from the soul like an electric spark, that wounds the feelings with a word and flees . . .'[17]. In his description or definition of popular poetry, Bécquer permitted himself the luxury of imprecision, and yet his terms constitute one of the best encapsulations of the essence of poetry. He locates this 'best poetry' within the *pueblo*, meaning here the group of people Unamuno was to envisage as the nameless (and for that reason worthy) protagonists of *intrahistoria*. But he did not enter into discussions of whether the traditional *romances* were composed by the group of people implied by the second meaning of *pueblo* (people who live humbly by manual labour), or whether they were fragments of poems produced by more *culto* ('cultured', or 'educated') poets.

Those who wrote *poesía popular* in the 1920s were, at the time of writing, relatively unconcerned with a political definition of that type of poetry. They used *poesía popular* to denote poetic style, but not to declare social commitment. The principal examples of *poesía popular* come from Alberti and Lorca.[18] The writing of *poesía popular* did not take place in a cultural vacuum. Lorca's poetic contribution, for example, was produced against a background of lectures on poetry which display his erudition, and his grasp (in the case of the *cante jondo*) of the sophisticated forms of poetry classified as *popular*. His lectures on the *cante jondo* and *las nanas infantiles* (children's lullabies) are the work of one who is a member of a cultural elite, but who also has attachment on an intuitive and emotional level to the value of these forms of poetry for the individual.[19] In particular, the lecture on the children's lullabies stresses the role of poetry to which one is exposed in early childhood in colouring and forming the personality, and in connecting man to essential and vital elements of his nation's folkloric riches. In 'Las nanas infantiles' Lorca spoke of journeys through Spain in which he sought 'los elementos vivos, perdurables, donde no se hiela el minuto, que viven un tembloroso presente' ('the vital, lasting elements, where time does not freeze, where a trembling present is lived'). For Lorca, the *pueblo* was not a rejected group of the underpriviledged, but a source of immense worth: nursemaids and servants had for a long time been carrying out the invaluable task of 'taking the ballad, the song and the story to the houses of the aristocracy and the bourgeoisie'.[20]

In the notion of the *pueblo* as the part of society which conserved vital forms one can see the beginnings of a political view, but in the early stages that diffuse political function consists of the *pueblo* safeguarding things of value which others (such as aware and educated elites) might cull and polish. The change which occurs in the 1930s is that the *pueblo* ceases to be regarded solely as a repository of things of cultural value, and becomes a section of society whose cause must be espoused. The elite, therefore, becomes defender of the *pueblo,* rather than just being that part of society which alone is able to see the true value of the *pueblo.*

Nineteen-thirty was a significant year. The regime of the dictator Primo de Rivera was foundering, and notable shifts occurred in the practice of literature. The literature of the 1920s, with the *Deshumanización* at the centre, had concentrated on art for itself, on 'pure' poetry, on essential qualities of art to be enjoyed by a select minority specially gifted for aesthetic creativity and enjoyment. The case of the *minoría* and its excellence was argued in the face of an undifferentiated and, for the artists concerned, boorish and ineducable bourgeoisie.[21] (An exception was the poet Emilio Prado, who showed a practical level of commitment by his enterprise in 1929 of teaching fishermen to read.)

The year 1930 marks the date when this attitude becomes inadequate as a response to political circumstance. This may have been acceptable while the dictatorship of Primo de Rivera precluded outspoken political comment, but not so after his departure. Thus when Ledesma Ramos published an article in July of that year condemning avant-garde artists, he invoked explicitly political criteria: 'The avant-garde was not interested in politics . . . the avant-garde did not even undertake a subversion of out-moded moral values, restricting its revolutionary activity to customs (!!) with talk of sport and the adoption of American fashions in dress . . .'.[22] César Vallejo, speaking from a politically committed position, rejected the intuitive, elusive notion of poetry that had inspired Bécquer: 'Art should be controlled by reason . . . It should always work for political propaganda, and work with clear, preconceived ideas, and should even develop a thesis, like an algebraic theorem.'[23] Arconada, a novelist who was to become prominent in the 1930s (but whose work today is little read) was more forgiving about the avant-garde writers than Ledesma Ramos, and said of the avant-garde that it was an army which had changed the front it was fighting on.[24] More concisely, the Caba brothers referred to the change imposed on artists in sartorial terms: 1934 had made aesthetes exchange their sports shirt for the worker's smock.[25] Lorca was to express this more dramatically on the eve of the Civil War: 'This concept of art for art's sake is something which would be cruel if it had not the good fortune to be vulgar . . . At this dramatic time, the artist must weep and laugh with his people. We must leave behind our bunch of lilies and enter the mud, waist-deep, to help those who want the lilies.'[26]

The calls for commitment were backed by works: not just words, but literary deeds. Through the years of the Second Republic and especially during the Civil War, specifically '*pueblo*-directed' works were produced, the way in which the *pueblo* was now treated bearing out most clearly the shift in attitude to literature and elitism brought by the move towards the change of political regime in 1931. Instead of interest in the *pueblo* consisting, as it had done in the case of *poesía popular,* of the location and distillation of the best elements of the country's traditional literature, the aim of artists now became predominantly to use the simplest forms of that literature in order to treat the *pueblo*'s specific (social and political) problems and concerns.[27]

There were also new journals of tremendous importance in showing the state of artistic and political awareness in the 1930s. Most notable were *Octubre* (June 1933–April 1934), the *Hoja literaria* (1932–July 1933) and *Caballo verde para la poesía* ('Green horse for poetry' 1935–6), founded by Neruda, and including in the prologue to the first number his famous declaration 'Sobre una poesía sin pureza' ('On poetry without purity').

Of the journals, *Octubre* declared most emphatically its commitment, not to an ill-defined *pueblo* that could be confused with the *pueblo* of Bécquer or Unamuno, a term which evaded the issues of class-division and class-awareness, but to a clearly defined proletariat that contrasted with a ruling, or oppressive minority. The first number of *Octubre* carried an epigraph entitled 'Por una literatura proletaria' ('For a proletarian literature'), and opened:

> Comrade workers of town and country: the review OCTOBER is not a review for minorities. It is a review for you. You should take part in it, sending us your impressions from the country and the factory, pieces of criticism, biographies, articles of struggle, drawings. Bourgeois culture is in its death-throes, incapable of creating new values. The only legitimate heirs of all the science, literature and art that have gathered through the centuries are the workers of town and country.[28]

Later, *Hora de España* ('Hour of Spain'), which began publication in January 1937 and continued until November 1938, carried on the tradition expressed by its subtitle: 'Ensayos, poesía, crítica al servicio de la causa popular' ('Essays, poetry, criticism in the service of the popular cause'). But its actual level shows that it is directed to, and appropriate for, intellectuals dedicated to the *pueblo,* rather than to the *pueblo* itself.

The epigraph to *Octubre* reveals the fundamental shift from the 1920s to the 1930s. The talk of minorities and of groups opposed to those minorities continues Ortega's awareness of divisions within society, and is equal with him in the condemnation of a flabby and mediocre bourgeoisie.

For Ortega, as for the *institucionistas,* the solution had been in sharper differentiation between groups. The elite then separated out were to rise above the level of bourgeois mediocrity and to carry out the true function of a minority. This was a double function of both acting as guardians of the culture that belonged to the nation and then as the medium for spreading that culture to the whole nation. For those committed to the Left in the turbulent years of the Second Republic and the Civil War, the solution was to recognise differentiation, and for the elite of intellectuals to then go below the bourgeoisie to unite with the proletariat. It constituted an accentuated version of the return to the *pueblo* for ultimate values that is evident in the Romantics and the Generation of 1898, but now also required that admiration and compassion be accompanied by practical commitment.

In the new atmosphere of political commitment, the *pueblo* acquired a further, and sharply focused role. For many writers of the 1930s, the *pueblo* was now conceived of as the new, indeed now the only possible form of public for art: 'the people, who are the ones possessed of a virgin sensibility for the plastic qualities of the stage and for high-level emotion'.[29] In 1934 Lorca reiterated the artistic capacities of the *pueblo,* and, by aligning it with the elite, envisaged a paradoxical synthesis of the two extremes:

> There is one audience we have found not to be fond of us: the middle one, the bourgeoisie, frivolous and given to materialism. Our audience, those who really grasp what the art of the theatre is about, is found at the two extremes: the cultured classes, university educated, or formed by their own artistic or intellectual cultural life, or the people, of the poorest and roughest, uncontaminated, virgin, a fertile ground for all the tremors of grief and the turns and reversals of grace.[30]

Lorca's own successful tours with *La Barraca* in 1932 were proof that art could indeed be taken down to the people, and without concession.

On a theoretical front, Manuel Abril showed how there did not have to be a division between the emphatic elitism of the 1920s, and in particular the elitism of Ortega's *Deshumanización,* and the level of concern for the *pueblo* that we find in the 1930s. He gave a committed and alternative gloss to the seven tendencies of the new art proposed by Ortega in 1925, and showed not just the positive potential of the essay, but also, in some measure, how it need not reduce art to the creation of sterile beauty. The first two tendencies, juxtaposed against Ortega's celebrated precepts, are:

> 1. The dehumanization of art (and we would say to the superhumanization of the human, including art. When art is too human it takes it down to man's level; the dehumanization of art raises man, and superhumanizes him to make him merge with Man). 2. To avoid living forms (and we would say – to

vitalize new forms. The new art does not seek what is alive to give life to itself, but itself gives life, since it creates).[31]

The Civil War was a cataclysmic interruption to the cultural and political developments we have been considering, although the movement to write literature for the *pueblo* continued with marked vitality throughout the course of the war.[32] It is difficult to estimate how far the censorship imposed by Franco after the war is responsible for the fact that the average Spaniard today is unlikely to be able to quote, or even to recognise, Civil War ballads, although most will be able to recite snatches of the 'Romance sonámbulo' ('Sleepwalking ballad') or 'La casada infiel' ('The faithless wife') from Lorca's *Romancero gitano* of the apparently elitist 1920s. Whether the cause of this is political or artistic, the aftermath of the Civil War brought a bitter disillusionment with the failure of both political revolution and artistic experiment. Luis Cernuda gives us a telling example of this disillusionment. His work *Los placeres prohibidos* ('Forbidden pleasures', 1931) had been Surrealist, and a gesture of social rebellion and nonconformism. And he had shown his allegiance to left-wing politics and consequent cultural commitment by his collaboration with the review *Hora de España* between the spring of 1937 and February 1938, although at all times he had maintained high literary and cultural standards. Nonetheless, with what is perhaps a mixture of bitterness and the wisdom of hindsight, in 1941 he expressed grave doubts about the relationship of the *pueblo* and poetry:

> It cannot be denied that poetry, whether popular or not, is above all a mental thing, and it seems materially impossible that since the *pueblo* is the social class with fewest opportunities to indulge in mental activity not through indifference but because of its sad condition of ignorance and servitude that the other two classes of society impose upon it, it should be the only class to provide an audience for poetry.

We may have doubts about his view of the potential for survival of *poesía popular,* but it is eloquent as a gauge of cultural mood in the aftermath of war: 'popular poetry, since it is addressed not so much to man in general, but to man as a member of a human caste, has, as a work of art, a fairly precarious basis'.[33] What is precarious is also, however, profoundly human.

Notes to chapter 13

1 Gabriel Alomar, 'Futurismo', *Renacimiento*, September–November 1907, reprinted in Paul Ilie, *Documents of the Spanish Vanguard,* University of North Carolina Studies in

the Romance Languages and Literatures, No. 78, Chapel Hill/Valencia, 1969, pp. 35–72.

2 *Prometeo*, No. 20, Madrid, 1910, reprinted in Jaime Brihuega, *Manifiestos, proclamas, panfletos y textos doctrinales: Las vanguardias artísticas en España. 1910–1931*, Madrid, 1979, pp. 89–90.

3 *Prometeo*, No. 20, 1910, reprinted in Paul Ilie, *op. cit.*, pp. 73–80.

4 Alberti, *Marinero en tierra* (1924), *La amante* (1926), *El alba del alhelí* (1927), *Cal y canto* (1929, written 1926–7), *Sobre los ángeles* (1929), *Sermones y moradas* (1930); Cernuda, *Perfil del aire* (1927), *Egloga, Elegía, Oda* (1927), *Un río un amor* (1929), *Los placeres prohibidos* (1931); Guillén, *Cántico* (1926); Salinas, *Presagios* (1924), *Víspera del gozo* (1926, written 1924–6), *Seguro azar* (1929), *Fábula y signo* (1931); García Lorca, *Libro de poemas* (1921), *Poema del cante jondo* (1922), *Canciones* (1924), *Romancero gitano* (1924–7), *El público* (1931), *Poeta en Nueva York* (1931).

5 José Ortega y Gasset, *La deshumanización del arte*, *Obras completas*, 12 vols., 4th edn, Madrid, 1957–83, III, p. 354.

6 Ortega, *Obras completas*, III, p. 355.

7 Ortega, *Obras completas*, III, pp. 357–8.

8 Ortega, *Obras completas*, III, p. 360.

9 Ortega, *Obras completas*, II, p. 146.

10 Ortega, *Obras completas*, II, p. 132.

11 Ortega had already expressed ideas about the masses in *España invertebrada* ('Invertebrate Spain', 1921), in a 1926 article in *El Sol*, 'Masas', and in two lectures given in Buenos Aires in 1928. Footnote by Ortega to *La Rebelión . . ., Obras completas*, II, p. 143.

12 Francisco Giner de los Ríos, 'Fragmentos del discurso inaugural de la *Institución Libre de Enseñanza*, en el curso de 1880–81', *En el cincuentenario de la Institución Libre de Enseñanza*, by Francisco Giner de los Ríos and others, Madrid, 1926, pp. 29–30.

13 See F. R. Leavis, *Mass Civilisation and Minority Culture*, Cambridge, 1930, and T. S. Eliot, *Notes towards the definition of Culture*, London, 1948.

14 A full list of major figures influenced by the *Institución* and its offshoots is given in Pablo Corbalán, *Informaciones*, suplemento de las artes y las letras del 13 de mayo de 1976, p. 2, cited by Elías Díaz, 'La Institución de la España del Nacional-Catolicismo', *En el centenario de la Institución Libre de Enseñanza*, by I. Avery, L. Bretsch, R. F. Brown and others (Associatión Española de Mujeres Universitarias), Madrid, 1977, p. 149.

15 Alberto Jiménez Fraud, *La Residencia de Estudiantes. Visita a Maquiavelo*, Barcelona, 1972, pp. 62–3. The section on the *Residencia* was a pamphlet originally produced by Jiménez Fraud in 1925 to celebrate the fiftieth anniversary of the *Residencia*.

16 See *En torno al casticismo*, ('The Authentic Tradition'), in *Obras completas*, ed. Escelicer, 9 vols, Madrid, 1966–71, ed. Manual García Blanco, I, pp. 775–856.

17 Gustavo Adolfo Bécquer, *Obras completas*, prologue by J. García Pérez, Barcelona, 1966, p. 539.

18 Rafael Alberti, *Marinero en tierra* ('Sailor on shore', 1924), *La amante* ('The lover', 1926), *El alba del alhelí* ('The dawn of the gillyflower', 1927); Lorca, *Poema del cante jondo* ('Deep song', 1922), *Canciones* ('Songs', 1924), *Romancero gitano* ('Gypsy ballads', 1924–7). See also Francisco Villalón, *Romances del 800* ('Ballads of 800', 1927).

19 'El cante jondo: primitivo canto andaluz' ('Deep song: primitive Andalusian song', 1922), 'Arquitectura del cante jondo' ('Architecture of deep song', 1931 – an amplification of the 1922 lecture), 'Las nanas infantiles' ('Children's lullabies', 1928, repeated at Vassar, 1930). These lectures are reproduced in García Lorca, *Obras completas*, 2 vols., Madrid, 1980, I, pp. 1003–24, 1025–30, 1073–91. See also *Federico García Lorca, 'Deep song' and other prose*, ed. and tr. Christopher Maurer, London/Boston,

1980, p. 138, and Norman C. Miller, *García Lorca's 'Poema del cante jondo'*, London, 1978, pp. 69–70.

20 'Las nanas infantiles', *Obras completas*, I, p. 1077. The labour of conservation of the vital forms of the *pueblo* was similarly to be stressed by Alberti in 'La poesía popular en la lírica española contemporánea', a lecture delivered in Berlin in 1932, collected in *Prosas encontradas*, ed. Robert Marrast, Madrid, 1970, pp. 87–103 (p. 87).

21 Valle-Inclán had protested about the impossibility of educating the bourgeoisie as early as 1915: in *La Esfera*, 6 March 1915, quoted in Dru Dougherty, 'Talía convulsa: la crisis teatral de los años 20', *Dos ensayos sobre teatro español de los 20*, by R. Lima and D. Dougherty, Murcia, 1984, p. 113. There are many points in this study which are illuminating on the atmosphere of opinion on public, *pueblo* and culture in the 1920s in Spain.

22 Ramiro Ledesma Ramos, *La gaceta literaria*, No. 85, 1 July 1930, p. 4 (the ironic exclamation marks are in the original). This forms part of a set of responses to a literary survey which began on 1 June 1930 in No. 83 of *La gaceta literaria* and which displays the new critical and political edges of artists. Much of the survey is quoted in J. Cano Ballesta, *La poesía pura española entre pureza y revolución (1930–1936)*, Madrid, 1972, pp. 45–6. See also Antonio Espina, '¿Incompatible? La cultura y el espíritu proletario', *El Sol*, 18 July 1930, p. 1, quoted in J. Cano Ballesta, *op. cit.*, p. 103.

23 César Vallejo, 'Un reportaje en Rusia. Vladimir Maiakovski', *Bolívar*, No. 6, 15 April 1930, p. 7, quoted in J. Cano Ballesta, *op. cit.*, p. 97. Interestingly, the greater part of Vallejo's own poetry is of high quality, and without doubt 'difficult' in all the best traditions of the 1920s.

24 Arconada's reply to the survey on 'Meaning and range of the avant-garde', *La gaceta literaria*, No. 84, 15 June 1930. Quoted in Brigitte Magnien, 'La obra de César María Arconada, de la "deshumanización" al compromiso: La novela rural bajo la segunda república', *Sociedad, política y cultura en la España de los siglos XIX–XX*, ed. M. Tuñon de Lara, Madrid, 1973, p. 337.

25 Carlos and Pedro Caba, 'La rehumanización del arte', *Eco. Revista de España*, No. 9, October 1934, pp. 1–5, quoted in J. Cano Ballesta, *op. cit.*, p. 157.

26 Interview with Bagaría, 1936, in Lorca, *Obras completas*, II, p. 1124. Oddly, Valle-Inclán, on this question, had been in the vanguard of the Spanish vanguard, and in 1920, in response to the question 'What is art?' had replied sharply, defining art as narrowly and exclusively as Ortega was to do, and immediately rejecting it as an indecent activity given the politics of his time: 'Art is a game – the supreme game – and its norms are dictated by numerical whimsy . . . Art is . . . form.' When asked what artists should do he replied: 'Not art. We should not be involved with Art now because to play in the times we have now is immoral, it's playing foul. First we must secure social justice.' Interview with Cipriano Rivas-Cherif, *La internacional*, 3 September 1920, quoted in M. Tuñon de Lara, *Medio siglo de cultura española*, p. 205.

27 Individual works produced in this context include Rafael Alberti, *Con los zapatos puestos tengo que morir: elegía cívica* ('I shall die with my shoes on: civic ode', January 1930), *El poeta en la calle* ('Poet in the street', 1931–6), *De un momento a otro* ('From one moment to the next', 1934–9), *Capital de la gloria* ('Capital of glory', 1936–8); Emilio Prados, *Calendario incompleto del pan y del pescado* ('Unfinished daybook of bread and fish', 1933); César Vallejo, *El Tungsteno* ('Tungsten' – a novel, 1931).

28 Epigraph to *Octubre*, No. 1, Madrid, June–July 1933, p. 21.

29 José Díaz Fernández, *El nuevo romanticismo*, Madrid, 1930, p. 207.

30 'Teatro para el pueblo', interview of Lorca by Octavio Ramírez, *La Nación*, Buenos Aires, 28 January 1934, p. 3 reprinted in María Laffranque, 'Federico García: encore trois textes oubliés', *Bulletin Hispanique*, 59, 1957, pp. 62–71 (p. 65).

31 Manuel Abril, 'Sobre la deshumanización del arte', *Cruz y raya*, 15 May 1933, pp. 162–3.

by a touch and leaves the stage red with blood and flames. In this unsubtle early instance we find some of the themes that will reappear in other forms elsewhere. Firstly, the energy, generated supposedly by the freedom to speak a new truth, which appears as anger, narcissism and violence; secondly, the universalisation of an exclusively male heterosexual voice; thirdly, the rudimentary attribution of power and voice to the woman, which is then immediately stifled. It is given to the 'Frau' to express sexuality as a deadly, vampiric exchange; but in the end, as in so much male writing, she dies and the man survives. His strength is premised no longer on her weakness or submissiveness, but on an absorption of her strength and a murder of her body.

Apollinaire is a much more central avant-garde writer, whose work is often both lyrical and obscure. But he is also quite capable of exploiting a crude and obvious metaphor, as in the war poetry, where he celebrates the 'virilités du siècle où nous sommes / O canons' ('virilities of our century, o cannons') or, again, 'Deux fusants / Rose éclatement / Comme deux seins que l'on dégrafe /Tendent leurs bouts insolemment / IL SUT AIMER / quelle épitaphe' ('Two time-shells / Pink bursting / Like two breasts as you undo her dress / Put forth their tips insolently / HE KNEW HOW TO LOVE / what an epitaph'). Here, as more relentlessly in his pornographic prose-writing, guns and bayonets are phalluses, shells are breasts exposed by a great lover, and war is a 'multiplication de l'amour' ('multiplication of love').[2] What does Apollinaire mean in this context by 'love'? Perhaps that odd combination of sentimentality typical of the soldier far away from his girl-next-door with the aggression that characterises all his waking thoughts at the front. What this mixture composes is a frank heroism of sexuality as violence.

My third text in this opening category is the editorial of the 1 October 1927 edition of the Surrealist journal *La Révolution surréaliste*, a polemic signed alphabetically by the group of thirty-two men. Entitled 'Hands off love', it concerns Charlie Chaplin, whose wife was suing him for divorce. The argument interestingly both exploits and inverts the Chaplin persona: no 'little man' but a shining genius, he is self-evidently strong and good, yet mercilessly exploited by a small-minded harridan. 'The married woman's condition', the Surrealists write, 'is a profession like any other, from the day the women claims as her due an alimentary and sexual ration. A man who is obliged by law to live with just one woman has no choice but to share his habits with that woman, to put himself at her mercy.'[3] Marriage here becomes a trap for men: one would think that wives could rape husbands. In counterbalance to Chaplin the genius, his wife (who has refused fellatio and objected to having an abortion) becomes a demon, and the state, if it censures his conduct, will inflict on him '*a tax*! imposed above all on his genius, and which even tends to dispossess him of that genius, or at least to discredit its very precious expression' (253). The use of the phallus against the woman has become the quintessential expression of genius. Chaplin 'is in truth the defender of love, purely and uniquely' (257), for 'genius serves to signify moral truth to the whole world, a truth which universal stupidity obscures and tries to nullify' (259). The demon wife ('nasty, hateful little bourgeoise' (259)) is the figurehead of this universal mediocrity. The article ends with a flourish of scarcely unconventional (and surely not ironic) courtesy to Chaplin – 'we are your humble servants' (259) – which contrasts nicely with the vituperative and vulgar terms used to describe Mrs Chaplin.

In these three examples, then, a dual value is invoked: the freedom to write with new frankness and energy about sexual desire and a new valuation of sexuality as supremely powerful, heroic and creative. But these impressive claims are vitiated by the concomitant nastiness and narrowness of the women's role in each: universalised as the beast from the unconscious, the target or attributes of cannonry, or the great bourgeois bitch, she serves as the victim of discourse whose modernist expansion often means little more than the inclusion, in 'respectable' publication, of schoolboy fantasy or adolescent slang. Most importantly, the energy characteristic of the erotics of avant-garde writing can be seen here as something less creative than destructive. The heroic phallus is an instrument not of love, but of rape.

I want to turn next to some rather different writings by the Surrealists for, as Roger Shattuck points out, the two most lasting legacies of Surrealism are in the domains of 'love and laughter' (though tellingly, his examples of the latter include the aphorisms: 'Beat your mother while she's still young' and 'One good mistress deserves another'). By 'love' Shattuck means not 'convulsive' desire, but something altogether more sentimental: 'against the background of misogyny, homosexuality, Don Juanism, and masculine confraternalism that formed part of the heritage from decadence and symbolism, the surrealist group takes on the status of modern troubadours. Their love poetry earns the comparison . . . they found in passionate devotion to a single woman over a long period of time the surest means of liberating desire. And for "desire" read "imagination".'[4] Liberation again; desire again; but whose? What does the lady do while her troubadour liberates himself? A lot of standing around, it seems.

Two illustrations from *La Révolution surréaliste* endorse this impression. The first (December 1924) portrays a woman murderer – an active female, one might presume – with, grouped around her picture, photographs of the Surrealists and their heroes; the whole thing is surmounted by a quotation from Baudelaire: 'Woman is the being who projects the greatest shadow or the greatest light into our dreams.' Thus, imprisoned in a cage of men all claiming to dream her, the powerful woman is transformed into a passive Muse. In the twelfth edition of the journal, a similar structure shows sixteen photographs of the Surrealist group, neatly collared-and-tied and with eyes closed, while in the centre a modest nude forms the missing noun in the sentence 'I do not see the . . . hidden in the forest' (Fig. 7). Here the woman has become merely a vocable, the image that completes their dream-like sentence: unseen, unnamed, yet standing presenting her unshielded body to the consumption of closed eyes. If in the Surrealists' love-poetry, then, we have the devoted husband that Charlie Chaplin was not, the wife is still kept indoors, confined to the palace or to the poem.

To see how this happens, let us look at two of the most famous modern French love-poems. The first, by Eluard, is 'L'Amoureuse':

> Elle est debout sur mes paupières
> Et ses cheveux sont dans les miens,
> Elle a la forme de mes mains,
> Elle a la couleur de mes yeux,
> Elle s'engloutit dans mon ombre
> Comme une pierre sur le ciel.
>
> Elle a toujours les yeux ouverts
> Et ne me laisse pas dormir.
> Ses rêves en pleine lumière
> Font s'évaporer les soleils,
> Me font rire, pleurer et rire,
> Parler sans avoir rien à dire.
>
> (She is standing on my eyelids
> And her hair is in my hair,
> She has the shape of my hands,
> She has the colour of my eyes,
> She is swallowed up in my shadow
> Like a stone upon the sky.
>
> Her eyes are always open
> And she does not let me sleep.
> Her dreams in broad daylight
> Make suns go up in steam,
> Make me laugh, weep and laugh,
> Speak without having anything to say.)

This, like the Kokoschka drama (though in every other way they differ),

(7) 'I do not see the . . . hidden in the forest'

presents sexuality as an intense interchange. The woman has the colour of the man's eyes, her wide-open eyes stop him sleeping, her dreams give him something to express. But two things make it clear that this togetherness is not true exchange, but always a one-way current. The first is the title: meaning primarily 'the woman in love', it suggests that the poem would be about her feelings; instead it is about his experience of being loved, what her love does for him. Secondly, the pronouns in the text are strangely reversed: unlike most love-poems, this is not between an 'I' and a 'you'. The female agent of the poem is a third-person, distanced figure, while the 'I', naturally central because of its logical appeal to reader-identification, is the object of her action. 'She' keeps her eyes open, 'I' shut mine (I must do, if she is to stand on my eyelids), but 'I' am the one who speaks without having anything to say: 'my' poem comes out of her silence.

Of course much of the appeal of this poem (like all writing depicting a love-relationship with a woman) lies in the fantasy, common to readers of both sexes, of unstinting nourishment received from the mother's body. For this reason, both male and female readers find it seductive. But it also works through a more covert fantasy: the woman seems the subject, the giver, but actually she is voiceless and actless, a myth. Woman readers may here, as in many other mythologising writings, find the portrait flattering, even powerful; but such readers end like the woman in the poem: ordered by a male fantasy, static and entrapped.

The second poem, by Breton, from *L'Union libre* (1931), also universalises the female body. In this long poem, physical parts of 'ma femme' are listed and given many surrealistic images as attributes. The presentation of the beloved's beauty seems as devotedly perverted as in Shakespeare's 'My mistress's eyes are nothing like the sun'. Here are the opening lines:

> Ma femme à la chevelure de feu de bois
> Aux pensées d'éclairs de chaleur
> A la taille de sablier
> Ma femme à la taille de loutre entre les dents du tigre
> Ma femme à la bouche de cocarde et de bouquet d'étoiles de dernière
>   grandeur
> Aux dents d'empreintes de souris blanche sur la terre blanche
> A la langue d'ambre et de verre frottés

> (My wife with her hair of fire of wood
> Her thoughts of lightning-flashes of warmth
> With her hour-glass figure
> My wife with her figure like an otter between the teeth of a tiger
> My wife with her rosette mouth like a bouquet of the largest stars
> With her teeth like the prints of a white mouse on the white earth
> With her tongue of the friction of amber and glass)

The poem goes on in this way, evoking such parts as the woman's shoulders, armpits, breasts, buttocks, sex organ and eyes. When read aloud on an American tour, it caused much surrealistic unease. But the love-poem genre is undermined in ways perhaps less under the author's control. The female body here exists purely as a series of *disjecta membra,* paraded before the reader by the poet. Mme Breton, demure or expressionless in her front-row seat, is not so much displaying her intimate charms as being dismembered; her belly and eyes no longer belong to a living person, but on a dissecting-table. Scarcely less incongruous is the heavy proprietorial term 'ma femme': Breton's irony is surely underlaid by a frank advertisement of ownership. These parts of a body are his, not hers.

In *Nadja* (1928), a woman is again central – the fey, ethereal girl of the streets whose self-chosen name is the book's title. But once again, a woman's place is in the dream. Breton opens his lengthy preamble with the arresting question: 'Who am I? If, exceptionally, I were to resort to an adage, could not the solution be after all to discover whom I "haunt"?'[5] Not 'who is Nadja?', not 'who inhabits my mind?'; but 'who am I?', 'whose mind do I inhabit?'. The value of Nadja is that she points Breton to himself. Shattuck blithely describes it thus: 'Breton implies that he discovers in Nadja his familiar spirit, an intercessor with whom he finally identifies himself at the moment she vacates her personality to enter an asylum' (28). Actually the narrator tires of Nadja – this is shown by his curiously aggressive reaction when she talks of occasions in her past when she was beaten or humiliated by men. He notes (in the terms exactly of a Romantic confessional novel): 'she was so touching at that moment, making no attempt to thwart the decision I had taken; on the contrary, her tears lent her the strength to urge me to carry it out!' (135). Here, when it is convenient, modernity is abandoned for a good old-fashioned renunciation scene. Some months later, the narrator learns Nadja has been locked up in a mental home; he inveighs for a few pages against psychiatry, and no more is heard of Nadja.

In these three texts, we have seen the tender troubadour revealed as a subtle exploiter. In its sentimentality as well as its violence, then, avant-garde writing bases its liberation on a further entrapment of the woman. The apparent mutuality of love rests on a mythologisation that is simply self-serving. Nadja only seems a spontaneous surrealist; actually, before even being locked up, she is sapped of her autonomy by her author's apparent tribute.

A third instance of the masculine bias of much avant-garde writing can be found in its key genre of the manifesto. Compare the following for two nicely nuanced versions of the phallic imagery of the new euphoria. The first comes from the first Futurist Manifesto (*Le Figaro*, 20 February 1909), where Marinetti lists the ten aims of the Movement; among them are 'the habit of energy and fearlessness', 'aggressive action, a feverish insomnia, the racer's stride, the mortal leap, the punch and the slap'. He praises 'a new beauty, the beauty of speed . . . we want to hymn the man at the wheel, who hurls the lance of his spirit across the Earth'. Or again, 'admiring an old picture is the same as pouring our sensibility into a funerary urn instead of hurling it far off, in violent spasms of action and creation'.[6] In this polemic, then, the new creativity is viewed on the model of a male orgasm, and everything beautiful or valuable gleams with the phallic narcissism of the new man.

William Wees describes how Vorticism grew out of an English reaction against Italian Futurism, adding: 'Vorticist sensibilities divided according to their preference for an aesthetic based on Boccioni's "in-and-out of a piston in a cylinder", or Hulme's "hard clean surface of a piston rod".'[7] What is a new element in the latter is a choice of stasis, a certain fastidious dislike of the obvious sexual image of thrust, and a marked preference for the 'clean'. The clean is very different from the 'pure' which Marinetti identifies with speed: equally founded in a misogynistic loathing for the viscous, it nevertheless points, with a sort of British modesty, to niceness rather than aggression.

What Hulme hated was Romanticism, defined thus: 'the concepts that are right and proper in their own sphere are spread over, and so mess up, falsify and blur the clear outlines of human experience. It is like pouring a pot of treacle over the dinner table. Romanticism then, and this is the best definition I can give of it, is spilt religion.'[8] Against the 'sloppiness which doesn't consider that a poem is a poem unless it is moaning or whining about something or other' (126), he advocates 'a poem which is all dry and hard, a properly classical poem' (126). The Vorticist manifesto (*Blast* 1, 1914) cursed 'sentimental Gallic gush', in another tellingly 'liquid' image. The machine was supremely an invention of the English – 'they are the inventors of this bareness and hardness' (Wees, 177) – and their chosen emblem of the Vortex, which one might think of as a concave, feminine alternative to the Futurist phallus, becomes another, less vulgar, explosion, 'stable and self-contained, yet suggesting whirling concentrations of energy' (Wees, 177). With the sexual politics of these two groups go the Fascist sympathies that unite them, as Judy Davies and Michael Long show in Chapters 5 and 6; as Woolf pointed out in *Three Guineas* (1938), this connection is not gratuitous.

So where does the light dawn in this gloomy scene? In my concluding section, I shall focus on two authors and two themes which together point the way to a different sexual politics and a genuinely fresh alternative to the posturing we have just seen. The two authors are Proust and Virginia Woolf, and the themes are secrecy and the trivial.

It is no coincidence that neither of these writers is a heterosexual man. Their interest in breaking down the stereotyping of patriarchal discourse is obvious. But neither favoured polemical writing just because of the rightness or personal urgency of the cause. We know that when Proust met Gide he insisted on the importance of not saying 'I', and Woolf, in *A Room of One's Own* (1929), argues against the special pleading of however good a cause.

In Proust's massive work *A la recherche du temps perdu* (*Remembrance of Things Past*, 1954), we find a theme of secrecy logically extrapolated from the circumstances of the homosexual, whose desire was not simply despised but illegal. It is the secret existence of homosexual connections – signals flashed and caught, furtive affairs in back rooms – that forms a society within a society. When the young protagonist gains access to the *monde,* whose glamour for him has long been embodied in the sonority of aristocratic names, he quickly becomes bored by the vapid inanity of the conversation: at the kernel of the glistening fruit there is, after all, nothing. But the discovery of homosexuality (for Marcel, purely a 'scientific' inter-est, since he himself is always vaguely heterosexual) restores the mystique and sense of quest. Enmeshed within one net is another; just as, at the time of Dreyfus, sudden alliances spring up or old ones collapse, so the homosex-ual secret is everywhere active but everywhere silent. And in another way, sexual secrecy becomes the key also to the enigma of individual personality. Jealousy is the keynote of love in Proust.

Jealousy in Proust is based on the anguished discovery that the self cannot be possessed or known. We change every minute; every moment of our lives marks a death of the self. Other people, similarly, cannot be known: no angle of view on a person is an adequate truth, and we have nothing but our partial gaze. If love is desire of the other, then jealousy is its quintessence, for jealousy is the impossible wish to possess the other perma-nently and fully. Even though such possession would quickly bring boredom and staleness, lack of it is painful, principally because the stable other (and this is especially true of the mother) might guarantee the per-manence and value of the self.

Jealousy in Proust is, interestingly, not a wish for revenge against a rival. It thus differs from Freud's Oedipus complex. The destructive urge is directed not at a rival male but towards the desired woman (for, despite Proust's own sexual experience, the detailed relationships all have a female as love-object). This destructive urge is, however, quite different from the sexual aggressiveness we have just observed in other writers: it has nothing to do with erotic violence, it is a wish to know.

The lover wants to possess as knowledge every moment of the beloved's life – including her past, and even after she is dead. Essentially, he wants to invade her subjectivity: she shall have no thoughts or wishes that do not point (like those of 'L'Amoureuse') towards him. He is a relentless detective, a tireless spy.

It is hardly surprising if the secret he suspects in her is a sexual one, not because the jealousy is about sex (as I said, it is scarcely erotic) but because what he is after is her desire. Nor is it very surprising that when a secret desire is uncovered, it turns out to be homosexual. By the Armageddon-like ending, practically every character except Marcel has proved to have a homosexual secret life, beginning with the key figure of the demonic Charlus. But much more important than the socially significant homosexuality of men is the (for Proust) purely psychologically significant homosexuality of women.

The mother is, of course, the first object of jealousy – not because, as Freud crudely suggests, she 'belongs to Daddy', but because of 'des plaisirs malfaisants et mortellement tristes parce que maman les goûtait loin de moi' ('pleasures which were evil and mortally sad because Mama was enjoying them far away from me').[9] Whatever she does after the child's bedtime is secret to him, and pleasure and secrecy become one. Particularly for a man whose sexual experience includes nothing female, women's pleasure, women's desire (which, in a repressed form, is inevitably identified with the body of the mother in which we all once safely dwelt) is the most extreme other, the ultimate object of his wish to know. For Freud and Lacan too, despite careers dedicated to the analysis of psychosexuality, there remained the unsolved riddle: 'What does a woman want?' ('Was will das Weib?').[10]

What women want may not be such a mystery. Neither Freud nor Proust seem to believe in the possibility of asking women, since to both, the female is the repository of secrecy: innately duplicitous, speaking with forked tongue, her avowals can be interpreted but not exactly listened to. This alone is the meaning of the myth of woman as enigma. Or to put it another way, what women want is, by definition, the unspoken of patriarchal discourse. Since, in public language, women are spoken of, rather than speak, it follows that women's potential speech or autonomy is the hidden, the secret, of patriarchy's language. A truly avant-garde use of language, a real liberation of desire, would come closer to this secret and let it speak.

There are signs in Proust's text (as well as in such heterosexual contemporaries as Rilke, Hofmannsthal or Sartre)[11] that this need is sensed. In much of the imagery used to describe literary creativity, comparison is with the female attributes of gestation and birth. For example, the recollection of the madeleine is likened to the rhythmic labour that eventually releases 'something' from subterranean waters; or, after writing a prose-poem, Marcel bursts out singing 'comme si j'avais été moi-même une poule et si je venais de pondre un œuf' (182) ('as if I were a hen that had just laid an egg'); or, finally, we can compare the single, limited recovery of the madeleine at the beginning of the text and the multiple and more conclusive series of involuntary memories at the end with the difference between male and female orgasms. The aim and the solution in *A la Recherche du temps perdu* is to know, and be, the mother's body; in writing, the man comes as close as he can to realising that fantasy. Thus Proust's work, with its massive motif of secrecy, refuses the sexual politics of patriarchy in a truly radical way.

What do women want? How can women speak? To seek an answer, we may turn to Woolf and the theme of the trivial. The use of the 'trivial' object or event is almost an identifying mark of the avant-garde, but I want to suggest that Woolf uses it rather differently from her male contemporaries. Let us glance at some of these first, and see how the trivial is used by them.

In Freud, the trivial appears as the psychopathology of everyday life: the umbrella forgotten, the key mischosen, the slip of the pen; as the seemingly insignificant detail in free association; or the nonsense of dream-material or the symptoms of the hysteric. Freud asserts that nothing is random, insignificant or innocent, all is utterance, everything means something. An obsessive smell of burnt cakes signifies that the hysteric smelt it at a moment of crisis; she displaced the emotional stress onto the contingent sensation, and the latter alone remains to haunt her. When the smell of burnt cakes is interpreted, the originating trauma is released. Proust's use of the banal is strikingly similar to this: the chance encounter with a trivial taste or smell can fully restore a past that had survived in abeyance, masked by the sensation. Through chance, in Proust, or the cultivation of free association, in Freud, the trivial is encountered, 'opened up' and dissolved. It is a sign, not a thing: interpreting it solves away the resistant present, revealing a true and creative self.

This attitude is religious, not political. The remembered madeleine or recovered trauma is more important than the present world in which the search for it originated. But the everyday bits-and-pieces are the unavoidable first step to reaching what is immaterial and true.

Apollinaire and Eliot specifically locate the trivial in the city. In *The Waste Land* or a poem like 'Lundi rue Christine', the verbal flotsam of Paris or London is pasted up in a collage along with intertextual borrowings from Baudelaire or Dante. It is no coincidence that these snippets are found most readily in the city streets: the promiscuity of classes and types rubbing shoulders is always full of a grim poetry. But this is not the whole story, as we shall see.

Aragon, too, finds in the cityscape a 'mythologie moderne'. In his Paris, the wanderer becomes a peasant, the text a neo-pastoral. What he describes as 'le sentiment du merveilleux quotidien' ('a sense of the wonderful in the everyday')[12] is available in flea-markets or obscure squares around unexpected corners. Joyce's 'epiphany' (the term means 'a revelation') is similarly outdoor: '– "Yes", said Stephen. "I will pass [the clock of the Ballast Office] time after time, allude to it, refer to it, catch a glimpse of it. It is only an item in the catalogue of Dublin's street furniture. Then all at once I see it and I know at once what it is: epiphany".'[13] Like Proust's madeleine, it is this object's very ordinariness and availability that paradoxically allow it to harbour an unsuspected truth.

Without a mystical turn of mind, it is perhaps difficult to see what Joyce or Aragon mean by this 'revelation'. It seems easier to follow the Freudian or Proustian argument of an acquired mythology which invests contingent objects with a personal privilege. But all these writers share a tendency to invest the interpretation of the trivial with metaphysical significance, to find it almost divine – even the staunchly atheistic Freud sees it as part of the 'royal road to the unconscious'.

In Virginia Woolf's autobiographical writings, she speaks of something similar in many ways to Joyce's 'epiphany' or Proust's 'moment bien-heureux' ('blissful moment'). She calls these experiences 'moments of being'.[14] They share a quality of 'shock' (83): 'I always feel instantly that [these moments] are particularly valuable. And so I go on to suppose that the shock-receiving capacity is what makes me a writer ... it is ... a revelation of some order; it is a token of some real thing behind appearances; and I make it real by putting it into words.' (84) She contrasts such moments with the rest of lived time: 'every day includes much more non-being than being ... one walks, eats, sees things, deals with what has to be done; the broken vacuum cleaner; ordering dinner; writing orders to Mabel; washing; cooking dinner; bookbinding' (81–2). Against this 'cotton wool of daily life' (83), the moments of being suggest that perhaps after all 'there is a pattern hid behind the cotton wool' (84).

Now we can see that, in this argument, Woolf is dividing experience into the revelatory, aesthetic mode (which, as in the male writers, is rare and arbitrary) and the world of specifically female work. At this point I must introduce another definition of the trivial. Whether consciously or unconsciously, this concept is commonly applied to women's pursuits. Domestic, unpaid work, for instance, is often dismissed as not really work – thus the answer 'No, I'm only a housewife' to the question 'Do you work?' gives little surprise. Similarly, women's arts like cooking or embroidery are classed as minor and decorative, unless practised by men. The trivial, then, is a term applied to the domestic: it is banal and insignificant because it belongs to the indoor world of women. In Woolf's writing, we find an interesting progression: while in a text like *Mrs Dalloway* (1925) she still has in mind something fairly close to the male writers' idea of the trivial as epiphany, two years later, in *To the Lighthouse,* she has taken the key step of locating 'moments of being' in the very activities she has called 'cotton wool'.

In the other writers, we observed how revelation was essentially out-door; all their protagonists are what Walter Benjamin calls *flâneurs.*[15] This aristocratic figure is free, irresponsibly, to wander the city-streets, picking up poetic impressions where he may. I say 'he' for good reason: a woman cannot be a *flâneur,* not only because often her work keeps her indoors, but because the city is not hers to move around in. Aragon describes the prostitutes of the Passage de l'Opéra as part of its fauna: they are not free to roam, they are on the streets for a reason. Nadja, however much the narrator might throw up his hands in horror, can run around freely by day principally because at night she, too, keeps herself and her daughter by prostitution.

Virginia Woolf had the typical agoraphobia of the anorexic. Despite her extreme beauty, people are said to have stared or laughed at her frequently in the street. In *The Years* (1937) she describes the hazards facing a girl venturing out unchaperoned; even today, women are effectively barred from many areas of cities at night. The trivial for women, then, belongs not to the holiday mood of the *flâneur,* but to the indoor world of domesticity.

Clarissa Dalloway takes a delighted walk across London, but even she has come out with a domestic purpose: buying flowers for her party. This party is her version of the domestic (trivial) art: 'she felt if only they could be brought together; so she did it. And it was an offering; to combine, to create; but to whom?'[16] As a definition of the aesthetic ('an offering . . . to whom?') this is exact. Mrs Dalloway's creation of harmony and coherence is quite other than the personalised metaphysics of the male writers – but it still shares some elements: the outdoors as stimulus, the religious termino-logy, however discreet. Something different happens in *To the Lighthouse.*

Lily Briscoe, the artist in this novel, has chosen not to be a domestic woman; Mrs Ramsay's absurd matchmaking, or her principle of always protecting the feelings of men, irritate Lily as they no doubt annoy her author. But Lily's final capacity to make the pattern appear is impoverished compared with the unknowing art of Mrs Ramsay, which is based simply in

her work as mother. As wife, she has limitations (the angry Oedipal viewpoint of James underlines this), but as mother, she is the cohering centre of everything.

Her whole life is what Woolf called 'cotton wool'. Unlike her throng of children and guests, 'one could not imagine Mrs Ramsay standing painting, lying reading, a whole morning on the lawn. It was unthinkable'.[17] Capable of an ironic endorsement of her work as trivial – 'for they were making the great expedition, she said, laughing' (15) – and convinced that her husband's contribution is far more important than hers, she is yet the centre of the world that makes his possible. As Woolf wrote of her own mother: 'her presence was large and austere, bringing with it not only joy and life, exquisite fleeting femininities, but the majesty of a nobly composed human being' (*Moments*, 41). Mrs Ramsay, like Julia Stephen, is the mother who died: 'she was central . . . She was the whole thing' (*Moments*, 96) . . . 'With mother's death the merry, various family life which she had held in being shut for ever' (*Moments*, 109). In exactly this way, the light goes out from the fictional world when Mrs Ramsay is suddenly, tangentially announced dead: the focus, the pattern, are hers.

Mrs Ramsay's beauty is frequently remarked on, but it does not make her a static object, like the Muses of Eluard or Breton. Her bringing-together of everything into a whole is not a given quality, but a perpetually-renewed activity: it is work. It devolves on her because she is a woman. As she is further developed than Mrs Dalloway, so her dinner is not just the act of assembling a group of people, but requires constant attention and activity: 'they all sat separate. And the whole of the effort of merging and flowing and creating rested on her. Again she felt, as a fact without hostility, the sterility of men, for if she did not do it, nobody would do it' (79). In the following twenty-five pages, we see her bringing one person out, listening to a second, letting a third have another helping of soup – all the trivial work of everyday, described in simple, practical language. But this language and these actions are inseparable now from a 'moment of being': 'there it was, all around them. It partook, she felt, carefully helping Mr Bankes to a specially tender piece, of eternity' (97). Out of the bathos of the ambiguous phrasing comes a new, consciously clumsy metaphysics.

Finally, how is it that, from the point of view of sexual politics, Proust and Woolf (in general terms, rather conservative thinkers) are more radical than the ostensible revolutionaries? To consider this, we would need to think again about the problem of women's speech. In such writing as Joyce's 'Nausicaa' episode in *Ulysses*, we find a *style indirect libre* reminiscent of Flaubert's and similarly dependent on the identification of an ironic distance between the wise male writer and the foolish female reader. In other male-authored texts that seek to reproduce women's voice (Lawrence's *Lady Chatterley's Lover,* Schnitzler's *Fräulein Else*) there is a tendency, more or less well integrated with a realist aim, to mythologise women into an archetypal 'flow' of thought. But in texts by sexual political 'deviants' – Proust the homosexual, Woolf the bisexual woman – we find a certain emancipation from the dominant discourse of patriarchy. Since for women and homosexuals of both sexes, language is always borrowed, alien and unfitting, it is they above all whose writings have that quality of literariness that the Russian Formalists called *ostranenye* ('making-strange'): in speaking of sexuality, or the theme of the trivial, they no longer privilege the voice of male heterosexuality. Or, to put this another way, perhaps all writers, in their most creative moments, temporarily become society's eunuchs, women and inverts. For we have seen that the identification of artistic creativity with womb-envy is not exclusive to Proust.

The alienation from patriarchal discourse that belongs to its creative deviants is perhaps, then, after all the true avant-garde – and it is in Proust and Woolf, rather than in all the 'blasting and bombardiering' of the Surrealists, Vorticists or Futurists, that we find the real revolution in that most fundamental aspect of language, its sexual politics.

Notes to chapter 14

All translations from French and German are my own: reference is to the original text, even where the translation alone is given. Further references to a text appear after quotations, in brackets.

1   O. Kokoschka, *Das schriftliche Werk, I,* Hamburg, 1973, pp. 33–41.
2   G. Apollinaire, *Calligrammes,* Paris, 1918; 1966, pp. 92, 101, 127.
3   Reproduced in M. Nadeau, *Histoire du surréalisme, suivie de Documents surréalistes,* Paris, 1964, p. 253.
4   R. Shattuck, Introduction to English translation of Nadeau, Harmondsworth, 1973, pp. 24–5, 26.
5   A. Breton, *Nadja,* Paris, 1928; 1964, p. 9.
6   *Marinetti, Selected Writings,* ed. R. W. Flint, London, 1972, pp. 41–2.
7   W. Wees, *Vorticism and the English Avant-garde,* Toronto, 1972, p. 114.
8   T. E. Hulme, *Speculations,* London, 1936, p. 118.
9   M. Proust, *A la Recherche du temps perdu,* I, Paris, 1954, p. 30.
10   Quoted in Ernest Jones, *The Life and Work of Sigmund Freud,* Harmondsworth, 1964, p. 474.
11   N. Segal, *The Banal Object,* London, 1981.
12   L. Aragon, *Le Paysan de Paris,* Paris, 1926; 1953, p. 16.
13   J. Joyce, *Stephen Hero,* London, 1969, p. 216.
14   V. Woolf, *Moments of Being,* ed. J. Schulkind, St Albans, 1978, p. 85.
15   W. Benjamin, 'On some motifs in Baudelaire', in *Illuminations,* ed. H. Arendt, London, 1968.
16   V. Woolf, *Mrs Dalloway,* London, 1925; 1976, p. 109.
17   V. Woolf, *To the Lighthouse,* London, 1927; 1977, p. 180.

PART IV

MEDIUM
AND MESSAGE

The triumph of the banal: art in Nazi Germany

I

In Munich on 18 July 1937, to the accompaniment of lengthy speech-making and elaborate ceremonial, Adolf Hitler opened the first exhibition ever held in the *Haus der deutschen Kunst* ('House of German Art'). The *Haus der deutschen Kunst* was a spacious, well-lit gallery designed in a robust version of the neo-classical style by Hitler's favourite architect Paul Ludwig Troost, previously best known for his luxurious interiors in several transatlantic liners. The new gallery replaced the famous Munich *Glaspalast,* a brilliantly engineered structure of iron and glass, which, until it burned down in 1931, had served a variety of purposes, not least the annual staging of the most important exhibition of contemporary art in southern Germany, the *Grosse Kunstausstellung* ('Big Art Exhibition'.) Now the *Haus der deutschen Kunst* was continuing the interrupted tradition; but the exhibition of 1937, renamed the *Grosse deutsche Kunstausstellung* (and the addition of the *deutsch* – 'German' – is, of course, significant) was rather different from its predecessors: it consisted exclusively of art that was to the Government's taste.

The exibition of 1937 was the first of a series which continued annually without a break until 1944. Although Munich was not the administrative capital of Germany, it was for all Nazis the *Hauptstadt der Bewegung* ('Capital of the Movement') and the national cultural centre. These exhibitions, unlike their frankly provincial predecessors, were therefore of truly national significance. For the visual arts they were the outstanding event of every year. Painters and sculptors realised that their careers depended on showing their work there and resorted to every possible ruse to ensure that they did so.

No one was left in any doubt about the importance placed on the Munich exhibitions by the authorities. Each show, even in the grim, penultimate year of the war, was opened by the Führer himself who almost always took the opportunity to make a major speech on a cultural topic. Each exhibition was extensively covered by the press and in the cinema newsreels. Although many other shows of similar art were regularly held throughout Germany, these *Grosse deutsche Kunstausstellungen* were far and away the most significant. They were larger than any other; they regularly attracted large numbers of visitors; and their duration was unusually long: six months was the norm. They were also the only such exhibitions to be hung in a purpose-built gallery designed in a government-approved style, providing the opportunity to view Nazi-inspired painting and sculpture against the background of a building shaped to embody the Fascist virtues.

We need look no further than the exhibits in the *Grosse deutsche Kunstausstellung* of any year to gain an impression of both the style and subject-matter of the art which the Nazi Government encouraged. Every year the walls of the *Haus der deutschen Kunst* were hung with paintings showing women who, both clothed and naked, embodied the Nazi ideal of Nordic physical beauty and, as Leda or Diana, gave that ideal a respectable, time-honoured pedigree (Fig. 8). Uniformed men in battle advertised the virtues of heroism and fortitude (Fig. 9). Peasants at work in the fields or relaxing at home announced the benefits of the simple life or illustrated the charm of regional costume (Fig. 10). Great moments in the nation's history such as the Battle of Tannenberg were dramatically recalled. Great moments in the party's history such as the Führer's imprisonment in the fortress of Landsberg zu Lech were presented in histrionic fashion. The German landscape was lovingly described, frequently, as when eagles were shown wheeling over Alpine peaks, in a fashion pregnant with meaning (an oak tree was a similarly loaded image.) Paintings of steelworks, dams under construction (Fig. 11), aircraft factories and autobahn bridges expressed and invited pride in the nation's material and military progress; while sculptures in the round and relief employed classical conventions on a monumental and often gigantic scale in order to suggest parallels between the Third Reich and Imperial Rome at the height of its influence (Fig. 12). Sculpture was indeed accorded an importance even greater than that given to painting, a logical result of its public character and of the major role it assumed in Nazi Germany as a vital component of architecture. Finally and inevitably, portraits of Adolf Hitler and his ministers presented their subjects in both two and three dimensions as determined, enlightened and inspired.

The subjects of the works shown at the *Grosse deutsche Kunstausstellungen* were more varied than the styles in which they were depicted. These styles were by no means uniform, however, and ranged from a consistently sharp-focus treatment of a myriad of tiny details to a softer, more suggestive kind of description; but they were all, in essence, varieties of Naturalism, and thus intended to be instantly accessible to the widest possible public. All of them gave the visitor, however unsophisticated, a reassuring sense of familiar, enduring values. No conventional view, either of art or of art history, was challenged; no unconventional view was permitted to disturb the mirrored surface of optimism and contentment. There was an absence of problems: no one had any trouble recognising what was represented or understanding what was being said.

Oskar Martin-Amorbach's *Evening Peace* (Fig. 10) was shown at the *Grosse deutsche Kunstausstellung* of 1944 and is a prime example, not simply of contemporary German painting of its type, but of Nazi-approved art in general. It is, of course, a kind of pastoral. The mood is calm, contented. Yet the relaxation described speaks clearly of work well done, and so does the title. The period is imprecise. It might be 1944 or 1844. The skill of the painter is manifest. The detail, the high technical accomplishment, would impress anyone for whom artistic achievement is synonymous with evidence of industry and the ability to create a convincing illusion of reality.

The message communicated by this painting is clear: labour has its reward; the old values, the simple rural life close to the soil are to be preferred to modern, sophisticated urban habits. The past is evoked in another way. Martin-Amorbach's painting belongs to a German (and specifically south German) tradition which has its roots in the paintings of peasants of Wilhelm Leibl, who was deeply impressed by Courbet's work when he saw it in an exhibition at the Munich *Glaspalast* in 1864.

There is a narrative element in such paintings by Leibl as *The Village Politicians* (1877, Oskar Reinhart Foundation, Winterthur) and *Three Women in Church* (1882, *Kunsthalle,* Hamburg) which, entirely absent from similar works by Courbet, verges on the sentimental. In Martin-Amorbach's *Evening Peace* the narrative has degenerated into anecdote, the sugar-sweetness of which, exemplified by the cat washing its paws and the child sucking his thumb in sleep, betrays a general lack of sincerity. We do not need to be reminded of what was happening in the real world while this false idyll was being created, in order to hear its hollow ring.

II

On 19 July 1937, the day following the inauguration of the *Haus der deutschen Kunst,* Adolf Hitler opened another art exhibition in Munich.

(facing 8) Padua, *Sleeping Diana* (*and* 9) Lipus, *Warriors*

(*facing* 10) Martin-Amorbach, *Evening Peace* (*and* 11) Gessner, *Castles of our Time*
(*this page* 12) Breker, *Revenge*

rassischer Querschnitt

Man beachte besonders auch die unten stehenden drei Malerbildnisse. Es sind von links nach rechts: Der Maler Morgner, gesehen von sich selbst. Der Maler Radziwill, gesehen von Otto Dix. Der Maler Schlemmer, gesehen von E. L. Kirchner.

Welche von diesen drei

Zeichnungen ist wohl eine Dilettantenarbeit vom Insassen eines Irrenhauses?

Staunen Sie: Die rechte obere! Die beiden anderen dagegen wurden einst als meisterliche Graphiken Kokoschkas bezeichnet.

The publicity which attended this event was possibly greater than that attracted by the *Grosse deutsche Kunstaustellung*. Also devoted to contemporary art, the second exhibition was dramatically different from the first. Hung in badly-lit rooms in the Hofgarten Arcade a few steps to the rear of the *Haus der deutschen Kunst*, it consisted not only of badly-hung paintings and sculpture, but also of placards on which texts and sensational photographs urged the visitor to make comparisons between, for example, the works on show and the products of both the mentally deranged and the primitive tribes of Africa and Oceania (Figs. 13 & 14). The treatment of faces and bodies in some of the painting and sculpture was similarly compared to the appearance of the physically deformed. The title of this exhibition, unique in the history of art, was the *Entartete Kunstausstellung* – the 'Degenerate Art Exhibition'.

If the exhibition at the *Haus der deutschen Kunst* presented examples of government-approved art, the sideshow in the Hofgarten Arcade was intended, as its title implied, to be a chamber of horrors. Here was eloquent proof of the lunacy, disease and danger which the Nazi Party had been founded to combat; here was abundant evidence of the cancer at the heart of German society which it was committed to eradicate.

Between the placards the *Entartete Kunstausstellung* showed the work of artists who, until comparatively recently, had been widely regarded in Germany and abroad as modern masters and were represented in many of the world's most important museums: painters such as Nolde, Kirchner and Kokoschka; sculptors such as Barlach, Lehmbruck and Marcks. Their work, by almost total contrast to that in the *Grosse deutsche Kunstausstellung*, was heterogeneous in the extreme. Brilliant colours, exaggerated forms and energetic handling characterised many of the paintings, while the sculptures employed unnatural proportions and, in conventional terms, showed scant respect for technique. Nor were the subjects easy to categorise. Some of the work was non-figurative; some of it was politically inspired; some of it took remarkable liberties with the appearance of the human form; much of it was extremely subjective. All of it was challenging, unsettling and difficult. Most of it seemed to issue a strident challenge to all familiar categories of thought and to the conventional mind at home in them. All of it belonged to state and other public collections and had recently been confiscated.

The two Munich exhibitions of 1937 were the clearest and best advertised expressions of official government policy towards the visual arts in Nazi Germany. Never has a government worked so hard to encourage the art of which it approved, or to suppress that by which it felt threatened. Hitler, who had unsuccessfully applied to study at the Art Academy in

(*facing* 13) From the catalogue of 'Degenerate Art': works by Kokoschka and by a lunatic (*and* 14) From the catalogue of 'Degenerate Art': works by Nolde, Schmidt-Rottluff, Morgner, Dix and Kirchner

Vienna in both 1907 and 1908, who subsequently tried to make a living by making water-colour copies of picture postcards and who now saw himself as an architect *manqué*, was deeply interested in art policy. The party architect and designer of important events such as the Nuremberg rallies, Albert Speer, was but one of several of Hitler's intimates to recall that art was often the subject of the Führer's table talk.

For that reason alone it is surprising that both the exhibitions of 1937 were the first of their kind (the *Entartete Kunstausstellung* was also the last), that it took so long for party policy to be fully formulated and even longer completely to take effect. Whilst it is true that the party set about controlling all cultural activity in Germany from the movement Hitler became Chancellor in January 1933, and that in regions where the Nazis had gained parliamentary control before that – in the State of Thuringia for example – the process began even earlier, the fact remains that, even by 1936, by no means all activity in the visual arts had come fully under official scrutiny. Although there was a series of *Schandausstellungen* ('Exhibitions of Infamy'), which as early as 1933 put on show the 'decadent' parts of public collections in, among other places, Karlsruhe, Dessau, Mannheim and Chemnitz, museums in other cities such as Hamburg continued for at least two years to give places of honour to Expressionists and representatives of other modern schools. As late as 1937 inconsistencies persisted in official attitudes, and gratifyingly hilarious contradictions could still occur. Thus the sculptor Rudolf Belling, who worked concurrently in abstract and figurative modes, was represented in both the *Grosse deutsche Kunstausstellung* and the *Entartete Kunstausstellung* of the same year.

By the time of these exhibitions, however, control was almost total. Every independent artists' organisation had been absorbed by a union under direct state influence. Artists deemed 'degenerate' or, in a virtually synonymous phrase, 'culturally Bolshevik', had been expelled or persuaded to resign from national and regional academies, dismissed from teaching posts at art schools and universities, forbidden to exhibit and in some cases to acquire materials and therefore to work. Every museum official was invited to implement government policy or tender his resignation. That meant co-operating with the authorities sent by Berlin throughout the Reich to confiscate everything unacceptable. It also meant, in future, purchasing only what was officially approved. Art critics and historians were left in no doubt that they, too, were expected to follow the party line. In 1936 *Kunstkritik*, art criticism, was actually banned, replaced by *Kunstbetrachtung*, reflection on art, a blander kind of writing in which all expression of opinion disappeared in favour of sympathetic description. Journalists were in any case told what to say about current exhibitions, which artists to mention and in what terms, and of which artists the deaths and anniversaries could be marked. Artists out of favour could therefore be *totgeschwiegen* – killed by silence – while others were kept firmly in the public eye. Art historians learned that the more distant the period in which they specialised, the safer they were from interference. Those who insisted on thinking about the art of the previous hundred years were obliged to acknowledge a tradition in which major roles were played by painters such as Menzel, Leibl, Thoma and Hodler, and not even walk-on parts were given to the likes of Cézanne, Van Gogh, Seurat and Gauguin.

The *Entartete Kunstausstellung* of 1937 provided the last opportunity before 1945 for contemporary art unpalatable to the Government to be publicly viewed in Germany. It was the climax of a series of events during which such art was either removed from public collections, burned, appropriated by members of the Government (especially Hermann Goering) or auctioned off in Switzerland. On 30 June 1939 most of the contents of the *Entartete Kunstausstellung* was sold by auction at Lucerne.

The 'Degenerate Art Exhibition' proved enormously popular. When it closed in Munich on 30 November it had been seen by more than two million people (many more than saw the *Grosse deutsche Kunstausstellung*), and more still saw it in a slightly different form when it travelled on to other cities in Germany and, after the Anschluss, in Vienna, too. Its striking popularity is usually explained as the result of the desire of so many people to see original and challenging things for the last time, before the banal celebrated its final victory. There may be something to this view; but another explanation is more likely: the general public enjoyed the spectacle of the humiliation of something which they did not understand, consequently feared and fervently hoped was a confidence trick. By no means did the general public alone relish what they believed to be the exposure of the modern art swindle. Some art critics, no longer embarrassed by their failure to grasp the point of something which had apparently struck most of their peers with the force of a spiritual revelation, also hugely enjoyed themselves.

Since it may be thought that there was something peculiarly German about this reaction to 'degenerate' art by professional critics, an account of a related event in England will prove instructive. In 1938 Herbert Read and others organised an exhibition of modern German art at the New Burlington Galleries in London as a propaganda exercise, as an answer given by a democratic nation to the 'Degenerate Art Exhibition'. At least one of those invited to exhibit, Oskar Kokoschka, then living in exile in Prague, feared that the effort would prove counter-productive, since most of the visitors to the exhibition would have little sympathy for what was shown.

Kokoschka's fears were justified: even usually enlightened critics expressed their hostility. One of them was Raymond Mortimer, who wrote in the *New Statesman and Nation* that the 'people who go to see the exhibition are only too likely to say: "if Hitler doesn't like these pictures, it's the best thing I've heard about Hitler." ' Mortimer went on to describe the impression made on ordinary people as one of 'extraordinary ugliness'.[1]

In Germany the *Entartete Kunstausstellung* had made the man in the street feel that the Government was on his side against the self-appointed experts, that the Government had ensured that in art, as in other matters, common sense had triumphed. Authorities more reliable than self-appointed art experts now told him that if he found something difficult to understand, contrary to his perception of things or otherwise offensive, it was necessarily devoid of quality. Abstraction was indeed nothing more than pattern-making; distortions of the human form or of any other aspect of nature were the product of a diseased mind. The popular success of Nazi art policy ensured the victory of banality.

III

The Nazi Government implemented all its cultural policies with singular energy; but its efforts to control artistic activity throughout the nation were hardly without precedent, nor was it the first government in history to claim the right to define the nature of art. Many of its attitudes and methods were anticipated by and may even have been borrowed from the Soviet Union, which during the 1920s reversed its liberal policy towards literature, music and the visual arts, attacked experimentation of every kind and declared Socialist Realism to be the only acceptable style.

The only significant difference between Soviet and Nazi art policies is that the Soviets prescribed as well as proscribed. In practice, however, as any comparison between Nazi and Soviet art will show (battle scene for battle scene, popular hero for popular hero, tractor for tractor, contented peasant for contented peasant), both the subject-matter, style and apparent purpose of the majority of paintings and sculptures are strikingly similar.

That it should be the Soviet Union which offers the closest parallel to the Third Reich in this respect is surprising. There was, after all, another Fascist state in Europe whose leader, Mussolini, had provided the Führer with one of his earliest role models. In cultural matters, however, Italy was considerably more liberal than its ally at the northern pole of the Axis. Although directly and enthusiastically involved in artistic affairs, Italy was less consistent and less thorough in its application of norms. Most obviously it was less hostile to experimental styles and even encouraged two of them, the *scuola metafisica* ('the 'metaphysical' painting invented by Giorgio de Chirico), and Futurism. In spite of the fact that both styles had seen better days, and that Futurism was the invention of one of the pioneers of theoretical Fascism, F. T. Marinetti, both were unconventional enough. In Germany they were indeed execrated as violently as every other example of *Kunst-ismus* ('ism-art'), virtually a synonym for degeneracy. Occasionally this conflict of ideas caused diplomatic problems at a high level, as when a large exhibition of Italian art 'from 1800 to the present day', sponsored by the Italian Government, was staged in Berlin in December 1937. It included a small Futurist section which would not have looked out of place in the *Entartete Kunstausstellung*.

Inconsistencies in official attitudes to German and foreign art were numerous and inevitable (especially after the fall of France) and make the completeness of the control over cultural activities within Germany itself seem remarkable. Although it is difficult to be sure, it seems likely that Nazi art policy enjoyed widespread support. What is certainly true is that many of the arguments the Government employed in its effort to define the nature of the nation's culture were not new. Some of them were intellectually respectable and commonplace long before they were borrowed and frequently perverted by the theorists of National Socialism.

The most important of them concerned national cultural identity. Although the debate about an art that might be regarded as quintessentially 'German' began during the Romantic Revival (where it was given extra edge by the Nationalist Movement), the terms on which it was conducted became less rarified during the years following unification in 1871. To many Germans none of 'their' painting and sculpture seemed more than third-rate beside the achievement of the French. While the *Siegessäule* in Berlin proclaimed the nation's military superiority, by displaying the gilded cannons captured from the French at Sedan, the National Gallery was abjectly bowing the knee to the enemy by acquiring more art by French than German artists.

Kaiser Wilhelm II characteristically met the problem head-on: he not only publicly attacked all contemporary painting tainted by foreign influences as *Rinnsteinskunst* (literally, 'gutter art'), but in 1896 sacked the director of the Berlin National Gallery, Hugo von Tschudi, for buying too many French paintings. That event must have sprung unbidden to the minds of those museum officials dismissed by the Nazi Government some four decades later for a broadly similar reason. Appropriately enough, some of the paintings included in the Lucerne auction of 1939 had first entered Germany when acquired for Berlin by von Tschudi.

A broadside of 1911, the *Protest deutscher Künstler* ('A Protest by German Artists'), written by Karl Vinnen, an unsuccessful provincial painter, and signed by 120 other artists, asserted that too much attention was being paid not only to foreign but also to 'modern' and experimental art at the expense of native and conservative talent. The counter-argument was put by another publication (*Im Kampf um die Kunst* – 'Fighting for Art') by artists of the kind Vinnen had attacked. Significantly, several of the signatories to the former protest enjoyed some success after 1933, while almost all of the contributors to the latter found themselves in the 'degenerate' camp.

One prominent aspect of the long and continuing debate about national art and national culture was decidedly sinister. The attempt to define national characteristics in art became inextricably bound up with racial theories. Germans, it was argued in a series of books and articles dating back at least as far as the last quarter of the nineteenth century, were members of the Nordic race and were thus quite different from the Latin peoples with whom they shared the western part of Europe. This difference, evident in physical traits, emerged in art, literature and music. Climate, geography and genes ensured that the Nordic artist was concerned with issues fundamentally at variance with those pursued by his Latin counterpart.

Later tracts went beyond the notion of racial difference and even of Nordic superiority and claimed to discern connections between art and the mental and physical state of those who produced it: degenerates produced degenerate art. Possibly the most sensational of such publications was *Kunst und Rasse* ('Art and Race', 1928) by the architect and cultural activist Paul Schulze-Naumburg. Thirty-two of the 175 illustrations in Schulze's book compared the work of such artists as Modigliani, Schmidt-Rottluff, Kokoschka, Picasso and Nolde (later inevitably branded 'degenerate' to a man) with photographs of men and women suffering from encephalitis, elephantiasis or mongoloidism (Fig. 15). Clearly, such comparisons provided inspiration for the organisers of the *Entartete Kunstausstellung*.

There is yet another, more telling aspect to the artistic debate as it was conducted before the Nazi period. French art was not rejected by the Kaiser and other reactionary Germans simply because it was French. Indeed Wilhelm II did not feel strongly about *all* recent French art and may well have been an admirer of some of it, the work of Meissonier, for example. Most of what had been acquired by the museums and celebrated by the most vociferous critics was avant-garde. In other words it was (if good of its kind) original, critical of established conventions, and as a result largely

(*facing* 15) Two pages from *Art and Race*, contrasting portraits by Schmidt-Rottluff with photographs of people with physical abnormalities.

Was hatte es aber für ein Volksleben zu sagen, wenn eine gewisse Schicht sich künstlerisch so ausdrückte und ein weit größerer Teil es hinnahm und wie jede andere Mode anbetete?

Es ist für einen denkenden Menschen schwer, nicht nach der Ursache dieser Erscheinungen zu fragen, die sich aufdringlich genug innerhalb eines Volkes zeigen, das bisher als vorwiegend nordisch eingestellt galt, zum mindesten soweit es seine geistig führende Schicht betrifft, und

Abb. 129. Paralyse, 130. Mongoloide Idiotypie, 131. Lähmung der Augenbewegungsnerven, 132. Mikrozephalie, Idiotie

Abb. 125.

Abb. 126.

Abb. 127.

Abb. 128.

Die Abb. 125–128, 133–135, 139–141, 145–146 und 149–152 sind Ausschnitte aus Bildern von 1918–33, die besonders bezeichnende Gestalten darstellen. Die ihnen gegenüberstehenden Abb. 129–132, 136–138, 142–144, 147–148 und 153 bis 156 zeigen körperliche und geistige Gebrechen aus der Sammlung einer Klinik.

incomprehensible to the conventional mind. Avant-garde art could by its very nature speak only to a minority of open-minded, unprejudiced people. It could not satisfy the spiritual needs of most of the population who, through their taxes, were enabling the museums to pay for it.

In France, its country of origin, the avant-garde was fully established before the turn of the century. It almost destroyed the academic system by confronting it with an impermanent, anarchic pageant of styles and opinions which appeared and disappeared with bewildering speed. In Germany, by contrast, the avant-garde had scarcely begun to drive out academic forms of art by 1900, although the emergence of alternative exhibiting bodies in all the major German cities during the 1890s (the Secession Movement) marked the beginning of a growing commitment to experimentation, often under direct influence from France.

Not until the inter-war years, the period of the Weimar Republic, did the German avant-garde celebrate its victory. It suddenly became clear to foreign taste-makers that German art, architecture and design were making a major contribution to international Modernism, the avant-garde style in evidence everywhere from New York to Prague. This was of little comfort to the common man in Germany, who was as bemused as his counterpart abroad by Kandinsky's non-figurative paintings and the flat-roofed, concrete houses of the Bauhaus. What distinguished the German from his foreign counterpart, however, was the background against which he viewed the activities of the avant-garde. For many people there appeared to be eloquent affinities between the seeming irrationality of abstract art, or the excesses of Expressionism, and the political instability, economic crises and collapse of moral values during the Weimar Republic.

The Nazis exploited the prejudices of the common man with some sophistication. Presenting themselves as the saviours of the nation from the spirit of Weimar, they asserted that between 1919 and 1933 vast sums of money had been spent by a backrupted exchequer on the acquisition of painting and sculpture by artists, mostly foreign, which only a few claimed to understand. The Nazis declared solidarity with the uncomprehending and war on those artists and dealers who had allegedly grown fat on the deception. Significantly, the prices of the exhibits at the *Grosse deutsche Kunstausstellung* were kept low so that ordinary people might afford modest collections of contemporary German art.

There were, of course, objections to the avant-garde, other than the claim that it embodied the spirit of Weimar. From the moment of its emergence in the France of the 1840s the avant-garde had been inextricably linked with radical politics. Many of the leading avant-garde painters, Courbet, Pissarro and Seurat among them, were active on the far left of the political spectrum. The restless search for alternatives to convention by means of the subjects and styles of such artists' work encouraged the desire for continuous questioning and – what was worse – continuous change. Avant-garde art was revolutionary at several levels. Not only in Germany were conservative politicians afraid of it.

IV

In one important respect the German avant-garde proved to be different from most, if not all, of its foreign counterparts. For the debate in Germany about the nation's cultural identity, about vitality and degeneracy in art, was in part conducted by the avant-garde itself.

Several of the Expressionist painters who came to maturity around 1910 were determined simultaneously to destroy existing conventions and introduce thoroughly 'Germanic' or 'Nordic' qualities into their art. Drawing heavily on nineteenth-century romantic theory and on several of the ideas which had emerged during the more recent debate about the national cultural identity, they wanted to be original and obviously German, to be avant-garde without appearing to be indebted to the French.

The most telling example of such an artist is provided by the north German Emil Nolde, whose thinking reveals in extreme form the contradictions and confusions current at the time. In his search for racial characteristics Nolde was attracted not only to the Gothic, then believed by many Germans to be the quintessential 'Nordic' style, but also to a wide range of exotic, primitive art, in which he claimed to find the direct and authentic expression of race. In developing a new style capable of an equally direct expression of his own 'Nordic' soul, Nolde arrived at a combination of exaggerated colour and distorted forms, to which the closest parallels were, paradoxically, French. Yet another contradiction was Nolde's simultaneous admiration for the culture of primitive races and his crude racialism.

Nolde was by no means the only Expressionist to aim for a thoroughly German and thoroughly modern style around 1910. Most notably the artists of the *Brücke,* the Dresden group of which Nolde was briefly a member, sought to revive the medieval and in their view characteristically Germanic art of the woodcut; and they occasionally alluded in their painting to works by the great German masters of the past, such as Cranach. Nolde was nevertheless unusual because he, alone of the major Expressionist painters, joined the Nazi Party, in 1920 (the same year as Hitler), believing that its programme was the political equivalent of his artistic philosophy. He remained a fervent Nazi even after he was condemned by the Government as 'degenerate' and forbidden not only to exhibit but also even to paint.

Nolde's theories, heavy with racialism and mysticism of the *Blut und Boden* variety, might suggest that there are links between Expressionism and Nazism. As David Midgley shows in Chapter 3, many of the left-wing intellectuals who sought refuge from the Third Reich in the Soviet Union argued that there were indeed such links: that the extreme subjectivity of Expressionism, the belief in the primacy of feeling and the scorn for logic and rationally, directly contributed to an atmosphere conducive to Fascism.

Appealing though such an argument is, it must be admitted that far more Expressionists were politically active on the left than on the right. Certainly true, however, is that many Nazis, some of them influential, believed that the kind of 'Nordic' Expressionism produced by Nolde and others was eminently qualified to become the new state art. One of them was no less a figure than Goebbels, who as late as 1934 argued that the Expressionist style should receive official blessing. Alois Schardt, the Nazi director of the Berlin National Gallery, also publicly stated that there were close links between the kind of figurative Expressionism represented by the work of Nolde and Kirchner and qualities discernible in the Germanic art of all periods. For a time Schardt continued to hang Expressionist paintings in the modern German section of the museum.

But, as the *Entartete Kunstausstellung* vividly illustrates, Expressionism did not achieve official status and was finally not even tolerated. Given Hitler's hosility to every form of contemporary art that was neither bland nor nugatory, it never could have been. Nevertheless in 1934 there was a major debate behind closed doors, in the course of which Goebbels was forced to concede defeat to the party theorist Rosenberg (who was supported by Hitler). At the party rally of 1934 Rosenberg made a speech in which the future of art in the new Germany was a major theme. He made it clear that the Government regarded every form of the avant-garde as un-German, socially evil and morally bankrupt. Party cultural policy was now more clearly formulated, and the authorities could begin more consistently to enforce it.

By 1937 the result was not only the most oppressive artistic climate ever known, but also a period in which in painting and sculpture the mediocre, the stale and clichéd were encouraged and nurtured. This much is clear, even though it is impossible to be objective about Nazi art, and any judgement of it is made doubly difficult because most of it remains hidden from view (very little has been exhibited or reproduced since 1945).

Perhaps at a future date it will be possible to take a more balanced view of the art produced in Nazi Germany, eventually to see it as unencumbered by political issues as we see the work of Jacques-Louis David today. Perhaps the affinities between Nazi art, and contemporary styles in Germany and abroad, will then become as clear as the differences.

The years between the two world wars are marked everywhere by a growing reaction against the headlong experimentation in which the avant-garde indulged before 1914. After 1918 Picasso was but one of many painters to return wholeheartedly to figuration and even to a neo-classical style. The work of Otto Dix and George Grosz, however challenging its political content, also reflected the desire not only to produce convincing illusions of aspects of the real world once again, but also to retrench, to return to artistic traditions whose merit had been proved by time. Significantly, the Old Masters, despised by the avant-garde, once again served as models for both technique and subject-matter.

The art sponsored by the Nazi Government was also a reaction against the avant-garde and an attempt to revive a tradition which the avant-garde had suffocated. Unlike Picasso's neo-classicism or Grosz's realism, however, Nazi painting and sculpture were content to imitate without modifying their models.

Nazi art was frankly populist in intention, and it is doubtful whether any populist art of any period can be regarded as considerable. This view was advanced by Thomas Mann in *Doktor Faustus,* a novel published ten years after the two exhibitions in Munich so dramatically illustrated Nazi attitudes to the visual arts. The reflections on art and society in this novel provide an appropriate epitaph to the story of art in Nazi Germany:

> Art is spirit and in no way whatsoever should the spirit feel beholden to society, to the community – in my view it must not feel so beholden for the sake of its own freedom and nobility. An art which 'goes to the people', meets the needs of the masses, of the little man, of the philistine, becomes weak and miserable [. . .] I am convinced that the spirit in its boldest, freest and least popular advances, researches and experiments will serve [. . .] not only the individual but, in the long run, even mankind.[2]

Notes to chapter 15

1 *New Statesman and Nation,* 16 July 1938.
2 *Doktor Faustus,* 1947, XXXI, p. 512.

De Stijl:
style and idea

After a long and contented period of dormancy Dutch literature was aroused in the 1880s by a young and confident voice, that of the poet Willem Kloos, who sweepingly rejected all but a few of his precedessors and heralded the coming of a great new literature. Between 1880 and 1889 a group of poets and writers, who became known as the *Tachtigers* ('Eightiers'), headed by Kloos, indeed changed the somnolence of Dutch letters into an atmosphere of lively and productive creativity. A period of almost imperceptible preparation for change had come to fruition; the arts in general were pervaded by a new and articulate enthusiasm, and Dutch culture as a whole suddenly came to life.

Kloos and his fellow artists can be viewed rather as a late romantic flowering than a truly revolutionary new beginning. Their philosophy was that art was divorced from society, since society no longer offered the artist a place and a function. They aimed at the most refined expression of their own individualistic perception of reality, and this was doomed to be overtaken quite rapidly by the artistic creative turmoil of the *fin de siècle,* in which a striving for synthesis and collectivity was a prominent feature.

The periodical founded by the Eightiers, *De Nieuwe Gids* ('The New Guide', 1885) showed from its very first issue that no lasting cohesion of viewpoints was possible. The individualism and the ivory tower of Kloos and some other poets soon came into conflict with the opinions of editors and contributors who wanted not only to change art, but society, and went in search of salvation in socialism or alternative modes of reform. The Eightiers poets had no other visions than those of themselves as the elevated worshippers of Beauty. The Eightiers novelists, many of them apostles of Zola, recorded the cracks in society but made no blueprints for their repair. The effect of the movement of the Eightiers and of Kloos in particular was a short-lived blaze of glory and a long aftermath in which successive generations of poets and writers wrested themselves free from the clinging embrace of past poetics. Even forty years later one encounters vehement condemnations of Eightiers in the pages of *De Stijl,* evidence of the much felt and lingering influence of the generation of 1880.

The conflict between individualism and collective ideals was particularly fierce in the Netherlands around the turn of the century.[1] It found expression in literature, the arts, politics and philosophy, and was mirrored in the career of one of the Eightiers, Herman Gorter (1864–1927).[2] Gorter was the author of what is still considered to be the highlight of the poetry of that generation, a long narrative poem called *Mei* ('May'),[3] published in *De Nieuwe Gids* in 1889. It was a delicious evocation and presentation of spring and an expression of the new literary revival which Kloos had so challengingly heralded in 1880. Its concern centred on the place and function of the poet and of poetry in a basically indifferent world, as well as on the conflict between the poet's contemplative inclinations towards the spiritual and his longing to be part of society; to achieve that the poet must compromise part of himself and his creativity. The poem thus reflects the increasingly strong tendency in late nineteenth-century Dutch society to find a balance between the individual and the community.

In the 1890s Gorter became stranded in his individualism and went in search of a new collective ideal to which he could dedicate himself. The nineteenth century had been lacking, he felt, in a great unifying and driving force which would inspire poets to create monumental epics and become the eulogists of an all-embracing ideal. Socialism now seemed set to take the place religion had vacated. Gorter was convinced he had found a cause to which he could dedicate himself and his poetry. He became a great propagandist for the Socialist cause and his contribution, both in writing and as a fiery public speaker, to the Dutch Social Democratic Workers Party, the SDAP, was marked by total dedication and a fanatic adherence to pure Marxist dogma, so much so that he caused a split in the SDAP and founded, with a few supporters, the Dutch Communist Party, the CPN. They accused the leadership of the SDAP of revisionism in their attempts to lay some practical foundations for a better society, thereby deviating from Marxist dogma. Gorter's loyalty to his principles was absolute and even caused him to be banned from the CPN in later years. This great individualist tried with persistence and utter integrity to combine political ideals and poetic ideas. After writing a great amount of 'Socialist' poetry, he embarked on a heroic venture, the creation of the epic of socialism; *Pan,* 12,000 lines long, and thus the longest poem in the Dutch language, appeared in 1916. The figure of the Greek God Pan symbolises nature, from which mankind, represented by a woman-figure, is estranged by private property, which has separated mankind from nature by means of power and money. Mankind, however, continues to strive for unity with nature and achieves this through communism. Gorter's tragedy was that he was far too much of an individualist and an aesthete to really live in the atmosphere of socialism. There are beautiful passages in this poem, precisely those where the poet becomes lyrical and expresses his own individual experiences, but as a work of effective political art *Pan* must be considered a failure.

Prominent in *Pan* is the feeling, akin to that of many Modernists, that the Great War, despite its limitless misery and despite the fact that the workers were abused by the rulers who wanted this war for their own benefit, was nevertheless a necessity, a cleansing operation which would lead to a golden era of domination by the workers. The slaughter of the war would incite people to strive for the establishment of a new world, in which the workers would attain victory after a massive revolution.[4] Gorter's vision of a world saved by socialism was not shared by many other poets in the Netherlands. The mood was more negative: many beheld the modern world with horror without being able to visualise salvation, either collectively or individually. Chaos and the disintegration of familiar reality play an important role in Modernist poetry. One encounters this, for instance, in the work of the Flemish Belgian poet Paul van Ostaijen (1896–1928),[5] whose collection of poems *Bezette Stad* ('Occupied City') was a poetic recording of and reaction to the horrors of the war. In his work the disintegration of reality is shown very clearly in his poetic form. He abandoned the sentence in favour of the word, and instead of neatly arranged phrases a tumble of splashed and scattered utterances, sometimes in different colours, occurs on the page.

In marked contrast with this is the work of the Dutch Modernist poet Martinus Nijhoff (1896–1953), whom A. L. Sötemann memorably described as 'a non-spectacular modernist'.[6] This was not meant as derogatory qualification, but concisely indicated that Nijhoff's Modernism lies in his sensibility rather than in any formal experiments. Nijhoff made his début in 1916 and in his measured, traditional verse, in which order reigns supreme, he cries out from the depth of the chaos. He was sharply aware of the fragmentation of experience and the isolation of the individual, whose helplessness is increased by the awareness of a great and cruel God. Reality and Self are reduced to near nothingness, hauntingly expressed in, for instance, the following lines:

> De dingen zijn niet meer dan hunne naam.
> Ik ben niet meer dan een ontdaan gelaat.
> (Things are no more than just their name.
> I am no more than a distraught visage.)

Nijhoff's struggle to accept and live life, and his search for a reason for existing and for a function for his poetry, found expression mainly in the balanced form of the sonnet or even older, medieval forms such as the *laisses,* groups of lines linked by assonance, of the *Chanson de Roland* or the short lines of the early Germanic epic. These Nijhoff used in two long narrative poems, *Awater* and *Het Uur U* ('Zero Hour') in which he probed the hidden reality beneath the superficial reality of everyday with imagery anticipating Surrealist poetry.[7]

Gorter, Van Ostaijen and Nijhoff each in their own way reflected and expressed formal and thematic aspects of Modernism. Yet there is a sense of no man's land between Dutch literature in the years leading up to the Great War and the avant-gardist ideas which manifested themselves in *De Stijl* from 1917 onwards. This is, of course, partly the fate of any avant-gardist position, but it was also due to the fact that after the Eightiers no clear group or movement had manifested itself as the representative and mouth-piece of Dutch literature. The first clearly identifiable group to do so would be that around the periodical *Forum* in the 1930s. *Forum* demanded the full participation of the artist in the world, a firm commitment to his or her convictions, political or otherwise, as long as they were not Nazis, and a clear declaration of faith and intentions.

In the years around the Great War a whole generation of rather elegiac poets established themselves, each of these attempting to find individual salvation and fulfilment in either ancient philosophy, mysticism, religion, mythology or, in some cases, socialism and communism.[8] None of these seemed to be a clear preparation for the startling outbreak of avant-gardist ideas expressed by the contributors to *De Stijl*.

Here we must distinguish between literary Modernism and Modernism in the visual arts. Literature did not play a major part in *De Stijl's* crusade to change and reform society by means of art; the message of reform was posed far more radically and much more explicitly by means of the visual arts, and that was very much part of the international Modernist movements. Dutch architecture and painting before *De Stijl* certainly informed and influenced some of the ideas expressed by the contributors to the periodical, but these preparations too were inseparable from those made in and by other European and American individuals and movements. The Socialist architect Berlage,[9] for instance, whose influence is clearly discernible in the work of some of *De Stijl* architects, and who was one of the first in the Netherlands to plead for and practise a co-operation between architecture, painting, sculpture and the decorative arts and whose aim it was to produce community buildings, was himself a great admirer of Frank Lloyd Wright.

Literature was a relatively minor part of *De Stijl*'s concerns and production, and the major and effective changes in Dutch literature are found in the work of poets such as Van Ostaijen and Nijhoff. The major changes in literary criticism, which at this time showed considerable developments, inspired by both modernist and a wide range of aesthetic, formal and political or social ideologies, are reflected in periodicals such *De Beweging* ('The Movement'), *Het Getij* ('The Tide') and *De Eenheid* ('Unity').[10] Moreover, truly radical change did not occur in Dutch literature until the early 1950s, when the experimental strands in the work of the *inter bellum* poets such as Van Ostaijen were picked up again and further developed.

In this climate of modest Modernism *De Stijl* was, and remained, exceptional. The periodical was the brainchild of Christiaan Marie Emil Küpper, better known under his adopted name Theo Van Doesburg, whose prismatic personality dominated the periodical until his death in 1931. He was a poet, a writer, critic, painter, designer, architect and the prime representative of Modernist theory and practice in the Netherlands from about 1914 until 1931. Van Doesburg had been writing and painting from at least 1908 onwards, but his true initiation into the arts came, ironically, when he was kicking his heels in military service between 1914 and 1916. The Dutch army, well equipped with bicycles, was posted along the frontiers, waiting to see whether the Germans were interested enough in their country to break its neutrality. As they did not seem to have a use for the Netherlands on this occasion, the army continued its stagnant watch. For Van Doesburg, however, these were seminal years, in which he met a number of people whose ideas about art were as Modernist as his own.[11] He met Mondriaan, the painter Bart van der Leck and the architect J. J. P. Oud, all future contributors to *De Stijl* and men who would determine the visual arts associated with the periodical.

It is difficult to see *De Stijl* as a movement; each of its contributors was building a career of his own and almost all of them would at one time or another fall out with Van Doesburg because their development did not stay in line with his own. Each of them had his own artistic vision, though they shared the desire to reform art and with it society, even though their aesthetic model turned out to be too rarefied to be accessible to the majority of people. Most of them saw as their object to use art to create an environment for living which would be harmonious and balanced, even serene. In principle they wanted such an environment to be created through the co-operation of architects, interior designers, furniture-makers, painters and sculptors. It was an ideal that was barely and only very partially realised. Creative individualism is not very conducive to successful co-operation.

Especially in Van Doesburg, the most fervent believer in the co-operatively created environment, there was a streak of abstract Utopianism which made his interior designs rather unsuitable for actual living, as his theories about the influence of art on life often went far beyond any possible applicability. The case of the Café Aubette illustrates this point. Van Doesburg, Hans Arp and Sophie Tauber Arp were given this assignment in the late twenties. It allowed them a completely free hand and the chance to realise their ideas of a totally coherent interior in which the architectural dimensions were made subject to the colours and forms of the interior decoration. There is no doubt about the historical and artistic importance of the project. And yet, here perhaps more clearly than anywhere else, van Doesburg showed that he was aiming at the creation of an abstract Utopia in which practical considerations had no place, and in which, therefore, people did not feel at home. Inhumanity was not an unknown component of some Modernist ideas, and the relentless application of theoretical concepts in the name of art is one of the more dubious aspects of *De Stijl*. Immediately after the completion of the Café Aubette the owners made changes in the interior due to complaints from clients, and in 1938 the café was totally and radically changed.[12] Van Doesburg's environment for living made no allowances for the practical rhythms of everyday life. The angular and geometric designs seemed oppressive and non-functional.

Yet one of the many paradoxes of *De Stijl* and of Van Doesburg is that the aims of this periodical are so didactic and so strongly presented as such. There is no doubt about Van Doesburg's goal in life: he wanted to transform art in order to reform mankind. The editor's preface to the first issue in August 1917 is very idealistic.[13] However irrelevant the periodical (with its 100 to 200 subscribers)[14] may have been to the cultured as a whole in the Netherlands, *De Stijl* had unmistakable Dutch characteristics: its didacticism, its longing for the pure and elementary forms and its zealous proclamation of its puritanical doctrines are typically Dutch,[15] even though there is no specific religious implication. Van Doesburg exhorted his readers to strive for a truly modern art; artists should create a universal language from the materials with which they work: concrete, wood, stone, paint should, quite literally, speak for themselves and dispense with the need for unnecessary frills, disguises or symbols. Artists should attempt to build up not a social, but a spiritual community, which would only be possible if they refrained from 'ambitious individualism'. Universality is the password: 'Only a universal new creativity can express itself as style in all objects.' That was the ideal: the co-operation of artists who wanted to create a harmonious environment by designing towns, houses, interiors, decoration, lighting, floors – decoration as a balanced composition, down to the smallest detail. An early attempt to do this was Van Doesburg's 'Attempt at colour composition in interior' (1919)'.

Apart from this programmatic credo Van Doesburg contributed with only modest articles to the first issues of *De Stijl*. It was the painter Mondriaan who carried the torch of abstract and universal art in a long series of articles: *De Nieuwe Beelding in de Schilderkunst* ('The New Creativity in Painting').

We have already noted the fragmentation of familiar reality which one encounters in the work of poets such as Nijhoff and Van Ostaijen, which is related to their despair about the human condition. In Mondriaan's paintings, as in those of Van Doesburg, we can also observe an inexorable process of reduction. The great difference, however, is that this is not a reduction inflicted by fate and experienced with horror, but a deliberate reduction as the logical consequence of the artists' rejection of mimetic art.

(16) Van Doesberg, *Composition in Dissonance*

It is a reduction in pursuit of ultimate purity, as in Van Doesburg's *Composition in Dissonance*, which in a sequence of six pictorical frames reduces the human figure to a geometrical abstraction, enhanced by dazzling colour effects which a half-tone illustration (Fig. 16) unfortunately cannot convey. Mondriaan, too, was searching to express the relationships between elements which had been abstracted as far as possible from their natural forms.[16] He believed that the balance and order which he sought could only be found in art in the composition of geometrical forms. Mondriaan's energy was thus directed towards expressing purity, balance and harmony. He aimed at order in all areas of life, beginning with the minutiae of one's own environment, and his atelier in Paris itself looked like an abstract painting in primary colours, in which the artist's work in progress on the easel is indistinguishable from the decorated walls of the room. To Mondriaan it was a sanctuary where he could live in the harmony which he hoped would one day pervade existence as a whole.

Mondriaan's concept of art and life was in fact static; his aim was ultimate stillness, and this was where he and Van Doesburg disagreed. The latter's concept of art and life was dynamic. Earlier movements in art had led to this particular phase which was called 'neo-plasticism', *nieuwe beelding*, a term coined by Van Doesburg and Mondriaan to indicate their own artistic programme; after this there would be other movements, other ideas. Time and space could not be ruled out as factors in human life. As they affected life, so they would affect and change artistic concepts. Van Doesburg's prolific writings, as well as his increasingly convoluted style, sometimes obscured the fact that his basic programme remained fundamentally the same throughout his life: to reform mankind by reforming art. The main tenets of his theory are clearly stated in his first substantial programmatic essay, published in the periodical *De Beweging* in 1916.

Van Doesburg judged that a break in art had occurred with the advent of Impressionism. Until then the visual arts in Europe had been mimetic and largely applied in the service of religious or secular powers. The fundamental change which the Impressionists brought about was that they saw their subjects as of minor importance in themselves; of prime interest was the potential contribution of the subjects as an element in the total composition of a painting or other work of art. Van Doesburg pleaded for an art which would become totally emancipated, that is, that its importance should be totally independent of and divorced from natural subjects. In fact, natural forms were seen as a hindrance to the perception of the spiritual value of a work of art. One should attempt to negate the natural value of an object in order to be able to see its artistic and spiritual value. Thus, Van Doesburg wrote, a painting of an apple will only be art if and when the spectator is able to experience the spiritual value which the artist has given the painting by transforming a well-known natural phenomenon such as 'apple' into an independent spiritual composition. The difference between the pre-Impressionists and modern art he judged to be 'that the former pour their emotion into a form derived from nature, whereas the artist of this time transmits his emotion into a *beeldende* ['expressive' or 'plastic'] form'. To distinguish between the two concepts of form, Van Doesburg gives the example of the natural form of a tree, which in *beeldende* form becomes a line; or that of a rose, which in expressive form is rendered as round and red.[17] Here too, a process of reduction is applied similar to that advocated by Mondriaan. Both men were aiming at an art which saw as its task to create paintings from which the natural form had been evicted, whose content was adequately transmitted by the *beeldende* form alone. All reference to natural reality should be banned, and that also implied that perspective, that great means of creating an illusion of reality, had to go. A painting consisted of a flat piece of canvas in a frame and had to remain so undisguisedly; its plane was to be filled by relating geometrical forms and colours to each other in a perfectly harmonious composition.[18]

It was one thing to apply such theories to painting, but it turned out to be much more difficult to use them in projects where practical considerations had to play a role, such as in architectural projects. The Café Aubette project had clearly created a space in which people definitely did not feel at home. Greater difficulties faced the architects connected with *De Stijl* and the case of J. J. P. Oud illustrates this.[19] For Oud the creation of an environment for living was not a theosophical ideal, as for Mondriaan, nor an absolute artistic concept, as for Van Doesburg. He was interested in the application of new building materials and in designing new kinds of housing not only from an artistic, but also from a social point of view. In 1918 Oud was appointed town architect of Rotterdam and faced with the massive task of providing much needed housing for the workers of Rotterdam's expanding industry. He was a pupil of the architect Berlage, the builder of the famous *Beurs* ('Exchange') in Amsterdam and the Kröller-Müller Museum of Modern Art, as well as a hunting lodge and several other houses for the wealthy Kröller-Müller family, who were great patrons of the arts. Notwithstanding these assignments, Berlage was a convinced Socialist who saw as the task of architecture to help build a better society. Oud was deeply influenced by his master in this respect, as well as sharing with him the feeling that in the co-operation of the various arts lay the possibility of giving new life to a monumental community art. Moreover Berlage, long before Mondriaan and Van Doesburg, had formulated the characteristics of a modern architecture: simplicity, the use of geometrical forms, order and regularity. Oud continued and developed Berlage's ideas, but instead of using the traditional bricks started to experiment with concrete, which created a revolution in building all over Europe and America, making possible shapes and sizes which had never been seen before. Above all, this allowed building materials to be produced on an industrial scale and allowed construction to proceed more rapidly.

Oud and Van Doesburg managed to work together for a number of years. Van Doesburg designed the colour schemes for a number of buildings, as well as interior decorative elements, such as tiled floors and stained-glass windows, features of *De Stijl* which really did become popular and can be seen in numerous *inter bellum* houses in the Netherlands. The break in their relationship and their co-operation was due to two things, and they were characteristic flaws. Oud, of necessity, had to take into account practical considerations; Van Doesburg, however, totally concentrated on the aesthetic elements and would not compromise. They also clashed in their individuality as artists. Oud did not take kindly to having his designs affected by Van Doesburg's colour schemes in such a way that the lines and the shapes of the buildings were obscured or interfered with; Van Doesburg was reluctant to have his theories about colours and lines subjected to the demands of the architectural structure.

This was a very typical situation: the artists of *De Stijl* were, inevitably, individualists. In principle they cherished a common ideal, the creation of a better world, but in practice their aims were worlds apart. It is not surprising that practically the only satisfactory and still existing creation of a total environment was accomplished by one man, the gifted furniture-maker Gerrit Rietveld (1888–1964).[20] The so-called Schröder House in Utrecht (1923), designed by Rietveld, formed a dramatic contrast to the adjacent houses build in more traditional style (Fig. 17). The Schröder house had a number of movable inner walls, which gave the interior (Fig. 18) an airy aspect. Free-standing furniture, amongst which was the famous Berlin chair, was in complete harmony, in colour and line, with the wall decorations and partitions. The only curved lines came from some of the light fixtures, vases and other small objects, and thus, notwithstanding the very varied colour schemes and the variations in space made possible by the movable walls a harmonious and peaceful atmosphere was created. Mrs Truus Schröder who herself contributed ideas for the design of the open-plan upper storey, was still living in the house in 1980 – proof of its viability.

An inhabitant of another house designed by an architect–designer connected with *De Stijl* once remarked that the mere entry of a person into the rooms with their careful detailed colour scheme was enough to disturb the whole arrangement; such an environment did not allow itself to be lived in, and remained merely the application of theoretical artistic principles: in effect a mockery of the stated aims of *De Stijl*. Thus the proclamation of a new environment for living in the pages of *De Stijl* remained a largely theoretical vision, and most of the blueprints that were designed were satisfactory only in an aesthetic respect. Moreover, *De Stijl* architects suffered from the same paradox as Berlage had: even though they did desire to create monumental community buildings, they often only had the chance to apply their artistic principles when building for a private, and wealthy, patron. Oud did manage to get some assignments where he could combine artistic with utilitarian principles, but his housing blocks for the workers of Rotterdam, even though a vast improvement on the existing housing for the working class, show how diluted the artistic ideals had become.

It is never simple to show explicit connections between social ideals and aesthetic aspirations. *De Stijl*'s ideals were not backed up in the periodical by any political manifestos. One does encounter calls for the artists of Europe to unite, but there is no support for the international Socialist Movement, let alone for revolution. Here we must distinguish between the apolitical views of Van Doesburg and a number of sympathisers who ultimately determined the professed outlook of the periodical, and the views of a number of others for whom *De Stijl*'s separation of political and artistic ideology was intolerable. The events connected with the reactions to the Russian Revolution caused quite a rift in *De Stijl*.[21] Amongst its contributors were two fervent and dedicated Communists, the architects Jan Wils[22] and Robert van 't Hoff.[23] Like many others, Van Doesburg and other non-Communists included, they expected the imminent collapse of Western Europe's decadent bourgeois capitalist society and its individualism. *De Stijl*'s very first manifesto in 1918 included an attack on bourgeois individualism:

Manifesto I,1:
There is an old and new consciousness of time. The old is directed towards the individual. The new is directed towards the universal. The struggle of the individual against the universal reveals itself both in the world struggle as well as in the art of our time.

Manifesto I,7:
The artists of today have been driven the whole world over by the same consciousness and therefore have taken part from an intellectual point of view in this war against the domination of individual despotism. They therefore sympathize with all who work for the formation of an international unity in Life, Culture, either intellectually or materially.[24]

(*facing* 17, 18) The Schröder House, exterior and interior

This manifesto, printed in four languages, meant to bring the periodical to the attention of an international audience, but for Wils and Van 't Hoff the 'struggle' meant a political struggle, and they mistakenly believed that the *De Stijl* editors were just as sympathetic to a politically engaged art as they themselves were.

This impression seemed confirmed when in 1919 *De Stijl* published a German version of a translation of a Soviet statement on their artistic policies, which was hailed as quite in accordance with some of the ideas forwarded by the periodical.[25] These included the levelling-out of the distinctions between the various arts and between craft and industrial workers; the artistic education of the population, and the legal protection of the arts. Such ideas had also been expressed and found sympathy outside the circles of *De Stijl*: various Dutch newspapers discussed these issues, and so did the most influential Communist art critic (and medievalist) Dr Jan Knuttel, the mouthpiece, in artistic matters, of the Dutch Communist Party. Knuttel too, like Wils, Van 't Hoff and others, confidently expected a Soviet form of government to be established in the Netherlands in the near future. It is curious how the medievalist Knuttel judged the past he knew and loved so well to be the model for the future of his society: 'When the foundation laid in Russia is also established in Western Europe in a relatively small number of years, then there will be the possibility to achieve that unity of the concept of life, that similarity of views, which the Middle Ages knew.'[26] It was very difficult to get information to and from Russia, as the Dutch Government, and other European powers, put a ban on postal traffic with the Soviet Union. In 1919 a group of artists, amongst them some members of *De Stijl*, took the initiative to present a petition to the Dutch House of Commons to lift the ban. Van Doesburg, with his international contacts and prestige, had been asked to lobby his foreign friends and colleagues to petition their governments. Van Doesburg, however, failed to send on the translations of the request and nothing came of it.[27] Van 't Hoff and Wils were so disgusted that they withdrew from *De Stijl*; Wils[28] remained true to its artistic principles, but Van 't Hoff,[29] on whom it had dawned that the proletarian Revolution was a mirage, even abandoned his profession and completely withdrew from public life. A great pity, as this talented architect was one of the members of *De Stijl* who really combined, with passion, both political and artistic beliefs, blueprints and visions.

It was clear, however, that for such believers *De Stijl* was not the right place. The periodical opted for a purely artistic position, wishing to remain above politics. Van Doesburg is reported to have mockingly spoken of all those 're-ra-revolutionaries, who stood in the way of that which was new'.[30] *De Stijl*, with so many practising artists amongst its members, was surprisingly theoretical and abstract, and one cannot help feeling that the avant-garde, in its very attempts to establish a new world for all, was isolating itself by creating constant gaps between the ideals and the realisation of those ideals. To give one example: the architect Vilmos Huszar[31] designed complete interiors even before his connection with *De Stijl*, but his designs were seldom carried out, as he would not allow his clients a say in the matter. There emanated from many of *De Stijl* members, besides Huszar, a strong sense of artistic superiority and elitism, which made their fulminations against the decadent bourgeois individualism of the 'The Eightiers' ring somewhat hollow.

Van Doesburg's literary effort also sagged under the weight of the aesthetic theories of which they were the practical application, though one cannot help admiring his versatility. Quite apart from his theoretical, philosophical and critical work, he wrote poetry, rhymed fables, a play, prose fiction and an 'automatically written' novel, *het andere gezicht* ('the other face'). *De Stijl* contains only a small portion of his fictional writings, many of which were written before 1917. It is Hannah L. Hedrick's[32] merit to have unearthed and studied Van Doesburg's early and largely unpublished fictional writings, as well as his widely scattered theoretical work. It is yet another paradox that this Modernist used a time-hallowed form to educate his readers: he wrote quite a number of moralistic–didactic tales, grotesque fables, entirely traditional in title and moral, reminiscent of Aesop, with titles such as *The Lark and the Sparrow* or *The Pipe and the Tobacco*, but experimental in structure and in the representation of sound. Equally moralistic is the title of his play, *Resurrection, an Historical Philosophical Play on Beauty and Love in One Act*, in which the artist is portrayed as the reformer of the imperfect world. Other prose tales demonstrate the use of the artist's God-given power to change his fellow-men. A theme which occurred here would prove to be a lasting preoccupation for Van Doesburg and other Modernists: that of the destructive power of the worship of beauty. In some of the tales the moral is explained by the time-honoured contrast between negative physical and positive spiritual beauty.

There is precious little humour or playfulness in Van Doesburg's writings; the light touch which makes Van Ostaijen's message so penetrating is utterly lacking. Some of his work is often classified as Dadaist, but this is perhaps valid only for his creation and use of different identities. He established two *alter egos* for himself, that of the poet I. K. Bonset, the name possibly an anagram of *ik ben sot* ('I am crazy'), and that of the Italian philosopher Aldo Camini. It was possibly due to his relationship with Mondriaan that Van Doesburg found it necessary to provide himself with these poetical and philosophical bolt-holes. In the guise of Bonset he published his poetry which he then, as Van Doesburg, was able to discuss and to praise as the successful embodiment of Modernist poetic theory. In the guise of Camini he was able to produce theories which deviated from those of Mondriaan, and as Van Doesburg he could debate aesthetic problems with Camini.

The introduction of Camini into the pages of *De Stijl* would not have been out of place in a Walter Scott novel. Van Doesburg had found, he wrote,[33] piles of dusty papers in an attic somewhere in Italy, and reading them he realised he had stumbled on the writings of an important philosopher, obviously not long dead, whose amazingly modern approach to art and life made him destined for publication in *De Stijl*. Thus Van Doesburg claimed to have found a means of having his own theories backed up by a poet and by a philosopher. In particular, Bonset's poetry and his abstract novel *het andere gezicht*[34] were supposed to be proof of an artist's ability to perceive the inner shape and significance of objects, living things or events. The artist has second sight with which he is able to see the other, spiritual face of reality. He can penetrate the natural forms with his X-ray vision. In his poems *X-beelden* ('X-images')[35] he tried to express the near mystical experience of the mingling of individual perception and of a kind of collective awareness of the world outside the individual, as in for instance *ik word doordrongen* ('i am penetrated'), in which the simultaneity of the experiences and of the creation of the poem is suggested by the absence of normal punctuation and capital letters; where the latter occur they indicate loudness or intensity. Not only is the poet here able to register and express reality, but he feels that he is merging with it, as is stated in the last line with its triumphant capital letters *RUIMTE BEN IK* ('INFINITE SPACE AM I'). Far from merging into space, the poet's ego seems here to stand out rather conspicuously. Van Doesburg's sense of self, of his elevated status as an artist, calls up echoes of the despised individualistic 'Eightiers'.

Van Doesburg's literary work did not inspire any followers. When in the early 1950s a truly experimental group of poets transformed poetry in the Netherlands, it was not to his work, but to that of Van Ostaijen they turned. In much of his interior designs, too, he remained aloof from human reality. And yet it was due to him that a number of artists and architects were given a forum and an identity by his initiative of founding *De Stijl*; it was Van Doesburg who acted as a travelling salesman for the Dutch Modernists and re-introduced the Netherlands, after the isolation of the war years, into modern artistic Europe. Nor must we forget the real influence Van Doesburg exerted on the ideas generated by the Bauhaus architects. Walter Gropius invited him to come to the Bauhaus in 1921, where Van Doesburg staged a revolution by attacking the teachings of Johannes Itten and opening a rival school of painting, sculpture and architecture. His lessons soon drew so many Bauhaus students that Gropius had to try and save his own school by forbidding the students to follow Van Doesburg's classes. Notwithstanding this prohibition the school continued to flourish until 1923, when Van Doesburg left for Paris. Many Bauhaus designs betray the influence of his architectural ideas, while even Gropius himself was not impervious to them.[36] The most tangible reminder of Van Doesburg's efforts, however, can be found in the Netherlands itself: in the ordinary streets of every town the expansion of the 1930s and 1940s owe a lot to *De Stijl*'s architectural idiom, and thus he did, though more indirectly perhaps than he would have wished, help to realise a bit of our brave new world.

Notes to chapter 16

1   E. H. Kossmann, *The Low Countries 1780–1940*, Oxford, 1978, Ch. VIII.
2   Kossmann, *op. cit.*, pp. 443–4.
3   Herman Gorter, 'Mei', in *Verzamelde Werken*, 8 vols., Bussum—Amsterdam, 1948–52, Vol. 1.
4   H. de Liagre Böhl, *Herman Gorter. Zijn politieke activiteiten van 1909 tot 1920 in de opkomende kommunistische beweging in Nederland*, Nijmegen, 1973.
5   Paul van Ostaijen, *Verzameld Werk*, ed. Gerrit Borgers, 6th revised edn, 4 vols., Amsterdam, 1979.
6   A. L. Sötemann, 'Non-spectacular modernism: Martinus Nijhoff's poetry in its European context', in *Nijhoff, Van Ostaijen, 'De Stijl': Modernism in the Netherlands and Belgium in the first quarter of the 20th century*, ed. Francis Bulhof, The Hague, 1976, pp. 95–116.
7   Martinus Nijhoff, *Verzamelde Gedichten*, Amsterdam, 1978.
8   Jan Brandt Corstius, 'The international context of Dutch literary modernism 1915–1930', in *Sölemann, op. cit.*, pp. 8–22.
9   Jan Romein and A. H. M. Romein-Verschoor, 'Hendrik Petrus Berlage, Bouw-meester der Beurs 1856–1934', in *Erflaters van onze Beschaving XIXe eeuw*, Amsterdam, 1941, pp. 276–307.
10 J. J. Oversteegen, *Vorm of Vent. Opvattingen over de aard van het literaire werk in de Nderlandse kritiek tussen de twee wereldoorlogen*, Amsterdam, 1969, Ch. II.
11 Carel Blotkamp, 'Theo van Doesburg', in *De Beginjaren van De Stijl 1917–1922*, eds. Carel Blotkamp *et al.*, Utrecht, 1982, pp. 13–46.
12 'Café Aubette', in *De Stijl 1917–1931*, eds. H. L. C. Jaffe *et al.*, Amsterdam, 1982, pp. 191–6.
13 *De Stijl* 1, August 1917, No. 1.
14 Blotkamp, *ed. cit.*, p. 10.
15 Jaffe, *ed. cit.*, p. 13.
16 Els Hoek, 'Piet Mondriaan', in Blotkamp, *op. cit.*, pp. 47–82; 'Mondriaans atelier in Parijs 1926–1931', in pp. 80–6.
17 *De Beweging* 12.1(1916) 5, pp. 124–31; 12.1(1916) 6, pp. 219–27.
18 *De Beweging*.

19   Hans Esser, 'J. J. P. Oud', in Blotkamp, *ed. cit.*, pp. 125–54.
20   Marijke Küper, 'Gerrit Rietveld', in *ibid.*, pp. 263–86; Martin Filler, 'De meubels van Gerrit Rietveld: Manifesten voor een nieuwe revolutie', in Jaffe, *ed. cit.*, pp. 125–36; 'Het Rietveld-Schröder huis', in *De Stijl 1917–1931*, pp. 137–46.
21   Ger Harmsen, 'De Stijl en de Russische Revolutie', in Jaffe, *ed. cit.*, pp. 45–50.
22   Sjarel Ex and Els Hoek, 'Jan Wils', in Blotkamp, *ed. cit.*, pp. 187–206.
23   Eveline Vermeulen, 'Robert van 't Hoff', in *ibid.*, pp. 207–32.
24   Manifest I, in *De Stijl* 2, November 1918, No. 1, pp. 2–5.
25   'Russisch Manifest', in *De Stijl* 2, April 1919, No. 6, pp. 68–9.
26   Jaffe, *ed. cit.*, pp. 45–6.
27   *Ibid.*, p. 46.
28   Blotkamp, *ed. cit.*, pp. 200–1.
29   *Ibid.*, pp. 228–9.
30   *Ibid.*, p. 201.
31   Sjarel Ex, 'Vilmos Huszar', in *ibid.*, pp. 83–124.
32   Hannah L. Hedrick, *Theo van Doesburg. Propagandist and Practioner of the Avant Garde, 1909–1923*, Ann Arbor, 1980.
33   *De Stiji* 4, July 1921, No. 7, p. 97.
34   I. K. Bonset, 'het andere gezicht', in *De Stijl*, 1926–8.
35   I. K. Bonset, 'X-beelden', in *De Stijl* 4, November 1921, No. 11.
36   Kenneth Frampton, '*De Stijl*. The Evolution and Dissolution of Neoplasticism: 1917–31' in *Concepts of Modern Art*, ed. Nikos Stangos, London, 1985, pp. 147–8.

Politics and the silent cinema: *The Cabinet of Dr Caligari* and *Battleship Potemkin*

In his influential book on the early German cinema, *From Caligari to Hitler*, Siegfried Kracauer describes the original scenario of *The Cabinet of Dr Caligari*[1] as 'an outspoken revolutionary story'.[2] This revolutionary story, Kracauer argues, was turned into a 'conformist' one by the people at the production company, Decla Bioscop. They added a framework narrative to the original idea by Carl Mayer and Hans Janowitz, redefining the action as the delusion of a madman and thus neutralising the anti-authoritarian thrust of the original.

It is now clear that Kracauer's account of the circumstances surrounding the production of this film is misleading. In the first place, Janowitz himself has acknowledged (in an unpublished memoir) that he and Mayer were not fully conscious of the political implications of their original idea. The possibility of interpreting the film as an allegory of the abuse of state authority only dawned on them retrospectively.[3] Furthermore, Kracauer had no access to the original scenario itself, a copy of which has come to light since his book was published.[4] The screenplay is less susceptible to political interpretation than even Janowitz suggests. As S. S. Prawer has pointed out: 'the typescript [of the screenplay] asks us to regard Caligari as a dedicated scientist whose mind has given way, as a man to be pitied, as a tragic figure. It offers little support for Kracauer's thesis of a revolutionary or anti-tyrannical tendency that those who made the film then prevented.'[5]

The original typescript concerns a mysterious showman who exhibits a somnambulist at a fair by day, and directs his exhibit – Cesare – to commit murders by night, under the influence of hypnosis. The story is narrated by a young man named Francis, whose friend is one of the murderer's victims. The narrator's enquiries lead to the identification of the showman as none other than the director of a nearby lunatic asylum. Janowitz later interpreted this as an allegory of insane state authority – an attack on the system which had directed *its* helpless victims to commit murder, as conscripts in the Great War.

A close examination of the original script reveals that it, too, had a framework narrative which was in its own way no less conservative than that later imposed by Decla. In the original, the story is told after what has evidently been a congenial bourgeois dinner party, from the veranda of a comfortable country residence. Francis, who was to become the deranged narrator of the film version, has in this script been happily married to Jane (the principal female role in the main story) for twenty years. In other words, the disturbance in the bourgeois order of things, which is recounted in the main story, is compensated for by the reassuring stability of the framework. The whole script has a decidedly nineteenth-century feel about it.

What, on the other hand, are not nineteenth-century about the script are the distinctly cinematic elements introduced by Janowitz and Mayer (Mayer was to become the most significant screenwriter of the early German cinema). Apart from the ideas for many of the most striking visual effects of the film, these elements included the following: the focus on the beautiful, prone heroine, the rooftop chase, and the narrative structure of the detective story. It is notable, however, that none of these elements contributes to the political dimension of the film.

What is interesting about *Caligari* from the political point of view is the subsequent psychologisation of the original anti-authoritarian idea. This resulted from two market-determined production decisions made at Decla: first, the interpolation of a deranged narrator, which internalises the action and undermines the notion that it is authority which is really insane; and secondly, the use of stylised flat painted sets, which further displace the action – and the bodies which are its agents – from the plane of mundane reality. The Decla poster (Fig. 19) served to accentuate the disorientating effect of the sets.

Kracauer's most valid point is that it is precisely this internalisation of a tale of political rebelliousness which makes the film characteristic of the state of the German political imagination around 1919: 'There could be no better configuration of symbols for that uprising against the authoritarian dispositions which apparently occurred under the cover of a behaviour rejecting uprising' (p. 67). What Kracauer is saying here is that the various components of the production of *Caligari* acted together (though without any unified intention) to produce a representation of the plight of the German bourgeois imagination. The film reflects the convergent effects of the interrelated technologies of the World War and the capitalist film industry.

Far from distorting the political content of the original script, the actual film brings out its underlying substance: a substance which is essentially

(facing 19) *The Cabinet of Doctor Caligari,* poster *(and* 20) Distorted visions of authority: Caligari and the Town Clerk

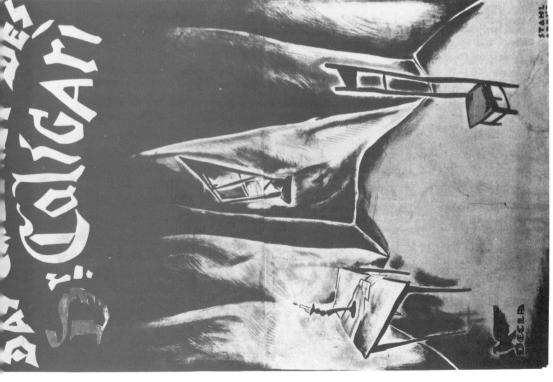

(*facing* 21) External world or the subconscious? Caligari enters the Fairground
(*and* 22) Caligari exhibiting Cesare: the secret impossible to disclose
(*this page* 23) *Battleship Potemkin*, poster for display in Germany

self-subversive. Janowitz explains the political meaning of the psychological tale by saying that it intuitively reflected objective reality, as they (and millions of others of their generation) had endured its imprint: 'world history . . . experienced on our bodies and in our innermost hearts'.[6] But they were also writing within the context of inherited bourgeois culture, from which they derived both the motifs of the fantastic[7] and the compensating counter-structure of the stable narrative framework. Hence their script, in its political semi-consciousness, was couched in the language of the Romantic and bourgeois traditions of the nineteenth century. But it also made concessions to the market demands of popular cinema, caught up in the aftermath of the First World War with its crisis of national self-confidence. No wonder the film's anti-tyrannical impulse becomes displaced by a visionary mode of expression which is ultimately subordinated to the objective authority under attack.

All these ambiguous elements converge, under Robert Wiene's direction, to transform an unremarkable script into a compelling film. The framework narrative seeks to render the main story uncontroversial, but it is at the same time an excuse for telling it. The painted sets, which are a brilliant way of marketing bourgeois culture (in the then popular form of Expressionism), displace not just the story, but also the very status of the images. They transform secure identity into a space in which reality and illusion have to make their claims and counter-claims without the benefit of a stable meta-language. That the framework narrative does not fulfil this function has often been noted.[8]

These conflicting determinations pose the problem of the value of depth psychology as an artistic perspective, indeed of the value of individualism as a focus for understanding and evaluating the world at large. The film's style, in other words, produces its effects by confusing the distinction between 'inside' and 'outside'.

The film resolutely internalises the original story, and by this inward movement reveals the space of interiority as problematic. As Thomas Elsaesser says in his excellent analysis of the film: 'It would be inaccurate to say that in the German silent cinema all social conflicts become internalised, "psychologised" – unless one added that this interiorisation is of such a virulent kind that it tends to threaten and disturb the very process of psychological containment or resolution.'[9]

One might object that the film does produce a stable metaphorical language with which to express distorted visions of authority, such as the town clerk perched on his impossibly high stool (Fig. 20); or the inturned aggression of a deranged mind, in the form of jagged and threatening shapes and an architecture that seems on the point of implosion. This point of view has been persuasively argued by Noel Carroll.[10] But the actual experience of watching the film is more confusing. It is very difficult to tell whether the figure of Werner Krauss, as Caligari shuffling towards his appointment with the town clerk, is in a street or a corridor. Similarly, the courtyard of the lunatic asylum is not clearly interior or exterior, indeed, it is *both* interior and exterior to Francis's narrative.[11] Then again, what spatial connotation for the viewer does the celebrated iris-in to the Holstenwall fair have? This intensification of camera focus remains ambiguous. Are we moving *out* into the hurly burly of the real world, or *down* into the subconscious areas from which the film so memorably has Caligari make his entrance? (See Fig. 21.)

'Outside' thus develops into an impossible but inescapable mental fact. To attempt to escape out into the countryside (as Cesare does) is to collapse from exhaustion and die amidst the painted grass. To attempt to unravel a plot (as Francis does), is to become hopelessly involved oneself (a familiar motif!). To provide a normalising frame is to permit the uncertainty to make further inroads.

The medium of film itself resists the attempt to de-documentarise or de-technologise it. What is meant by this can be illustrated by reference to that image which most memorably conveys the ambiguity of 'inside' and 'outside': the human head, especially in close-up. There is a memorable sequence in which the viewer is moved with inexorable cinematic logic towards the disclosure of Caligari's exhibit (see Fig. 22). First the tent opens, then the curtain, then the coffin-like box. Herein stands Cesare, his head the most secret, fascinating place of all, and the opening of his eyes is the drawing aside of the curtain of the soul. But, of course no magical revelation of interiority takes place, no secret landscape of the mind, only the hypnotised gaze of the actor, Veidt, directed straight at the camera. This blank face functions as a block to the spectator's eagerness for ever more intimate disclosure. The audience now finds itself transfixed by a gaze which re-enacts its own hypnotised enslavement to the lure of the camera. The eyes reveal only captivity, not security and satisfied repose.

In the silent film there is no dialogue to produce the sort of linguistic alibi which, in the sound film, compensates for the impenetrability of the human face.[12] The closing shot of Krauss as the asylum director illustrates this point. Here, the overt meaning, namely that the deviation of Francis can now be corrected by society, has to be read against the resistance of an actual face, in this case presented as authentic by virtue of the fact that Krauss appears without his make-up. What is going on inside that head, behind that face, remains a mystery. Thus an uncertainty is produced about the relation between psychology and social power; and this uncertainty has the profoundest political implications, exactly as Janowitz envisaged.[13] Moreover, the very dwelling on the face, without speech, posits the head as a place of incarceration like the others which feature so prominently in the film: cabinet, cell, strait-jacket. This again pushes the viewer up against the question of inside and outside: is the film 'out there', begun, finished and closed by a long close-up of the face of normality? Or is it all in the head, my head, a place from which there is no escape *outside,* into the world of social and political action?

Caligari's political implications derive from its strategic attempts to do without any. It is highly significant that its central motif – like that of Thomas Mann's allegory of fascism, *Mario and the Magician* (1930) – is the abuse of hypnotism. But where Mann's ironic narrative criticially distances us from the seductive manipulations of the hypnotist, the visual medium of Wiene's film precludes this kind of detachment. What becomes evident instead is a kind of complicity between the artistic medium of film and the ideological potential of the cinema as a medium for the collective manipulation of consciousness. *Caligari* projects the image of its own functioning: the hypnotic power of the cinema. This power is both exploited and exposed to critical scrutiny. This is the source both of the film's political ambivalence and of its aesthetic radicalism.

Battleship Potemkin was made in the Soviet Union in 1925, as part of the official twentieth-anniversary celebrations of the 1905 Revolution. It was orginally intended as a chronicle of the whole revolutionary year, to which end Nina Agadzanova-Sutko had prepared a lengthy literary scenario. Eisenstein, his cameraman Edward Tissé and their collaborators decided in the course of their work to restrict their film to the events at Odessa of the summer of 1905, and particularly to the uprising of the sailors of the Black Sea fleet. The mutiny aboard the cruiser *Potemkin* became representative of the year as a whole.[14] And the success of the film, particularly in Germany, brought Eisenstein world fame.[15]

Battleship Potemkin[16] is explicitly a political film. It is the product of the new approach to art possible in a post-revolutionary situation, where a new frankness prevails with regard to the sacred topic of art itself, and where finance is available independently of market constraints. Eisenstein's art is the antithesis to *Caligari,* a film which he regarded as negative, unhealthy and representative of a futureless introspection which affronted the vibrant young medium of film.[17] He decared that a film without a message was an artistic non-starter,[18] and worked in the context of an intellectual and cultural milieu which made it possible to say: 'Our cultural creative work is now entirely purpose orientated. . . . The concepts of "pure science", "pure art" and "self-valuable truths and beauties" are foreign to us.'[19] His views on art and culture, like those of others in avant-garde post-revolutionary circles, were steadfastly anti-individualist, because they saw in individualism the hallmark of the bourgeois culture they rejected.[20]

Lion Feuchtwanger, in his novel *Erfolg* (Berlin, 1930), described the stunning effect this Soviet propaganda film had on the smart audiences of Berlin. Word was about that here was something genuinely new: 'a film without structure, without women, without plot action; tension replaced by political direction'.[21] These terms convey rather well some ways in which collectivist art can or might differ from individualist art. The German poster for *Potemkin* (Fig. 23) conveys dynamic action, not brooding introspection. The accusation that the film has no structure is of course not true, but it does lack the sort of structure a bourgeois audience expects: a narrative, characteristically involving the exploitation of women. *Caligari* has both these elements, although they are somewhat estranged. *Potemkin* dispenses with these constituents of individualist culture in favour of the construction of a collectivist vision.

How does Eisenstein set about this task? Perhaps one can pursue the contrast with *Caligari* a little further in order to answer this question. Each of the two films invites its audience to respond in a distinctive way. Their modes of self-consciousness are divergent (whilst they are both distinctly modern in that they *are* self-conscious). The self-consciousness of *Caligari* is aesthetic rather than technical. It reflects film only in its alienated psychological form as hypnotism. It raises profound questions of an epistemological nature by juxtaposing theatrical flats with real people: an image of problematic depth projected on to a flat screen.[22]

Potemkin, however, is self-conscious in a technical sense; it openly acknowledges its technological basis. Film is produced by creating the impression of a moving picture by means of the rapid succession of static ones. Tissé and Eisenstein announce this frankly and wittily in the celebrated sequence of the stone lion, in which static images of three different statues succeed one another in such a way as to seem to make the stone lion stir, awake and then rise to its feet.

The lions draw attention to the activity of editing, and this self-conscious activity of montage is the key to the film's style. We are always aware of the medium of film being used to a certain end, and in this way the film dispenses with the illusionism characteristic of the realist novel and the narrative cinema.

Caligari is about illusionism: Caligari's various deceptions; the film's own 'trick' of passing off a delusion as reality until the end. *Potemkin* is about the *use* of technology: about seizing control of the machines that

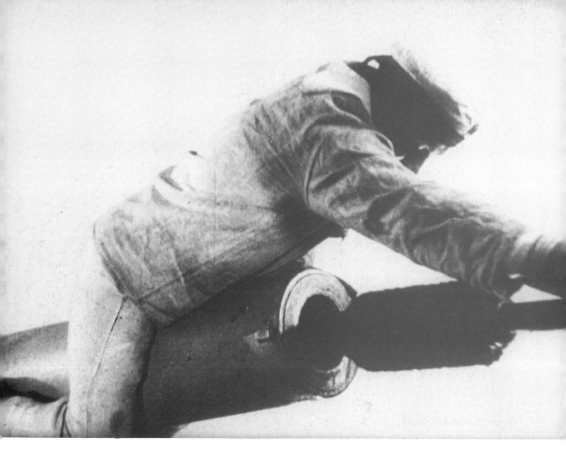

confer power in the material world. The one film celebrates the power of the illusionist's 'Cabinet'. The other treats the battleship, with its awesome technology, as the setting for a struggle for power. *Potemkin* is dedicated to the overthrow of illusions and to liberation from oppression.

There is a parallel here between the gun and the camera. Both represent technologies which have a crucial function in the constitution of reality. And both must be wrested from the wrong hands, by which they are conventionally used to enforce systems of alienation, politically through tsarist oppression, aesthetically through illusionist narrative. They must be restored to their role as mediators between subject and object, so that they may contribute to the construction of non-alienated reality: 'The Machine is no longer an enemy, but a partner and a "comrade" of man.'[23] One felicitous contemporary German review of *Potemkin* said: 'Hier spricht der Film seine Muttersprache' ('Here film is speaking its native language').[24] Eisenstein's language of montage combines the documentary force of cinema with extreme artistic control of means and effects. '*Potemkin* looks like a chronicle (or newsreel) of an event, but it functions as a drama', as Eisenstein himself noted.[25]

(*this page* 24) Cleaning the guns of the *Potemkin*: the relatedness of people and things
(*facing* 25, 26) Quarter-deck of the *Potemkin*: order and energy

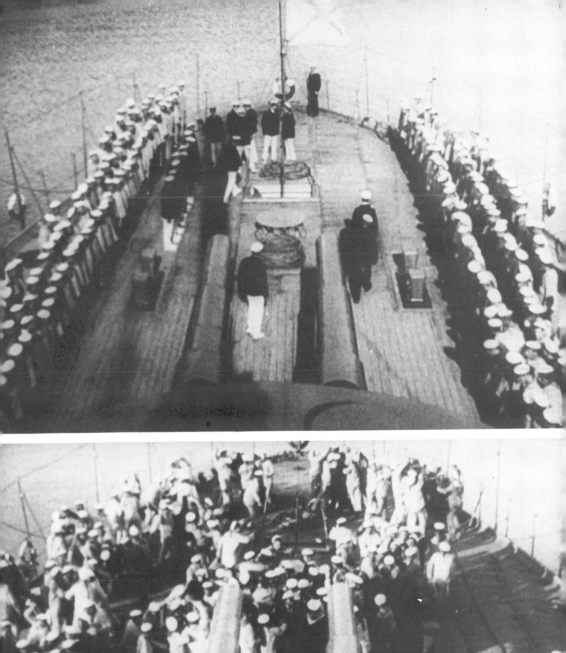
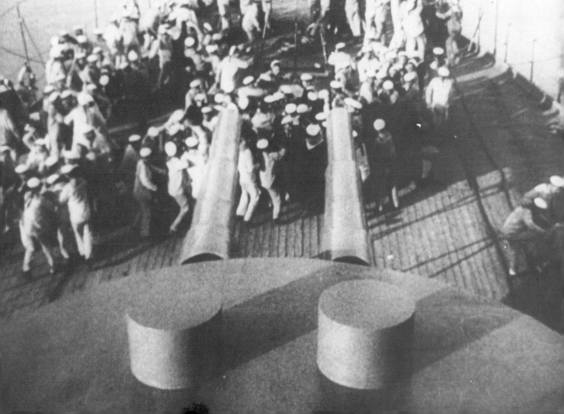

In effect, Eisenstein's use of montage gives to each shot a double function. First, it preserves the immediacy of the photographic image and thus the trace of its own technology; and secondly, it places this sense of immediacy within a higher order of coherence, by means of juxtaposition.

On the level of the individual shot (or sequence of closely related shots), Eisenstein is able to produce images of the immediate connectedness of things and people. Not only does each edited shot bear the trace of its own technology (the relation between image, camera, scissors), but also *within* each shot simple aspects of the relatedness of people and things stand forth clearly. The emphasis is on practical human interaction: eating, forming up on parade, sleeping, cleaning the barrel of a gun (see Fig. 24). Ceremonial symbols are revealed in their functioning as social: pince-nez, cross, or ceremonial sword.

These moments, conveying a sense of being immediate impressions of reality, are organised into a higher coherence, in accordance with the film-makers' sense of the objective constitution of the world. They are made representative of the dynamics of political oppression and the resistance it calls forth; of reality as constituted by class struggle.

Hence, in place of the sort of *Spannung* ('tension') missed by Feucht-wanger's Berlin audiences, one has instead the strong rhythmic play of energies which supply the architectonic structure of the film. Initially, control is exercised by the dominant order in various forms of uniformity, designed to repress the agitation, the disordered movement, amongst the sailors (once roused from their aesthetically composed sleep). This agitation reaches a climax in an anticipatory outburst of actual violence: the sudden breaking of a plate. The decisive struggle between uniform order and dynamic movement is carried out on the quarterdeck. The agitated movement of the sailors is contained in rank and file, only to break free again (see Figs. 25 & 26). Pressure from above, resistance from below, result in the implicit violence of the prevailing order becoming explicit violence: the tarpaulin, thrown over the cowering band of sailors who are about to be shot, replaces discipline. The symbolic violence of the parade ground verges upon the real violence of the firing squad, only to be contained. One cry countermands another: the spontaneous voice of fraternal resistance replaces the routine shout of oppression, which is thereby forced to reveal its latent violence as a scream.

To the compressed violence of the naval establishment, the liberating violence of the sailors now provides an answer. The sweep of this rhythm of violence and containment is carried throughout the film by the motif of the discharge or silence of guns: the muted rifles of the firing squad are answered by the methodical and inhumanly regular firing of the cossacks' rifles. This illicit explicitness of institutionalised violence is answered by the spontaneous and liberating firing of the ship's armaments. Yet the ability to control, contain, and institutionalise power passes to the other side when the admiral's fleet *holds* its fire, in a gesture which suggests revolutionary control of real power, and thus the inauguration of a new law, after a passage through the chaos of lawlessness.

The documentary style of the individual shots and sequences of shots, together with the choice of an authentic historical topic rather than a fictional motif, are formal indications of the film's own relationship to the reality beyond it. Obviously the film is staged or composed and not really documentary at all. But its commitment is to 'fact' rather than 'fiction', to 'contemporaneity' rather than to the past.[26] For through its formal constitution it redefines the historically authentic past in terms directed towards the political future.

This is virtually the antithesis of *The Cabinet of Dr Caligari,* which seeks to deny its connectedness with its material and political contexts, exhibiting them only in an internalised and distorted form (hypnotism; the fairground as the market place of spectacle; absolute authority abused).

Where *Caligari* had moved inwards, *Potemkin* moves outwards. After arguing against the introspective gloom of Wiene's film, Eisenstein goes on to say: 'Our spirit drove us out into life, amongst the masses, out, into the pulsating reality of our country's revival.'[27] Both films feature near the beginning an image of conversation, an image with special resonance in the silent cinema. These images, precisely because they are not supported by audible dialogue, memorably express the divergent functions of linguistic exchange in the two films (see Figs, 27 & 28). The talk in *Caligari* is an exchange of obsessions. The interlocutors do not face each other; they are darkly dressed and shot from slightly above: passive, prone, anonymous and enigmatic. The bulk of the action of the film turns out, of course, to be the content of one of those obsessions (that of Francis, the deranged narrator).

The exchange in *Potemkin* is between interlocutors named by intertitle, Matjusenko and Vaculnicuk. These names are not 'individualising' but documentary (Vaculnicuk becomes most effective as an individual after he is dead, and can serve as a focus for mass feeling!). The shot is from a low angle, giving priority to the situation, rather than to the hypnotic power of film to capture and subjugate through images. The sailors are in uniform, that is to say historically and socially identified. They are talking on the battleship, the metonym of political might. What they say concerns themselves, their fellow-sailors and the revolutionary cause as a whole.

The implications of their words subsequently spread to their

fellow-sailors, then to the good people of Odessa, finally to the entire imperial fleet. This mode of communication ultimately overflows into the auditorium, as the prow of the cruiser, shot from the lowest possible angle, fills the screen at the end of the film to indicate the wave of brotherhood passing beyond the confines of the film. As Eisenstein wrote: 'Over the heads of the battleship's commanders, over the heads of the admirals of the Tsar's fleet, and finally over the heads of the foreign censors, rushes the whole film with its fraternal "Hurrah!" just as within the film the feeling of brotherhood flies from the rebellious battleship over the sea to the shore.'[28]

In retrospect, this euphoria is somewhat problematic. Clearly, the further *Battleship Potemkin* becomes detached from the Soviet Union of the New Economic Policy, the less political its impact.[29] It is not *really* a case of the fraternal 'Hurrah!' spreading throughout the world (although there will always be the possibility of the film functioning politically in a different time and place).

The problem is one of the thorniest in political aesthetics, namely that of emotionalism. Eisenstein, coming as he did from a cultural background (Agit-Prop, *Proletkult,* behaviourism[30]) which approved of the role of emotion in the conveying of propaganda messages, made extensive use of it in both his practice and as a term within his theory. Obviously, *Potemkin* has an enormous emotional appeal, although this is of course the result of careful calculation on the part of its makers. As Brecht observed in an oft-quoted poem on the film, not even the exploiters are immune from the excitement generated by the spontaneous uprising of the sailors.[31] It is impossible to watch the Odessa steps sequence without a most vivid emotional participation; nor is it easy not to rejoice at the slow, deliberate turn of a battleship gun-turret in preparation for the taking of righteous revenge.

Eisenstein explained this manipulation of emotional responses as 'the construction of a Pathos' which, far from repeating the passivity of bourgeois 'psychologism',[32] actually allowed or enabled the audience to feel itself fuse with the historical process represented in the events of the film.[33] Now while this may be true in certain times and places, there is no *necessary* link between the intensity of the emotion and any specific intellectual/political position. Peter Wollen has argued persuasively that Eisenstein's most intractable problem was how 'to reconcile his "idealist" preoccupation with the dialectic with the materialist inheritance he carried with him from the Proletkult theatre',[34] in other words, how to forge a necessary link between the emotions he was able to generate through the art, and a particular *form* of knowing.

In its affirmation of technology (witness the last 'act' especially), in its

(facing 27, 28) Contrasting conversations: *Caligari* and *Potemkin*

self-conscious 'formalism' and its collectivist hostility to narrative illusionism, *Potemkin* bears characteristic features of the European avant-garde of the first decades of the twentieth century. Yet in many crucial aspects it is aesthetically a very conservative work, still essentially remaining 'within the bounds of ordinary aesthetic cinema', as a contemporary Soviet theorist put it.[35] Unlike the work of the more consistently avant-garde film-maker Vertov, it is unashamedly narrative at times; and it reconstructs the past, rather than analysing the present. It may well be informed by a rhythmical structure of energy and restraint, but it is also schematic in its construction. Eisenstein's theoretical account of the way the film is composed in the essay 'The organic and pathos in the composition of *Battleship Potemkin*' sounds more like Aristotle than Marinetti, revealing Eisenstein's dependence on notions like the golden section, or that of the organic itself, which are part of the classical inheritance of European art.

If we seek a counter example of the relationship between artistic experiment, political commitment, and the technology of film, then we should turn to the practice of Erwin Piscator. Piscator was a committed Communist as well as a pioneer of the political theatre. He was conscious, in Weimar Germany, of working in a 'pre-revolutionary' society, towards an actual influence upon his audience, about whose non-proletarian constitution he had no illusions.[36] In the debate about revolutionary art he occupied a more radical position than that of Eisenstein, believing in the primacy of rational argument, and disapproving of the emotionalism of *Potemkin*.[37] But he supported, and was influenced by, the great Russian director in substantial ways. Eisenstein's practice with the *Prolekult* theatre, before his move into full-time film work, in some ways resembled that of Piscator, notably in the anti-illusionist 'review'-like montage of sketches, and the use of film as part of theatrical production.

The production of *Hoppla, wir leben!* by Ernst Toller,[38] with which Piscator opened his own theatre in the Nollendorfplatz, Berlin, in 1927 (the first independent political revolutionary theatre to be established in Germany), was a crucial one in many ways for the themes of this book. As Raymond Williams explains in Chapter 18, its revolutionary stage design made possible a multiplicity of dramatic action on different levels. Figures 29 and 30 show the basic structure of the multi-level set Piscator had specially built for the production, and suggest the kinds of effects which could be achieved with the help of film-projection and stage-acting in eight possible separate areas, each one of which was itself internally adjustable in a variety of ways.

What is relevant here is, first, the way in which film, as technology, was

Hoppla, wir leben! (*facing* 29) Reconstruction of Piscator's stage set, made in 1971 by Werner Schwenke and students of the Schiller Colleg in Berlin (*and* 30) Design by Traugott Müller (1927) for the set showing the various projection areas

used not to *replace* an individualist perspective, as was the case with *Potemkin*, but rather to place the agony of individualist politics in a wider context. Piscator trimmed back the Expressionist despair of Toller's original play, and expanded Toller's suggestions for cinematic illustration of its historical background. The play hinges upon the notion of a Socialist revolutionary, committed to a mental asylum in 1918 and released nine years later, who is traumatically confronted with the 'stabilised' reality of the Weimar Republic in 1927. The main filmic episode of Piscator's production provided documentary illustration of the social, economic and political developments missed by Toller's protagonist during his years of internment. It consisted of a rapid montage of poverty and high life, revolution and reaction. *Hoppla*, incorporating elements from both *Caligari* (the political contradictoriness of Expressionism; the motif of the insane psychiatrist), and *Potemkin* (which Piscator described as 'exemplary proletarian theatre'[39]), seeks to mediate between these two modes of representing cultural and political reality. In *Hoppla* film thus functioned both as a two-dimensional technological alienation of conventional theatre, and as documentary correction to the subjective disorientation suffered by the post-Expressionist protagonist.

Furthermore, Piscator escaped a drawback intrinsic to film constituted as 'a film', rather than film as one medium amongst many. Notwithstanding the care and research which went into the footage used in *Hoppla*,[40] no attempt was made to preserve it after the production. Like the text of Toller's play, the film footage was exploited for its value as material in making a specific series of points about the circumstances of the political life of the Weimar Republic, rather than a work with its own self-sufficient artistic integrity. *Caligari* survives as the ambiguous masterpiece of the Expressionist cinema. *Potemkin* is still the *Monumentalfilm* as which it was advertised in Germany in 1926. But in the very irrecoverable nature of Piscator's experimentation, in its massive investment in the ephemeral, one may discern most distinctly the possibilities and limitations of a genuinely avant-garde politicul culture.

Notes to chapter 17

1 Germany, 1919. Directed by Robert Wiene.
2 Princeton, 1947, p. 64.
3 'The Story of a Famous Story', unpublished manuscript by Hans Janowitz, p. 8. The *Stiftung Deutsche Kinemathek*, Berlin, kindly allowed me to consult the copy of the typescript held in their archive.
4 It is now in the possession of the *Stiftung Deutsche Kinemathek*, who kindly allowed me to read it.

5   S. S. Prawer, *Caligari's Children. The Film as Tale of Terror*, Oxford, 1980, p. 169.

6   Janowitz, *op. cit.*, p. 93.

7   Cf. Lotte Eisner, *Dämonische Leinwand*, Wiesbaden-Biebrich, 1955, p. 11; Thomas Elsaesser, 'Social mobility and the fantastic', *Wide Angle*, Vol. 5, No. 2, 1982, pp. 15–25 (pp. 16, 21–3).

8   For instance, by John D. Barlow, *German Expressionist Film*, Boston, 1982, pp. 45–53.

9   Elsaesser, *op. cit.*, p. 23.

10   'The Cabinet of Dr Kracauer', *Millenium Film Journal*, Vol. 1, No, 2, 1978, pp. 77–85.

11   For further examples, see Carroll, *op. cit.*, p. 84.

12   Cf. Stephen Heath, *Questions of Cinema*, London, 1981, p. 191.

13   Cf. Prawer, *op. cit.*, p. 174.

14   See Werner Sudendorf, *Sergej Eisenstein: Materialien zu Leben und Werk*, Munich and Vienna, 1975, p. 55.

15   For the reception of *Potemkin*, see Hans-Joachim Schlegel, 'Eisensteins filmische Konstruktion des revolutionären Pathos. Eine Einführung in den "Panzerkreuzer Potemkin" ' in Sergej M. Eisenstein, *Schriften 2: Panzerkreuzer Potemkin*, ed. Hans-Joachim Schlegel, Munich, 1973, pp. 7–22; Hermann Herlinghaus, 'Eisensteins Matrosen bedrohten Preußens Ordnung' and 'Eisensteins Matrosen siegten', *Deutsche Filmkunst*, No. 11, 1956, pp. 325–7 and No. 12, pp. 373–7; also Sudendorf, *op. cit.*, pp. 63–71.

16   Soviet Union, 1925. The illustrations for *Potemkin* are photographs made especially for this chapter from a copy of the film, and thus lack the clarity of production stills.

17   *Sergei Eisenstein. Ausgewählte Aufsätze*, ed. R. Juvenew, Berlin (East), 1960, p. 166.

18   'Sergej Eisenstein über Sergej Eisenstein, den "Potemkin"-Regisseur', in Sergej M. Eisenstein, *Schriften 2: Panzerkreuzer Potemkin*, ed. Hans-Joachim Schlegel, Munich, 1973, pp. 121–5 (p. 123).

19   O. Brik, 'From picture to calico-print' (*Lef*, Vol. 6, pp. 27, 30–1, 34), *Screen*, Vol. 12, No. 4, 1971/2, pp. 48–51, (p. 48).

20   For Eisenstein's position *vis-à-vis* contemporary socialist–aesthetic debate, see Schlegel, *op. cit.*, pp. 11–17; and Chapter 1 ('Eisenstein's aesthetics') of Peter Wollen's *Signs and Meaning in the Cinema*, London, 1972, pp. 19–70.

21   Lion Feuchtwanger, *Erfolg*, Berlin, 1930. Vol. 2, p. 15.

22   Cf. Noel Burch and Jorge Dana, 'Propositions', *Afterimage*, Vol. 5, 1975, pp. 40–66 (pp. 43–44).

23   Schlegel, *op. cit.*, p. 19 (my translation).

24   Quoted in Sudendorf, *op. cit.*, 1975, p. 68.

25   From Eisenstein's essay 'The Organic and Pathos in the Composition of the Film "Battleship Potemkin" ' (1939), quoted in Jan Leyda, *Kino. A History of the Russian and Soviet Film*, London, 1960, p. 198.

26   The words are those of S. Tretyakov, from a discussion in *Novy Lef*, No. 11–12, 1927, *Screen*, Vol. 12, No. 4, p. 77.

27   Juvenew, *ed. cit.*, p. 166 (my translation from the German).

28   From Eisenstein, 'The Organic and Pathos . . .', quoted in Leyda, *op. cit.*, p. 199.

29   For the contemporary political reasons behind Eisenstein's aesthetic choices, see his essay 'Constanza. The Destination of the "Battleship Potemkin" ' (1926), Schlegel, *op. cit.*, pp. 128–33.

30   Wollen, *op. cit.*, p. 47.

31   'Keinen Gedanken verschwenden an das Unabänderbare', *Gesammelte Werke*, Vol. 8, Frankfurt am Main, 1967, pp. 390–2.

32   Eisenstein, 'Constanza . . .', p. 219.

33   Eisenstein, 'The Organic and Pathos . . .', Schlegel, p. 185.

34   Wollen, *op. cit.*, p. 47.

L

35 *Screen*, vol. 12, No. 4, p. 82.
36 See Erwin Picator, *Das politische Theater*, neu bearbeitet von Felix Gasbarra, Reinbek bei Hamburg, 1979, p. 122.
37 Erwin Piscator, *Theater, Film. Politik. Ausgewählte Schriften*, ed. Ludwig Hoffman, Berlin (East), 1980, p. 48.
38 The *Regiebuch* of this production survives and is held by the Abteilung Darstellende Kunst der Akademie der Künste der DDR, Berlin. I am grateful to the Erwin Piscator-Center, Akademie der Künste in West Berlin for permission to consult their copy. A very detailed reconstruction of the performance is to be found in Friedrich Wolfgang Knellessen, *Agitation auf der Bühne. Das politische Theater der Weimarer Republik*, Emsdetten, 1970, pp. 115–33.
39 Piscator, *Das politische Theater*, p. 41.
40 See *ibid.*, pp. 150–1.

Theatre
as a political forum

In neutral Zurich, in 1916, a cabaret of Dadaism –

> Gadji, beri bimba
> Gadji, beri bimba

and similar items, deliberately meaningless words repeated slowly and solemnly, or bizarre disjunctions of a hated normality –

> The cows sit on telegraph poles
> and play chess

– was being performed in Number One, Spiegelgasse. One of the founders of Dada, Hugo Ball, recalled that at Number Six, Spiegelgasse, 'directly across from us . . . there lived, if I am not mistaken, Herr Ulianov/Lenin. Every evening he must surely have heard our music-making and our tirades.' Ball went on to put this question: 'Is Dadaism something of a mark and gesture of a counterplay to Bolshevism? Does it oppose to the destruction and thorough settling of accounts the utterly quixotic, unpurposeful, incomprehensible side of the world? It will be interesting to see what happens'.[1] Indeed it has been, especially when we remember that Dada also, for a time, had a Revolutionary Central Committee and was proposing a new culture to include circuses and the use of Dada verse as a Communist state prayer.

In fact, within five years, in Lenin's Soviet Union, there was a revolutionary avant-garde theatre. Alexander Tairov was pioneering the extraordinarily influential constructivist sets of scaffolding and platforms, and was using exaggerated make-up to emphasise theatricality. Vsevolod Meyerhold was moving drama and theatre away from what he saw as trivial personalia towards the deliberately unidividual. Meanwhile Nikolai Okhlopkov was developing large open-air productions, intended to break down the conventional separation between actors and audiences. A similarly experimental vigour was evident also in Soviet film-making: in one direction moving out to crowds and actual locations and away from actors and sets; in another, controlling and planning the juxtaposition of images, in some versions as an identification of montage with the dialectic: shot A interacts with shot B to produce a new concept C. During the same years, in the turbulence of post-war Germany, Expressionist theatre and cinema were moving very actively in related avant-garde directions. And in England, too, D. H. Lawrence was writing; 'drama is enacted by symbolic creatures formed out of human consciousness: puppets if you like: but not human individuals. Our stage is all wrong, so boring in its personality.'[2] W. B. Yeats had already produced his *Plays for Dancers*, on similar principles, influenced by the Japanese *Noh* theatre.

These developments could be described in a historical narrative. But that legendary, perhaps apocryphal moment in the Spiegelgasse gives a more truthful insight into the complex relations between avant-garde theatre and radical or revolutionary politics. More generally, in avant-garde art as a whole, comparable or at least negatively related innovations and technical experiments, founded on an angry rejection of bourgeois culture and its enclosed, personalised, reproductive works and institutions, contained, within themselves, profoundly different social principles and almost equally different conceptions even of the basic purposes of art. Ball's question is perceptive. There was indeed a counterplay between the conception of theatre which was associated with Bolshevik practice – a movement beyond bourgeois concepts of the sources of human action and a corresponding transformation of the relations between producers and audiences – and on the other hand the conception, as marked in Lawrence and Yeats as in what seems the special case of Dada, of forms of writing, acting and presentation which would explore, or as often simply assert, all that was 'unpurposeful, incomprehensible', not only in acknowledgement of this human dimension but in its acceptance, even its celebration.

The diversity of early Soviet experiments was in fact first reduced, then cut short, by political developments and eventually by repression, from the late 1920s. The central site of the whole remarkable history is then the Germany of the Weimar Republic, later ended by Hitler but continuing to be influential in exile, in ways that come down to our own time.

We can best look at the early German experience through two figures: Ernst Toller and Erwin Piscator. There is then a later and very significant climax in the changing work of Bertolt Brecht. Yet before we enter these details, it is necessary to look more generally at the development of modernist drama, before the crisis and new opportunities after 1917. The main reason for this is that the rhetoric of the avant-garde, characteristically rejecting even the immediate past, has survived into what appears to be scholarly and critical discussion, with deeply negative effects not only on the work of that earlier period but, more to the present point, on the understanding of the complex character of avant-garde theatre itself and especially its relations to politics.

One word sums up the diverse rejection: *naturalism*. There is hardly a new dramatic or theatrical movement, down to our own day, which fails to announce, in manifesto, programme note or press release, that it is rejecting or moving beyond 'naturalism'. And this is especially surprising since the overwhelming majority of theatrical works and productions continue, in relatively obvious senses, to be naturalist, or at least (for there can be a difference), naturalistic. To untie this tangle we must attend to its history.

The key moment, not surprisingly, is that most neglected period of dramatic and theatrical history in which bourgeois influence and bourgeois forms made their decisive appearance. In England, where this was early, this period is the mid-eighteenth century. Much can be missed if we interpret this new influence in terms only of its evident and at first crude morality and ideology. It is important that the bourgeoisie had moved from its earlier rejections of late feudal, courtly and aristocratic theatre – because of its inherently misleading fictions, its lewdness and amorality, its function as a mere distraction from the serious and the utilitarian – to positive interventions in its own image, sentimental and conformist as these undoubtedly were. But the most fundamental cultural history is always a history of forms, and what we actually find, as we examine this period in its long and slow lines of development towards our own century, is one of the two major transformations in the whole history of drama (the first was that of the Renaissance).

We can identify five factors, of an immensely influential kind in all subsequent drama. First, there was the radical admission of the *contemporary* as legitimate material for drama. In the major periods of Greek and Renaissance drama the inherent choice of material was overwhelmingly legendary or historical, with at most some insertions of the contemporary at the margins of these distanced events. Second, there was an admission of the *indigenous*, as part of the same movement; the widespread convention of an at least nominally exotic site for drama began to be loosened, and the ground for the now equally widespread convention of the *contemporary indigenous* began to be prepared. Third, there was an increasing emphasis on *everyday speech-forms* as the basis for dramatic language: in practice at first a reduction from the extraordinary linguistic range, including the colloquial, which had marked the English Renaissance, but eventually a decisive point of reference for the nature of all dramatic speech, formally rhetorical, choral and monological types being steadily abandoned. Fourth, there was an emphasis on *social extension*: a deliberate breach of the convention that at least the principal personages of drama should be of elevated social rank. As in the novel, this process of extension moved in stages, from the court to the bourgeois home, and then, first in melodrama, to the poor. Fifth, there was the completion of a decisive *secularism*: not, in its early stages, necessarily a rejection of or indifference to religious belief, but a steady exclusion *from the dramatic action* of all supernatural or metaphysical agencies. Drama was now, explicitly, to be a human action played in exclusively human terms.

The success of this major bourgeois intervention is easily overlooked just because it has been so complete. For the last two hundred years, and as clearly in the modernist and avant-garde theatres as in those of the successive mainline bourgeois establishments, these five factors have been fundamentally defining. What has then really to be traced is the string of variations and tensions within these norms, in different phases of experimental drama and theatre. We can then approach the question of the real nature of the avant-garde revolt against what it called 'bourgeois' drama and theatre.

For our present purpose the naturalist variation is decisive. It is true that 'naturalism' might be used as a summary of the effects of these five bourgeois factors, but historically this was not the way the term went. Late nineteenth-century naturalism, in practice, was the first phase of modernist theatre. It was in many ways an intensification – in its period a shocking intensification – of the five factors, but in its immediate development it rested on a more specific base. At its centre was the humanist and secular – and, in political terms, Liberal and later Socialist – proposition that human nature was not, or at least not decisively, unchanging and timeless, but was socially and culturally specific.

There was always a decisive action and interaction between what was still residually called 'character' and a specific 'environment', physical and social. The new use of 'naturalism', as distinct from earlier broadly secular emphases, was formed by the new natural history, with a clear borrowing of language to describe the adaptation, or failure of adaptation, of old and new social and human types; and with an explicit emphasis on the evolutionary process, commonly seen as a struggle for existence, by which a new kind of life tried and as often failed to come through. Thus the best-known technical innovation of naturalism – the building of 'lifelike' stage sets (though this had actually already been pioneered in society drama as a form of luxurious display) – was now a dramatic convention in its own right. A real environment had to be reproduced on the stage, because within this perspective an actual environment – a particular kind of room, particular furnishing, a particular relation to street or office or landscape – was in effect one of the actors: one of the true agencies of the action. This is especially clear in Ibsen, but in many subsequent plays and films this essential relationship is common, and is even taken for granted.

Thus real and often new social locations were put on stage, and within the same purpose there was ever more careful attention to the reproduction, within them, of everyday speech and behaviour. These new conventions passed ever more widely into drama as a whole, but it is then necessary to distinguish between what can still properly be called the naturalist convention and what became, in the more general change, the naturalist habit. This is in practice a distinction between the naturalist drama which was actually the first phase of modernism, and that naturalist – or shall we now say 'naturalistic'? – accommodation to the norms of the orthodox culture. What is most clear in modernist naturalism – from Ibsen through early Strindberg to Chekhov – is its challenging selection of the crises, the contradictions, the unexplored dark areas of the bourgeois human order of its time.

These challenges were met by furious denunciation. The new drama was low and vulgar or filthy; it threatened the standards of decent society by subversion or indifference to accepted norms. Plays which questioned prevailing conceptions of feminity, such as Ibsen's *Doll's House* and Strindberg's *Miss Julie,* provoked particular indignation. In this sense there is a direct continuity from modernist naturalism to the work and reception of the avant-garde. Moreover their social bases are directly comparable, in that each is the work of dissident fractions of the bourgeoisie itself, which became grouped – especially from the 1890s – in new independent and progressive theatres.

Yet there was an early crisis within the chosen form of modernist naturalism. Its version of the environment within which human lives were formed and deformed – the domestic bourgeois household in which the social and financial insecurities and above all the sexual tensions were most immediately experienced – was at once physically convincing and intellectually insufficient. Beyond this key site of the living room there were, in opposite directions, crucial areas of experience which the language and behaviour of the living room could not articulate or fully interpret. Social and economic crises in the wider society had their effects back in the living room, but dramatically only as reports from elsewhere, off-stage, or at best as things seen from the window or as shouts from the street. Similarly, crises of subjectivity – the privacies of sexuality, the uncertainties and disturbances of fantasies and dreams – could not be fully articulated within the norms of language and behaviour which, for its central purposes, the form had selected.

This was an ironic result in a form which had gained its main energies from its selection and exposure of deep crises and hitherto dark areas. And in fact each of the three major naturalist dramatists moved to continuing experiment to overcome these limitations. Ibsen and Chekhov used visual images beyond the room to suggest or define larger forces (*The Wild Duck, The Cherry Orchard*). Ibsen, in his last plays, and especially in *When We Dead Awaken,* and Strindberg, from *The Road to Damascus* through *Dreamplay* to *Ghost Sonata,* acually inaugurated the methods, later known as Expressionism, which were to be main elememts of the drama and theatre of the avant-garde. Here again, and centrally, the essential continuity between the thrust of modernist naturalism and the campaigns of the avant-garde is historically evident.

There is then need for a further distinction. The drama of the living room had unreachable areas of experience in what must continue to be seen as two *opposite* directions. Theoretically there were then two choices. Either the drama could become fully public again, reversing the bourgeois evacuation of the sites of social power, which had been a consequence of its rejection of the monopoly of rank. But where now would these sites of power be? Or the drama could explore subjectivity more intensively, drawing back from conscious representation and reproduction of public life in favour of the dramatisation, by any available means, of what was taken to be an inner consciousness or indeed an unconscious. The key to the politics of avant-garde theatre is that both these very different directions were taken, of course with quite different results. The spurious unity which is conferred by what appears the common negative element – the 'rejection of naturalism', which by this stage could mean almost anything, including the respectable mainline accommodations of the unchallenging naturalist habit – has long concealed the only important question: that of the *alternative* directions in which a continuing bourgeois dissidence might go, and of the very different and ultimately transformed positions which were waiting at the end of each of these directions.

These alternative but at first overlapping directions are especially clear in German drama. Sternheim's *Scenes from Bourgeois Life* (trilogy, 1911–14) was a relatively simple form of bourgeois dissidence: scandals and shocks within the outwardly respectable. But in *Earth Spirit* (1895) and *Pandora's Box* (1904) by Frank Wedekind there was a more radical break: the bourgeois world is grotesque, haunted by dead customs and laws, choked by its self-repressions; but now this is challenged by an elementary life-force, primarily but not exclusively sexual, which will at once disrupt and liberate. One of the most influential consciously Expressionist plays, Kaiser's *From Morn to Midnight* (1916), showed, through twelve hours in the life of an absconding bank clerk, the insecurities and miseries of a conforming *petite bourgeoisie* breaking into petty revolt. Meanwhile Brecht, in *Baal* (written in 1918), selected the strong and ruthless individual, unafraid of the social conventions, as a form of liberation of human nature and desire. The essential overlaps in what is customarily perceived as an avant-garde now seem very clear. There was at once a continuation, often by new methods, of the naturalist project of exposing the dark places of bourgeois life, and a break to a new emphasis of the agency which will disrupt it, an elemental and uncontainable force identified primarily as an intense subjectivity.

It is then already insufficient to rest on the 'anti-bourgeois' definition: above all because other new work was moving in a quite different direction. Ernst Toller, in gaol for his part in the Bavarian Revolution of 1919, was writing *Man and the Masses* (1921). Erwin Piscator was moving from the Spartakus League to found the Proletarian Theatre as 'the stage of the revolutionary working man'. The two decisively different directions of what could be grouped as the avant-garde, and indeed more narrowly as Expressionism, can be seen in two contrasting statements of these years. Theodor Däubler wrote in 1919: 'Our times have a grand design: a new eruption of the soul! The I creates the world.'[3] Somewhat later, Piscator wrote: 'No longer is the individual with his private, personal fate the heroic factor of the new drama, but Time itself, the fate of the masses.'[4]

It is from these wholly alternative emphases that we can define, within the vigorous and overlapping experimental drama and theatre, the eventually distinguishable forms of 'subjective' and 'social' Expressionism. New names were eventually found for these avant-garde methods, mainly because of these differences and complications of purpose. What was still there in common was the refusal of reproduction: in staging, in language, in character presentation. But one tendency was moving towards that new form of bourgeois dissidence which, in its very emphasis on subjectivity, rejected the discourse of any public world as irrelevant to its deeper concerns. Sexual liberation, the emancipation of dream and fantasy, a new interest in madness as an alternative to repressive sanity, a rejection of ordered language as a form of concealed but routine domination: these were now seen, in this tendency, which culminated in Surrealism and Artaud's 'theatre of cruelty', as the real dissidence, breaking alike from bourgeois society and from the forms of opposition to it which had been generated within its terms. On the other hand, the opposite, more political tendency offered to renounce the bourgeoisie altogether: to move from dissidence to conscious affiliation with the working class: in early Soviet theatre, Piscator and Toller, eventually Brecht.

The concept of 'political theatre', for obvious reasons, is associated mainly with the second tendency. But it would be wrong to overlook altogether the political effects of the first tendency which, with an increasing emphasis on themes of madness, disruptive violence and liberating sexuality, came through to dominate Western avant-garde theatre in a later period, especially after 1950. One element in this domination has been what can be seen as a failure in that most extreme political tendency – the Bolshevik variant of socialism – which had attached itself to the ideas and projects of the working class. Post-war history, and especially the Soviet experience, has made the brave early affiliations evidently problematic. Yet, since both tendencies are still active, and in changing proportions, it is important to identify them, within the generalities of avant-garde theatre, at the point where they most clearly began to diverge.

Piscator's production of *Fahnen* ('Flags') in 1924 is exemplary of that movement in which 'our pieces were incitements with which we wished to engage in living history and "act" politics'.[5] It was based on a bombing incident in Chicago after which four anarchists were hanged. Described by Piscator as 'epic drama', it had fifty-six characters, in a deliberately open, public action. There was a minimum of stage furniture; playing areas were constructed and isolated by lighting, on a basis of the scaffolding and platforms pioneered by Tairov in Constructivism, and with further mechanical developments. Film excerpts and titles were inserted in the action, and there could be direct audience address. The whole emphasis was on a fluidity and simultaneity of otherwise distanced actions; newsreels and radio announcements cut in to the direct dramatisation of an acted group.

This production can be directly related to Toller's *Hoppla!* of 1927. The prologue shows a group of condemned revolutionaries in 1919, waiting for execution; at the last moment one of them, Wilhelm Kilman, is released, while the sentence on the others – including Kilman's friend Karl Thomas – is commuted to a long term of imprisonment. The action then switches to 1927. Thomas has just been released; meanwhile Kilman has become Prime Minister. Thomas explores the altered political world; in the end he is rearrested, on a false charge, and commits suicide.

The general history of these eight decisive years is projected by newsreel extracts and titles, and by radio reports. The stage itself is a scaffolding divided into floors (see Figs. 29 & 30); any part of this structure can become a room on which the action settles by lighting. At different times the structure is hotel, asylum and prison. The successive scenes are of political, financial and sexual corruption; there is also sharp satire of a group of 'philosophical revolutionaries' intent on their own class-based forms of male sexual liberation. Karl Thomas, who has become a waiter, plans to shoot Kilman; but a student shoots the Prime Minister first.

Two main points arise from *Hoppla!* First, that it is a decisive reoccupation of that public space which the bourgeois domestic drama had evacuated. Moreover, its fluidity of scene and staging allows the virtually simultaneous presentation of otherwise separated and concealed areas of social action. The play invokes the widest possible contemporary history and then moves through more localised situations to exposure and confrontation.

Secondly, the reoccupation of this public space is accompanied by a dilution of the substantial social relationships which modernist naturalism had explored. The relationships in *Hoppla!* are sharp and diagrammatic: modes of presentation and analysis rather than of substantiation. Moreover, and this can be seen as an inner link with the subjectivist tendency, the revolutionary affiliation is primarily an exposure of the corruption of the bourgeois world – sexual as well as financial and political – against which the heroic individual struggles to act, but fails. It is relevant in this context that the decisive act is not a communal rising (as already, within naturalism, in Hauptmann's *The Weavers* of the 1890s) but an individual assassination, within the militant anarchist tradition.

These points can be related to the changes of direction made by Brecht who, coming out of this theatrical world of the 1920s, at first with less clear political commitments, was to become the major practitioner of the drama and theatre of the political avant-garde.

The early Brecht, of *Baal* and *Drums in the Night,* is radical and anti-bourgeois within the subjectivist tendency; even the revolution in *Drums in the Night* is essentially a disconnected background to a subjective history. In a following phase, that of *Mahagonny* and *The Threepenny Opera,* the critique of specifically bourgeois society is more explicit and more vigorous, but the dominant mode of response is still a cynicism linked with individual accommodation and survival. There is a transition in *St Joan of the Stockyards* and especially in his adaptation of Gorki's *Mother,* where the elements of a positive and eventually collective response begin to come through. This is also the period of his deliberate movement away from the experimental bourgeois theatre towards a possible working-class theatre. This was a period, in the late 1920s, of intensified theatrical enterprise of this kind, in mass pageants, in street theatre, in performances in pubs and factories, and in the touring of such groups as the Red Shirts and the Red Rockets. Brecht, who had moved much closer to Marxism, contributed his 'teaching plays'. The most significant of these, *The Measures Taken* (already analysed by Edward Timms in Chapter 1), was performed by the Workers' Choirs in Berlin before a mainly working-class audience.

This phase was in fact the climax of what is, historically, a relatively unusual situation: the direct interaction of avant-garde theatre with a militant working-class movement which has found its appropriate cultural institutions. It is thus different in kind from the dissident bourgeois avant-garde working within dissident bourgeois minority theatres. Yet the change cuts both ways. There is a movement beyond a knowing and self-regarding cynicism, and beyond ever wilder gestures of theatrical revolt within basically conformist institutions in unaltered social relationships. At the same time, the mediation of the new drama and new audiences through a party and a theory, at one level the sources of its strength, produced (as in *The Measures Taken*) a certain applied angularity, indeed a core of over-bearing demonstration within what was consciously offered as a shared, participating exploration of the profound and authentic problems of struggle.

We cannot now say what would have happened if this whole development had not been aborted by the coming to power of the Nazis. An immensely self-confident cultural movement was overborne by political history. Shock and denunciation were replaced by repression and terror. It is within this experience of dislocation and defeat that the next and best-known phase of Brecht's work developed: one that is very significant for understanding the changing politics of avant-garde theatre. It is mainly within this situation, and from exile, that Brecht developed the new techniques of distancing and of 'estrangement' (a term which he probably took directly from early Russian Formalism). It is true that within the 'teaching plays' he had been moving towards the idea of the consciously partici-pating, critical audience, but there was then still both an actual and a potential comradely public of that kind. Deprived of such a public, and having tried and largely failed to produce a drama which could confront contemporary Fascism directly, Brecht moved, both in technique and in choice of subject, towards new and deliberate forms of distance. In doing so, it happened that he cancelled two factors of the long development of bourgeois drama: the indigenous and the contemporary. This can be taken, in one perspective, as the radical break from 'naturalism' or 'realism': within avant-garde theory the two are conflated. But of course it is also the reconstruction, within the forced conditions of exile, of the determining social conditions of the original avant-garde: the chosen forms of the marginal artist, drawing away from reproduction of a contemporary world that is hostile to art.

The brilliance of Brecht's development of these forms is not to be doubted. *Mother Courage* and *Galileo* are the profoundly divided, even self-dissolving figures of mature modernist naturalism, now given broad and clear historical and ideological perspectives. *The Caucasian Chalk Circle* breaks new ground in moving towards the Utopian elements of the fairy-tale, when an unlooked-for and literally impossible human justice prevails over the hard lines of necessity typically demonstrated in both myth and realism. In one direction there are the ambiguities of survival through defeat and destruction, in which positive consciousness is available only through critical response to the action, which the form invites but does not enforce. This has been brought out by productions of Brecht which – against his intention – have emphasised the self-interested virtues of survival. In another direction, whether in the songs of pleasure and defiance, or in the Utopian realisation of a rare and happy justice, the collective impulse survives and communicates.

It is in this kind of complex analysis, which corresponds to what Brecht himself described as his new method, that of 'complex seeing' of a multivalent and both dynamic and uncertain social process, that Brecht's significance must be defined. To abstract the specific methods, or the theoretical phrases attached to them, as determining forms without reference to their very specific and limiting social situation, is to confirm the actual development of the avant-garde, culturally and politically, towards a new aestheticism. By this means unresolvable social problems are bypassed in what seems an autonomous, self-dependent and self-renewing artistic enterprise. The often successful attempt to depoliticise Brecht, by bringing up the elements of cynical survival and unspecific liberation and playing down the firm attachments to a common condition and common struggle, is characteristic of that phase of accommodation and incorporation of the avant-garde which happened so widely, in the West, after 1950.

By contrast with developments in Germany, the English theatre of the twenties and thirties never acquired real political momentum. The dominating figure was Bernard Shaw; but his drama of ideas lacks the leading edge of formal innovation. For developments which run parallel (and may in part be indebted) to German Expressionism, we must turn first to Sean O'Casey, and then to Auden and Isherwood. O'Casey, after the distinctive realism of his Abbey Theatre plays, wrote in 1927 *The Silver Tassie*, which in its central sections is an attempt at a new form: the use of songs, slogans, reduced speech to express the alienation of war; a movement that is accomplished in the play as a whole by the transformation of the hero from popular football star to mutilated war victim.

Auden and Isherwood, in their plays, adapted elements of Expressionist theatre in combination with the more familiar forms of musical comedy and pantomime. *The Ascent of F6* (1937) mixes motifs of social and psychological struggle. Caricatured figures from the political Establishment persuade an idealistic climber to conquer the haunted mountain 'F6' in the British colony of Sudoland, in order to impress the unruly natives. A downtrodden, gullible suburban family, speaking comic verse, acts as chorus. Although modernist techniques (like the split stage, where politicians, climbers, native monks and the British public unwittingly interact) help to underline the revolutionary tendency, the play's hybrid borrowings – from Symbolist as well as from Expressionist theatre – form an uneasy synthesis. The same disjunction is evident thematically in the attempt to combine Marxist and Freudian motifs – so characteristic of the avant-garde in this period. The climber, who disapproves of his tendentious mission, attempts to scale the mountain for more personal reasons – in order to win his mother's love. As he is dying, the figure of his mother appears as the shrouded divinity haunting the mountain-top. His dying fantasy is projected on stage in Expressionist fashion: his politician brother becomes a dragon, and masked Establishment figures enact a pantomimic chess game. This mingling of popular and experimental forms, resulting in a Brechtian sense of alienation, provides a panoramic critique of the social order juxtaposed with the spiritual crisis of the failed idealist.

On the Frontier (1938) portrays two warring countries, in which the troops mutiny and the workers revolt, as they overcome their misguided mutual hostility (which is largely attributable to the press and radio). Again the revolutionary theme is highlighted by both music-hall caricature and Brechtian montage. The Fascist leader is a failed revolutionary, feeble and insane, who is manipulated by big business. And the warring families living on either side of the invisible 'frontier' (centre-stage) respond unwittingly in ironic antiphony. But, in a significant shift of emphasis, the young lovers who have been separated by the frontier throughout the play affirm the supremacy of love, as they die. They have abjured their earlier pacifism to become respectively an insurgent and a nurse, in support of those who 'build the city where / The will of love is done'. The lovers thus 'die to make man just / And worthy of the earth'.[6] Despite this expression of faith in the justness of their cause, the effect of this ending is to eclipse the political impact of the popular rising, which had earlier been powerfully foregrounded by satirical newspaper-readings in front of the curtain. The play ends on a note of lyrical individual lament.

These were the best-known English Left plays of the 1930s, mainly because they were produced within the most effective cultural formation: that of the politically dissident bourgeoisie. Yet work of a different kind, seeking out working-class audiences and direct workers' production, was also being done: not only through the agitational forms of the living newspaper but over a range of methods, including reconstructed popular history and contemporary social realism. This tendency, often interrupted by its institutional weaknesses, has continued to appear and has strengthened.

Yet it is on what has happened since to the cultural politics of the self-conscious avant-garde that we must place our final emphasis. The fragmented ego in a fragmented world has survived as a dominant structure of feeling. In the overlapping phases of Surrealist theatre, the theatre of cruelty, the theatre of the Absurd and the theatre of 'non-communication', distinct original strains of the avant-garde formation have deepened and intensified. There is still an element of revolt in the challenge to bourgeois society (later renamed 'mass society' or even 'society' as such, including, in a later phase, 'male patriarchal society') on the grounds of its monopoly of consciousness: a monopoly typically expressed in its forms of language and of representation.

The cutting edge of this critique can still move towards forms of more general revolt (as in some examples of feminist theatre); but more characteristically it settles in the attempted breakthrough to authentic individual experience from below this standardised consciousness, or in the wry demonstration of the impossibility of any such break. There is then a movement from presenting the bourgeois world as at once domineering and grotesque to an insistence – in certain forms a satisfied and even happy insistence – that changing this is impossible, is indeed literally inconceivable while the dominant consciousness bears down. This takes a special form in theatre in what is offered as a rejection of language. If words 'arrest and paralyse thought' it may be possible, as Artaud hoped, to substitute 'for the spoken language a different language of nature, whose expressive possibilities will be equal to verbal language':[7] a theatre of visual movement and of the body. In such ways, the fixed forms of representation can be perpetually broken, not by establishing new forms but by showing their persistent pressures and tyranny. One main emphasis within this is to render all activity and speech as illusory and to value theatre, in its frankly illusory character, as the privileged bearer of this universal truth.

Yet what has to be said as we look at this latest and in practice diverse theatre of the avant-garde is that it has also been, in its own ways, a politics. It has continued to shock and to challenge. It has often illuminated, with its own forms of sympathy, the dislocations, the disturbances, the forms of what are accounted madness, which orthodox society in all its political colours has crudely dismissed. At the same time, as in the earliest subjectivism, it has often been profoundly equivocal about violence, and has at times converted it to subjectivist spectacle and to what are in effect cruel forms of pornography (the element of *male* liberation and rejection of women in the earliest subjectivism has been powerfully maintained). Further, in some of its most beguiling examples, from the genius of Beckett to the incoherent black comedies of the new boulevards, it has programmatically reduced the scale of human possibility and human action, converting a dynamism of form which had flirted with a dynamic of action to a repetitious, mutually misunderstanding stasis of condition. These are not then the politics of an avant-garde, in any but the most limited sense, but, as was always possible (and as had happened earlier in Eliot, Yeats and Claudel), of an avant-garde as *arrière-garde*: the impossible, unacceptable condition now taken to be inevitable and requiring submission: a defeat rationalised by cancelling its human ground and moving first its theatre and then its politics elsewhere.

Notes to chapter 18

1   Quoted in F. Ewen, *Bertolt Brecht*, London, 1970, p. 74.
2   D. H. Lawrence, *Sea and Sardinia*, London, 1921, p. 189.
3   Quoted in Ewen, *op. cit.*, p. 174.
4   Quoted in Ewen, *op. cit.*, p. 151.
5   Quoted in Ewen, *op. cit.*, p. 149.
6   W. H. Auden and Christopher Isherwood, *The Ascent of F6* and *On the Frontier*, London, 1958, pp. 190–1.
7   A. Artaud, *The Theatre and its Double*, New York, 1958, p. 110.

Acknowledgements

The editors are grateful to Gonville and Caius College and to the Faculty of Modern Languages, University of Cambridge, for contributions towards the cost of illustrations.

Thanks are also due the following for permission to reproduce illustrations: Fig. 4, DACS ©; Fig. 6, Abidin Dino (Paris); Figs. 19–22 & Fig. 27, Stiftung Deutsche Kinematek, Berlin; Figs. 24–26 & Fig. 28, photographs made by Peter Magdowski from a copy of *Battleship Potemkin* supplied by Stiftung Deutsche Kinematek; Fig. 29, Erwin-Piscator-Center, Akademie der Künste, Berlin; Fig. 30, Edition Hentrich, Fröhlich & Kaufmann, Berlin. Fig. 23 is a reproduction of the original poster for the 1926 première of *Battleship Potemkin* and is the property of the Landsbildestelle, Berlin. Other illustrations are based on printed sources.

Additional photographic work was undertaken by Don Manning (Audio Visual Aids Unit), and the index was prepared by Beatrix Bown (Literary and Linguistic Computing Centre, University of Cambridge).

Index